D1327188

Aging, Media, and Culture

Aging, Media, and Culture

Edited by
C. Lee Harrington,
Denise D. Bielby, and Anthony R. Bardo

LEXINGTON BOOKS
Lanham • Boulder • New York • London

Published by Lexington Books
An imprint of The Rowman & Littlefield Publishing Group, Inc.
4501 Forbes Boulevard, Suite 200, Lanham, Maryland 20706
www.rowman.com

16 Carlisle Street, London W1D 3BT, United Kingdom

British Library Cataloguing in Publication Information Available

Library of Congress Cataloging-in-Publication Data

Aging, media, and culture / edited by C. Lee Harrington, Denise D. Bielby, and Anthony R. Bardo.
pages cm
Includes bibliographical references and index.
ISBN 978-0-7391-8363-2 (cloth : alk. paper) — ISBN 978-0-7391-8364-9 (electronic)
1. Older people. 2. Mass media and older people. 3. Mass media and culture. I. Harrington, C. Lee,
1964– editor of compilation.
HQ1061.A42953 2014
302.23084'6—dc23

2014013772

Printed in the United States of America

Contents

1 New Areas of Inquiry in Aging, Media, and Culture   1
    C. Lee Harrington, Denise D. Bielby, and Anthony R. Bardo

I: Advertising and Marketing   **11**

2 Aspiration and Compromise: Portrayals of Older Adults in
    Television Advertising   13
    Shyon Baumann and Kim de Laat

3 Forever Young: The New Aging Consumer in the Marketplace   25
    Anne L. Balazs

II: Age Identities   **37**

4 Reflections of Old Age, Constructions of Aging Selves:
    Drawing Links between Media Images and Views of Aging   39
    Anne E. Barrett, Alexandra Raphael, and Justine Gunderson

5 Age and Gender in Film and Television: The Case of Huong Hoang   51
    Anthony R. Bardo

III: Celebrity   **63**

6 Growing Old in Celebrity Culture   65
    Hilde Van den Bulck

7 Social Meaning of Celebrities in the Everyday Lives of Nursing
    Home Residents: An Exploratory Study   77
    Nathalie Claessens

IV: Music   **91**

8 Music, Performance, and Generation: The Making of Boomer
Rock and Roll Biographies   93
Stephen Katz

9 "The Long Strange Trip" Continues: Aging Deadheads   107
Rebecca G. Adams and Justin T. Harmon

V: Fandom   **121**

10 A Life Course Perspective on Fandom   123
C. Lee Harrington and Denise D. Bielby

11 Breaking Dusk: Fandom, Gender/Age Intersectionality, and the
"Twilight Moms"   143
Christine Scodari

VI: Gender and Sexuality   **155**

12 "Let's Do It Like Grown-Ups": A Filmic *Mènage* of Age,
Gender, and Sexuality   157
Leni Marshall and Aagje Swinnen

13 Sexualizing the Third Age   169
Barbara L. Marshall

VII: Social/New Media   **181**

14 Learning New Tricks: The Use of Social Media in Later Life   183
Kelly Quinn

15 Polite Pigs and Emotional Elves: Age in Digital Worlds   193
Rosa Mikeal Martey

16 Afterword: A View from Media Studies   205
Cornel Sandvoss

17 Afterword: A View from Gerontology   211
Merril Silverstein

References   217

Index   251

About the Contributors   255

Chapter One

New Areas of Inquiry in Aging, Media, and Culture

C. Lee Harrington,
Denise D. Bielby, and Anthony R. Bardo

The producer-consumer relationship is consequential for the life course of all parties to the transaction, yet is hidden from view in everyday social life, and has been largely ignored by life-course research.

—Dannefer and Miklowski (2006, 38)

The media mediate everything, entering into and shaping the mundane yet significant relations among individuals and between individuals and society.

—Livingstone (2009, xi)

The general idea for a collection on aging and media grew out of a session we organized for the 2012 American Sociological Association (ASA) meetings that was jointly sponsored, for the first time ever, by both the Culture Section and the Aging and the Life Course Section of the ASA. Recognizing the importance of the interplay between rapid global population aging and increasing mediation in shaping the organization and meanings of everyday life, this resulting anthology of original, invited chapters (along with one reprint) aims to bridge the gap between media studies and life course scholarship by bringing together a diverse set of voices around core issues of aging, media, and culture. In their recent consideration of the futures of old age, Dale Dannefer and Casey Miklowski (quoted above) emphasize the salience of linked lives in navigating new twenty-first-century landscapes. The notion of linked lives highlights the role of interpersonal relations and relational contexts in shaping life journeys—including the context(s) of production, distribution, and consumption of cultural commodities, an understudied but increasingly important aspect of life course research. Relatedly, in her 2008 presidential address to the International Communication Association, media scholar Sonia Livingstone (also quoted above) addresses the widespread claim in the field of communications that "everything is mediated," and encourages her colleagues to consider the implications—empirical, historical, political (and demographic, we would add)—of such a claim. What does it mean to live a mediated life? More specifically, what does it mean to grow old(er) in a thoroughly mediated world?[1]

Elsewhere we have argued (Harrington and Bielby 2010; Harrington, Bielby, and Bardo 2011) that the rapid mediation of everyday life is an overlooked aspect of twenty-first-century aging, and that the emotional anchoring offered by media engagement in general, and media fandom in particular, has joined with more traditional personal attachments to help reshape the life course through their influence on social identity. We believe that the shared interests of media fan communities—formed around actors, singers, television shows, politicians, and even Grumpy cat—provide a key resource for navigating identity transformations through adulthood and late(r) life. As the expectable twentieth-century life course dismantles and we enter an era of unprecedented flexibility "for people of every age to live lives that are congruent with their personal interests and wishes" (Settersten 2008, 22), the media provide "an important framework in all spheres of society for such an institutionalization of the individual biography" (Hjarvard 2009, 175). Here we call for a new line of inquiry located at the *intersections* of life course studies and media studies that explores the present status and future directions of aging, media, and culture.

In general, we find these two bodies of research are rarely in direct dialogue with one another. On one hand, media/cultural studies is underinformed about gerontological (or aging) theory and subsequently tends to: treat age as little more than a basic demographic variable; assume that chronological age has predictive power in media tastes and preferences; overlook other meanings of age; and assume homogeneity of older users/audiences. On the other hand, we find aging/life course studies to be underinformed about: differences in consumer/user/audience experiences; the influences of media forms and industries on the social and cultural aspects of the aging process; and media consumption itself as a meaning-making activity. Aging studies thus underengage the role of media/mediation in both its recent theoretical development and its current and future practical applications. This collection represents our own contribution toward bridging the divide between media/cultural and aging/life course studies and adds a unique perspective to recent literature on aging, performance, and stardom (Swinnen and Stotesbury 2012), aging and celebrity (*Celebrity Studies*, Issue 1, 2012), and media imagery and age-based identity (Ylanne 2012), among others.

Of particular interest to us and one of the distinctive features of our collection is how the institutional logics and practices of major culture industries "produce" older consumers—as in how culture industries formulate the association between themselves and the aging individual—in order to better understand how age is produced by these industries *as a social category.* Market constructions of adulthood and late(r) life set increasingly inescapable parameters for how adults navigate twenty-first-century aging, a reality that calls for considering how major culture industries themselves conceptualize aging and the life course as commodities. We examine a variety of media in this collection, both "old" and "new"—advertising, marketing, music, and social media, among others—and explore a range of questions about age/aging, identities, consumption practices, and affective engagement with media. We focus in this Introduction on the prominent culture industry of *television* as an exemplar and do so for four reasons: first, television's centrality in the mass media landscape of the past sixty years and thus in the lives of many older adults today; second, its centrality in Harrington and Bielby's long history of collaborative research; third, as an (unfortunate) model of the gap between media/cultural studies and aging/life course approaches; finally, as a mass media form whose days (some say) are numbered—not in terms of content but platform (how long will we still watch television on a TV?). As such, television is uniquely illustrative in terms of its rich history with the twentieth-century aging process and its bridge to the new media landscape, as well as the new landscape of aging.

Our discussion of television below is loosely informed by the production of culture perspective which focuses on the industrial systems within which the symbolic elements of culture are created, distributed, evaluated, taught, and preserved (Peterson and Anand 2004). This perspective offers insights into the institutional logics of the industries that produce culture and *how* they produce symbolic elements of culture, and thus is useful as we evaluate existing scholarship on the TV industry for how it conceptualizes the aging individual, and for how change in the social construction of age identification is related to how the industry engages consumers as individuals. We conclude with a brief overview of the contents of this collection.

MEDIA AND THE AGING SELF

At the core of the relationship between media industries, media engagement, and the individual as a viewer/listener/consumer/user is the aging self. Life span developmental psychologists have long noted the stability of personality traits that comprise the self throughout adulthood (Costa and McCrae 1980) and recognize the continuities in the self that appear as personality coherence from infancy to adulthood (Caspi 2000). They also suggest that long-term identity changes can take place in the characteristics associated with an identity, through a shift in the salience hierarchy of an identity, or from the outright gain or loss of an identity (Deaux 1991). This is especially relevant when we consider the demographic and other structural transformations of the twentieth-century tripartite life course (education, work/family, retirement) and the rewriting of established life-stage transitions such that individuals can no longer expect their lives to unfold chronologically as they once did (or were assumed to). The consequences of these structural level changes on the twenty-first-century self are reflected in the individualization thesis which emphasizes the tension between self/identity construction and the blurring of age-based norms (Waters et al. 2011). This tension is particularly evident in light of recent age identity research which finds that differences between actual age and subjective age become more pronounced with advancing chronological age (i.e., Montepare 2009, 42; Westerhof, Whitbourne, and Freeman 2012, 52), a disconnect highly pertinent to media industries as they struggle to identify and retain audiences in an expanding media landscape. Age identity research is explored by multiple authors in this collection.

Empirical research on age identity or perceived age dates back to the 1950s, and is commonly measured by subjective age and/or ideal age (Montepare 2009). Subjective age typically refers to "the age I feel," whereas ideal age represents "the age I would most like to be." In general, adults tend to feel younger and would like to be younger than their chronological age (Montepare 2009), and this disconnect is similar across cultures and intensifies across adulthood (Barak 2009). While perceived age represents only a facet of self/identity, its potential to capture self/identity shifts associated with major life course revisioning is unparalleled (Schafer and Shippee 2010). Offering additional insight into some of the complexities related to aging and self/identity construction, reconstruction, and maintenance is Westerhof's (2010) notion of lives "migrating in time." The idea of movement implied by temporal migration suggests that rapid cultural change can complicate how individuals adapt to social change under conditions of uncertainty and further affect what it means to grow old. Despite this interest by aging scholars in the effect of social change on self/identity, we believe (as noted earlier) that insufficient scholarly attention has been given to the *interplay* between rapid global aging and increasing mediation (see Harrington, Bielby, and Bardo 2011).

A key theme of this collection is that the interconnections between media-related activities and identities and the restructuring of the life course do not occur on their own. Market constructions of adulthood and late(r) life set increasingly inescapable parameters for how adults negotiate twenty-first-century aging, a reality that calls for considering how major culture industries themselves conceptualize aging and the life course as commodities. As noted above, we focus on the culture industry of television as our exemplar.

SCHOLARSHIP ON TELEVISION AND AGING

Two decades ago, media scholar George Gerbner (1993) observed that "Mass media, particularly television, form the common mainstream of contemporary culture. They present a steady, repetitive, and compelling system of images and messages. For the first time in human history, most of the stories are told to most of the children not by their parents, their school, or their church but by a group of distant corporations that have something to sell" (207). At the other end of the life span, media images of late(r) life increasingly serve as resources for older adults' identity work in the context of unprecedented population aging and the shortage of real-life role models for twenty-first-century aging (Harrington, Bielby, and Bardo 2011; Westerhof 2010), and corporations struggle to clarify what types of aging images will resonate with consumers. Conventional mass communication approaches to the study of media, especially of television's images of aging and late(r) life, target how older adults "use the media and how the media portray them" (Gantz, Gartenberg, and Rainbow 1980, 56). This research trajectory, which emerged in the United States in the 1950s and reached its peak in the 1970s, relies mainly on content analysis for its insights and is concerned with the representativeness of media images to the demography of the general population, both in the United States (Cassata, Anderson, and Skill 1983; Lauzen and Dozier 2005a, 2005b; Robinson and Skill 1995a) and abroad (Grajczyk and Zollner 1998; Kessler, Rakoczy, and Staudinger 2004). In general, both children and older adults are underrepresented on television; when older men and women appear, they tend to occupy peripheral or minor positions, have an absent or platonic relationship status, live alone, play comedic or eccentric roles, and are more likely to uphold traditional gender stereotypes (Healey and Ross 2002). This body of research drew on social learning theory as formulated by Albert Bandura and Richard Walters (1963) to account for the socializing effects of observed (stereotypical and other negative) behaviors, particularly on children, while cultivation theory (Gerbner et al. 2002)—the audiences' shared worldview that is anchored through "common stereotypes [deployed] though a relatively restrictive set of programs, images, and messages" (Signorielli 2004, 281)—was used to account for television's influence. "Because television has a limited amount of time to tell a story, it relies on stereotypical portrayals to get points across quickly with the intent of appealing to the emotions of viewers rather than their intellect" (Robinson and Anderson 2006, 287).

The basic premise of these traditional mass communication approaches is that television's images and representations are read *literally* by viewers and are taken at face value and out of context, not as the fictionalized, symbolic constructions they are known to be, or for the literary license that is central to their creation and production. These approaches also rest on the assumption that there is a direct and unmediated causal relationship between screen images and representations and audience beliefs in them as signifiers of social reality. While younger age groups (children and teens) are typically more susceptible to the influence of stereotypes, studies of their effect on older viewers yield contradictory results, with some researchers (Healey and Ross 2002) finding a negative outcome (older viewers are concerned about stereotypes) and others finding the opposite (older viewers are unfazed by belittling images) (Hofstetter et al. 1993), although some scholars do find negative stereotypes to be more common among older respondents in diminished economic, health, and living arrangements. Unresolved in these studies is whether heavier TV viewing overall is a cause or an outcome of life circumstances, as well as consideration of the intermediary processes that shape viewers' particular responses.

A contrasting body of research on media audiences recognizes that there is variance in life-stage-related television-viewing patterns, that high levels of TV viewing among the elderly can be a positive indicator of the relational bonds that viewing builds, and that most studies of elderly viewing practices are cross sectional in design and thus capture only cohort-specific effects whose generalizability is unknown. Because all aging occurs in social and historical contexts that shape the distinctive elements and outcomes of a generation (Elder, Kirkpatrick, and Crosnoe 2003), incorporating these factors is important to clarifying how older viewers as a demographic group that contains considerable individual variation actually use television or are affected by it. As Mary Chayko (1993) states, "a heightened sensitivity to the *meaning* of the viewing experience for persons . . . may help us develop the understanding that our complex modern social situations require [and provide scholars with] richer, more fully explanatory theories of social behavior" (588; emphasis in original). Finally, research on the association between differences in measured cognitive ability in use of the Internet (Freese, Rivas, and Hargittai 2006; van Deursen, van Dijk, and Peters 2011) suggests the importance of individual differences in predisposition to adoption and use of new media technologies (see also Gilly and Zeithaml 1985; Hilt and Lipschultz 2004; Mellor, Firth, and Moore 2008) and with the skills and abilities necessary for information processing more generally (John and Cole 1986; see also Slegers, van Boxtel, and Jolles 2009; van Deursen, van Dijk, and Peters 2011). As changes in distribution platforms and other "new rules" for the ways we watch television make finding one's preferred programming more difficult and/or the viewing experience more complicated (Carr 2011), technological comfort and facility become increasingly relevant for older audiences.

The long line of research that dates back to the seminal work by Stuart Hall (1980) and his colleagues on what audiences actually *do* with media content challenges the direct, unmediated effects presumed by generalizing theoretical approaches to the impact of media on viewer interpretation. As Chayko (1993) notes, onscreen representations are one thing, the active (not passive) meanings that viewers *make* of those representations are quite another thing, and the vast majority of research on TV and aging since the 1950s has focused on the former not the latter. How do meaning-making practices (re)shape our understanding of television, age, and aging? When we move beyond the assumption that TV watching is an inherently passive experience, what new insights emerge? In a study of older adults' daily lives, Paige E. Goodwin and colleagues (2005) found watching television to be a critical mechanism through which older adults work "to maintain an optimum range of emotional experience" (69). For older adults in their study, television is an activity "that can be used either to enhance positive affect or avoid negative affect" (68). Moreover, in a qualitative study of older Dutch TV viewers, Margot van der Goot and colleagues (2012) found that personal experiences over the life span lead to lifelong content interests *and* aversions, that differences in available time, health, and need for diverse activities lead to both more *and* less TV viewing (not just more) among older adults, and that television "has a variety of meanings as people age" (162). Finally, the first editor of this volume and a colleague explored how older US soap opera watchers deliberately weigh onscreen representations that they find dissatisfying against their awareness of the realities of soaps' aging audience base, the target demographics of soaps' corporate sponsors, and the economic struggles of the genre as a whole (Harrington and Brothers 2011). Part of their consumption experience is thus keen insight into the complexities of their identity and status *as* aging consumers of a product with a long history and a dwindling shelf life. In short, the outcome of a focus on media effects alone, without attention to audience practices, can yield contradictory outcomes.

Our point is this: *that* older adults watch television and *how much* and *what* they watch—the still-extant research focus dominant from the 1950s to the 1970s—must be more carefully balanced with empirical insight into *how* they watch and the personal meanings *made* of consumption practices, a research focus dating back to Hall's (1980) classic work but still too frequently overlooked by scholars and practitioners of both media *and* aging. Indeed, we were dismayed at the experience had by one of us serving as an expert advisor to the National Institute of Aging/National Academies of Sciences in 2011: a leading administrator dismissed television as a relevant funding priority for NAS by claiming that "everything to know" about TV and aging had been learned by the 1970s, thus negating several decades of research on media audiences/fans and the now taken-for-granted active audiences/users/consumers approach launched thirty-plus years ago. George Gerbner points out that "The need is not to regulate the image of aging—or anything else—on television but to loosen the constraints distorting it" (1993, 218). We need both a broader diversity of images of aging "in a visually and age-conscious society" (Featherstone and Hepworth 2009, 136)—acknowledging that alternative or emancipatory images are difficult to construct (Richards, Warren, and Gott 2012)—along with greater consideration of the role of imaginative engagement in generating the meanings of television for older adults.

CONCLUSION: BROADENING
AN UNDERSTANDING OF MEDIA ENGAGEMENT

Our goal in the prior section was to critique scholarship on television for overlooking how the logics and practices of the television industry socially construct aging and older consumers as a social category. The TV industry is crucial to the contemporary aging experience because of the important role it plays in cultural typecasting through the assumptions it makes about age and aging, because scholarly inattention undermines a deeper understanding of how these industries construct age, aging, and the life course as cultural products, and because little is understood about the experience of older consumers when they become the focus of the television industry. In short, continued neglect of the influential contributions this industry makes to the saturated presence of media in contemporary society limits understanding of the important role it plays in producing age.

Before briefly introducing the contents of this collection, which widen our scope of inquiry far beyond television, we return to our opening quotations—to what Dannefer and Miklowski (2006) observed about the consequentiality of the producer-consumer relationship for the life course, and to what Livingstone (2009) proposes about mediation. As media grow in importance as a crucial site for the formulation, management, and maintenance of identity and the self, the significance of "why media?" moves increasingly to the foreground. Research on fans has found that the potential for emotional authenticity is central to the media's growing cultural importance (Bielby and Bielby 2004; Harrington and Bielby 1995), but as Peterson and Anand (2004) observed, the autoproduction of authenticity leads to a complicated tension between producers and consumers. In one of his final contributions to the production of culture perspective, sociologist Richard Peterson observed that "This complex interplay between the artifice of manufacture and the fans' experience of authenticity is arguably the most important unresolved paradox of cultural sociology" (Peterson and Anand 2004, 326). So, what *is* the authenticity of age in the twenty-first century? How that intersects with consumer identities, tastes for various products, and media consumption in our media saturated society invites intriguing questions to explore in this anthology.

We have designed the volume to include paired contributions around seven core topics related to aging, media, and culture in the twenty-first century: advertising/marketing, age/identity, celebrity, music, fandom, gender/sexuality, and social/new media. The pairings were designed to allow for different disciplinary perspectives on these seven topics as well as multiple theoretical and empirical orientations. Overall we are pleased with the diversity represented herein—the chapters are situated in media/cultural studies, film studies, sociology, celebrity and fan studies, feminism/postfeminism, gerontology, aging studies, communications, and marketing discourse, among others. Some authors draw on their own biographical narratives while others study consumption experiences at very specific sites such as nursing homes and online communities. Elements of media production, distribution and consumption are explored throughout the collection, with particular attention paid to how media industries engage audiences as aged/aging individuals. As rapid mediation and rapid global aging converge in complex and unexpected ways, we hope this collection provides insight into the myriad of questions surrounding aging, media, and culture.

NOTE

1. Media/communications scholars are debating the suitability of two related terms to describe this phenomenon: mediation vs. mediatization. Mediation implies that "we moved from a social analysis in which the mass media comprise one among many influential but interdependent institutions whose relations with the media can be usefully analyzed to a social analysis in which everything is mediated, the consequence being that all influential institutions in society have themselves been transformed, reconstituted by contemporary processes of mediation" (Livingstone 2009, 2). In contrast, mediatization, drawn from the German Laws of Mediatization in the early nineteenth century, implies that "the media not only get between any and all participants in society but also, crucially, annex a sizeable part of their power by mediatizing—subordinating—the previously powerful authorities of government, education, the church, the family, and so forth" (2009, 6). For our purposes here, mediation is the more apt term (acknowledging the limitations outlined by Livingstone [2009]).

I

Advertising and Marketing

Chapter Two

Aspiration and Compromise

Portrayals of Older Adults in Television Advertising

Shyon Baumann and Kim de Laat

There is a vast literature on the portrayals of people in advertising, with major veins of research on gender and race. The literature on the portrayal of age groups in advertising is comparatively limited. However, one enduring finding of the research is that older people are underrepresented in advertising (and in the media more generally). We find this underrepresentation as well. In this chapter, we take this underrepresentation as the starting point for delving further into the nature of representations of older adults in advertising.

We analyze a sample of prime-time television commercials featuring older adults (fifty or older) as marketing discourse on the imagined older consumer. The literature on consumption has not taken up the case of older consumers as a distinct group with distinct ways of consuming (Simcock and Sudbury 2006). Discourse analysis of marketing content can provide multidimensional insights into cultural ideals about forms of consumption that are linked to particular social groups. Through a discursive and visual analysis, in this chapter we explore depictions of older adults in television advertising in order to make claims about a specific form of consumption among older adults. This analysis, built on observations of physical, personality, and behavioral dimensions of older characters in commercials, allows us to outline how consumption works for and is enacted by older adults in a form that is different from younger age groups.

The question of the nature of representations of older adults in advertising has two main motivations. On one level, we are interested to know more about these portrayals because of the potential for messages in the media to influence cultural schemas about social groups. Stereotypical and negative portrayals can reproduce limiting and damaging dominant understandings of the proper place of people in society. On another level, we are interested to know more about these portrayals because they present somewhat of a puzzle for advertisers. Advertisers typically employ aspirational marketing strategies, linking their goods and services to people consumers are assumed to aspire to be, or to qualities that consumers are assumed to aspire to possess (Richins 1991; Schudson 1984). And yet old age is devalued in society, rather than an aspirational quality (Nelson 2004). Given that most advertising is "aspirational," and depicts people and lifestyles that audiences are assumed to aspire to, and given that old age is predominantly devalued in our culture, what schemas/themes/strategies are used to portray older people in commercials?

We proceed by first explaining the empirical and analytical payoffs of analyzing the content of advertising. We then review prior work that has examined the portrayal of older adults in advertising, in order to show how our findings build on and innovate from earlier research. We present our main findings in the next section, before concluding with a discussion of the significance of our findings for understanding how advertising participates in the reproduction of cultural schemas for old age as an identity.

Based on our findings, we argue that advertisers recognize that old age is not aspirational and cannot be easily converted to something positive in the current cultural climate. This is precisely the point at which advertising's business imperatives trump any notions of social responsibility, as advertising reproduces dominant (and mostly negative) cultural schemas for older adults. Most obviously and most directly, advertisers manage the devaluation of old age through overall underrepresentation of older adults and by omitting older adults from straightforwardly aspirational advertising. However, when older adults are present, old age is most often tackled head on, insofar as for most of these characters, their age is not incidental but rather is central to their role in the commercial. Our main findings are a description of these modes of portrayal that rely on characters' old age, and we argue that these modes have not been identified in prior research. These modes of portrayal are 1) old age as comedic condition, 2) old age as treatable condition, 3) old age as context for occupational relationships, and 4) old age as context for familial relationships. We identify a fifth, minor mode of portrayal within our sample where age is incidental to the mode of portrayal of older characters. We interpret the significance of these findings to argue that these modes of portrayal are employed to allow advertisers to manage the tension between the culturally dominant devaluation of old age and the need to avoid negative and stereotypical portrayals of older adults.

CULTURAL SCHEMAS AND MARKETING STRATEGIES

Studies of media content are important for the inherent value in describing and understanding the complicated and voluminous products that are generated by the media industry. Just as importantly, the study of media content is valuable because of its links to the broader culture in which it is produced and consumed. We view patterns in advertising content as informed by dominant cultural schemas, the "rules of social life" (Sewell 1992, 7) that are automatic and unconscious, and that shape perception and interpretation in everyday cognitive processes (Vaisey 2009, 1686). Among the many cultural schemas that exist, those that apply to people are strongly structured by salient social categories such as age and gender, among others. Cultural schemas about people provide a cognitive framework that sets expectations and suggests how to best understand information we have about people, based on the social categories to which they are perceived to belong (Ridgeway and Correll 2004a). Indeed, scholars in cultural sociology recognize that the media are both reflective of dominant cultural schemas and a source from which individuals learn schematic knowledge (for example, see Bielby and Bielby 2001; DiMaggio 1997, 280; Ridgeway and Correll 2004b, 513; Vaisey 2008, 610).

Advertising exists to persuade audiences, and marketing, as both a field of knowledge and a business practice, has developed many strategies for achieving this goal. Aspirational advertising is one such strategy, and it accounts for the general tendency of advertising to present idealized people, contexts, and relationships (Schudson 1984). An investigation of advertising content, then, reveals not just raw cultural schemas, but cultural schemas that have been conditioned in order to fit into common marketing strategies, such as aspirational advertising. We interpret our findings as produced by the confluence of cultural schemas and marketing strategies.

This research is motivated by a broader social context where enduring inequalities are patterned by age. Through shaping expectations and perceptions of people (Macrae and Bodenhausen 2000), dominant cultural schemas can contribute to the reproduction of unequal social outcomes. Accordingly, understanding the nature of cultural schemas for age can improve our understanding of how these inequalities persist.

OLDER ADULTS IN ADVERTISING: UNDERREPRESENTATION IN THE ABSENCE OF OVERT NEGATIVITY

With a couple of exceptions (Lee, Carpenter, and Meyers 2007; Robinson 1998), prior research from various nations finds that older adults are underrepresented in advertising relative to their presence in the population, and also that older women are even more dramatically underrepresented than older men (Carrigan and Szmigin 1998; Furnham and Mak 1999; Ganahl, Prinsen, and Netzley 2003; Gantz, Gartenberg, and Rainbow 1980; Hiemstra et al. 1983; Harwood and Anderson 2002; Harwood and Roy 1999; Langmeyer 1993; Ong and Chang 2009; Prieler et al. 2011; Robinson and Skill 1995b; Roy and Harwood 1997; Swayne and Greco 1986). The rates of underrepresentation vary, and comparisons across studies are made difficult by variations in the age categories used and in the nature of the data sources (both medium and national context). However, most studies find fairly dramatic rates of underrepresentation.

Regarding the modes of representation, studies conducted in the 1970s and 1980s tend to find negative depictions of older adults in advertising. Vasil and Wass (1993) review and summarize these studies and find that the vast majority of them report that older characters are constrained to marginalized and stereotypical roles. However, many of the more recent studies find that older adults are portrayed positively and avoid negative stereotypes (Roy and Harwood 1997), with some even finding generally more positive portrayals relative to younger age groups. Roberts and Zhou (1997) find that characters over fifty in advertisements in the UK are generally portrayed as capable, important, healthy, and physically and socially active. Simcock and Sudbury (2006) find that while models fifty or older in advertising are more likely to appear in incidental roles, they are not portrayed negatively and generally avoid stereotyping.

In a comprehensive overview of the research, Harwood (2007, 167), a leading researcher in the area of media depictions of older adults, concludes, "Overall, though, advertising does appear to be one area in which positive portrayals are fairly common. Indeed, there are some indications that advertising may be at the leading edge of genuinely positive, and even liberating, portrayals of older adults."

We have two interpretations of this trend toward positive portrayals. It is possible that as overt stereotyping of all types (e.g., gender, race, disability, age, etc.) has become less socially acceptable in society, media depictions are reflecting these changing norms. It is also possible that as populations age, advertisers either consciously or subconsciously are creating advertising that is more appealing to or resonates more with older audience members.

We also think that there is more work to be done to accurately characterize the modes of portrayals for older adults. Although we do not disagree with the general research findings regarding the lack of overtly negative and stereotypical portrayals of older adults in advertising, we think that this research is hampered by a tendency to measure the presence of stereotypes. Although a valuable endeavor, stereotype measurement must be supplemented by an analysis that is open to seeing new ways in which portrayals are patterned. Moreover, an understanding of the portrayal of older adults needs to reconceptualize the context in which these portrayals appear. In particular, we think it is imperative to incorporate an important aspect of the larger cultural context, as well as an important aspect of the specific organizational and market context, especially insofar as these two aspects are in tension. Culturally, we recognize that old age is devalued while youth is glorified. Organizationally, we recognize that advertising is predominantly oriented toward a strategy of aspirational marketing, where advertising associates goods and services with people and lifestyles that audiences aspire to be or to have. How do advertisements manage this tension when depicting older people? What kinds of depictions does it tend to produce? How does the problem of age resolve?

METHODS

Television commercials are an ideal data source for investigating cultural schemas. Advertisers must deliver messages that resonate with as large an audience as possible and under tight time constraints. Compared to other media content producers (i.e., television and film production), they have less opportunity for character development and so have greater incentive to rely on dominant schematic or stereotypical depictions to present characters in their narratives. Moreover, and as we discuss further below, time constraints can encourage the use of exaggerated or extreme versions of cultural schemas (Goffman 1979), which can render them more readily identifiable. The study of television commercials, then, is ideal for uncovering the dominant, yet implicit, social "rules" for classifying and understanding the nature of the identities of women and men of different ages (Baumann and de Laat 2012).

We draw our qualitative analysis from a dataset of more than 5,800 advertisements aired during primetime programming on Canada's three primary television networks. Each advertisement was coded for a variety of factors, such as character age, gender, race, whether they are depicted as a (grand)parent, at work, and the product type being advertised. Three different coders worked independently to ensure that variable coding was reliable. Intercoder reliability was calculated using Cohen's kappa in Stata, and an agreement rate of 0.90 or higher was achieved for most variables. For the present analysis, we isolated all ads in which a character aged fifty or older appeared as a primary character. Primary characters receive more than five seconds of screen time. The plotline of the advertisement revolves around them, and they typically have a speaking role.

Once duplicate ads were removed, we were left with a sample of seventy-four advertisements. The qualitative analysis was inductive in nature. We documented the plotlines and dialogue occurring in each ad, and undertook an in-depth reading of advertorial content. We paid attention to many of the traditional Goffmanian signals (Goffman 1979), such as the use of ritualistic touch, as well as to whether characters addressed the camera directly when they spoke, or whether a voiceover was instead responsible for conveying information. A detailed description of our methodological approach can be found in Baumann and de Laat (2012). Although we were attendant to the presence of stereotypes as identified in prior research, the themes that we present as our findings emerged from repeated viewings and discussions of the nature of the portrayals.

FIVE MODES OF PORTRAYAL TO MAKE
OLDER AGE A MANAGEABLE CATEGORY

Before describing our modes of portrayal, it is important to understand the context in which these portrayals are occurring. In particular, the context is one of dramatic underrepresentation of older adults. Within our sample of 5,854 visible characters, 19.8 percent are children and teenagers, 17.1 percent are in their twenties, 29.9 percent are in their thirties, 20.9 percent are in their forties, 6.8 percent are in their fifties, 3.9 percent are in their sixties, and 1.5 percent are seventy or older. Among those over the age of fifty, 73 percent are men, and 27 percent are women. In the broadest terms, people fifty or older are strongly underrepresented, while people less than fifty are strongly overrepresented.

The seventy-four commercials in our sample featured portrayals of older adults that assume one or more of five modes of portrayal. Older adult characters generally did not assume multiple modes of portrayal, however different characters within the same commercial could assume different modes of portrayal. It must be noted also that, as with other demographic characteristics such as gender and race, age was rarely left ambiguous. Characters in commercials are presented as clear "types," of which age is a defining component. For men, baldness is a clear signal for old age, with the majority of our older male characters depicted as bald. For both women and men, outdated or "old people clothes" are used to signal old age, such as old-fashioned cardigans for men and floral prints for women. As an appearance-focused genre, advertising is quite effective at employing visual cues to characterize people.

The most common mode of portrayal for older adults is to frame age as a comedic condition. Humor is employed in 54 percent of the ads, where older adult characters facilitate a comedic goal of the commercial through their being old.[1] Their old age becomes part of the narrative that generates interest and appeal, through humor. In none of the commercials in our sample was age directly ridiculed or explicitly denigrated. Overt ageism is becoming increasingly socially unacceptable, and the commercials reflect that. However, as has been documented with sexism in the media, when overtly negative stereotypical or offensive depictions are essentially off limits, social expressions of differential valuation and preference are often expressed more subtly. We find that this is the case with the portrayal of age, where comedy is used to buffer what would otherwise be offensive or harsh commentaries on age. A good example can be found in a commercial for TD Canada Trust: Two white men in their seventies are sitting on a bench on the street. The audience eavesdrops on their conversation, and we hear that they are talking about how awful it is that this bank is open for so long (the bank's extended business hours being the focus of the commercial). "What's wrong with the way it used to be?" one asks. Both men are dressed in clothes that typify old age, with one in an old-fashioned cardigan. One of the men is hunched over from age, and both men speak with disgruntled and raspy voices.

This commercial is focusing on the useful innovation of extending the bank's business hours. It is clearly an idea that many customers will find appealing and rational. The older adults in the commercial find the change difficult, but the humor in the commercial allows us to both focus on the marketing message and to subtly comment on the silliness of the stubborn and inefficient ways of older people, but without being overtly offensive. There is a winking acknowledgement of the slightly sad behavior of the older adults, one that seems both accepting and at the same time mocking.

While humor can be used to smooth over otherwise offensive stereotypical portrayals, it can also be used to present counter-stereotypical portrayals. A good example of a counter-stereotypical portrayal is found in a commercial for the Honda Pilot SUV: An older white man is driving down the road with his teenaged son beside him when he comes across a downed hot air balloon in the road. We see that there are six elderly people (of multiple races) in the balloon, all nudists. The driver offers them a ride, with the marketing message made that they all fit in the large vehicle. The driver and his son make it clear that they are hard to look at since they are nude, and their nudity is humorous rather than sexualized. At the same time, the elderly balloonists are framed as incompetent for having crashed, and perhaps slightly deranged for being nude. They even look a little confused about what they are doing. The driver is shown before the end of the commercial looking a little disgusted, while his son looks both mortified and clearly disgusted.

Because sexuality is so strongly associated with youth in the general culture, nude depictions of older adults are not only unexpected, but also ridiculous, and even disgusting. On the surface, showing a great deal of skin of older adults is liberating because it is counter-stereotypical, as is depicting older adults hot air ballooning. Of course, this strategy eventually just reinforces the stereotype. Harwood (2007, 159) notes that "older people and aging are used a lot for comic effect, often in less-than-flattering ways.

Comedy can be achieved by having a stereotypical older character who is the butt of other characters' jokes (e.g., the dirty old man, the forgetful aging parent). Such messages obviously rely on shared knowledge of the stereotype for their humor and almost certainly serve to reinforce that stereotype." What is missing are depictions that are counter-stereotypical without being humorous. In their article specifically on the progressive possibilities of the show *The Golden Girls*, Harwood and Giles (1992) argue that in that show, humorous portrayals frame counter-stereotypical portrayals as literally laughable, with the final effect being to simply restate the stereotypical understanding as legitimate, however implicitly.

The second mode of portrayal we identified in our sample of commercials is for older adults to engage in consumption to "treat" or deal with age and/or age-related consumption needs. Consumption among these characters tends not to be glamorous or high status. Interestingly, we note that in our sample of commercials with older adult primary characters, just under half the commercials feature older adults consuming or using the advertised products for themselves. In the commercials where older adults are consuming for themselves, nearly one-third of the commercials are for old-age-related conditions or experiences, mostly implicating health, bodily function, or appearance. In the commercials where older adults are present but not consuming or using the product advertised, none of the commercials are for age-related conditions or experiences. In other words, the portrayal of consumption among older adults in commercials is strongly related to marketing products directly toward older purchasers. Older adults are not shown consuming products that are for all ages, and certainly not for products that are targeting younger markets. A good example of this mode of portrayal is Nivea DNAge: A white woman in her early fifties quickly walks down the stairs as a voice-over intended to represent her own voice says, "Beauty is embracing all my experiences." She steps outside to meet her twenty-something daughter, who is waiting in the driver's seat of her convertible. She continues, "I feel wiser. I feel confident." Mother and daughter drive away in the car. They pull up to traffic lights and in the car next to them are two young attractive men. They gaze over at the women in the convertible, however, it is left to the viewers to decide whether the men are gazing at the daughter or the mother. "But I certainly don't feel older." The mother then glances at her daughter and smiles. Another female voice-over comes on to introduce the product—an antiaging cream that firms up skin and reduces the look of wrinkles.

On the one hand, the older woman is empowered by her appearance as she is depicted as attractive. Nevertheless, the older woman in this commercial is treating her age in order to correct what is being put forward as a deficiency or as decay caused by wrinkles. Other products that appeared in our sample and that illustrate this mode of portrayal include Viagra (erectile dysfunction medication) and Restoralax (laxative), as well as retirement-related financial instruments.

In the third mode of portrayal, age was emphasized as an important aspect for understanding occupational relationships. In these portrayals, age is neither overtly positive nor negative. For these older adults, age can be a tool for establishing occupational authority and supervisory capacity. Sometimes they are depicted on the job, and sometimes they are spokespeople for a brand, company, or product. One example of the former is a hockey coach managing players in a commercial for McDonald's, where the coach is seen to be using his vast experience in hockey to be deciding on players' careers. Another example is the depiction of a traditional, Old World candy maker in a commercial for Werther's caramels, where the older adult character is implied to carry generations of vocational experience and knowledge. For depictions on the job, we observed this mode of portrayal only for men. An advertisement for Dyson vacuum cleaners is particularly illustrative of this mode: The commercial features a male voice-over discussing the difficulties of vacuuming as well as the advantages of Dyson vacuums in managing these difficulties. It is revealed that the voice-over is the inventor of the vacuum cleaner and owner of the company, an older White man who demonstrates the science that makes the brand innovative. As he talks, we are shown a montage of women vacuuming over successive decades, signaling technological advancements over time.

Another example of the spokesperson portrayal is a senior lawyer in a law firm portrayed as the spokesperson for the firm, explaining the firm's areas of expertise in a serious tone. Thirty-two percent of characters are depicted as spokespeople (both celebrities and noncelebrities). Among spokespeople, the ratio of men to women is 3:1.

The fourth mode of portrayal relies on age to establish the nature of familial relationships, most often as a parent or grandparent. (Nineteen percent of characters are portrayed as grandparents, and this is evenly split between men and women.) However, consumption among these characters is not particularly glamorous or high status. Instead, the characters engage in consumption within their relationships as parents/grandparents or employees. The focus is not on the self or indulgence, as is often the case with younger characters. Consider the following example for Royal Bank of Canada: An upper-middle-class white man and East Asian woman are shown flying and then arriving at their destination airport. The man says in voice-over, "I wasn't ready for the rocking chair," and explains that they received personalized advice to achieve an idealized retirement. They are depicted as savvy and sophisticated travelers and for the moment it looks like they are going on an expensive travel adventure. However, at the airport their grandchildren greet them and the emotional greeting demonstrates a great deal of fulfillment on their part.

This was one of many ads showing older people with their grandkids. In this particular instance, the identity of these characters centers on their roles as grandparents in their retirement, not as their independent selves or as adventurous travelers. Another example of this mode of portrayal is found in a couple of commercials for Kleenex tissues, where a series of older women are presented as competing to care for the needs of younger adult relatives, so as to be "chosen" as the "right" mom.

A fifth theme, which applies to a small minority of characters, and they are often the younger characters among those who are older, is for age to actually be incidental. In these portrayals, the older adult is not linked to a product that is specifically for older consumers, and there are no familial or occupational relationships conditioned by their older age. In these ads, humor is also not employed. In short, there are a small number of ads where older adults are presented as people, not as older people. An example of this is a commercial for Blinds To Go, where an older woman is shown shopping for blinds for her house. Although shopping for the home is gendered labor, people of all ages need and use blinds, and no mention is made of her age. Another example is a commercial for Casino Rama, a Toronto-area casino, where two of the patrons of the casino are older adults. Adults of all age groups patronize casinos, and there is no age distinction being made in the way that these older adults are depicted as customers of the casino.

CONCLUSION

In this study of the representation of older adults in television advertising, we replicate prior findings on the underrepresenation of older adults (fifty or older), where the underrepresentation of older women is more severe than the underrepresentation of older men. But we also generate new findings about the portrayal of older adults. We argue that five modes of portrayal characterize the primary ways in which older adults currently appear in television advertising.

Overall, how should we characterize these portrayals? When age is not incidental to, but rather, the focus of the character, there is a strong tendency for advertisers to portray age according to hegemonic cultural schemas for age. These schemas differ across the modes.

These schemas are present, however implicitly, in comedic portrayals, where ageist stereotypes (e.g., incompentent, desexualized) are subtly employed, or employed counterhegemonically (but to the same effect). When counterhegemonic portrayals are employed in a humorous context, the advertisements ultimately confirm that these counterhegemonic ideas are laughable. All deviation is humorous, and this humor undermines any progressive or innovative portrayals. In the mode of "treating" old age, schemas of deficiency and the social unacceptability of ageing are present.

The third mode of portrayal, where age is used to position a character within an occupational relationship as authoritative, is hegemonic but also ostensibly a positive depiction, since authority is a valued trait and resource. However, the mode of portrayal is sexist insofar as the portrayal is available only to older men. Again, there is strong conformity to existing cultural schemas for age, and in this case also for gender. In the familial mode, schemas are reinforced because old age as an identity matters only insofar as the older adults can fulfill some warm, familial function for others (e.g., caring for others), thereby also constraining the range of consumer identities available to them.

In essence, there are virtually no counterhegemonic age portrayals, while there are a great number of regressive dominant cultural schemas reinforced for old age identity. In their portrayal of older adults, advertising relies on characters that almost never deviate from a narrow range of age-specific behaviors in a straightforward way. Taken together, these modes of portrayal do not overtly stereotype or denigrate older adults (notwithstanding a couple of egregious examples). However, our analysis shows that these portrayals cannot be considered liberating and instead reinforce damaging and constraining cultural schemas.

How can we account for these portrayals? We argue that these modes balance preexisting dominant cultural schemas for identity of older adults' with marketers' imperatives to persuade audiences and to generate positive affect toward the advertised good or service. On the one hand, the portrayal of older adults is rational from a marketing perspective, in order to advance a narrative within the commercial (e.g., dinner with the whole family) or to depict a typical consumer for a product (e.g., Viagra), or just to portray a "realistic" workplace. They cannot be entirely absent from advertising. On the other hand, marketing strives to be aspirational and to depict idealized people and lifestyles (Schudson 1984). Given that ageism is pervasive, insofar as old age is culturally devalued relative to youth (Perdue and Gurtman 1990), marketers must strategize, however consciously or subconsciously, about how to portray older adults within this marketing context. We argue that the portrayals do not necessarily solve marketers' quandary, but they are compromises that deal with their main constraints. The first compromise is to minimize the appearance of this troublesome category of character. Beyond that, when portraying older adults, advertisers employ modes of portrayal that neutralize the negative cultural valence of age through humor (first mode), or that position age as a condition that is "treatable" by the specific goods and services being advertised (second mode), or that use age to establish occupational and familial relationships to advance a narrative within a commercial (third and fourth modes). In a very small number of cases, age is incidental to the portrayal of an older adult. It is possible that this fifth mode will grow in importance over time, which would be a progressive development in the depiction of age in advertising.

Finally, what do these modes of portrayals tell us about older adults *as consumers*? We interpret these portrayals as producing a picture of older adults as "compromised" consumers. In contrast to younger adults, older adults are never depicted in straightforwardly aspirational modes. In aspirational modes, younger characters are portrayed as though age is incidental to their identity, although this really just means that young age is the default age identity. These younger characters are presented as full consumers, for whom consumption is about status, enjoyment, independence, and achievement. Older adult characters, for whom age is almost always central to their characters, and is a stigmatized identity that has to be managed in some way within the commercial. Consumption is less often for the self, more often for others, and when it is self-oriented, it is related to "treating" age and age-related "problems." Rather than hedonistic, consumption for older adults is "compromised," producing the modes of portrayals we identify, because of the status disadvantage and practical constraints of older age.

NOTE

1. Although we do not have a reliable measure of the use of humor for the larger sample of commercials from which this paper's sample was taken, our subjective impression is that humor is dramatically more frequent in this smaller sample with older adults as primary characters.

Chapter Three

Forever Young

The New Aging Consumer in the Marketplace

Anne L. Balazs

This chapter will summarize the research in marketing and communication that deals with portrayals of older consumers in various media and advertising channels. As the US population has aged, and those who control the media and marketplace have aged as well, the representation of baby boomers and seniors has become more realistic and positive. Increasing political, social, and economic power has led to greater visibility, and a more sensitive portrayal of older Americans. In fact, the rise of an ageless cohort is part of this trend as well.

MARKETING TO A NEW GENERATION

The industrial capacity and economies of scale realized in the first half of the twentieth century led to mass production and the introduction of a consumer society. Scientific breakthroughs in synthetic materials allowed for lighter, more durable and less expensive goods to flood the market. The largesse of manufacturers was finding its way to the burgeoning populace of post–World War II. The baby boom generation (the largest cohort heretofore in world history) was born during the years 1946–1964 and the art and science of marketing became more sophisticated. Household formation and construction starts led to increased spending on durable goods (vehicles, appliances) and soft goods (home furnishings, sporting/leisure goods). Mass merchandising was the most common method of meeting consumer demand through discount department stores and other modern retail formats. At the same time, advertising media were expanding, as were the points of data capture.

The population growth and buying patterns warranted a closer look and new areas of inquiry (e.g., consumer research) and methodologies, such as telephone surveys, took off. As computer and satellite technology spilled over into academic and commercial arenas, it became possible to track TV viewing behavior, magazine readership, and mail order frequency. Marketing segmentation methods were employed to better understand consumers based on finer demographic, psychographic, and behavioral details.

Of course, the seventy-six million baby boomers were a market force to be reckoned with and many manufacturers and brands were born in the 1960s and 1970s in an attempt to capture the attention (and brand loyalty) of the new youth culture. The music, apparel, and automobile industries helped to support the revolutionary changes brought on by the tsunami of young adults. At the same time, the boomers' parents were aging and reaping the benefits of a prosperous economy, advances in health care, and the bounty of agricultural output. In fact, the boomers' parents were achieving sizeable gains in longevity and economic well-being. However, there was little attention paid to this group, having been successfully overshadowed by their progeny. It has since been recognized that the older market segments are indeed engaged in consumption behavior, that they are growing faster than younger cohorts, and that they have the disposable income that makes them attractive to retailers and service providers (Meiners and Seeberger 2010). In addition, as the population ages, the definition of what is "old" is continually being addressed and reevaluated. Thus we are able to point to a time when the senior market was "invisible" and now to a very different set of circumstances.

This chapter addresses the fall and rise of the elderly as a market segment via their portrayal in advertising. As the first line of baby boomers have reached retirement age and the population as a whole is aging, more images of well-preserved seniors are evident and a greater effort to remain ageless is being promoted. Recommendations for marketing to these consumers in the future are offered in light of this paradigmatic shift.

THE GROWTH OF THE MATURE MARKET

There have been multiple markers of old age in the United States, but the convention has been age sixty-five because of its association with retirement and eligibility for Medicare and Social Security benefits. The monikers "senior citizens," "senior market," or "mature market" have been used extensively and interchangeably in the marketing literature with attempts to further discriminate based on cognitive age, social roles, attitudes, health factors, wealth, and mobility. The notion of what qualifies as elderly continues to be addressed (Orimo, Ito, Suzuki, Araki, Hosoi, and Sawabe 2006) with the recommendation that "elderly" now refer to those over the age of seventy-five. The physical well-being (and indeed life expectancy) of those between sixty-five and seventy-five has improved that much over time as to suggest a redefinition of what is old. The dynamics of modern aging are creating new segments of seniors. For the purposes of this chapter, the terms elderly, older, mature, and senior will be used to refer to those who are chronologically aged sixty-five and over.

The Older Consumer as a New Market Segment

Beginning in the 1970s, marketing researchers started to explore the senior market and foretold of its potential impact. While the population was aging, there was limited use of people over sixty-five in the media, print advertising, general readership magazines and prime-time television. The assumption was that the elderly were no longer actively engaged in personal and household consumption, indeed that they were likely to be institutionalized, infirm, and impoverished. Not only were seniors underrepresented, but discounted as well.

The treatment of the elderly in advertising in the late twentieth century did not accurately reflect their position in American society. The whole world was aging, as birth rates were slowing, life spans were increasing, and the nature of old age was being redefined. Groups such as the American Association of Retired Persons (AARP, founded in 1958) and the Gray Panthers (founded in 1972) formed vocal lobbying groups to advocate for greater protection. The field of geriatrics was growing as a medical specialty and informing the social sciences and business.

With an aging group of "new old" (sixty-five to seventy-four years old), "old old" (seventy-five to ninety) and even the "oldest old" (ninety-one to one hundred) senior citizens, a market for travel and leisure, housing, personal care services, financial services, exercise equipment and classes, ergonomically designed homes and adaptive products was born. Seniors were more likely to choose "aging in place," defined by the Centers for Disease Control (2013) as "the ability to live in one's own home and community safely, independently, and comfortably, regardless of age, income, or ability level." While many more options for senior living exist now, from communal complexes to upscale assisted living communities, the preference remains for most older adults to live at home, rather than be institutionalized. This has spawned new industries, services, and a greater sensitivity to personal decision making in later life.

Impact of an Aging Society

The aging of the US population has been decades in the making. Social scientists and other researchers have anticipated and tracked the "age wave" and its potentially deleterious effects on the economy. The concerns of this demographic imperative have ranged from an insufficient labor force unable to support a burgeoning segment of retirees, to the dramatic increase in health care costs, to limitations on productivity and growth. As of 2011, almost forty million Americans were over sixty-five years old. That number is expected to almost double to 72.1 million by 2030, when the youngest baby boomers reach sixty-five (US Census Bureau 2011). This coincides with a decreasing birth rate to result in a long anticipated "graying" of America and redefinition of the population pyramid. That said, there will be a socialization effect over time that will likely assuage fears of growing old and may even lead to greater levels of life satisfaction. A new paradigm of healthy aging will develop (Agogo, Milne, and Schewe 2013). The heterogeneity of this group is important to acknowledge as well. While 12.8 percent of the US population is over sixty-five, there are significant differences within this group. Socioeconomic indicators and health status can be used to further segment the elderly population and yet, with increasing levels of education and retirement savings, some of these effects are mitigated over time. In addition, Fry, Cohn, Livingston, and Taylor (2011, 3) point out that "older Americans have been the beneficiaries of good timing" with respect to home ownership and the accumulation of equity in their investment.

The fact is that the elderly control the majority of the nation's wealth. According to Fry et al. (2011, 1): "In 2009, households headed by adults ages sixty-five and older possessed 42 percent more median net worth (assets minus debt) than households headed by their same-aged counterparts had in 1984." Furthermore, expenditure patterns of those over sixty-five do not change as dramatically as some might think. The percentage of household income spent on clothing and entertainment stay relatively the same as do a few other categories. Surprisingly food, housing, and transportation expenditures as a percentage of household income also remain relatively stable. As one might expect, health care expenditures go up and savings and investments are drawn down over time (US Bureau of Labor Statistics 2006).

As for buying behavior, the quality of decision making by the elderly and their preference for relying on friends and word of mouth for referrals is of concern (Perry and Wolburg 2011). The limited search activity and use of technology until recently has led to less than optimal outcomes when wealth, health, and personal safety are at stake. Seniors are often targeted by unscrupulous business practices regarding their financial investments, health insurance, medical treatment options, and charitable giving. Public policy, legislation, and banking reform have served to protect this vulnerability. Perhaps in a compensating fashion, seniors have been found to involve others more so than other age groups in their purchasing processes. Family members and professionals are often called upon for input, whether the purchase is for themselves or for others (Meiners and Seeburger 2010). Personalized customer service, risk disclosure, and responsible advertising would further protect vulnerable consumers from bogus offers. In the case of "age defying" beauty products and the like, do the same concerns hold true? Is the buying process rational and informed?

THE ETERNAL PURSUIT OF YOUTH

In his historical analysis of the elderly consumer market, Branchik (2010, 193) indicated that "one factor that has not changed in over one hundred years is American society's overall obsession with youth." This of course has fueled many an advertising campaign and the race to erase the negative effects of aging. Products to minimize or ameliorate wrinkles, ailments, and hair loss have been sold via direct and indirect channels since the nineteenth century and advertisements for creams, elixirs, and cures can be found dating back to the early days of print material. (See the John W. Hartman Center for Sales, Advertising and Marketing History collection of digital ads at Duke University [library.duke.edu/rubenstein/hartman] for examples.)

There have been potions and over-the-counter remedies for more than a century to relieve the discomforts of arthritis, indigestion, aches, and pains brought on by old age. What is new is the type of products and services devoted to staving off the aging process, many of which are difficult to evaluate. While many of the products' claims have been debunked, there is still a formidable market to address the effects of aging. As consumers clamor for new ways to maintain a youthful appearance, a wide-ranging array of products has been marketed to appeal to the fears of an aging population. There is a demand for products and services to support a healthy, productive lifestyle, along with its physical benefits, and many marketing campaigns appealing to this desire have been launched.

There are "fountain of youth" health and beauty aids, dietary supplements, and "cosmeceuticals" to eliminate or mask what has been part of the natural aging process. These "breakthrough" products are often brought to market by pharmaceutical companies after clinical testing and have a halo of medical claims to support them. The patented products, while sold over the counter, are premium priced and expensively packaged. Expected results, testimonials and before-and-after photos are often part of the marketing message. Virtually every cosmetic company has an antiaging skincare line (for men and women). The difference lies in the way they are advertised. The pro-age Dove soap campaign for women, with the tagline "beauty has no age limit" is one example of a new direction in marketing using real models, in this case older, multicultural, and often unclothed women who defy the younger-is-better strategy. (See www.dove.us/social-mission/campaign-for-real-beauty.aspx.)

Another class of remedies includes prescription drugs and supplements to enhance performance, reduce pain, and extend vitality and require the consultation of a physician. Print, television, and online advertising abound for new products to treat the natural by-products of aging. Arthritis, high blood pressure, and diabetes are common in the aging population. Electric wheelchairs, prescription weight loss pills, blood sugar testing strips, and other products to promote independence and self-awareness are found online, in stores, and through direct marketing channels. The more sensitive adult-related products are now commonly featured in all media outlets. Ads for erectile dysfunction medication are ubiquitous during prime-time television programming and typically include over-fifty models enjoying each other's company. For the most part, these ads are targeted toward men, who would need to see a doctor for what is currently a prescription medication. Female partners also feature prominently as coagents in this opportunity to enjoy life more fully. The subtext is a positive one, that sexuality extends across the life span and any physical difficulties in achieving sexual satisfaction can be treated.

Medical professionals and estheticians have profited from the vanity trend. Plastic surgery, laser technology, and other invasive procedures to sculpt a more youthful physique, remove signs of aging, or tighten slack skin can significantly change appearance and create an ageless look that has been cited by some as extreme (Baumann and de Laat 2012). More futuristic measures such as cryogenics and stem cell research are in their development phase as scientists explore atomic level ways to increase longevity.

PAST STUDIES OF THE ELDERLY IN ADVERTISING

Cultivation theory, developed by Gerbner (Morgan and Shanahan 2010) suggests that we are what we view, that over time we are shaped by advertising images and accept them as realistic. Cultivation theory espouses that the more time spent consuming media, the closer the audience's perception of reality matches the media-constructed images. So, with an increase in media consumption in older age, increased exposure to multimedia images, and a lifetime of media involvement, the constructed reality and perceptions of reality merge. If this holds true and remains unchecked, the unrealistic representation of the elderly (either negative or unachievable) would create a downward spiral of demoralization.

There is an extensive history of research examining the representation of the elderly in advertising. Lack of older models in general readership magazines was found by Bramlett-Solomon and Wilson (1989), Gantz, Gartenberg, and Rainbow (1980), Langmeyer (1983), Peterson (1992), Ursic, Ursic, and Ursic (1986), and in television by Gerbner et al. (1980), Vernon,

Williams, Phillips, and Wilson (1990), and in television commercials (Miller, Leyell, and Mazachek 2004).

The cultivation of ageism was supported by repeated viewing of negative stereotypes of the elderly. Past representations of the elderly often showed them as wise or frail, impaired or out of touch. Almerico and Fillmer (1989) warned that the consistent negative portrayals in print media produced a fear of aging and fear of the elderly by younger readers. Certain campaigns capitalized on these deficiencies, such as ineptness with technology ("What the heck is electronic mail?"—Honeywell), crankiness (Where's the beef?—Wendy's) and weakness ("I've fallen and I can't get up!"—LifeCall). Indeed they were so successful as to become iconic. Very few ads included minority models and males far outnumbered females. This is a worldwide phenomenon in advertising (Kohlbacher, Prieler, and Hagiwara 2011; Szmigin and Carrigan 2000; Zhang et al. 2006). Rotfeld, Reid, and Wilcox (1982) found in their study of models in print ads that older models were not rejected per se, but that model age and product orientation needed to be congruent for the ad to be effective. Product categories and advertising campaigns were often unimaginative and condescending (Carrigan and Szmigin 1999; Szmigin and Carrigan 2000). In the Miller, Leyell, and Mazachek (2004) study which covered a fifty year period, the most frequent product categories noted were food and beverages, and cameras and film. Ursic, Ursic, and Ursic (1986) found the elderly featured in advertising for such products as liquor, automobiles, banks, and cameras. (It should be noted that these ads were drawn from an era when consumer products were mass produced and mass communicated via a few television networks and print advertising, with very little effort to segment on the basis of any meaningful variables.)

Stereotypical portrayals were cited in several studies including Hummert (1993) and Miller, Leyell, and Mazachek (2004); however some of these were of a positive nature (i.e., the older and wiser person, the sweet grandma). Certain fictional characters who happened to be older were depicted as benevolent and affable such as Santa Claus, Colonel Sanders, and Chef Boyardee. The Adventurous Golden Ager, the Productive Golden Ager, and the Perfect Grandparent were three such types found by Hummert (1993) to have persisted over time. Vernon et al. (1990) concluded that while negative stereotypes were diminishing, female characterizations on television remained ageist and limited. The perpetuation of such backward portrayals during prime-time served to cultivate outdated role perceptions for women (Morgan and Shanahan 2010), developing skewed notions of age appropriate behavior and reinforced traditional gender roles.

More recently, Baumann and de Laat (2012) conducted an extensive study of the portrayal of older women in television advertising. They found that older women were underrepresented, as in the past, and unlike younger women (as sexualized or with limited roles related to housework and child-care), they are seemingly without status. They have no useful role. In the few cases where older women were more prominently featured, it was in stereotypical fashion as either aged or ageless. The effect of this devaluation only serves to perpetuate what for some women has been a lifetime of gender discrimination in the media. The cultivation of this discrimination may be changing however, as the study revealed also a greater frequency of younger women in work-related settings, a more realistic representation of women's participation in the labor force.

THE ROLE OF COGNITIVE AGE

Blau (1956) first recognized the phenomenon of identifying as younger than one's chronological age. This had implications for role enactment, determining appropriate behavior, and recognizing reference groups. Barak and Schiffman (1981) expanded this idea of cognitive age to expand upon the demographic variables that were regularly used in segmentation studies. The chronological age of an individual may be less meaningful in explaining demand and purchasing behavior than the age one identifies with, which in this case of older subjects was significantly younger than their biological age, often as many as fifteen years. The concept stuck as an important one in addressing older consumers. Stephens (1991) suggested cognitive age as a valuable concept for advertising to elders. Twenty years later this is precisely the practice we are reviewing. Have we created products, services, and corresponding advertising copy to appeal to the cognitive age of the older viewer? Over time, cognitive age has only become a more profound concept that has implications beyond purchasing behavior. Demakakos, Gjonca, and Nazroo (2007, 285) examined the relationship between cognitive age and health status with positive results: that "a younger age identity and positive age perceptions catalyze an increase in psychosocial resources that can benefit later health and extend life." The direction of the relationship was not determined. Good health may in fact contribute to a younger cognitive age or perceiving oneself as younger may lead to better health outcomes.

As an extension, Fagerstrom's (2010) research on positive life orientation demonstrates the vital and rewarding consequences of positivity, maintaining one's dignity, finding meaning in life, planning for the future and being needed. Increased exposure to marketing messages can contribute to these outcomes. Older consumers of today are more savvy, experienced, and educated than in the past. Myers and Lumbers (2007) point out the "sea change in attitude" between mature (fifty-five and older) shoppers and the generations who came before them. The differences are not age related, as much as the role changes and life stages they have experienced. Schewe and Balazs (1992) pointed out the importance of role transitions and for marketers to be aware of the profile of their customers. For example, it is entirely possible to be a "newlywed" or even a first time parent at an advanced age. These roles require some form of orientation, relevant information, multiple methods to achieve success, and even props to support their enactment. Fortunately, consumers have access to social media, online resources, and multiple forms of media from which to evaluate their options, form opinions, and comparison shop. This critical perspective has led to a market expertise that will serve these experienced consumers well in the future.

One such example of consumers' enlightened rationale is found in a study by La Ferle and Edwards (2013, 12). They explored the response by women over forty years old to digitally retouched ads and whether they are perceived as deceptive. In fact, there was a level of acceptability to the use of touching up photos in ads for cosmetics. The factors that were considered reasonable uses of digital manipulation of a photo were to "enhance/add a background image," "erase stray hairs/pimples/blemishes," and "change lighting/clothing." Those cases that were deemed unacceptable were "altering a woman's chest size," "changing body parts on a model," and "changing the shape of the face/legs/torso/arm/waist." There was support for disclaimers and regulatory oversight on advertising claims to limit deceptive practices. Whether because people are more knowledgeable about digital photography, or the beauty industry, or the realities of aging, this is a more tempered response than what we might have expected in the past. The American Society for Aesthetic Plastic Surgery (2012) claims that women are having minimally invasive cosmetic procedures, not in an attempt to regain youth, but to preserve "familiarity" with the face they have known for decades. This is a generation of women who do not hide the fact that they dye their hair (estimates are as high as 75 percent, according to Klara [2013]), use Botox to erase lines and wrinkles (a $1.7 billion dollar product line by Allergan [Allergan Annual Report 2012]), and wear slimming undergarments (e.g., Spanx, another billion dollar product line [O'Connor 2012]) to improve their appearance.

The goal for the marketer is to appeal to their audience in the appropriate way, with the appropriate appeal, in the channels and outlets they use. There needs to be an understanding of what the cohort values and to incorporate that into the value proposition (Migliaccio 2004–2005). Advertising campaigns do this often with the use of music, cultural references, and celebrity endorsers who are familiar to the targeted audience. As baby boomers age and are aware of the use of fashion photography techniques, products designed to reduce wrinkles, and stretch fabrics that improve their appearance, then there will be an acceptance of similar products within reason. The consistent recommendation in the entire aging and advertising literature stream has been to increase the use of older models, show realistic role portrayals, and consider cognitive age as a variable in the creative process.

There is evidence of some progress in the portrayal of the elderly in advertising of products and services. Balazs (1995) found realistic, relatively positive images in health care advertising where the elderly were featured prominently and as relaxed and happy. Zhang et al. (2006, 278) expressed some optimism in their findings: "advertising images of older adults in the past few decades have been quite positive. The positive portrayals are probably an effect of advertisers' motive of not alienating the older market or invoking negative affect in consumers."

A study by Darnell, Mason, and Prifti (2010) found a significantly more positive representation of the elderly in electronic and print media. They also predicted that as we become more accustomed to the growing number of elderly in society, we will form our attitudes less so by media depictions and more from personal experience. Thus through cultivation of a more positive imagery and an aging population in general, we will create a "kinder and gentler" orientation toward the elderly. Indeed Agogo, Milne, and Schewe (2013) suggest that baby boomers will drive a "new normal" of what to expect as we age and that healthy behaviors will lead to longer, more active lives.

DYNAMIC DEMOGRAPHICS

One could argue that as the population has aged, the balance of power has shifted. There is strength in numbers and social, economic, and political power has led to greater visibility and a more sensitive portrayal of the elderly in the media (Meiners and Seeburger 2010). Future representations of the elderly will hopefully remain positive; however it is not assured. The rapid growth in the over sixty-five population in the next twenty years, with more retirees and a smaller workforce will likely lead to some friction. An increase in health care spending, retirement housing, and the products and services to support an older population will be the focus of more creative product development and advertising.

Hopkins, Roster, and Wood (2006) addressed an additional dimension to the retirement role transition that is, how retirement is perceived (as negative or positive), the resulting retirement "style" and subsequent changes in purchasing based on that style. As one example, those who anticipate a negative retirement transition, likely view the experience as a disruption in their lifestyle, and the result may be a consumption pattern to replace the loss of the work role and actively engage in the new retirement "space." Purchases to fill the void with entertainment, hobbies, and exploratory activities would be a positive reaction to what was originally perceived as negative. For those who positively anticipate the retirement role as a "new start," they too will likely activate a new purchasing pattern to support their desire for novel experiences and new beginnings. Both types of responses to retirement may lead to experimentation with the new role and the opportunity to alter the direction of their aging process in a proactive fashion. Hopkins, Roster, and Wood (2006) question whether this hopefulness might lead to higher, and perhaps unachievable expectations. Resources would play a part in the ability to realize postretirement plans and unfulfilled dreams (Fry et al. 2011). Logan, Ward, and Spitze (1992) suggest that retirement is more complex than working versus not working. The options may include active volunteerism, education, and other work.

As seniors are portrayed as successful, energetic, youthful, and sexually attractive in the media, expectations are being formed at a higher level than in previous decades. These portrayals will continue to shift as baby boomers leave the workforce and Gen X and Y create media images and messages. A different understanding of how the elderly live, what the elderly want, and what it means to age should develop. New social roles for the elderly may form as they continue healthy and productive lives. Advertising will be more and more data driven and depict consumer behavior more accurately. Thus a more complete understanding of the new aging consumer in the marketplace will arise.

CONCLUSION: FUTURE RESEARCH

This chapter attempted to explore the evolution of advertising to the elderly and the direction it is headed. It does not address the ethicality of such advertising and the lack of representativeness that has been cited often. Marketers would be wise to rethink their assumptions of who the "elderly" are these days and to retest the concept of cognitive age. This might establish more accurate model specifications for advertising consumer products. Further, if the baby boomers are about to become the oldest cohort, then reassessing that cohort's values and history are necessary to create the most compelling advertising appeals. They are, after all, not their parents.

As the global population ages, more products and services will be developed to meet the needs of this heterogeneous group and correspondingly, more advertising (Kohlbacher, Prieler, and Hagiwara 2011). Marketers need to revisit their assumptions about the behavior, values, and age identity that the elderly (however defined) hold. If past research is a guide, then the message is clear: Incorporate more women and minorities into ads, portray them more accurately in their work and relationship roles, limit the use of the ageless, airbrushed models who are not remotely realistic, and connect with the deeply held values of your target market. Finally, evaluate the effectiveness of "uber human" models. Just as negative portrayals condition consumers to adapt negative attitudes, the Superman/woman models lead to unrealistic expectations, consumer dissatisfaction, and cognitive dissonance. With respect to the consumers who wish to pursue greater longevity and long lasting youthfulness, there are ways to creatively satisfy their needs with products and services that push the envelope of natural aging without the aura of science fiction or worse, deception.

II

Age Identities

Chapter Four

Reflections of Old Age, Constructions of Aging Selves

Drawing Links between
Media Images and Views of Aging

Anne E. Barrett,
Alexandra Raphael, and Justine Gunderson

Messages about aging and older adults permeate the culture, an omnipresent source of which is the media. The portrayals—in television, magazines, newspapers, films, advertisements, and the Internet—are often negative, implying that aging primarily involves decline. These images resonate with not only widely held attitudes toward older adults (Hummert 2011; Kite et al. 2005) but also individuals' perceptions of their own aging, including their reluctance, even at advanced ages, to identify themselves as old (Kleinspehn-Ammerlahn, Kotter-Gruhn, and Smith 2008). Although these patterns suggest that media images influence people's views of older adults and their self-perceptions of aging, relatively few studies examine this link.

This chapter develops this literature by examining the link between media images of older adults and attitudes and self-perceptions of aging. We bring together several strands of research. First, we review literature examining media images of older adults. Second, we review research on attitudes toward this group held by people of varying ages, followed by studies of self-perceptions of aging. Our review reveals that studies of predictors of attitudes or self-perceptions focus on either individual-level characteristics like age or health or, to a lesser extent, cross-national variation. They give limited attention to the media as an institution contributing to variation—across individuals or nation-states, as well as other levels of social structure—in both attitudes toward older adults and self-perceptions of aging. Following these reviews, we summarize studies examining links between media images and views of aging. We close by discussing four directions for research: (1) interpretation of media images, (2) timing and scope of media effects, (3) processes underlying links between images and views of aging, and (4) variation in interpretation, effects, or processes across images, media types, and individuals.

MEDIA IMAGES OF OLDER ADULTS

Older adults are underrepresented across media, including magazines (Williams, Wadeigh, and Ylänne 2010), television (Gerbner et al. 1980), and films (Lauzen and Dozier 2005). This pattern appears in media targeting different ages, as illustrated by studies of children's films (Robinson, Callister, Magoffin, and Moore 2007) and adults' magazines (Williams, Wadeigh, and Ylänne 2010). Older adult media, such as *AARP: The Magazine* in the United States and *Choice* in the United Kingdom, are exceptions; however, their messages reflect a similar valuation of youth over old age. Both magazines downplay aging, as illustrated by the removal of "retirement" from their titles and the more frequent portrayals of the younger end of the demographic (Featherstone and Hepworth 1995). Although representation remains low, recent studies find greater parity. For example, while only 16 percent of children's books published between 1967 and 1977 contained older characters (Ansello 1977), 40 percent of those between 2000 and 2010 did (Danowski and Robinson 2012).

Studies also have examined balances of negative versus positive depictions. For example, Robinson and colleagues (2007) find that the majority of older characters in Disney films are portrayed positively. Images may have become more positive, fueled by recognition of older adults' purchasing power (Featherstone and Hepworth 1995); however, an image shift from "frail" to "remarkably youthful" implies a limited range of later life depictions (Hodgetts, Chamberlain, and Bassett 2003, 417).

A consistent finding centers on gender. Older women are depicted less often than older men. As an illustration, women appear in less than 40 percent of television advertisements containing older adults (Lee, Carpenter, and Meyers 2007). Older women are often portrayed in gender stereotypic ways and fulfill supporting, not primary, roles (Lauzen and Dozier 2005b; Robinson et al. 2007). For example, among the top one hundred films in 2002, 37 percent of older male characters played leadership roles compared with 9 percent of older female characters (Lauzen and Dozier 2005b). Gender differences also are reported in one of the few studies of Internet images of older adults. In her study of antiaging websites, Calasanti (2007) found that aging was portrayed as a disease causing decline in women's attractiveness and men's physical, particularly sexual, functioning. Taken together, these patterns reflect a "double standard of aging"—the more rapid decline in women's than men's status as they grow older, stemming from the centrality of youthful beauty standards to women's social capital.

Our review reveals trends that may have implications for individuals' views of older adults and their own aging process. Although older adults are more often depicted in the media today than in the past, this rapidly growing segment of the population remains underrepresented across media types and targeted age groups. Media images are unrealistic in their portrayal of demographic contours of aging, including the higher proportion of women than men reaching advanced ages and the rapid increase in the "oldest-old" (US Census Bureau 2011). Research should examine how these images affect two categories of individuals' views of aging, both of which may shift with age— their attitudes toward older adults and perceptions of their own aging. Though conceptually related, they are reviewed separately, as most studies examine one or the other.

ATTITUDES TOWARD OLDER ADULTS

Consistent with the often negative stereotypes of older adults in popular media, people tend to hold fairly negative attitudes toward older adults—a pattern found not only among the young but also older adults themselves. Studies documenting these patterns examine stereotypes and attitudes, including evaluations along positive and negative dimensions. Compared with younger people, older adults are viewed as angrier, frailer, and less attractive and competent (Kite et al. 2005). Negative views, emerging in childhood, are found in studies of explicit and implicit attitudes, though they are stronger for implicit ones (Hummert 2011).

People hold numerous, complex stereotypes of older adults, a conclusion drawn from original research on aging stereotypes (e.g., Hummert 1990) and more recent studies (e.g., Fiske et al. 2002). Early research by Hummert (1990), for example, found using a trait-sorting task that young adults hold negative and positive stereotypes of older adults (e.g., shrew/curmudgeon, perfect grandparent). A recent framework—the stereotype content model— also highlights individuals' complex beliefs about older adults (Fiske et al. 2002). The model focuses on two dimensions of stereotypes—warmth and competence. It posits, and empirical studies find, that older adults are viewed as warm but incompetent (Cuddy, Norton, and Fiske 2005).

Research also has examined variation in attitudes, with studies focusing on individual-level characteristics, like sociodemographics. Research finds that, while negative views of older adults are observed across the age spectrum, more complex attitudes are found among older adults themselves (Hummert et al. 1994). Studies also find more positive attitudes toward older adults among women, race-ethnic minorities, and married people, and those with more children, better perceived income adequacy, and more interaction with older adults (Barrett and von Rohr 2008; Connidis 1989).

A few studies point to macrolevel factors producing cross-national variation in attitudes (e.g., Ayalon et al. 2013; O'Brien-Suric 2013). For example, a study comparing five nations finds that over three-quarters of people in the United States, United Kingdom, and Dominican Republic report that older adults receive too little respect, compared with less than half of Japanese and French participants (O'Brien-Suric 2013). The study also finds variation in conceptions of the beginning of old age. For example, 34 percent of Americans, compared with only 15 percent of participants from the Dominican Republic see mental decline as an old age marker. Further evidence of cross-national variation is found in a study comparing twenty-eight nations, revealing later ages of old age entrance in countries with higher education and greater income inequality (Ayalon et al. 2013).

Research also finds that aging attitudes affect older adults' well-being (e.g., Wurm, Tesch-Romer, and Tomasik 2007). For example, individuals who view aging as associated with physical losses tend to report greater accumulation of physical health problems over time, while those viewing it as ongoing development experience lower increase, or even decline, in physical illness (Wurm, Tesch-Romer, and Tomasik 2007). A recent meta-analysis found that negative age stereotypes' detrimental effects on behavior (e.g., memory) are almost three times greater than the salubrious effects of positive age stereotypes (Meisner 2012). However, experiments suggest that these health effects can be modified by altering aging attitudes. For example, participants primed with positive age words felt younger and were less likely to apply negative age stereotypes to themselves, compared with those exposed to negative age words (Eibach, Mock, and Courtney 2010). Effects even extend to young adults, as college students primed with negative age words walked more slowly (Bargh, Chen, and Burrows 1996).

SELF-PERCEPTIONS OF AGING

Much like attitudes toward older adults, self-perceptions of aging resonate with media images of aging adults, revealing a devaluation of later life stages. However, little is known about the role of the media in shaping these self-perceptions. Studies examining predictors have focused either on individual-level characteristics, like sociodemographics, or cross-national variation. Greater attention should be given to understanding media-related factors shaping self-perceptions of aging, given their health implications.

People hold not only attitudes toward older adults in general but also perceptions of their own aging selves. As people age and experience heightened awareness of their own aging process, they often self-stereotype (Levy 2003). However, they view themselves more positively than others their age and are more optimistic about their own later years (Heckhausen and Brim 1997). Research also finds that as people age, they maintain youthful identities, though there are limits to this youthful bias: Beyond age forty, age identities remain around 20 percent younger than actual ages (Rubin and Berntsen 2006). Birthday proximity influences age identity: Older adults feel less youthful nearer their birthdays (Montepare 1996). Age patterns also are found in other self-perceptions of aging. For example, older age predicts less anxiety about one's own aging (Barrett and Robbins 2008; Lynch 2000).

Many individual-level characteristics are associated with self-perceptions of aging. Women tend to maintain more youthful identities (Barrett 2005) but also have more anxiety about their own aging (Lynch 2000). Findings are more mixed for race-ethnic variation, with some finding that non-Whites hold older identities (Johnson, Berg, and Sirotzski 2007), others finding no differences (Barrett 2003), and still others reporting younger identities among some groups of non-Whites (Hispanics and Asians; Johnson, Berg, and Sirotzski 2007). Similarly, some research finds higher aging anxiety among non-Whites (Lynch 2000), while other work finds the opposite (Barrett and Robbins 2008). Findings on the relationship between socioeconomic status and self-perceptions of aging are more consistent, revealing that greater disadvantage predicts older identities and greater aging anxiety (Barrett 2003; Barrett and Robbins 2008; Johnson, Berg, and Sirotzski 2007). Social roles and relationships also appear to influence these self-perceptions. Having more children is associated with older identities (Karp 1988) but lower odds of worrying about growing older (Connidis 1989). Younger identities and less aging anxiety also are associated with having better relationship quality and health (Barrett 2003, 2005; Barrett and Robbins 2008).

Cross-national comparisons point to broader structural forces influencing self-perceptions of aging. They reveal that identification with younger ages is found across disparate cultures (Barak 2009). However, magnitudes of the youthful bias vary, with studies reporting younger identities among Americans, compared with German adults (Westerhof, Barrett, and Steverink 2003). Taken together, evidence of variation, across cultural and social structural contexts, points to the malleability of self-perceptions of aging.

Experiments corroborate this conclusion. For example, Stephan and colleagues' (2013) study found that older women told they performed better on a physical task than age peers felt younger, and did better on a subsequent test, than those receiving no relative performance feedback. Similar conclusions are drawn from Eibach and colleagues' (2010) experiment using exposure to visual decline to induce older (or "less youthful") identities. They found that participants experiencing simulated visual decline without any forewarning felt less youthful than did those either not exposed to visual decline or exposed but forewarned.

These self-perceptions have wide-ranging health consequences. For example, more positive self-perceptions of aging predict longer life expectancy and better functioning (Levy, Slade, and Kasl 2002). Younger identities predict lower mortality and reduced risk of disability and hypertension (Demakakos, Gjonca, and Nazroo 2007; Kotter-Grühn et al. 2009). Having more anxiety about aging-related declines in health and physical attractiveness is associated with greater psychological distress (Barrett and Robbins 2008), while higher satisfaction with one's own aging extends longevity (Kotter-Grühn et al. 2009). Research also finds that being primed to feel older strengthens the effect of aging attitudes on subjective well-being (Eibach, Mock, and Courtney 2010). The health implications of views of aging, including general attitudes and self-perceptions, underscore the importance of examining potential determinants, like media, receiving limited attention in prior research.

CONNECTING MEDIA IMAGES
WITH ATTITUDES AND SELF-PERCEPTIONS

Research examining media effects on attitudes toward older adults began several decades ago, but this literature remains small. This observation is surprising, given the centrality of the topic to the development of one of the major theories used in media studies—cultivation theory. This theory posits that television, "the common storyteller of our age," cultivates "shared conceptions of reality among otherwise diverse publics" (Gerbner et al. 2002, 44). Some of the studies leading to the theory's formulation centered on how frequency of television viewing affects attitudes toward older adults (Gerbner et al. 1980). This relationship, including its focus on television, has been at the center of much of the research in this area. However, recent studies have attended to other issues, including processes underlying the association between media exposure and attitudes toward older adults (Haboush, Warren, and Benuto 2012; Slevec and Tiggemann 2010) and variation in effects by image and viewer characteristics (Mares and Cantor 1992; Westerhof et al. 2010).

Some of the earliest studies in the area reported a link between television exposure and aging beliefs. Using a sample of over 4,000 Americans, Gerbner and colleagues (1980) found that greater television consumption predicted several aging views, including lower knowledge about aging trends, more negative views of older adults, and conceptions of the start of old age, particularly for women, as occurring earlier. An association between television exposure and views of older adults also was found in a study by Korzenny and Neuendorf (1980), using a quota sample of 112 older adults. Respondents were asked about television portrayals of older adults, as well as the extent to which several statements reflected "some general things about yourself, and other senior citizens in real life" (e.g., "the older I get the lonelier I get" and "senior citizens are generally happy with their lives"). Greater television exposure was associated with reporting that older adults were portrayed as a hindrance to society. Further, respondents perceiving them to be portrayed as societal assets had more positive aging views, while those perceiving them to be portrayed as hindrances had more negative views. The association between television exposure and aging views also is reported in a more recent study by Donlon, Ashman, and Levy (2005), finding that this predictor of negative age stereotypes is stronger than all others examined (e.g., education, age).

Other studies examine processes underlying the media-attitude link. Using a sample of 108 women between thirty-five and fifty-five years old, Slevec and Tiggemann (2010) examined body dissatisfaction, appearance investment, and aging anxiety as mediators of the relationship between media exposure and attitudes toward an aging-related issue—cosmetic surgery. More television exposure predicted greater personal social motivations and actual consideration of surgery; however, television was associated with none of the hypothesized mediators. In contrast, results for magazine exposure suggest that greater exposure may increase personal social motivations and actual consideration of surgery by magnifying appearance investment. Another study addressing processes focuses on internalization of media ideals. Using a sample of college women, Haboush and colleagues (2012) found that greater internalization of appearance ideals is associated with reporting worse attitudes toward older adults. They also examined race-ethnic differences, finding lower levels of internalization among African American women, compared with all other groups; however, its link with attitudes did not vary by race/ethnicity.

Some studies, however, do find variation in media exposure's effects—depending on characteristics of not only ads but also viewers. In an experiment comparing effects of negative versus positive portrayals of older adults (in a scripted video), Mares and Cantor (1992) found variation by viewers' mood. Lonely people preferred—and felt better after viewing—negative portrayals. In contrast, nonlonely people preferred—and felt better after viewing—positive portrayals. An explanation drawing on social comparison theory suggests that lonely people were motivated to make downward comparisons to enhance their self-perceptions and well-being, while nonlonely people made upward comparisons to inspire themselves or boost self-image. These findings suggest a role of both selection and causation processes, as mood influenced not only viewing preferences but also their effects.

A more recent experiment, using exposure to television commercials, finds further support for media effects—in particular, on age-related tasks. Westerhof and colleagues (2010) primed sixty-five- to seventy-five-year-olds with commercials portraying older adults in one of three ways, drawing on the stereotype content model: warm/competent, cold/competent, and warm/incompetent. Consistent with self-stereotyping theory (Levy 2003), priming had no effect on memory performance among older adults not identifying with their age group, while adults identifying with their group performed worse after being primed with warm/incompetent portrayals. Priming with the other negative stereotype—cold/competent—did not affect performance, while the positive stereotype—warm/competent—*did* impair it. The authors suggest that identification with characters in ads may explain these patterns, as respondents assessed more favorably the two ads affecting memory performance, though all three ads were rated fairly unfavorably.

In sum, studies linking media images with either attitudes toward older adults or self-perceptions of aging are relatively few—and limited in several ways. Studies, particularly the recent ones, tend to involve experimental methods, raising questions about the findings' generalizability to media exposure in people's everyday lives. The only study of which we are aware that addresses this issue using a large-scale survey (i.e., Gerbner et al. 1980), was conducted several decades ago, long before the proliferation of new media. These and other limitations point to directions for future research.

CONCLUSION: DIRECTIONS FOR RESEARCH

The small body of work leaves numerous questions underexamined. We focus on four issues: (1) interpretation of media images, (2) timing and scope of media effects, (3) processes underlying these effects, and (4) variation in interpretation, effects, or processes—across images, media types, and individuals. Consideration of these issues points to the utility of research involving a variety of methods and theoretical perspectives.

While copious research documents media images of older adults, few studies examine their interpretation and evaluation by older adults themselves. The findings of Westerhof and colleagues' (2010) study suggest that researchers' assumptions about the valence of stereotypes present in ads may be misguided. They found the most favorable assessments of ads *negatively* affecting memory performance. Interpretive research, using qualitative methods, is needed to better understand not only how older adults assess these images but also whether they use them for social comparisons. Some insight is provided by research on media consumption by other groups. Studies of adolescent girls' and young women's consumption of mainstream media are illuminating—and relevant to aging—given their portrayal of a thin, youthful body as an ideal. Research finds, for example, that young women often compare their bodies with celebrities' (Strahan et al. 2006). Studies should examine whether older women—and men—use media images of their age group as standards against which to assess their own and others' aging experiences and aging bodies, as well as under what conditions they make upward versus downward comparisons, which have implications for their effects.

Our review also points to unanswered questions about the timing of media effects. While cultivation theory implies that greater media exposure over time produces more negative views of older adults, research on this topic tends to involve either cross-sectional designs (e.g., Gerbner et al. 1980; Korzenny and Neurendorf 1980) or longitudinal designs with short time frames (e.g., Donlon, Ashman, and Levy 2005). Experimental studies also involve short durations (e.g., Westerhof et al. 2010), raising the question of whether observed media effects are lasting ones. Addressing this question will require prospective studies following individuals of varying ages over long time spans, tracking their consumption of various media along with their attitudes and self-perceptions of aging.

The utility of a prospective approach is underscored by two theoretical frameworks highlighting temporal dimensions of human lives—that is, life course (Elder, Johnson, and Crosnoe 2003) and life span developmental perspectives (Baltes, Lindenberger, and Staudinger 2006). The life course perspective, highlighting several dimensions of time, including historical, social, and lifetime, raises numerous questions about media effects on attitudes and self-perceptions of aging. As illustrations, how do historical time and place shape media images of older adults and their effects? How does age and duration of media exposure affect views of aging? And how are media exposure and its effects shaped by people's movement through the socially patterned, and socially intertwined, transitions that constitute the life course? Other questions are raised by a life span developmental model, focusing on processes producing constancy and change within individuals from birth to death. As examples, how might various regulatory strategies, like individuals' selective optimization of their developmental potential and compensation for losses as they age (Baltes 1997), affect their processing of media images of older adults? And how might they shape media effects on attitudes or self-perceptions of aging?

In addition to widening the temporal scope, future studies should consider a wider range of media effects. As our review revealed, studies examining the link between media and views of aging have focused on beliefs about or attitudes toward older adults (e.g., Donlon, Ashman, and Levy 2005; Gerbner et al. 1980; Haboush, Warren, and Benuto 2012; Korzenny and Neuendorf 1980), giving less attention to self-perceptions of aging. However, if media images are used as points of reference for evaluating one's own experiences, as suggested by studies of young adults (e.g., Strahan et al. 2006), they are likely to shape self-perceptions of aging, including age identities and anxieties. Media images also could affect more general conceptions of the life course—for example, when various stages begin and end and what events or ages mark them—as well as behaviors influenced by these conceptions, such as retirement and end-of-life planning. In addition, they may influence social relationships, both across (e.g., parent-child) and within generations (e.g., spousal relationships). Future research also should consider an expanded range of health and well-being measures, a possibility suggested by research on not only the effects of attitudes and self-perceptions of aging (e.g., Levy et al. 2002; Wurm, Tesch-Romer, and Tomasik 2007) but also the (negative) effects of media exposure on women's emotional well-being and body image (e.g., Tiggemann and McGill 2004).

Another avenue for research centers on the range of possible processes underlying links between media images of older adults and attitudes and self-perceptions of aging. While studies have explored potential mediators (e.g., Slevec and Tiggemann 2010), they have identified few processes. Some possibilities are suggested by the more extensive research on media's impact on women's body image, though young women are often the focus of these studies. Providing an illustration, Milkie's (1999) qualitative study of teen girls' interpretations of media images developed an argument reconciling people's belief they are not affected by media—but others are (i.e., "third person effects" [Davison 1983]). She posits that people may be affected indirectly by media images—namely, through a process involving reflected appraisals. In short, people may assume that others are less critical of media portrayals and, therefore, more apt to use them when making assessments of themselves and others. More macrolevel processes to be explored are suggested by cross-national studies finding that views of aging vary along dimensions like income inequality and education level (Ayalon et al. 2013). This research raises the possibility that cross-national variation in the representation of older adults in various media may contribute to national, and individual, differences in attitudes and self-perceptions of aging.

Another topic deserving further investigation centers on variation—in interpretations, effects, and processes—across images and types of media. A direction for research is suggested by the increasing portrayals of "remarkably youthful elderly" (Hodgetts, Chamberlain, and Bassett 2003, 417). Studies are needed to assess not only how adults of different ages and levels of health and functioning assess these images (e.g., negative or positive) but also how they affect their attitudes, self-perceptions, and behavior. The negative-positive dimension has been the focus of studies of media images and their effects; however, other dimensions should be explored. An example is suggested by socioemotional selectivity theory, positing that people shift in later life from information acquisition goals to emotional regulation goals, in response to a shrinking time horizon (Carstensen, Issacowitz, and Charles

1999). Supporting the theory, experiments find that older adults prefer, and better remember, advertisements promising emotional rewards over those promising informational rewards; but, when a longer time horizon is induced, older adults' preferences are similar to younger adults' (Fung, Carstensen, and Lutz 1999). Not only advertisements but other media may convey messages about time horizons, affecting older adults' interpretations of them and shaping their effects on aging attitudes, self-perceptions, and behavior. Future research also should examine variation in interpretations, media effects, and underlying processes across media types. While content analyses of images of older adults include multiple media, studies linking them to attitudes and self-perceptions of aging focus on television. The importance of considering new media is highlighted by the observation that half of adults age sixty-five and older are online (Zickuhr and Madden 2012).

Other sources of possible variation center on differences across individuals. A likely source of difference is age, a prediction derived from not only variation in the self-relevance of images of older adults but also research finding age differences in information processing. For example, studies find that older adults pay less attention to—and process less deeply—negative than positive information (Mather and Carstensen 2005), raising the possibility that some media images of older adults may more strongly affect the middle-aged. Another source of variation to be addressed further is gender, with prior studies suggesting different possibilities. Research on young women finds they often make upward social comparisons related to their bodies, using media images as reference points (Strahan et al. 2006). The same pattern may be found among older women, given the salience of attractiveness in women's social valuation. However, older women's underrepresentation in the media might limit its use in self-evaluations. This prediction is drawn from Milkie's (1999) study reporting that African American girls were more critical of teen magazines and less likely to use them for making social comparisons than were their White peers. This study also suggests the importance of considering other factors—like race, class, and sexual orientation—that shape not only the degree and type of representations of older adults in various media outlets but also their effects on a range of attitudes, self-perceptions, and behaviors.

Pursuing these and other avenues for research will illuminate the link between media images and individuals' views of aging. An assumption of a causal link motivates much of the research in this area and appears in more general public discourse on media's social impacts; however, more research is needed to determine key aspects of the association, including the magnitude, scope, and timing of effects, the processes generating them, and variation across images, media types, and individuals. Clarifying the link is a precursor to promoting media messages fostering views of aging that maximize not only the individual experience of growing older but also the social contributions of aging adults.

Chapter Five

Age and Gender in Film and Television

The Case of Huong Hoang

Anthony R. Bardo

Huong Hoang, who goes by her stage name Junie Hoang, is an American actress who sued Internet Movie Database (IMDb) for revealing her chronological age. According to her formal complaint document, filed with the United States District Court in January 2012, Hoang subscribed to IMDb's professional services (IMDbPro) in 2003, and began entering her acting profile information to increase her exposure to the media industries. In order to subscribe to these services Hoang had to provide detailed personal and credit card information to pay for the subscription. Shortly after subscribing to IMDbPro, she realized that her legal date of birth had been added to her public acting profile on IMDb.com, which she had intentionally not entered herself. Hoang argued that her date of birth is associated with her legal name, Huong Hoang, and was not public information prior to her subscribing to IMDbPro. She requested that IMDb, the company owned by Amazon that operates both IMDb and IMDbPro, remove her date of birth, but the company refused. Hoang claimed she has rigorously protected this information to benefit her acting career, and she anonymously filed a $1,000,000 lawsuit in 2011 against IMDb and its owner Amazon. The news media quickly began coverage of this case as a story about "ageism in Hollywood." This chapter draws on Hoang's legal battle against IMDb as a platform from which to explore issues of age and gender inequalities in film and television and their implications for life course scholarship in general and age identities in particular.

BACKGROUND

Internet Movie Database (IMDb)

IMDb, a subsidiary of Amazon, is an online database of films, television programs, and video games, which includes filmographies, resumes, biographical sketches and photos of actors, production personnel, and fictional characters. IMDb provides at least two distinct services, IMDb.com and IMDBPro.com. IMDb.com is a free website that acts as a link between media consumers/fans and media producers. This website includes information about actors, media personnel, and interactive functions such as user film ratings, message boards, and instant viewing. It is one of the most popular entertainment sites on the web, with over 100 million unique users every month and over forty-one million registered users (www.alexa.com/siteinfo/imdb.com). IMDbPro.com is a subscription service that provides more detailed information designed to meet the information needs of people who work in the entertainment industry. Actors and media personnel subscribe to this service so they have some control over the information provided on their personal page. For example, an up-and-coming actor who subscribed to IMDbPro would be able to list his or her own resume or post head shots, whereas IMDb, which controls what information is included, may only provide minimal information or the actor may not be listed. For others in the industry, such as casting personnel, IMDbPro provides access to additional information that is not available on the free site (IMDb.com), such as contact details and in-development and in-production information.

The Actress

Junie Hoang was born in Saigon, Vietnam, in 1971, and immigrated to the United States at an early age. She was interested in the arts, and began taking dance lessons at age sixteen. Hoang excelled in academics, as she graduated salutatorian from her high school and later earned a BS in Biomedical Science from Texas A&M University. Her interests include studying martial arts and learning different languages. According to her IMDb biography, she is fluent in Vietnamese and English, conversational in Spanish, and has some experience in French. She began her professional acting career in 1992 at the age of twenty-one.

The first ten years of Hoang's career (1992–2001) consisted mostly of voice work for minor roles (e.g., credited as "additional voices") in animated television shows and videos, and she eventually achieved a recurring role in an animated television series. In addition to her early voice work, Hoang also made onscreen appearances in two television shows and a TV movie. In 1998 she began appearing in films directed by Greg Carter—a director/producer for Nexus Films with a body of work that mostly includes low budget films that target the urban male audience. Since 2002 Hoang's career has mostly consisted of actress roles in films and TV shows, with occasional voice work for animated media, and a few television commercials and print advertisements. However, the bulk of her work has been with Carter, as she appeared in twenty of his films between 1998 and 2013. Some of her most recent work (2012–2014) has been with reality TV shows such as *Exotic Dancers of Houston*, and *Coast to Coast Cheerleaders*.

IMDb and Age-Related Issues

IMDb faced age-related issues before the Junie Hoang case. In June 2010, the Writers Guild of America launched a campaign against the website to remove all ages and birth dates, and the Screen Actors Guild (SAG) requested IMDb to remove ages of lesser-known actors (Kenneally 2011a). Additionally, there has been some concern about inaccurate age listings (Kenneally 2011a). The American Federation of Television and Radio Artists (AFTRA) and SAG "believe that businesses like IMDb have a moral and legal obligation not to facilitate age discrimination in employment," arguing an actor's chronological age is not relevant to casting (SAG-AFTRA 2011). In general, SAG-AFTRA argues that it is an actor's job to portray someone else, and when personal information is made public, such as a birth date, it can harm creativity and limit what type of characters an actor can portray (NewsCore 2012). Furthermore, SAG and AFTRA claim actors are losing work because of personal information being published on IMDb without the actor's consent (BBC News 2011).

THE LAWSUIT AND RELATED MEDIA COVERAGE

Junie Hoang's initial suit against IMDb and Amazon was filed anonymously in October 2011 for the sum of $1,000,0000 (Kenneally 2011a). She claimed IMDb violated her privacy by misusing her credit card information to cross-reference with public records to determine her date of birth and breached their Subscriber Agreement and Privacy Policy by publishing her age without her consent (UPI 2011). Even though the suit was filed in "Jane Doe" fashion, SAG and AFTRA came out in support of the "unnamed" actress (SAG-AFTRA 2011), as her lawyers argued that "youth is king" in Hollywood and that by revealing her actual age she is rendered vulnerable to age discrimination and could lose future jobs in movies and TV (Molloy 2011). IMDb responded by stating the forty-year-old actress was "selfish," trying to commit fraud by distorting her age and unjustly censor IMDb, and requested that her identity be revealed (Molloy 2011). Shortly after the initial suit was filed, the judge granted IMDb's request for Hoang to reveal herself and threatened to throw out the case if the plaintiff did not agree to come forward (Kenneally 2011b).

In January 2012 Hoang amended the suit by revealing her name, and SAG supported her decision in the following statement:

> Ms. Hoang has shown great courage in stepping forward and pursuing her claims despite efforts to deter her by demanding she be publicly identified. Thousands of actors have had their careers harmed by the unauthorized publication of their birth dates by IMDb against their wishes. The Screen Actors Guild and its members stand in support of efforts to curtail this invasion of privacy done to enhance a corporate balance sheet. (Kenneally and Chelin 2012)

Some of the press covering this case expressed supportive opinions as well. For example, a casting agent told *The Hollywood Reporter* "whenever I am asked how old a client is—and I am asked occasionally—we laugh together about how it isn't legal to ask or answer that question, yet people expect an answer. So they go to IMDb, which is only too willing to aid and abet age discrimination" (Haeusler 2012). Other sources, such as *National Public Radio*, picked up on issues of gender inequality in Hollywood based on age discrimination, stating "Male actors over forty—Harrison Ford, Daniel Craig, Morgan Freeman, and Christopher Plummer—play cowboys, spies and heroes, whereas filmmakers seem to pass all roles for women over forty between Dame Helen Mirren, Meryl Streep and Dame Judie Dench" (Simon 2012).

A trial date was set for January 7, 2013 (Gardner 2012a). Despite the major focus on age discrimination, the crux of Hoang's case rested on claims of a privacy violation over mining credit card data. In an interview with the *New York Times*, legal scholar Jonathan Turley argued "The age claim is so tenuous that it distracts from a legitimate concern over the mining of such information" (Cieply 2012). In fact, after several weeks of the discovery of evidence phase in the legal process the judge dismissed claims of alleged privacy violation but granted Hoang the right to pursue her case for breach of contract, concluding that "The plain language of the contract does not permit defendants' unfettered use of the personal information that plaintiff provided for the purpose of processing payment" (Gardner 2012b). However, the judge also required the compensatory damages be reduced to an unspecified amount from the original request of $1,000,000. In response, Hoang's lawyers amended their claims to focus on IMDb's breach of contract and violation of consumer protection laws, claiming that if Hoang was aware IMDb would mine her credit card information she would not have used their services (Gardner 2012c).

In August 2012, Hoang's case faced a major setback with the unexpected death of her lawyer (Gardner 2012d), and by October 2012, Hoang's new lawyers demanded they be allowed to reopen the discovery process, with a fuller investigation into the misuse of their client's personal information. They also planned to bring forward witnesses to attest to the negative impacts on Hoang's future earnings, as well as others who claimed to have been negatively impacted by IMDb publishing their ages (Gardner 2012e). This opened the door for a possible class action lawsuit.

IMDb, in November 2012, attempted to have the case dismissed by filing the claim that Hoang lied about her age at least twice before. In the first instance they claimed she provided a false birth date, one that was seven years younger than she actually was, when she signed up for IMDbPro (Kenneally 2012). In the second instance IMDb claimed Hoang contacted their office and requested her published birth date be replaced with one that made her seem even younger than the initial false birth date that she provided, and demanded they check her records for the discrepancy. IMDb checked her records, and recovered her actual date of birth—July 16, 1971. Subsequently, IMDb filed a motion to dismiss the case on the grounds that Hoang could not prove economic loss because of IMDb's actions, and she could not prove that IMDb engaged in "unfair" or "deceptive" practices (Kenneally 2012). However, the case went to trial. At trial, Hoang testified that "When a casting director knows my real age, I am either not called for an audition for a youthful role, or I don't get the part after I audition. When I audition for roles that are near my age, casting directors reject me for looking too young" (Gardner 2012f). This brought the case back full circle from one of alleged privacy violations and breach of contract to ageism in Hollywood and the implications for how chronological age is perceived by an industry that trades in cultural idioms.

Before the trial began, IMDb requested to exclude "testimony about ageism in Hollywood," and the court ordered both parties to refrain from using the term "age discrimination" during the trial.[1] IMDb also requested that third-party opinions about their practice of revealing actors' dates of birth be excluded as well, and this, too, was granted by the court (Gardner and Balasubramani 2013). Thus, all ageist and age discrimination claims were off the table, and the trial rested solely on Hoang's accusations of IMDb's breach of contract. However, when Hoang testified she managed to tell the jury "The entertainment industry is based on perception . . . your age, how you look; if you tell someone your age, it will affect their perception." In short, while her lawyers couldn't mention age discrimination as the basis for the lawsuit, they could more broadly introduce how information on an IMDb profile could have a negative impact on an acting career (Balasubramani 2013). The trial lasted a little more than two days, and despite Hoang's effort, she lost the case when the jury determined IMDb had not breached their contract (Gardner 2013).

After the trial Hoang spoke with reporters and discussed her disappointment in the loss and frustration with the inability to control her on- and offscreen age identity.

> Everybody uses it [IMDb.com] in the entertainment business and it's like having your age in every job resume. You're not really allowed to ask someone's age in a job interview but the way IMDb works is you have a profile where you have a resume and your picture and all the work you have done. And having your age there is basically exposing how old you are anytime you apply for a job. It's very hurtful. There's a lot of age bias in Hollywood. We are looking to a chance to appeal it and the unions [SAG and AFTRA] have been very supportive with the lawsuit. (American Free Press 2013)

FRAMING LITERATURE

The Intersections of Aging, Media, and Culture

Hoang stressed that she has rigorously attempted to protect information that could reveal her actual date of birth. She allegedly lied numerous times, before and after her birth date was publically posted on her IMDb profile without her consent, to make herself seem younger than she actually was. In her case against IMDb, Hoang argued it is more difficult for "older" actresses, compared to their male counterparts and "younger" actresses, to land onscreen roles. However, are Hoang's concerns about age/ing and her lawyer's claim that "youth is king" in Hollywood valid? In other words, are such age and gender inequalities reflected in the contemporary landscape for onscreen actors? What are the broader implications surrounding age and gender in the media? Is there a link between the portrayal of age and aging onscreen and their interpretation and performance in everyday life? Hoang's lawsuit provides a case study for exploring these questions by linking the pertinent literatures in communications, media/cultural studies, sociology, and gerontology to examine the role of age and gender in film and television and its influence on age identities.

Actor's Age and Audience

In her case against IMDb Hoang claimed, "When a casting director knows my real age, I am either not called for an audition for a youthful role, or I don't get the part after I audition. When I audition for roles that are near my age, casting directors reject me for looking too young" (Gardner 2012f). Unfortunately, there is no academic research regarding the discrepancy between an actor's chronological age and their character's age. However, there is a growing body of literature concerned with the relationship between age and media content selection by audiences (Mares and Sun 2010). Media consumers in general tend to prefer material with *characters* around their same age group (Mares and Sun 2010). Other research in this area is particularly interested in the type of media genre and character that is appealing to certain age groups. For example, some studies suggest older adults tend to prefer more heartwarming and uplifting content, with little of the violence and sexuality (Gauntlett and Hill 1999) that appeals to younger audiences. In contrast, younger adults tend to prefer the emotionally intense content (Bartsch 2012) that is found in horror films and in media with violent characters (Fischoff et al. 2002).

Despite Hoang's inability to land a role playing a character of a distinctly different age than her own (or even a role for a character around her own age), there are many examples of age discrepancies between actors and their characters. Dustin Hoffman was thirty years old when he played Benjamin Braddock, a recent college graduate who was seduced by an "older woman," in the 1967 film *The Graduate*, while Braddock's seductress, Mrs. Robinson, the mother of his girlfriend, was played by Anne Bancroft, who was only six years his senior. In the popular TV sitcom, *The Golden Girls*, Estelle Getty was sixty-two years old when she began playing Sophia, a character who was supposed to be in her eighties, while Sophia's daughter, Dorothy, was played by Bea Arthur who was actually a year older than Getty. These are just a few examples of the unpredictable nature of age casting; future research should investigate age discrepancies between actors and their characters. In sum, while there is emerging research on age and media content selection by audiences, and limited evidence that suggests age discrepancies between actors and their characters is not "uncommon," there is a growing body of research which demonstrates that the intersection of aging and gender is more consequential to actresses' future employability than it is for actors' future employability.

The Distribution of Age and Gender in Film and Television

Over the last four decades communication scholars have documented the gender and age representation of characters in film and television (Gerbner et al. 1980). In general, women in younger age groups (twenties and thirties) are overrepresented, while older age groups (sixty and older) are underrepresented, in both television (Greenberg and Collette 1997) and film (Lauzen and Dozier 2005b; Lauzen, Dozier, and Reyes 2007) productions, and until recently relatively little research has examined the possible causes of this pattern. Lauzen and Dozier (2002), in their analysis of prime-time television programs that aired on the networks between 1999 and 2000, suggest that the fact that relatively few women work behind the scenes as producers may be key to the lopsided distribution of female characters. Lincoln and Allen (2004) have suggested that age/gender disparities among actors may be related to attractiveness stereotypes that are consistent with Sontag's (1979, 473) assertion that "a woman's fortunes depend, far more than a man's, on being at least 'acceptable' looking." Such reasoning is consistent with Bielby and Bielby's (2002, 27) conclusion that because "cultural stereotypes are embodied in the industry's product, [they] figure prominently in its marketing strategies, and therefore become rules of thumb for making decisions about writers and other creative professionals" who hold influential positions in determining who and what gets to appear onscreen (also see Bielby and Bielby 1996; 1999).

A handful of studies have found that macrolevel socioeconomic factors are associated with the age and gender distribution of roles in film and television (Pettijohn 2003; Treme and Craig 2013). Pettijohn (2003) examined the relationship between social and economic hard times and audiences' preferences for an actor's age and gender, and found young male actors are preferred during hard economic times, which suggest that Hoang's difficulties could have been exacerbated by the economic recession. These findings are in line with others that indicate male actors' exposure increases box office sales, but female actors' exposure doesn't (Treme and Craig 2013). Also, it is more difficult for older male actors to carry a film (as opposed to younger male actors), and it is harder for an older female actor to actually land a role (Treme and Craig 2013). However, this area of research is underdeveloped, and future studies should also consider how macrolevel socioeconomic factors may influence age and gender in film and television, as well as other media.

Other studies have noted that "in the entertainment industry after a certain age women have a harder time being as successful as men" (Gilberg and Hines 2000, 175). In an analysis of 1,169 Oscar nominees for Best Actress/Actor and Best Supporting Actress/Actor from 1928 through 1990, Markson and Taylor (1993) found men over the age of thirty-nine have accounted for 67 percent of all Best Actor winners, while women of the same age category only accounted for 27 percent of all Best Actress winners. In a more recent analysis of age and gender distributions of Best Actress/Actor Oscars, Pardoe and Simonton (2008) found the median age of Best Actress winners was thirty-three, while over this same time period (1928–2006) the median age for Best Actor was forty-two years old. The overrepresentation of women in younger age groups (twenty to thirty years old) and the underrepresentation of older actors (sixty or older) on television and in film, as well as the age/gender inequalities across the distribution of major awards, not only substantiates Hoang's concerns about age/ing but reaches beyond the Hollywood community as "they may interact with other factors to influence and reinforce perceptions of gender and age" (Lauzen and Dozier 2005b, 437).

Representations of Age and Aging in the Media

Examining the historical distribution of onscreen actors' age and gender is useful for understanding some of the demographics associated with inequality in film and television, but examining the portrayal of such social categories reveals more about the intersections of aging, media, and culture. As Bielby (2009, 250) notes, "Hollywood's culture industries of film and television are sites where symbolic representations of gender," and I would add age, "are literally produced, and they provide new challenges for understanding the persistence of gender [and age] inequality." Goldie Hawn's character in the film *The First Wives Club* exclaimed, "There are only three ages for women in Hollywood: babe, district attorney, and driving Miss Daisy" (cited in Lauzen and Dozier 2005b, 437).

In regard to the representation of age and gender in film, an examination of the one hundred top-grossing motion pictures from the 1940s through the 1980s found ageist and sexist stereotypes interacted in a way that portrayed older female characters more negatively than their male counterparts (Bazzini et al. 1997). These ageist and sexist stereotypes have been found to persist across time, as a study of the one hundred top-grossing films of 2002 found older female characters were less likely to have goals, and their male counterparts (male actors forty to sixty-nine years old) were more likely to play characters with leadership roles and occupational power (Lauzen and Dozier 2005b). The portrayal of age and gender in film is important, but television may represent a more pervasive conduit of age/gender stereotypes as "one of the most significant disseminators of cultural messages" (Lauzen and Dozier 2002, 138).

> Television, with its cast of characters in all phases of the life cycle, provides an almost inescapable set of messages about aging, gender, and race, and serves as one of the major sources for age-role socialization and resocialization in our society. (Signorielli 2004, 280)

The pervasiveness of television and the role it plays in socialization, particularly age-role socialization, is particularly cognizant in light of the age-segregated structure of contemporary society, where people of distinctly different ages rarely interact with one another outside of the family unit (Hagestad and Uhlenberg 2005).

Television programming, since at least the 1970s, has reinforced stereotypical age/gender roles (Gerbner et al. 1980), as female characters perpetually inhabit interpersonal roles (i.e., family, friends, romance) (Lauzen, Dozier, and Horan 2008). Additionally, in her analysis of prime-time network programs between 1993 and 2002, Signorielli (2004) found that women on television tend to age faster than their male counterparts—more women between fifty and sixty-four years old were characterized as "elderly," older female characters were typically less relevant to the storyline and less likely to have defined roles. Similarly, Lauzen, Dozier, and Reyes (2007) found that scripted prime-time television programs provide a truncated view of adulthood; one in which characters in their twenties participate in an extended adolescence, with a greater amount of leisure time and sexual activity than other adult age groups, and a lack of occupational power coupled with less leisure activities for characters over sixty, particularly women.

These age/gender stereotypes, premised by the historically persistent age/gender gaps in the availability of roles for onscreen actors, and the skewed distribution of prominent acting awards for relatively older male and younger female actors suggest that age matters in Hollywood. There is substantial evidence to support Hoang's concerns about age/ing in Hollywood, but what are the broader implications surrounding age and gender in the media? Is there a link between the portrayal of age and aging onscreen and their interpretation and performance in everyday life? Lauzen, Dozier, and Reyes (2007) warn that cultural representations of adulthood may reinforce ageist stereotypes, and portrayals of extended adolescence as an age intended for leisure and sexual activities may devalue the transition to adulthood—in a time where the transition to adulthood may be more complicated and stressful than it ever has before (Settersten and Ray 2010).

LINKING AGING THEORY
AND MEDIA/CULTURAL STUDIES

Media and Age Identities

As noted in this anthology's introduction, "The producer-consumer relationship is consequential for the life course of all parties to the transaction, yet is hidden from view in everyday social life, and has been largely ignored by life-course research" (Dannefer and Miklowski 2006, 38). To this regard, the depiction of age and gender in the media is particularly salient, especially when considering that the media "provides some of the few available sources of information about aging and age-role socialization" (Signorielli 2004, 280). Sociologists and gerontologists have long recognized the importance of, and interplay between, age and sex categories in relation to social structure (Linton 1942). Harrington, Bielby, and Bardo (2011) suggest that Westerhof's (2010) notion of "migrating in time" points toward the potential role media may play in anchoring individual identities in the radically transforming contemporary landscape defined by the shift from the twentieth- to twenty-first-century life course—represented by the growing ability "for people of every age to live lives that are congruent with their personal interests and wishes" (Settersten 2008, 22). Central to implications surrounding age and gender in the media and the blurring of traditional age-based norms is the concept of age identity (Lauzen, Dozier, and Reyes 2007), which refers to how people perceive themselves, or how others perceive them, in terms of age.

Two of the most common age identity constructs are subjective age (the age I feel), and ideal age (the age I would most like to be). A large body of aging research indicates there is a growing disconnect between chronological age and age identity, with adults feeling younger than their chronological age—especially as they become chronologically older (see Montepare 2009). Youthful age identities have been associated with positive psychological states (e.g., higher life satisfaction and positive affect), and lower levels of negative affect (Westerhof and Barrett 2005). Yet, gendered inequalities, similar to those represented in the age distribution of film and television actors, are evident across age identities—as "old age" is often perceived as beginning at an earlier age for women than for men (Barrett and von Rohr 2008). As media engagement plays an increasingly important role in age identity formation, given the deinstitutionalization of the normative twenti-eth-century life course (education, work/family, retirement) (Harrington, Bielby, and Bardo 2011), the truncated view of adulthood portrayed in popu-lar media and the lack of relevance assigned to older characters, particularly women (Lauzen, Dozier, and Reyes 2007), should be of concern to life course scholars.

CONCLUSION: LINKING ONSCREEN
AND OFFSCREEN AGE IDENTITIES

This chapter drew on Huong Hoang's legal battle against IMDb as a platform from which to explore issues of age and gender inequalities in film and television and their implications for life course scholarship in general and age identities in particular. The unwarranted publication of Hoang's date of birth by IMDb denied her the ability to maintain a distinction between her on- and offscreen age identities. While there is a bourgeoning literature on age and media content selection (Mares and Sun 2010), the lack of empirical studies on age discrepancies between actors and their characters makes this a fruitful area for future aging research. The relatively more substantial litera-ture on age and gender distributions and their portrayal in film and television points toward alarming inequalities that offer a truncated view of adulthood and a devalued old age, especially for women (Lauzen and Dozier 2005b; Lauzen, Dozier, and Reyes 2007). However, this literature has been dominat-ed by communication and media/cultural studies. While sociologists have explored various mechanisms to better understand age/gender inequalities across culture industries (Bielby and Bielby 1996; 1999; Lincoln and Allen 2004), life course scholarship and gerontology has given little regard to such issues. Yet, a call for collaborative research between these disparate disciplines has gone relatively unanswered since at least the 1970s:

> The neglect of communication is unfortunate for that field [gerontology] as well as our own [communications]. Gerontology represents an area of investigation and curricular development in communication that is not only socially important, but is also promising in terms of useful research and theory advancement. (Carmichael 1976, 121)

One promising area of useful research and theory advancement concerns age identities (Lauzen, Dozier, and Reyes 2007). As we face an unprecedented time of population aging and cultural transformation "identifying with contemporary culture without losing one's identification with one's past" (Westerhof 2010; 13) has become an important developmental challenge for the maintenance of self-identity in general and age identity specifically. Future aging research should give more consideration to the role of media in the twenty-first century.

NOTE

1. The request for both parties to refrain from using the term "age discrimination" is based on the court's reasoning that Hoang's case against IMDb is for breach of contract and not age discrimination. Thus, such "age discrimination" language could have confused the jury about the legality of the case.

III

Celebrity

Chapter Six

Growing Old in Celebrity Culture

Hilde Van den Bulck

"Bo Derek appears ageless at fifty-six" (*NY Daily News* 2013a). "Celebrity youth secrets revealed" (*Celebrity Beauty Buzz* 2012). "Madonna jealous of daughter's youth and beauty?" (Trevorrow 2009). Aging does not sit well with celebrity culture. On the one hand, celebrity culture worships youth and beauty and presents celebrities as icons with an aura of godly and timeless perfection defined as youthful beauty. At the same time, and following the aging of society at large, the celebrity industry experiences shifts that put people of any age in the limelight and allow (life)long celebrity careers. Together with an increasing attention of the gossip industry on the private and "real" celebrity, this results in a complex relationship between the celebrity ideal of youthfulness and the reality of aging.

This chapter combines insights from celebrity studies, sociology, postfeminism, and aging studies in order to discuss the reality and discourses of growing old in celebrity culture. How does celebrity culture and its main protagonists—celebrities and their entourage, media, and audiences—deal with growing older? How does this fit societal shifts that embrace aging and the "makeable self?" This chapter argues that age-related changes in both society and the celebrity industry have led to a greater prominence of aging in the reality and representation of celebrity, resulting in a "hegemonic struggle for the meaning of old age" (Dolan 2011, 14). This chapter explores how this can be witnessed in the mediated discussions of celebrities, focusing on the body, the main vehicle through which discourses of aging are articulated. It argues that while old concepts such as the pathological gaze and the gender double standard regarding aging seem replaced with a notion of youthful aging, getting older is still considered problematic, particularly for women, thus indicating that the battle over the definition of the meaning of age and aging is ongoing.

THE CELEBRITY CONSTRUCT AND AGE

Understanding how age is played out in celebrity culture requires insight into the nature of celebrity. Celebrity is constructed within the celebrity apparatus, an industrial complex behind celebrity culture that is responsible for the production, distribution, and consumption of celebrity and that is based on complex relationships and interactions between its main antagonists: the person wanting to be or to remain famous and his or her entourage, the media, and audiences (Van den Bulck and Tambuyzer 2008). All actors need to be present to guarantee the (ongoing) construction of a celebrity; that is, celebritization (Turner 2004). This celebrity construct is a combination of a public persona or image—the roles she or he plays, the music she or he performs, the products and good causes she or he endorses; a private image—the presentation of the private life of the celebrity as single or engaged, married or divorced, mother or loving uncle; and the "real" celebrity—the paparazzi glimpses of the actual person behind this double façade (Holmes 2005). Typical of the process of celebritization is that the public figure's private life and behavior—the official and the real—increasingly become (at least) as important as his or her professional activities to media and audiences. In all three aspects, a celebrity is presented and discussed against the celebrity norm and benchmark of youthfulness. Celebrities further distinguish themselves by the paradoxical combination of ordinariness and extraordinariness (Dyer 1998) and a certain habitus that separates them from other people (Gorin and Dubied 2011). This constructed, multi-image, exceptional, and ideological character of celebrity does not prevent a notion of authenticity (Tolson 2001) but points to the fact that authenticity is not just determined by the celebrity, but by all meaning-creating players in the apparatus, including media and audiences.

Indeed, virtually all communication with and about celebrities is mediated, turning celebrities into mediated personae (Evans and Hesmondalgh 2005). Media exposure is like oxygen to celebrities who, in turn, help media compete for shares of audiences eager to read about them (Drake and Miah 2010; Gamson 1994; Marshall 2006a; Rojek 2001). For a long time, celebrity news was restricted to specialized gossip magazines (*Heat; OK!*). Today it is part of all (news) media including daily and weekly popular and quality media and their online equivalents, current affairs programming and talk shows (*The Tonight Show*) and online celebrity gossip websites (justjared.com) and blogs (Perez Hilton; Lainey).

The media focus on the private (Gorin and Dubied 2011), aiming to reveal the "real" celebrity (Holmes 2005; Marshall 2006b), results in celebrity scandals and paparazzi photographs becoming mainstream news content, tying in with shifts toward sensationalism, entertainment, and the realm of private affairs, in short tabloidization (Turner 2004, 2010). In this mediated celebrity gossip, female celebrities in particular are under hyperscrutiny by celebrity gossip journalists, bloggers, and audiences. Age is key in this as, according to Fairclough (2012, 91), "the age narrative is a central trope in gossip culture [with] perpetual discussion of the age of female celebrities and whether their behaviour, lifestyle and look are 'age appropriate.'" In discussing this, media show a complex interplay of the stereotype of natural beauty (nature) and the workings of medical and other enhancements (culture) (e.g., "good genes or good docs" item on TMZ.com). Particularly the paparazzi version behind the constructed image of a celebrity focuses on sloppy hairdos, revealing plastic surgery scars, bikini pictures suggesting cellulite, and the like. Aging has thus become part of celebrity culture, constructed through mediated discussion with audiences.

Audiences, the final actor in the celebrity apparatus, are dependent on media for news about celebrities they almost never meet in person (Cashmore 2006). Despite the apparent triviality of the topic, the construction and media coverage of celebrities help shape audiences' understanding of the social world (Evans and Hesmondalgh 2005; Gorin and Dubied 2011) and their cultural identities (Dyer 1998). As Rojek (2007, 73) explains, "the lives of celebrities provide parables of instruction for fans and general audiences." To some extent, audiences' interest in celebrity news compensates for their anonymity and alienation, and for their frustrations in capitalist society; that is, for failing to reach the dream of becoming rich and glamorous. This is the celebrity-as-commodity thesis (Cashmore 2006; Marshall 1997; Rojek 2001). However, the meaning of celebrity goes beyond the consumer capitalism argument as celebrity coverage provides media and society with a forum for discussion of a wide range of social and moral topics and issues, including age: how aging should be interpreted, what it is to become old, and what constitute "correct" and "incorrect" versions of aging (Fairclough 2012; Marshall 2006a; Weber 2012).

THE MAKEABLE SELF AND AGING

Growing old in celebrity culture is in a complex relationship with aging in contemporary society. As people live longer and baby boomers have claimed a new, active, and healthy interpretation of what it is to grow old (Gilleard and Higgs 2007), showing the commercial potential of older consumers (Biggs et al. 2007; Jermyn 2012a), so representations of aging have changed. According to Dolan (2011, 4), this has resulted in a shift away from "the clinical gaze that constructs older people as physically frail, as needing care and support." This has been replaced, still according to Dolan (2011, 4) by a notion of "youthful aging" or "successful aging" that focuses not on the pathologized old age but on positive images of the active and healthy aging process as something joyous, energetic, and vibrant, thus blurring the boundaries between young and old.

This new image of aging goes hand in hand with the focus in contemporary postmodern society on the "makeable" self. Modernity was based on stable social relationships and cultural ideals, with predetermined and more or less fixed life paths, and with clear limits to ambitions and possibilities, including those based on age. The demise of the grand narratives and institutions today results in an increased stress on diversity and change (Jameson 1991; Lash 1999). In a diverse and fragmented culture, each person needs to actively construct his or her own identity and to express it in the choice for a certain lifestyle, including the choice of how to grow old (Giddens 1991). Mediatized culture is the glue that holds this fragmented society together, as media provide access to a global culture (Kellner 1995) and, importantly, to celebrity culture. Celebrities function as icons and trendsetters (Van den Bulck and Tambuyzer 2008). Media and celebrities tell us continually that we are "makeable," that we can and must do something about who we are.

The combination of aging societies, a neoliberal view on person and identity—also dominating postfeminism (Fairclough 2012)—and the accompanying lifestyle industries has resulted in new discourses about aging, new ways in which people are invited to experience growing old, and in new ways in which older people, especially aging women, are represented. Aging—and particularly influencing and resisting it—is today presented in popular and celebrity culture as a life choice rather than a biological certainty. Aging parameters are blurring (Jermyn 2012a). As Fairclough (2012, 92) states, today "ageing is not something to be feared, but must be both celebrated and fought," with the consumer industries providing the means toward youthful aging and the promise of successful aging if not an ageless society. This is not to say that society, through popular culture discourses including celebrity, is seen to embrace old age. Rather age has become an issue under constant cultural scrutiny, as interpretations of "right" and "wrong" ways of growing old fight it out on the battlefield of celebrity culture (Dolan 2011; Weber 2012). As such, the extreme attention to body and soul of the aging celebrity as positive or negative role model is no coincidence.

THE SHIFTING AGE OF CELEBRITY
CULTURE AND THE DOUBLE STANDARD

Traditionally, growing old in celebrity culture, particularly in the Hollywood star system, was the domain of men. For male stars, growing old seemed easy and could be done graciously (Dyer 1998). They continued to play lead roles, with actors like Cary Grant remaining a heartthrob image, playing romantic love interests to young women/actresses well into middle and even old age.

As older actresses started to show "their age" and thus no longer confirmed the youthful beauty norm, they found it more difficult to find work in the Hollywood system. If Hollywood did produce films about older women, these focused on portrayals of aging female stars such as Norma Desmond (played by Gloria Swanson) in *Sunset Boulevard* (1950) (Jermyn 2012a). These films showed famous Hollywood actresses "playing out exaggerated and discomforting performances of female ageing" in which getting older itself was shown as horrific and traumatic and elder female celebrities as grotesque (Jermyn 2012a, 4). A similar process could be witnessed in other sections of celebrity culture such as music and television. The only way for aging female celebrities to remain in the public eye was to function as endorsers of antiaging products such as mature cosmetic lines. As such, celebrity culture echoed Susan Sontag's notion of the double standard of aging that dominated Western culture until quite recently and by which women are considered "old" from menopause onwards while men are not considered old or judged by their age until much later (Swinnen 2012).

Following societal trends mentioned above, celebrity culture has witnessed a shift in this regard. Fairclough (2012) points to the growing visibility of older women in cinema, even in leading roles. The breakdown of barriers between cinema (and its "distant" star system) and television (and its "friend of the family" personality system), has provided fertile ground for aging female celebrities. Jermyn (2012a) refers to former film stars gaining new credibility and celebrity status through television work like Glenn Close in *Damages* (FX, 2007–present). In music, too, there are increasing numbers of female performers growing older while staying at the top of their game, with pop icon Madonna leading a whole range of female singers and musicians such as Sheryl Crow, Debbie Harry, and Kylie Minogue. The same applies to other fields of celebrity culture.

This greater visibility of older female celebrities in public performances is accompanied by an exploding media attention that focuses mainly on the private and the real. As such, older female stars seem to have gained inclusivity which questions the old notion of a gender double standard when it comes to age in celebrity culture. However, gender differences persist in that aging remains a key topic discussed about female far more than about male celebrities, even resulting in different notions of privacy for reporting on older male and female celebrities (Negra and Holmes, 2008). Fairclough (2012, 94) goes as far as to state that "the discourses about ageing women are first and foremost framed in terms of narratives of ageing." While there are indications that for male celebrities too, age is increasingly part of how they are talked about (e.g., "Brad Pitt's Wrinkles 'Killing' His Career?" [*Gossip Cop* 2013]), overall their age is rarely part of the characters they play or the issues they are associated with in celebrity gossip. For female celebrities, age is inherent in the discourses about their public and private performances and persona. Is she acting "appropriate" to her age? Is she managing her aging process "properly," with "dignity?"

HOW OLD IS CELEBRITY CULTURE?

Regardless of these surviving aspects of a double standard, old age no longer seems an obstacle to maintain visibility, success, and status in celebrity culture (see also Jermyn 2012a), as can be witnessed from the success of seventy-something and older actors Judi Dench, Morgan Freeman, Shirley MacLaine, and Maggie Smith; musical celebrities Shirley Bassey, Bob Dylan, Roberta Flack, and Tom Jones; comedian Joan Rivers; and television host Barbara Walters. Several "old" celebrities even manage to become more celebrated in ways that reinforce their career, as can be witnessed from Eastwood's new career as a director (Cornell 2009) and Diane Keaton's resurfacing as a mature romantic comedy actress (Jermyn 2012b).

However, most discourses of age and celebrity situate getting older much earlier in a celebrity's life and deal with celebrities in their forties and fifties, focusing on how good they "still" look, how they deal with turning forty and fifty, and how energetic they still are. Age is thus a central trope in gossip discourses surrounding actresses such as Gwyneth Paltrow, Courtney Cox, and Angelina Jolie; actors Brad Pitt, George Clooney, and Hugh Jackman; and musical stars like Jon Bon Jovi, Madonna, Bono, and Kylie Minogue. As such, most celebrity discourses "project ageing only in terms of a kind of extended middle age" (Jermyn 2012a, 1). The fact that these celebrities often become endorsers or spokespersons for consumer products geared at retired people (Weber 2012), while official retirement in most Western countries is set around sixty to sixty-five, paints a very partial picture of "old age" and confirms the continued fear of "real" old age.

Looking at these, at times contradictory, trends, it becomes clear that celebrity culture today is witnessing a "hegemonic struggle for the meaning of old age" (Dolan 2011, 14). No longer made invisible (in the case of female) or ignored (in the case of male celebrities), age, the acceptance of aging and "appropriate ways" of aging in celebrity culture are part of a discursive battle focusing on celebrities. The rest of this chapter explores key areas in which this struggle can be seen to take place.

THE CELEBRITY BODY AND AGE

Crucial to the discussion of age in celebrity culture—and beyond—is the body. The body is considered as an indicator of personality, talent, capacities, character, and social skills and as a key instrument in the building and presentation of identity, image, and lifestyle (Blum 2003; Featherstone 1991;

Hancock, Hughes, and Jagger 2000). The body is the main tool through which to present oneself to others. It is an "action system" that needs to be put into battle and played out. This is the body as commodity, editable with the help of cosmetics, dietary habits, sports, and garments that strengthen a certain image and delineate a certain lifestyle.

What can and should happen with that body, what is beautiful, and what is ugly, is not an inherent quality but is determined by a particular view held by a particular society at a particular point in time. Celebrities are socially appropriate vehicles to articulate and promote these views. The beauty ideals they present to us today are strict and difficult (Feasey 2006; Turner 2004). For women this includes a look that is youthful and very slender, with smooth, wrinkle-free skin, long legs, and narrow hips. The "ideal man" is mainly presented as toned and even muscled, youthful and with a V-shaped body, big biceps, broad chest, and shoulders. These beauty ideals go against the natural process of bodily aging.

Considering the "supposedly natural and rather austere semiotic relationship between ageing and bodies" (Weber 2012, 65), the body is the main indicator from which to read a celebrity's age and aging celebrities cannot naturally maintain the beauty ideals. With "the young body constituted as the healthy norm" (Dolan 2011, 3), the aging body is its unhealthy semiotic opposite, indicative of physical and psychological decline. The "newly sanctioned discourse of 'youthful' ageing" (Dolan 2011, 8) expects both male and female celebrities to maintain their body—and thus their beauty—nonstop as part of their job and responsibility as a celebrity. Celebrities are under permanent scrutiny by media and audiences in this regard. Visible wrinkles, cellulite, fat, and saggy breasts and bottoms are presented as nonpermissible shortcomings, unworthy of a celebrity (Van den Bulck and Tambuyzer 2008). When a famous body presents the audience not with the usual constructed perfection but more true to nature, media and audiences rebel. Conversely, a famous body that appears to stand the test of time is praised, as in the case of actresses Goldie Hawn (Tincknell 2012) and Jane Fonda: "Jane Fonda: Seventy-three and a half, and almost certainly hotter than you" (Butt 2011). Youthful aging in celebrity culture is equated with successful aging.

AGING CELEBRITY WEIGHT ISSUES

Key to the beauty ideal of youth, and thus of youthful aging, is the notion of a slender, svelte, "hard" (trained) body. Blum (2003, 232–33), in reference to (the close media scrutiny of) former actress and celebrity activist Elizabeth Taylor, states that the weight issue "'embodies' the intrinsic paradoxes of celebrity culture" as it shows the difficulty between the reality of weight gain at later age and the idealized version of celebrities.

With the apparent cutoff age at forty for female ("Fit and fabulous celebrities over forty" [*NY Daily News* 2013b] and fifty for male celebrities ["Foxy over fifty" (Silverstein 2011], media scrutinize the weight of aging celebrities, congratulating the continued "healthy" physique of female celebrities such as actresses Sharon Stone and Christie Brinkley and male counterparts Harrison Ford and Denzel Washington, and singers like Tom Jones. The "ideal" older female celebrity body is epitomized by the 2008 paparazzi bikini picture of Helen Mirren, then in her early sixties, made iconic by its viral spread through media worldwide (Dolan 2011). Interestingly, Mirren herself criticized the photograph, saying, "In and of itself, it is a lie because I don't actually look like that and I know that that is going to haunt me forever and I'll be forever trying to bury it unsuccessfully" (Bull 2011).

While some more realistic older celebrity bodies such as Meryl Streep or Jack Nicholson's seem to be accepted by the media on account of their talents, overall failure to live up to the firm, svelty body ideal as age progresses is heavily commented on and harshly evaluated with disregard for age or ill health. As a result, Kathleen Turner is nominated into the "fifty fat celebrities" list of the *New York Post* (1999), despite her weight being related to rheumatic disorder treatment. Many other aging female celebrities are commented on, sometimes through euphemistic reference to "envious curves," more often by criticizing them for "having forgotten to make trips to the gym" and advising it is "high time she did something about her weight gain." Similarly, male actors Val Kilmer and Steven Seagal, former sports star Mike Tyson, and Guns and Roses' singer Axl Rose are criticized for having lost their once perfect V-shaped physique. Long-term public battles with weight issues such as those of Elizabeth Taylor, Kirstie Alley, or Oprah Winfrey are followed at close range (Smith 2012; Wilson 2003).

As such, the "overweight" body of aging celebrities, particularly women, "is a site where numerous discourses intersect, including . . . beauty and sexuality, health and pathology, morality, anxieties about excess, and the centrality of the individual in the project of self-governance" (Murray 2008, 4–5, quoted in Weber 2012, 71). Kissling, in her discourse analysis of celebrity diet books, identifies a number of key themes which also apply to media coverage of celebrity weight issues (2006; see also Van den Bulck and Tambuyzer 2008). Central is the control of mind over body. Behind vague quotes about how it is to feel good in one's skin is a notion of the body as an object that needs to be controlled, sometimes even an enemy that needs to be fought. A nonperfect body is a sign of weakness, illustrated by stories of aging celebrities that "let themselves go" or "feel guilty" because they "sinned." So, aging is the celebrity's own fault, the result of a lack of discipline. Self-appreciation is thus associated with beauty. Fitness and dieting are motivated by a sense of good looks rather than good health. Weight gain is presented as leading to a feeling of ugliness, the main motivation to do something about it. Weight loss is then the basis to be happy again. Beyond that, excess weight is considered not just pathological but immoral, and dieting or exercise as the path to moral superiority. In these stories about aging celebrities' weight, the relationships between health, fitness, and beauty merge. Being slim or skinny is equated with being healthy and most of all happy. Beauty is obtained through health and physical fitness; mental and physical health results from beauty.

FADING LOOKS, PLASTIC SURGERY, AND AUTHENTICITY

Even more than with weight, youthful beauty is equated with firm skin, that is "skin unwrinkled, unmarked by expression, environment and/or genetic pre-disposition" (Dolan 2011, 10). The youthful aging of celebrities, therefore, is crucially concentrated on avoiding, delaying, and getting rid of signs of aging "through the inscriptions of 'youth' on the bodily flesh" (Dolan 2011, 10). As a result, cosmetic and plastic surgery have become intrinsically linked with celebrity culture (Blum 2003; Davis 1995).

This link, according to Blum (2003), goes as far back as the late nineteenth century when surgeons used hypodermic paraffin injections to fight bags under the eyes and wrinkles of celebrities. Facial peeling was developed in 1886 to treat aging actresses. Stars such as Joan Crawford, Rita Hayworth, Robert Mitchum, and John Wayne reverted to cosmetic surgery to stretch their dwindling careers with a rejuvenated look. In the 1960s, actress Raquel Welch obtained the reputation that there is very little left that is natural about her body, a reputation she passed on in the 1970s to legendary actress Mae West.

Today, cosmetic surgery is part and parcel of celebrities' fight against the natural forces of aging, making Botox and collagen injections to remove wrinkles standard procedures in the world of actors such as Sylvester Stallone and Teri Hatcher, singer Céline Dion, and style guru Trinny Woodall. Often, this is combined with implants to compensate for a lack of chin or cheek, such as in the case of Arnold Schwarzenegger and Priscilla Presley. Many others move on to more far-reaching surgical interventions to maintain the eternally youthful look. This becomes apparent from the new, youthful face of media magnate Martha Stewart or country singer Kenny Rogers.

This is accompanied by a battle over the meaning of authenticity. In the old Hollywood star system, facelifts and other interventions were among the best kept secrets as stars' semidivine aura was centrally built around authenticity defined as natural qualities, part of what made them exceptional (super) human beings. The mask presented itself as a reality, in those days not contradicted by the paparazzi lens aimed at the "real" celebrity (Blum 2003). This reverberates in "surviving" representatives of the old Hollywood studio system such as Sophia Loren, who denies having had any cosmetic surgery, "espousing a version of femininity and glamour that is both seemingly natural and which can be maintained through a healthy living regime" (Fairclough 2012, 93).

Today cosmetic treatment is discussed at length in the media. Photo galleries and extensive analyses of old and recent photographs suggest who has undergone treatment. In the media evaluation of such treatments, Fairclough (2012, 93) distinguishes the "gruesome," the "desperate," and the "sanctioned." Gruesome examples such as Mickey Rourke and Jocelyn Wildenstein are rejected, while "desperate" cases such as Meg Ryan or Nicole Kidman are met with harsh criticism: "Nicole's face looks like a bat!" (Mendoza 2008). Often the media are quite positive about an obviously worked-on famous face, sanctioning it in the process. The new nose of actress Winona Ryder is considered to add to her youthful appearance and French actress Catherine Deneuve is praised for managing to look natural with well-performed cosmetic surgery (Zender 2010). Celebrities too have changed as many talk openly about how they deal with cosmetic and plastic surgery. For media magnate and television personality Simon Cowell, "Botox is no more unusual than toothpaste. It works, you do it once a year—who cares?" (Anisiobi 2012). In her autobiography, reality television and talk show celebrity Sharon Osbourne (2006) writes extensively about her tummy correction, hip liposuction, butt lift, thigh lift, facelift, eyelid lift, and breast lift and has her Botox administered in front of the reality television cameras.

This openness of celebrities, media, and audiences toward cosmetic surgery impacts on the relationship between the celebrity body and authenticity (Blum 2003; Van den Bulck and Tambuyzer 2008). Authenticity no longer refers to natural physical perfection, but to the extent to which the celebrity abidingly fulfills an ideal and, as he or she gets older, maintains its youthfulness—if need be through plastic surgery. It makes us accept that celebrities postsurgery do not necessarily resemble themselves (Blum 2003). Examples include comedian Joan Rivers, who has made her surgically reworked face the subject of self-deprecating witticisms. Or the new eyelids, cheek implants, liposuction, facelift, nose job, chin implant, breast and belly reduction of actress Rosanne Barr. The result is that she looks simply like another person (Van den Bulck and Tambuyzer 2008). In their never-ending attempts to keep looking the same or even better, these aging celebrities stop looking like themselves. The audience does not seem to have a problem with this as it wants the two-dimensional images of the perfect celebrities to align with what they know. It is the audience itself that does not want the celebrity to age, encouraged by the media.

Today, then, anxiety is not focused on youthful aging as such, which seems widely accepted, but on those occasions when "the always already pathologized signs of old age rupture the embodied construction of youthful ageing" (Dolan 2011, 13). A well-known example is pop icon Madonna, whose career spans several decades. For many years the musical celebrity was celebrated for her age-defying looks, established by nonstop workouts and subtle cosmetic and plastic surgery, resulting in her svelte figure, firm body, and youthful face. However, since reaching her fifties, she is increasingly criticized for "her sinewy arms, her gnarled, bony, wrinkly and veiny hands" (Dolan 2011, 13), indicating the actual, natural aging of the celebrity body. In showing the ultimate inevitability of bodily aging, this clash between "eternal youth" and "real old age" in one celebrity body is confronting and therefore criticized and deplored.

THE AILING CELEBRITY

The latter example indicates that even in contemporary celebrity culture, the inevitable alteration of youthful aging cannot be ignored. This is the most obvious in the illness that befalls aging celebrities such as actors Michael Douglas' throat cancer (later identified as tongue cancer) and Zsa Zsa Gabor's strokes, hip replacement, leg amputation, and slow decline. Bonner and McKay (2000), in their diachronic analysis of women's magazines' health stories, show that media follow celebrities through the decades as they age, providing discussions of their health and medical conditions that accompany "changing life events": "miscarriages, cancer scares, coping with widowhood, dealing with a parent's ageing, not to mention endless weight loss stories and sponsorship of health campaigns" (Bonner and McKay 2000, 139–40).

The focus in these stories is, on the one hand, on biomedical models of health issues, as something that cannot be helped and that the celebrity needs to endure, just like "normal" human beings (Bonner and McKay 2000). On the other hand there is a stress on the inspirational: the aging celebrity's determination, perseverance, and courage in his or her darkest hour, in turn becoming an example and symbol of inspiration and hope. Discourses of aging celebrities' health concerns thus help readers identify with and understand health issues but also perform a political function as they help put the issue on the public agenda. In the latter context, celebrities who deal with illness are considered good celebrity endorsers for all kinds of medial concerns, as their own fragility and personal experience provides them a legitimate stance (Panis and Van den Bulck 2012).

However, media discussing aging celebrities' health issues speak with forked tongues, with hints to the personal responsibility of a celebrity for his or her health and well-being and references to "excesses" of the celebrities in their early lives (Van den Bulck and Tambuyzer 2008). In the case of Michael Douglas's cancer, next to a dominant discourse of personal bravery throughout the ordeal, the media are keen to spread the story that the affliction resulted from too much oral sex, a reference to Douglas's alleged past as a sex addict. This illustrates the focus of celebrity gossip on the scandalous but also the difficulty of celebrity culture to deal with the clinical and pathological aspects of old age.

CONCLUSION

It appears contemporary celebrity culture is a culture in transition when it comes to dealing with age. Much of the "old" discursive notions of age are being undermined as the fear of old age and the gender double standard are replaced by a celebrity world in which both men and women can remain current well into old age. However, the question as to what constitutes "acceptable" old age seems more difficult to answer. The complexity of the issue, as becomes clear from the above analysis, indicates that aging is part of a hegemonic battle fought around the notion of youthful aging as successful aging with the celebrity body as main and moldable instrument. For Dolan (2011, 14) this is "a struggle between biological essentialism and cultural constructionist positions." As the aging of celebrity culture, like that of society, is not yet at an end, this struggle will continue, and thus requires future academic attention. Combining insights from different disciplines including celebrity studies, cultural studies, and gerontology will prove fruitful and crucial in gaining further understanding of this complex phenomenon.

The above analysis further suggests a mutual responsibility of the different actors in the celebrity apparatus: despite having "freed" themselves from the old, controlling Hollywood star system, actors and actresses, guided by their entourage, seem keen to abide by the new, and equally strict rules of "youthful aging." Media act as crucial mediators, communicating the new notions of successful aging to audiences which, in turn, appear happy to embrace them, including the treatment of aging bodies that comes with it. However, more research is needed to better deconstruct the different relationships and roles of the actors in the apparatus behind this celebrity culture. Such research can contribute to an understanding of ways for celebrity culture and society to embrace age in a healthy and respectful fashion.

Chapter Seven

Social Meaning of Celebrities in the Everyday Lives of Nursing Home Residents

An Exploratory Study

Nathalie Claessens

While contemporary Western societies are increasingly characterized by processes of global aging and an omnipresent celebrity culture, academic research has hardly addressed the combination of these issues—celebrities in the lives of older adults—with some notable exceptions (e.g., Harrington and Bielby 2010; Harrington, Bielby, and Bardo 2011; Van den Bulck and Van Gorp 2011). However, this topic needs to be explored extensively because, as people live longer and grow older, they have more time to potentially invest in celebrity (news) culture. This is especially the case for a specific subgroup—nursing home residents—who are the focus of this study because their circumstances (more leisure time, less mobility, and smaller social networks) may increase their mediated encounters with celebrities and the importance of celebrities in their lives.

Celebrities have proven to be important for nursing home residents as food for gossip—strengthening social relationships—and replacements for lost real-life social contacts—in the form of parasocial relationships (De Backer et al. 2007). For the general audience, celebrities are believed to not just provide food for entertainment or gossip, but to fulfill social functions and have meaning beyond mere pleasure: as a topic for conversation, a lead into moral discussions, or social companions (Dyer 1998; Giles 2003; Marshall 2006a; Rojek 2001; Turner 2004). A qualitative approach is used here to examine whether these functions can be translated to the nursing home

context. Combining individual and focus group interviews, the celebrity preferences of the individual residents as well as the meanings of celebrity in a
social space (nursing home) are examined.

CELEBRITY IN THE LIVES OF OLDER ADULTS

The academic neglect of older adults in media research has been criticized
before (Carmichael 1976; Van der Goot 2009) and can be extended to celebrity studies (Harrington and Bielby 2010). Indeed, although there are several
studies on celebrities and older fans (e.g., Harrington, Bielby, and Bardo
2011; Van den Bulck and Van Gorp 2011), their applicability to the general
older adult population is limited as they focus on a very specific audience
segment. This is why this chapter wishes to provide insight in the functions
of celebrity for the—not necessarily fan—older audience.

As stated above, this chapter focuses on nursing home residents as they
tend to have a lot of leisure time, be restricted in terms of mobility, and have
decreasing social networks (Drageset 2004), all factors which may increase
their use of celebrity media. In Flanders (the northern part of Belgium),
nursing home residents are mostly female (75 percent) and on average
eighty-four years old. More than a quarter of the Flemish nursing home
population suffers from dementia and 82 percent are physically and mentally
dependent on nursing staff (Callens and Pauwels 2006). Within the diverse
older adult population, nursing home residents often represent the old-old
(eighty and older) (Carmichael 1976) and/or the dependent and unhealthy
(Harrington, Bielby, and Bardo 2011). Misleadingly, most research focuses
on losses related to old age (Vandebosch and Eggermont 2002; Van der Goot
2009; Van der Goot, Beentjes, and van Selm 2012), whereas aging also
entails advantages which should be considered, such as more free time, leisure possibilities, (life) knowledge, social confidence, and emotional experience and skills (Carstensen, Fung, and Charles 2003; Harrington, Bielby, and
Bardo 2011; Vandebosch and Eggermont 2002). As such, the present chapter
focuses on how the consumption of celebrity can positively influence older
nursing home residents' lives.

Contemporary Western societies are characterized by an omnipresent celebrity culture, not limited to gossip magazines and popular television talk
shows, but extending to almost every medium and domain of life (Holmes
and Redmond 2010; Marshall 2006a). This can be linked to changing news
values, where personalization and soft news—embodied in celebrity news—
are gaining importance (Turner 2004). Celebrity can be defined as a construction created and maintained by the famous person and his or her entourage, the media, and the audience—the celebrity apparatus (Marshall 2006a;
Rojek 2001). This process is described as celebritization (Turner 2004), in

which a public figure's private life becomes (at least) as important to media and audiences as the professional activities. The celebrity construct consists of three personae, namely a public (professional), private (official), and real persona (behind the celebrity façade) (Dyer 1987; Holmes 2005). Within the large variety of celebrities, Rojek (2001) distinguishes between at least 3 different forms; (1) ascribed (predetermined by birth, e.g., royalty), (2) achieved (based on accomplishments or talent, e.g., sportsmen), and (3) attributed (result of extensive mass media attention, e.g., reality TV).

Despite its apparent triviality, celebrities have meaning for audiences beyond entertainment which includes food for social interactions, means to discuss moral issues, and social companions in the form of parasocial relationships (Dyer 1998; Giles 2003; Harrington, Bielby, and Bardo 2011; Marshall 2006a; Rojek 2001; Turner 2004). The latter are relationships in which audience members have the illusion of friendship with a celebrity, which is mediated and one-sided, but entails an emotional connection and is similar to traditional social relationships (Claessens 2013a; Giles 2002). Celebrities thus fulfill important social functions that are theoretically accepted within celebrity studies. However, with the exception of several case studies (e.g., Feasey 2008; Van den Bulck and Claessens 2013), there is little empirical research into the functions of celebrities in audience members' everyday lives. Even fewer academics have examined the meaning of celebrities for older adults or nursing home residents. Therefore, this chapter examines whether the social functions described above are also relevant for nursing home residents and whether there are any additional meanings for this group. For instance, considering the heightened need for reminiscence and memory-related issues that many older adults, in particular, nursing home residents are faced with, celebrities may act as an "aide-memoire," a means to foster reminiscence in a positive, fun, and light manner and thereby enhance self-esteem (Bender, Bauckham, and Norris 1999; Van der Goot, Beentjes, and van Selm 2012).

In addition, little is known about older adults' celebrity preferences. Some exceptions are the studies by De Backer et al. (2007) and Vandebosch and Eggermont (2002) in Flanders (Belgium) in which a preference for local celebrities and royals, soap actors, and sportspeople was found among nursing home residents. Van der Goot (2009) further found a preference for older (TV) characters. In this chapter, nursing home residents' celebrity preferences are studied through individual interviews, while celebrities' social functions for residents—as food for conversation, leads into moral discussions, social companions, and aide-memoires—are examined through focus groups.

METHOD

Individual and focus group interviews are employed in this study, as previous studies on nursing home residents have found these to be effective methods (Barrett and Kirk 2000; Hajjar 1998). Indeed, focus groups tend to fit into nursing home residents' daily schedules quite easily, mimic animation activities, and are more time-efficient in comparison to participant observation (Morgan 1997). Combining in-depth individual interviews and interactive focus groups helps to understand residents' personal preferences as well as underlying group meanings, processes, and norms. Selecting residents who live together further enhances the natural character of the focus groups. However, conducting interviews with nursing home residents is more time- and labor-intensive than with other groups as multiple health-related factors complicate interviews (Barrett and Kirk 2000).

This study is situated in Flanders (Belgium), where forty semistructured individual interviews were conducted to gain insight in residents' celebrity preferences and select participants for focus groups (e.g., Bender, Bauckham, and Norris 1999). The respondents were asked about sociodemographic variables and their favorite celebrities. Residents of two similar (in size and population) nursing homes—one rural and one urban—participated in the interviews, including thirty-five women and five men between the ages of 68 and 101 ($M = 85$). Following nursing home staff instructions, only residents with relatively good mental capacities were selected. Indeed, it was difficult to interview less healthy residents or those suffering from dementia, because of their limited (mental or physical) capacities or unwillingness to participate (Callens and Pauwels 2006; Claessens 2013b; Lloyd, Gatherer, and Kalsy 2006). Therefore, the results below do not represent the whole range of nursing home residents, which (unfortunately) is common practice in research on this group (Hajjar 1998).

Four focus groups of approximately 1.5 hours were conducted in the nursing homes, each with six to seven residents. The total twenty-seven focus group participants live in the two nursing homes described above (thirteen rural; fourteen urban) and have an average age of 85.6 (range: sixty-five to ninety-seven). There was a large overlap between the participants in the individual and focus group interviews. With regard to group composition, there were no male residents in the first focus group (rural), one man in the second (rural) and third (urban), and two men in the fourth (urban). The focus groups were conducted by the researcher (a young woman), assisted by a female activities staff member and a female student who took notes and transcribed the interviews *verbatim*. The combination of the young female researcher and assistants and the older, female nursing home residents (aside from the few men) in the focus groups facilitated the discussions. Indeed, research material is more easily elicited when both the researcher(s) and the participants are female (Finch 1993). In addition, the intergenerational approach enhanced the trust between (older) participants and (young) researcher because it mimicked grandparent/grandchild relations (Grenier 2007). After an introduction, the focus group discussion was opened with a general question ("what comes to mind first when you think about celebrities?"), followed by the presentation of twenty celebrity pictures. For each picture, a set of questions was asked: "Who is this? What do you know about [celebrity]? Do you like [celebrity]? What do you think about [topic]? How old were you when [celebrity] was famous? Did/do you talk about [celebrity]?" These questions related to the residents' knowledge of celebrities as well as celebrities' social functions: social companionship, lead into moral discussions, aide-memoire, and food for conversation.

Table 7.1. Selection of Celebrities

No.	Name	Topic
1	Prince Charles and Princess Diana	Adultery, divorce, accident
2	King Albert and Queen Paola	Adultery
3	Elizabeth Taylor	Divorce
4	Rock Hudson	Homosexuality
5	Luc Appermont and Bart Kaëll	Homosexuality
6	Walter Capiau	Child abuse (sexual)
7	Elvis Presley	Drug abuse, divorce
8	Yasmine	Homosexuality, suicide
9	Will Ferdy	Homosexuality
10	Eddy Merckx	Drugs
11	Tom Boonen	Drugs
12	Prince Filip and Princess Mathilde	/
13	Prince William and Princess Kate	/
14	John Wayne	/
15	Greta Garbo	/
16	Tony Corsari	/
17	Eddy Wally	/
18	Kim Clijsters	/
19	Rik Coppens	/
20	Roger Federer	/

The celebrity pictures were selected on the basis of the residents' preferences and the sample was composed of eleven celebrities who obtained extensive media coverage in the context of a social or moral topic and nine celebrities who did not obtain such media attention. Efforts were made to balance male/female, past/contemporary, local/global, and royalty/film/music/TV/sports celebrities (see table 7.1). The social/moral topics were varied, with a focus on adultery and homosexuality. This resulted from the social/moral topics' association with the residents' favorite celebrities. The celebrity pictures were ordered according to domain (royalty, film, music, TV, sports), each with a global and local example. In the first and third focus groups, eleven celebrities (linked to a social/moral topic) came first, followed by the other nine celebrities. In the second and fourth focus groups, this was reversed.

The focus groups were transcribed and qualitatively analyzed by means of open and axial coding to identify celebrities' social functions. The segments covering the celebrity preferences and each celebrity function were analyzed separately. In the following segments, residents' celebrity preferences are described, followed by an analysis of celebrities facilitating social interaction in the nursing home as well as fostering meaning-making processes. Then, celebrities' meaning as close yet distant friends, with whom nursing home residents maintain parasocial relationships is examined. Finally, celebrities' ability to help nursing home residents with reminiscence is investigated.

CELEBRITY PREFERENCES

In the individual interviews, thirty-one of forty residents named a favorite celebrity and these included both local and legendary international celebrities (table 7.1). Several residents felt distance toward international celebrities and closer to local ones (e.g., De Backer et al. 2007).

Researcher: Were you sad when she [Princess Diana] had the accident?

. . .

Ma. (♀ 88): It was another country.

Researcher: What if it happened in Belgium? Would it be different?

M. (♀ 76): Yes.

Mad. (♀ 90): Yes.

. . .

Researcher: So it is different because she comes from Great Britain?

Ma.: Yes.

D. (♀ 91): It is quite distant. (FG1)

This can be linked to the relevance of cultural proximity in parasocial relationships (Claessens 2013a; Tian and Hoffner 2010) and the local nature of
celebrity culture during the residents' youth, when globalization was not yet
dominant (Chapman 2005). In this context, it is interesting that the residents
mostly indicated celebrities of their own generation as favorites (e.g., Van
der Goot 2009). Both cultural proximity and the local nature of celebrity
culture in the past thus appear to play a role here. The preference for older
celebrities can be explained by the persistence of earlier media habits in later
life (e.g., Hajjar 1998). However, when residents referred to sports, the
younger celebrities—still competing today—were mentioned more often.
This may be related to their higher media coverage and the possibility to
cheer for them in competitions. In the focus groups, there was almost no
difference in the discussions of older and younger celebrities, indicating that,
even though they tend to indicate the older ones as their favorites, they know
a lot about both.

The residents mentioned a variety of celebrity domains—music, TV, film,
royals, and sports—but the ultimate ascribed celebrity, royalty, clearly dominated, which can be linked to the stability of royals throughout Belgian
history (e.g., De Backer et al. 2007; Vandebosch and Eggermont 2002). This
was especially strong for the female residents, for whom kings, queens,
princes, and princesses were among the first things that came to mind when
thinking about celebrities. Sportspeople—the archetypical achieved celebrity—were the most-mentioned celebrities among the male participants (e.g.,
De Backer et al. 2007; Gantz and Wenner 1991). Interestingly, all celebrities
discussed by the residents were ascribed or achieved (Rojek 2001), despite
the multitude of attributed celebrities (famous for being famous; Rojek 2001)
in contemporary society.

Most male residents stated that they mainly talk about the (clean) public
or professional celebrity persona because "you can never hurt anyone this
way" (L. ♂ 78 FG2). Women, however, happily discussed all three personae:
public, private, and real. This distinction also applied to the residents' display
of knowledge throughout the focus groups. Whereas both male and female
residents knew a lot about the celebrities in the pictures and were keen to
show it, for men, this was usually limited to the professional careers of
sportsmen. Women, however, demonstrated knowledge of all personae, with
a preference for the private and real. This is not surprising considering how
celebrity gossip, focusing on the private and real, stems from women's week-
lies (Feasey 2008), and gossip is traditionally associated with women, linking
the personal and trivial to the feminine (Hermes 1995; Turner, Bonner, and
Marshall 2000).

SOCIAL FUNCTIONS OF CELEBRITY
FOR NURSING HOME RESIDENTS

Food for Conversation

One of celebrities' social functions is the celebrity as a topic for conversation (De Backer et al. 2007; Feasey 2008). Here, the focus groups demonstrated that, by showing a celebrity picture, social interaction was evoked. Most residents explicitly stated that they (frequently) use celebrity as a topic for conversation, but some were more reluctant: "I don't really talk about it with other people" (M. ♀ 87 FG2). This can be linked to the low cultural status of celebrity magazines (Hermes 1995). They further stated that "those are no profound conversations, rather a *fait divers*" (R. ♂ 92 FG3), triggered by "big news" (M. ♀ 88 FG1) which is "the talk of the town" for a day or two but "passes rapidly" (L. ♀ 85 FG4). The media were important here as discussions are often triggered "in the nursing home when we read something about it or see it on TV" (J. ♀ 78 FG1). Media thus play a powerful role in terms of access to celebrities.

Moral Discussions

Celebrities are important as an easy lead into moral discussions and help residents give meaning to the world and construct their own identities. Indeed, discussing celebrities as shared parasocial acquaintances can safely lead to wider moral discussions as there is little real-life risk for criticizing them (Feasey 2008). A large variety of topics were discussed, both anticipated by the researcher and introduced by the residents. The topics varied from celebrities' appearances and personalities, to moral topics such as adultery, homosexuality, health, addiction, divorce, suicide, or child abuse. In addition, the residents introduced new topics such as the celebrity system and the toll of fame, money, and the changing world. Discussions usually started specific but led to general topics, such as cultural or societal changes, or long-lasting truths, such as "there are three things [in life]: money, sex, and God" (M. ♀ 79 FG2).

The celebrities' appearances were mainly discussed by the female residents, but sometimes men also offered their evaluation. Both male and female celebrities' looks were evaluated, mostly positively. Some female residents had a crush on actors: "I thought he was very handsome. I always told my husband that he [Rock Hudson] would not have to propose twice" (J. ♀ 78 FG1). The celebrities' personalities were usually discussed positively, when they are humble and normal. However, when celebrities were perceived as arrogant or hypocritical, they were criticized.

Several moral topics were discussed, both provoked by the celebrity selection and introduced by the residents. For the former group, adultery and homosexuality were the most-discussed topics (as provoked). Adultery was mostly evaluated critically, but the residents accepted it as a part of life, beyond their control. This acquiescence can be linked to older adults' life experiences and higher emotional complexity, which helps to put things in perspective (Carstensen, Fung, and Charles 2003; Harrington, Bielby, and Bardo 2011). The second most-discussed moral topic introduced in the focus groups was homosexuality. Here, the residents stated that they do not discuss it because "it is bad enough the way it is" (M. ♀ 87 FG2). They further referred to the sensitivity of homosexuality in the past: "Taboo, and if you talked about it, you got a severe punishment" (C. ♂ 77 FG4). The overall tendency was to support celebrities' coming out and accept homosexuality, although most residents considered it to be a sad illness as a result of "wrong hormones" (I. ♀ 85 FG3).

Interestingly, the residents introduced new topics beyond the context of specific celebrities. Residents discussed the celebrity system by stating that royalty "are in such a strict system that, in fact, they are directed by the government and their environment" (R. ♂ 93 FG4). A resident further explained that "there are a lot of tragic figures among the famous people . . . because they are glorified too much and lead lives that are too hectic" (R. ♂ 93 FG4). Celebrities were thus considered victims of the system (e.g., Van den Bulck and Van Gorp 2011). Further, the residents discussed the decreased solidarity in contemporary society: "In the past the people were happy when they could help each other. . . . But now, you can no longer make a child happy" (M. ♀ 79 FG2).

Throughout these discussions, residents often referred to their personal experiences or social networks. Discussing homosexuality, a resident stated: "I have a cousin and . . . she told her daughter 'there is something about you' and she is a lesbian" (L. ♀ 85 FG4). Further, the use of doping in sports evoked personal stories: "My father had pigeons, oo and . . . he did it in their food and their water" (M. ♀ 79 FG2). These residents' personal stories and the similarity between celebrity and real-life acquaintance gossip indicated that there is an analogy between celebrities and (real) social companions.

Social Companions

Celebrities were also meaningful socially and morally for nursing home residents as a parasocial connection in particular ways. In the focus groups, the residents referred to both positive and negative parasocial relationships with celebrities and this distinction was linked to the ordinary-extraordinary celebrity paradox (Dyer 1998). Residents' positive expressions were toward humble and ordinary celebrities and the negative expressions toward arrogant celebrities who behave extraordinarily, like "stars."

Most residents had favorite celebrities and some women stated that "you were always in love with those men" (D. ♀ 91 FG1). However, they were reluctant to label themselves as fans which can be linked to fandom's low cultural status (Jensen 1992). Further, residents referred to feelings of shock after a favorite celebrity's death: "Queen Astrid. I can never forget that she died when the car hit that tree [in 1935]" (I. ♀ 85 FG3). Similarly, the residents felt sad when celebrities quit their job and were disappointed after the outing of a homosexual celebrity, the confession of drug use in sports, or child abuse. Here, the residents were aware that their image of the celebrities highly depends on media coverage, indicating their insight into the celebrity construction (Marshall 2006a):

> R. (♂ 92): As an outsider, you cannot decide . . . whether someone is sympathetic or not. You let the press guide you, right?

> G. (♀ 94): That is the way it is, we only see them on film or on . . . and you never really know . . . what she is really like. (FG3)

They stated that they did not really know the celebrities, but this did not hold them back to express personal feelings: "Without knowing the man of course, but he looks trustworthy and sympathetic" (R. ♂ 92 FG3) or "I don't know her personally but I never liked her" (L. ♀ 84 FG3). Further, they were aware of the one-sided nature of parasocial relationships: "He doesn't listen to me. I look at him, but not the other way around, right" (L. ♀ 85 FG4).

Aide-Memoire

Finally, celebrities helped residents to reminisce. However, the residents found it hard to situate celebrities' life events in their own life histories which can be explained by memory issues (Vandebosch and Eggermont 2002; Van der Goot 2009). The residents tried to outweigh this by pointing to other elements: "I don't remember the year in which they married, but I know they have not been married for long" (J. ♀ 78 FG1). Further, they compared the celebrity's age to their own or that of their siblings. Another compensating strategy was to think in terms of being married, having (young/older) children, or being at home or at the nursing home. At times, the media played a role in reminiscence: "Wasn't it black and white televi-sion back then?" (M. ♀ 88 FG1) or "I went to the cinema with my children then" (J. ♀ 86 FG1). Some residents remembered watching specific movies or TV programs featuring celebrities: "I remember her well in the role of Cleopatra" (R. ♂ 92 FG3). For two female residents, the picture of John

Wayne brought up memories of their late husband's fandom: "My husband had a picture of him in his office . . . and then those porcelain plates of John Wayne in cowboy movies and my husband put them on a cupboard, which irritated me because it did not fit there. I had Louis XIV and then John Wayne, Haha" (J. ♀78 FG1).

When able to fully place the timing of the reminiscence, the residents often used celebrities to compare the present and past, for instance with regard to sports: "In the current state of soccer, he probably would not have been a great talent, because he went drinking too often and did not take care of himself" (R. ♂ 93 FG4). Further, Elvis's divorce led to a discussion of the status of divorce:

Researcher: And he divorced his wife

M. (♀ 79): Yes, but that is nowadays warp and weft

Staff member: But back then it wasn't, right?

M.: No

L. (♂ 78): The Americans brought it here. We have to be honest, when we look at the past

Researcher: Who brought it in?

L.: The movie stars, marrying multiple times. And now the families here are almost all reconstituted families. One week at dad, one week there (FG2)

CONCLUSION

To compensate for the gaps in gerontology and celebrity studies, this chapter aimed at providing insight into the meaning of celebrities for nursing home residents by means of individual and focus group interviews. The current knowledge of nursing home residents' celebrity preferences is scarce but provides some valuable findings which are mainly confirmed and expanded by this study. Thus, cultural proximity was important for the residents under study as they felt closer to local celebrities (e.g., De Backer et al. 2007). Respondents preferred celebrities of their own generation (e.g., Van der Goot's 2009), but the sports celebrities included the younger ones who are still competing today. Respondents' preference for older celebrities was further put in perspective as they knew (at least) as much about current celebrities. The residents' favorite celebrities were mostly royalty (for women) and sportspeople (for men) (e.g., De Backer et al. 2007; Gantz and Wenner 1991; Vandebosch and Eggermont 2002). Interestingly, all favorite celebrities were ascribed or achieved, which can be explained by their long-standing history in contrast to attributed celebrities. It can also be linked to the persistence of earlier media habits and preferences (Hajjar 1998).

Further, the existing (limited) knowledge of the social functions of celebrities for nursing home residents—as food for conversation and as social companions (De Backer et al. 2007)—was confirmed and extended. Indeed, celebrities fulfill a variety of social functions for nursing home residents, some of which were found for the general celebrity audience—food for conversations, moral discussions, and social companions—and a new, age group–specific function—aide-memoire. With regard to the first three functions, the nursing home population thus appears to be similar to the general audience—although the specific interpretation of the functions is likely to differ—whereas, for the latter, the nursing home population is a distinct group in society, with its own needs (e.g., higher physical and mental dependence) and wishes (e.g., more reminiscing).

The significance of celebrities as food for conversations (De Backer et al. 2007) was clearly demonstrated by the discussions, with celebrity pictures evoking social interaction and residents explicitly confirming it. However, some residents were rather reluctant about this celebrity function which can be explained by the lasting view of celebrity as low culture, despite its omnipresence in all domains of life (Hermes 1995; Marshall 2006a). When residents used celebrities as food for conversations, big media-covered events were usually the talk of the town for a few days. This confirms the importance of media as the primary link between celebrities and audiences (Marshall 2006a; Rojek 2001).

Celebrities further helped nursing home residents to make meaning of the world by evoking moral discussions on various topics. Celebrities as shared (parasocial) acquaintances evoke discussions of (sensitive) moral topics with lower risks for real-life consequences of criticizing an acquaintance (Feasey 2008). The moral topics' prevalence varied widely and was present whether they were provoked by the researcher or introduced by the residents, regardless of whether they covered a specific celebrity or broadly incorporated society, or whether they were superficial or more profound. Interestingly, residents' moral judgments were more relativistic than critical, which can be related to the acquiescence that is linked to older adults' myriad of life experiences and emotional complexity (Carstensen, Fung, and Charles 2003; Harrington, Bielby, and Bardo 2011). Finally, the residents often discussed their personal experiences or social network, which implies a similarity between celebrities and real-life acquaintances.

The residents considered celebrities as social companions with whom they maintained parasocial relationships. The positive/negative nature of these relationships is linked to the ordinary-extraordinary celebrity paradox (Dyer 1998). When celebrities were perceived as ordinary, the residents had positive feelings, but when celebrities acted extraordinarily, they evoked negative feelings. Most residents indicated having a favorite celebrity, but refrained from labeling themselves as fans (e.g., low cultural status of fandom, Jensen [1992]). Interestingly, the residents showed awareness of the workings of the celebrity apparatus and discussed their dependence on the media for celebrity information and the one-sided nature of parasocial relationships.

Finally, a new social function was found for nursing home residents, as celebrities helped to reminisce as an aide-memoire. This function is expected to also apply to a younger community dwelling population, as reminiscence is important for all older adults (Kuhn 2002). However, considering how nursing home residents tend to be the least mentally healthy older adult group, the aide-memoire function may be especially relevant here as memory issues can hinder reminiscence processes for them (Barrett and Kirk 2000). Although it was hard to link celebrities' events to a specific time, the residents compensated by comparing the celebrities' age with their own or that of their siblings, thinking in broader life circumstances (marriage, children), and referring to media changes. Reminiscence triggered by celebrity pictures included memories of media consumption and the sharing of personal memories which resulted in a comparison of the past and present culture and society. This aide-memoire function is important as reminiscence enhances older adults' self-esteem and helps with identity construction (Bender, Bauckham, and Norris 1999).

This chapter thus provided exploratory insight into the junction of two major processes in contemporary Western societies: the meaning of celebrities for nursing home residents. Considering its societal relevance, this chapter is a valuable contribution to the limited knowledge of nursing home residents' celebrity preferences and celebrities' social functions in nursing homes and wishes to inspire future research. This study showed that celebrities fulfill similar functions for the general audience and nursing home residents with regard to food for conversation, means for meaning making, and social companions. However, celebrities perform a specific function adapted to the nursing home population as an aide-memoire to promote reminiscence despite memory issues.

More empirical studies are needed to understand the meaning of celebrities for older adults—nursing home residents as well as independently living older adults, both healthy and unhealthy. Further, the relevance of gender-, class-, location-, or age-related differences should be explored in the future. Finally, the social functions of celebrities that were found here should be explored in more detail in future research.

IV

Music

Chapter Eight

Music, Performance, and Generation

The Making of Boomer Rock and Roll Biographies

Stephen Katz

> Musical pleasure is unique in that it is derived from fantasies and daydreams
> while simultaneously being extremely real. And it's just this fusion of fantasy
> and reality that integrates the aesthetic judgment that something *sounds* good
> with the ethical judgment that something *is* good.
>
> —Bruford (2009, 281)

We owe it to C. Wright Mills to espouse the idea of a "sociological imagination" as a visionary method "to grasp history and biography and the relations
between the two within society" whereby "no study that does not come back
to the problems of biography, of history, and of their intersections within a
society has completed its intellectual journey" (Mills [1959] 2001, 12). For
Mills, sociologists need to *imagine*, not just analyze, how war or immigration
are embedded in experience and memory. Sociologists Anthony Giddens
(1991), and Jaber Gubrium and James A. Holstein (2009) have followed
Mills's "intellectual journey" to look more deeply at the narrative practices,
scripts, and plots by which lives are rendered meaningful. As Giddens says,
"A person's identity is not to be found in behavior . . . but in the capacity *to
keep a particular narrative going*" (original emphasis; 1991, 54). Particular
narratives, however intimately experienced, are also culturally grounded so
that our biographical accounts are the result of intersecting conversations
between self and society. This is why letters, songs, photos, and videos, and
increasingly electronic media, are such fertile sociological territory, where
stories and storytellers produce and reflect each other.

This chapter argues that the narrative and biographical emphases of the
sociological imagination can fruitfully be expanded to include the relation-

ships between age, generation, and music. In particular, I examine the powerful role of rock and roll music in the life course experiences of the baby boom generation. While there is a prolific literature on culture and music, such as Simon Frith's work on the boundaries between "high" and "low" popular musical forms (1998, 2007), such research rarely veers from youth cultures. Gerontology and aging studies, for their part, just do not rock at all. However, as Andy Bennett observes, "the fact that an individual becomes a follower of music as a 'young person' may matter far less than what that music continues to mean to them as they grow older" (2013, 20). For the boomers, there is little reason to assume that the intensity of emotion, time, money, fantasy, and identity which they have invested in rock music would diminish later in life. Music has become the boomer generation's way of representing itself to itself as a collective, as it has moved through families, jobs, places, illnesses, and losses. Thus, as this chapter observes, the generational and intergenerational pressure to keep classic rock timeless is connected to its ubiquity as an audionarrative that reiterates memories, relationships, and belongings as lifelong experiences.

While the boomer generation, as I discuss below, is generally represented as a structural and often static demographic entity, we cannot understand its unique cultural legacy without looking inside its forms of self-expression. Such forms include collective fantasies and dreams as articulating forces which bind together cultural and personal dimensions. In this vein, I also write this chapter as a sociologist and a middle-aged "boomer" rock drummer and music rock fan. Hence I am a subject as well as an author of this writing as it unfolds through a double lens of history and biography, and concludes with a personal account of my experience in a rock and roll fantasy club in order to illustrate the power of imagination in generational identity.

THE BOOMER GENERATION AND THE THIRD AGE

While I was working on this study, The Rolling Stones performed at Toronto's Air Canada Centre as part of their "fifty years and counting" tour, a phrase that otherwise decorates midagers' birthday cakes and retirement gifts. Much has been made of the Stones's capacity to capitalize on their longevity long after making their most relevant music. Survival has been more than a matter of music, however, because along the way lost souls have included original member Brian Jones who drowned in 1969, and 1970s record producer Jimmy Miller. As for the remaining core group, Ron Wood broke his legs in a car accident in 1990, Charlie Watts had two operations for throat cancer in 2004, and in addition to his years of steady drug and alcohol intake, Keith Richards suffered a head injury falling from a tree in Fiji in 2006. Only the indomitable Mick Jagger manages to age without growing older or succumbing to serious health or injury issues. The rejuvenating spirit of The Rolling Stones symbolizes an aging musical generational field consti- tuted by the enduring styles and cultural narratives of the youth groups who grew up during the 1960s to 1970s and became the baby boomers. Thus the group members, their audiences, their music, and their style together consti- tute an idealized living portrait of what it means to age as a boomer.

Born between 1946 and 1964, the boomers are defined by the bulging size of their cohort relative to adjacent generations, and by the particular postwar conditions in which they matured: national prosperity, the relative political peace of the Cold War, new media and communication networks, affluent consumerism, and rapid social change. In turn, the populous boomer genera- tion created new lifestyles and forms of expression that dismantled the tradi- tions separating young and old, producing an extendable "youth culture" unfettered by age and identified with rebellion. On the one hand, boomer discourse, itself a product of popular demography and marketing, stereotypes the very people it represents (along with a boomer kinship network of "emp- ty nesters," "snowbirds," "seniors," "zoomers," etc.). Yet few journalists, marketers, or popular demographers are prepared to delve into the detailed gerontological research on periods, cohorts, life course trajectories, and inter- generational relations or consult the critical perspectives stemming from feminism, disability studies, political economy, and the humanities that deep- en such research. As a result, a popular boomer vocabulary has become a pseudoauthority on aging, health care, housing, and retirement, even while it neglects important sociological data on inequality and population diversity. This homogenizing vocabulary also sidelines the realities that not all boom- ers are prosperous, healthy, educated, and politically empowered, and the lauded ideals of individual choice and liberating lifestyles are themselves part of a larger political economy of postwar and late capitalism.

On the other hand, I suggest that boomer language is a response to a discursive void about the "new aging" today, one that appeals to a public interest in understanding the aging experience in changing times. As Setter- sten Jr. and Trauten suggest, "Great shake-ups seem to be afoot in every period of life, so much so that the whole of human experience feels in flux" (2009, 455). If the human experience of aging "feels in flux," then so are the vocabularies, metaphors, and representations which articulate and animate it. According to some cultural gerontologists, these "shake-ups" include the blurring of conventional chronological boundaries and life course identities due to increased longevity, the allure of antiaging industries, and the global- ization of aging spaces. Retirement is also changing due to the reconfigura- tion of generational relations, the fragmentation of the workplace, and the contingencies around transitions in later life (Gilleard and Higgs 2005; Hock- ey and James 2003; Katz 2005, 2013; Levin 2013).[1] In turn, these changes intersect the rise of boomer culture to produce new life course experiences.

Most importantly for this study, the boomer generation, as it matures into retirement (in various forms) has and will carry forward the particular life-style expectations and consumer aspirations formed as part of the postwar "youth culture," which also became less class based and more defined by the framing of the new cohort as rebellious and in pursuit of the fashionably "new." As Gilleard and Higgs argue, "the desire to embrace what was new and reject what was old was felt at least as strongly by working-class youth as it was by the middle class. It focused upon sources of *horizontal* differenti-ation, eliding 'youth' with 'freedom' and 'leisure'" (original emphasis; Gil-leard and Higgs 2005, 152–53; see also Gilleard and Higgs 2011). Indeed, these expectations, aspirations, and identities have already become the fea-tures of a commercialized, posttraditional retirement culture, one labeled the "third age" by late British philosopher and demographer Peter Laslett (1987). For Laslett, the third age encapsulates a midlife period for which convention-al chronological and retirement ages are no longer adequate indicators. The third age, marked by midlife independence, activity, health, and lifestyle choice, has become a keyword in British gerontology and, like boomer dis-course, has sparked numerous debates about aging, social stratification, and the commercialization of "mature" lifestyles (see Carr and Komp 2011).[2]

What has been less developed, and which the following sections of this chapter elaborate, is the "inside" of the boomer experience as it enters the third age, in particular, the connections between narrative, biography, and music. Rock music is an important focus on the subjective dimension of this generation because it materializes generational identity in the historical con-ditions and life course trajectories of its time. As I argue, the preservation of specialized musical genres, the discourses of rock criticism, the technologies of music making, and the intergenerational reach of boomer musical emo-tionality, come together to provide the embodied elements that nurture the boomer generation's idealization of itself through feeling, dance, sensation, and volume. Thus the exploration of rock music is key to understanding the boomer phenomenon and its cultural consequences, while linking it to the wider changes in our aging societies pronounced by theorists and critics of the third age.

BOOMER ROCK AND ROLL: TALKING ABOUT MY GENERATION

Boomer rock and roll, in parallel with the third age boomer generation itself, is united around a timeless and ageless narrative accomplished through dis-courses of genre continuity and musical biography. Since the origins of rock music in the 1950s and its evolution as a dominant cultural form, it has animated every facet of postwar style, identity, technology, and sociability.[3]

Even a brief familiarity with the Linnaean table of rock bands, genres, musicians, discographies, concert histories, personnel lineups, equipment inventories, hits and failures, record companies, and breakups and reunions reveals a complex and obsessively detailed inventory spanning generations and local and global communities. Indeed, popular and rock musical genres constitute a classification system of their own by constantly identifying against what it is not (traditional music), whether the classifying agents are industry, the media, the musicians, or the audiences. This system is elaborated in Jennifer C. Lena's stellar book on the sociocultural classification of musical genres as "a thick history of musical change" (2012, 145) "that would help us to see and understand shared elements, not only among musical communities, but among other symbol-producing fields as well" (160). (See Lena [2012, 68] for a comprehensive genre inventory). And while rock and roll may have begun as music for younger audiences, that distinction has long since been discarded, as youth music has been appropriated by the boomer generation as *its* music, whose sense of ageless time is sought in and mirrored by extended musical lineages spawned during the 1960s to 1970s.[4]

In this ageless universe, rock obituaries form a powerful part of the classification system where they resettle musicians in the afterlife imaginary often referred to as "rock and roll heaven." When Richie Havens, who opened the Woodstock festival in 1969, died April 22, 2013, at the age of seventy-two, the *New York Times* noted that "for the baby-boom generation, he [Havens] will live forever on the stage of Woodstock" (Martin 2013). As a recent edition of *Guitar World* (2013) exemplifies, there is a pantheon of classic rock musicians who have "gone too soon," such as John Lennon, Jim Hendrix, Kurt Cobain, Stevie Ray Vaughan, Bob Marley, and Frank Zappa, who through accident, illness or misadventure, died "before their time." There are also popular bands which broke up prematurely because of key members dying; for example, Led Zeppelin's John Bonham, The Who's Keith Moon and John Entwhistle, Queen's Freddie Mercury, Chicago's Terry Kath, The Grateful Dead's Jerry Garcia, and The Doors' Jim Morrison. Some bands had already broken up when their famous members died, such as The Band's Levon Helm, Uriah Heep's Trevor Bolder, Ten Years After's Alvin Lee, and Deep Purple's Jon Lord. Even when obscure musicians such as Rick Huxley (bassist for the Dave Clark Five), Bob Welch (guitarist for early Fleetwood Mac), or Michael Clarke (drummer for the Byrds) pass away, they are duly added to the expansive musical clan as obituaries in the music media make their peace with them. Obituaries also emphasize special cases of rock royalty whose aristocratic status ensures a long afterlife, such as the death of Elvis Presley ("the king of rock and roll"), Donna Summer ("the queen of disco"), Michael Jackson ("the king of pop"), Solomon Burke ("the king of rock 'n' soul"), et cetera.

While popular acts that continue to tour with their traditional set lists are a lucrative market (e.g., The Eagles, The Rolling Stones), when such acts decide to create new music and reclaim their relevancy, the potential break with the past as another form of obituary is often met with disapproval. Thus media reviews of recent albums by classic rockers David Bowie, Black Sabbath, Rod Stewart, Creedence Clearwater, and Fleetwood Mac, oscillate between respectful appreciation and criticism about the fracturing of tradition. The review of Bowie's *The Next Day* (RCA 2013) in *The Observer* (London) pits the continuity of "old" Bowie's music against the new material (Empire 2013). *Rolling Stone* magazine praises John Fogerty's (age sixty-eight) new album, *Wrote a Song for Everyone*, as "the best new music Fogerty has made since, well, Creedence" and "it affirms the living history in his [Fogerty's] greatest hits—that of a great nation being born" (Fricke 2013). The magazine's review of the new Black Sabbath album *13* with sixty-four-year-old Ozzie Osbourne concludes that "above all, this reboot shows that the genre Sabbath helped birth remains timeless, insofar as the devil remains gainfully employed on Earth, and heavyweight rock shredding still kicks ass" (Hermes 2013). However, Todd Rundgren's (age sixty-five) new album *State* is slammed in *Uncut* because while "Rundgren's refusal to revisit the past is laudable. . . . We'd still like to hear how the Todd of 1972 would approach elegant ballads like 'Imagination'" (Lewis 2013, 76). Continuity, especially if rebooted, reprised, or remastered, is its own reward.[5] Not surprisingly, in one of the few studies that links musical tastes to aging, rock music was posited as the only exception to the narrowing of musical genre tastes with age (Harrison and Ryan 2010). Despite the heterogeneity of the rock classification system and its audiences, therefore, a timeless continuity bonds boomer audiences with the music they grew up with. This happens, as the next section argues, through the biographical work inherent in the boomer generation's horizons of its own longevity.

Musical Biography: Are We All Rolling Stones?

It would be straightforward to explain the importance of rock music to boomer identity as a case of late-capitalist cultural consumerism. Certainly the nostalgia industries encompassing classic rock radio and media, reunion concerts and reissued music, and heritage instruments and listening technologies are worth a fortune. And the musical saturation of lifestyle products and environments has made rock universally polysemic, capable of signifying and marketing anything. Musical consumerism is also part of the development of devices for listening, playing, recording, storing, and downloading music (records, tapes, cd/dvds, mp3 formats), the expansion of musical portability (transistor radio 1954, Sony Walkman 1979, iPod 2001), and the availability of sophisticated sound systems. Added to this critical perspective is the image of the boomer rocker, stereotyped as either a musical snob stuck in time who fails to appreciate musical innovation outside of classic rock, or a rather sad (usually male) ex-hippie whose middle-class lifestyle has been devoid of the rebellious spirit of rock and roll for decades, despite his or her pining nostalgia for it. This juvenile male image is also linked to the prevailing sexism of many rock genres and its pervasive guy culture. Thus, "refusing to grow up" is one of the most profitable identities for, rather than against, late-capitalist cultural and recreational industries.

However, arguments about musical elitism and nostalgia as gerontocratic aspirations fail to account for popular music as a lived experience.[6] In particular, questions of biography and self-identity, generational relations, gender and performance, and aging audiences tend to be sidelined. Again, as third age theorists have illustrated, the rise of a posttraditional aging culture has created special affective conditions embedded in the liberational lifestyles of the boomer generation. The soundtrack for these lifestyles is rock and roll and it does not fade with age. Joseph Kotarba believes that "rock 'n' roll music continues to serve a critical meaning resource for its adult fans as they continuously experience the becoming of self throughout life" (Kotarba and Vannini 2009, 114). Indeed, rock music continues to help boomers make sense of their lives as they age, including their politics, relationships, spirituality, and destinies. While certain songs may freeze moments in time, such as a couple's wedding song or the graduation song of a certain class cohort, music also extends the self into time (Kotarba 2013). According to Kotarba, not only can "our song" provide "meaning for benchmark events in the relationship," it also "can help the person feel like a lover" throughout the history of their relationship (Kotarba 2013, 22). Thus music and identity can be artfully and biographically navigated as meaningful patterns of growth, apart from a commercialized culture of nostalgia.

Robert J. Wiersema, in his autobiography, *Walk Like A Man: Coming of Age with the Music of Bruce Springsteen* (2011), goes farther into a rock-inspired life narrative by organizing his book like a Springsteen compilation tape, with fourteen chapters or "tracks" split into two parts or "sides," followed by a "bonus track" at the end. Each chapter is named for a Springsteen song. Although Wiersema was born in 1970 and Springsteen in 1949, the story of "coming of age" with Springsteen is made coherent because Wiersema had "grown up with Springsteen as the soundtrack of my life" (2011, 6). Much has been written already about Springsteen, yet Springsteen himself has also repeatedly written his own life of humble working-class origins from small-town New Jersey into some of the most powerful rock anthems of the last four decades. Rock and roll is nothing short of a messianic, religious experience in Springsteen's music and this is precisely how his fans experience him too. Therefore, Wiersema's layering of Springsteen's story into his own account of growing up heightens the author's ability to celebrate his joys and sorrows with new understanding. *Walk Like A Man* is a book rich with many examples (such as when Weirsema invokes the title of Springsteen's 1992 song "Living Proof" upon seeing his son for the first time), whereby Springsteen, the musician, and Wiersema, the fan, share a grid of reflexivity that reaches into the deepest intimacies of their lives. [7]

Music across Generations:
The Family That Plays Together

Unlike many other musical genres, a key characteristic of boomer rock and roll is its intergenerational appeal. Despite the image of rock music as a music that divides generations and families, research has demonstrated the opposite to be true in this case. Boomer rock demonstrates its timeless character and, thus the timelessness of the boomers themselves, by migrating across generations and assuming its seminal status as "classic" rock. This is borne out at concerts and social events where adult-child, mother-daughter, and father-son bonding is commonly achieved through the consuming and sharing of classic rock music (Kotarba and Vannini 2009). Indeed, in attendance at any classic rock concert or festival today are audiences of two and often three generations. Such events are multigenerational opportunities to learn about and relive the 1960s to 1970s together, including joining groups and playing music together as well. Andy Bennett notes that:

> The new perception of rock and pop as uni-age fields of musical practice appears to permeate all levels of music-making, right down to the local/informal level. This is evident not only in the growing number of multigenerational rock and pop bands observed in local scenes but also through the non-ageist sensibilities that appear to inform such bands and their creative pursuits. (2013, 138)

While Bennett's examples mostly focus on punk musicians and audiences, his words ring true for local classic rock bands as well, often populated by young, middle, and older players who appreciate each other's talents and experiences. I know from my own experience that many jam sessions and groups with which I have been involved have included players who range in age from sixteen to seventy. (I am always surprised when a young person knows "my" music better than I do). The local scene also reflects the larger musical world where older and younger musicians record and perform together. The fact that Led Zeppelin could replace drummer John Bonham with his son Jason Bonham, The Who could replace drummer Keith Moon with Zak Starr (Ringo Starr's son), or that Van Halen could replace bass player Michael Anthony with Eddie Van Halen's son Wolfgang, points to the intergenerational nature of classic rock in the most obvious way. [8]

Karl Mannheim, the first sociologist to theorize the concept of "generation" (1952/1998), wrote that only in an "Utopian, imaginary society" could social life be envisioned as one generation living on forever, because in reality we live in a society where "the transition from generation to generation is a continuous process" (170). Each subsequent generation has "fresh contact" with the legacies left by the generations before it. Further, "generations are in a state of constant interaction" (180) and "whether a *new generation style* emerges every year, every thirty, every hundred years, or whether it emerges rhythmically at all, depends entirely on the trigger action of the social and cultural process" (original emphasis; 191). But Mannheim also asked why some generations realize their potentialities and develop "a distinctive unity of style" (192), while others remain latent. No doubt the boomer generation, with its economic power, political clout, biographical consciousness, enduring musical narrativity, and fostering of "fresh" intergenerational contact, would have been seen by Mannheim as exemplary of a distinctive unity of cultural style and potentialities. What Mannheim did not foresee, however, is the role of generational fantasy as a social "trigger." Given the ubiquity of consumer rock industries and its capitalization on nostalgic youthful lifestyles, the role of fantasy in boomer identities appears obvious. However, as drummer Bill Bruford states at the beginning of this chapter, musical pleasure is a "fusion of fantasy and reality," it articulates daydreams with realities through the doing, listening, playing, and imagining of musical performance. As such, musical fantasy is a particularly powerful generational experience that transcends its social production, as the next section discusses.

MUSICAL FANTASY AND PERFORMING IDENTITY

As every boomer knows, on November 22, 1963, while riding through Dealey Plaza in Dallas, President John F. Kennedy was shot and killed. I was in my sixth grade class just after lunch when our Principal came in to tell us the news. The assassination was especially tragic because Kennedy was young (the second youngest president at age forty-three and the first to be born in the twentieth century), intelligent (Harvard educated), and stylish (the first president not to wear hats). He challenged the traditional geopolitics of war with a vision for peace (during the Cold War) and space exploration. He was the first president to win voters through a TV debate and it was on TV where we also saw Kennedy order state troops to a school in Alabama that would not allow two black women to enter, but it was also the TV coverage of Kennedy being shot over and over again that had people openly crying in the streets and shops. He was the boomer generation's first American president. But then on February 9, 1964, another massive media event occurred, which was the first appearance of The Beatles in America on the Ed Sullivan Show, counteracting the Kennedy tragedy with a joyous display of youthful optimism. Ed Sullivan, an awkward ex–radio announcer from New York with his own weekly variety show, had met with The Beatles' manager Brian Epstein in London on November 11, 1963, a few weeks before Kennedy's assassination. When The Beatles flew into JFK airport for the show (the old New York Idlewild Airport had just been renamed in honor of Kennedy on December 24, 1963), there was mass hysteria. And on the night of the show itself, seventy-three million viewers tuned into what many of them still claim was a life-transforming event. I was at home with my parents watching too and realized that The Beatles' music, hair, attitude, and style were inviting signs of a new way to grow up. For boomers, the Kennedy assassination and The Beatles on Ed Sullivan symbolically framed the making of a new generation and the start of its collective self-narrative.

The Beatles are also famously acknowledged for inspiring people not only to buy more music, but to play more music. Being on a stage, with a guitar or behind a drum kit, without the need for years of musical training, and performing in front of thousands of adoring fans, became an instant and enduring generational fantasy. This heady mix of performance, sexuality, freedom, and youthfulness has expanded to a point today where playing music is a way of imagining an identity that accommodates if not encourages rebellious experimentation. For example, in her account of being a member of a middle-aged "girl group" (The Hot Flashes), Lois Melina describes a gig where the negotiation between appearing to be "good" versus "bad" girls was reflected in their roles: "We wanted to be independent, uppity, sexy bad girls, but we didn't want to give up being smart or sweet or occasionally even goofy" (2008, 107). Her group is really about defying "rules that say we have to stay within our prescribed roles, honor precise boundaries" (109).[9]

But nowhere is this nonconforming and fantastical spirit of boomer rock more alive and evident than in the proliferation of adult rock camps and jam clubs. Adult rock camps, schools, and clubs, vary in terms of costs and programs. For example, the "Rock and Roll Fantasy Camp" is a short-term but very expensive opportunity for people to play with actual (but often aging) rock stars, such as Roger Daltrey from The Who (www.rockcamp.com/rrfc-1-23-13.php). Other camps are far less celebrity oriented, more affordable or are branches of central organizations in various cities. Some require musical screening and auditioning for new members, while others provide actual musical instruction and coaching. But all promote the idea that living out a rock and roll fantasy is linked to how old (young) one "feels." The promotional materials are full of testimonials about how stay-at-home moms become rock goddesses or shy guys alone with their guitars finally get the confidence to rock out with a band. The organizations also provide lots of pictures, videos, recordings, and prizes to keep the fantasy alive after the program is over. Equipment, rehearsal space, and refreshments, are usually included in the fees and members keep in touch with each other and sometimes form real bands of their own. Helen O'Shea's (2012) ethnography of a band in the "Weekend Warriors Program" in Melbourne is a relevant study of "lapsed" rockers (median age fifty-seven) who gather for six-week periods to upgrade their musical skills and learn (or relearn) how to get along in a band situation. As with most of these programs, the groups decide on a name, a song list (covers and/or originals), rehearsal scheduling, and performance expectations, all more difficult than they sound. The professional coaches work hard to improve the music and motivate the players. About one coach in her study, O'Shea says, "Jeff's focus was on musicianship" but "Jeff also monitored the musicians' feelings" (208). In the end, the program is a success (for the band Hot Vox) and O'Shea concludes that her project "challenges the assumption that ageing may be detrimental or a disadvantage to creative musical activity" (212). O'Shea's observations and those of others who look at the complicated worlds of boomer rock, certainly resonate with my own experiences, discussed below.

CONCLUSION: MY OWN WAY TO ROCK

I am a boomer drummer (sixty-one) who has been in bands since adolescence and well versed in the rock and roll songbook. My own identity and subjectivity are very obviously wrapped up in the temporal and musical plots of boomer rock music. Along with Joseph Kotarba or Robert Wiersema, I too could write a story of parallel tales where life and songs have intersected to build a durable soundtrack of my past into my present. As with many other boomer musicians, in my current groups my professional income subsidizes the purchase of music, equipment, drums and (too many) cymbals. So the irony that boomer amateurs can afford the fantasy denied to the struggling professional musician is not lost on me. But I want to conclude this chapter with a more specific autoethnographic exercise by looking at my experience in a boomer rock and roll fantasy club, in order to relay how fantasy continues to be an indispensable force in creating boomer musical identity. Hence, a few years ago I decided to join an adult rock camp in Toronto to see how the fantasy was produced firsthand. I was put into a band with other middle-age players, which decided on a name, an approach to rehearsing and musical selections to accommodate the various skill levels of the band members. I kept a journal as part of an ongoing autoethnography project. The organizers and coaches always stressed the team-building nature of the program and that "fun" was the prime objective. I was impressed with the program's organization of a complete musical experience: join a band, learn songs, perform on stage, learn from experienced coaches, record in a professional studio, and finish the program in rock and roll style with a boozy showcase party where the bands perform for friends and family.

In our first rehearsals, my band (four men and two women) became dominated by two men who, as program veterans, assumed leadership roles. However, as our rehearsals progressed it became clear that I had to mediate growing tensions between the men and women and also impose some efficiency on the group if we were ever to get performance ready. Compared to the real bands I have been in I was stunned by the lack of discipline with this group, where some members showed up late or unprepared (or not at all). Indeed, all the focus on having fun and "leaving egos at the door" seemed to downplay the need for real musical supervision, which was detrimental to the novices and less experienced musicians. I began to fear that the fantasy of being in a band was going to be at the expense of sounding pathetically bad. At rehearsals the volume was all over the place and since members were paying for the fantasy, the coaches seemed far too mild in their criticism. But our first performance was passable and the audience responded positively (an audience of the other bands). Some band members had never performed before and so acted out rock performances according to how they imagined them to be (back to The Beatles perhaps). One woman imitated the rock video of her song (with her son filming a video of her doing it). The second performance was better and at this point, the bands had self-ranked their levels of competence. My group thought we were the best, based on image as much as sound, from what I could judge.

As the program developed, I also noticed group members acting more juvenile and sporting more rock paraphernalia (to which I am not immune). Some bands made their own T-shirts and websites. One woman updated her Facebook profile with a picture of herself in a sexy outfit and holding a guitar. Another nicknamed himself "The Hurricane." The imperative to allow the "real" (fantasy) rock and roll self to emerge seemed to be working, even if the music only gradually migrated from poor to mediocre. The recording session (for our chosen one song) took a long time. Most real bands would do our song in an hour or two, while it took us all day. Still, the pictures showed us as happy, relaxed, and accomplished. The final performance event was a real party as promised, lots of lights and rock volume, with the usual ultra-supportive audience. As the organization's musical director notes in a post-program email to our band, "You proved last night the talent is really amping up and your willingness to take chances and step out on a limb *within the safety of our community* makes all of the difference" (my emphasis). The end of the program meant the end of the bands and emails flew around about "withdrawal symptoms" and future "reunions." Our photos and CDs were reminders of what it felt like to be a celebrity.

Despite my suspicions about the program, its simulated bands and unreal audiences, being treated like a star even for a moment allowed me to experience the power of this particular rock fantasy to make coherent those spaces where music, identity, and the dreamy narrative of my generation are bound together. I believe this is the kind of experience that C. Wright Mills had in mind when he championed the "sociological imagination" mentioned in the introduction to this chapter, as a potent resource in understanding the relationship between biography and society. Further, as a case for understanding this relationship as it moves, or dances, its way through time, baby boomer rock and roll is an ideal "intellectual journey."

NOTES

1. British sociologists Mike Featherstone and Mike Hepworth (1991, 1998) inspired an extensive literature on "positive" and "new" aging cultures and "postmodern" and "post-traditional" life courses which today form the language of "critical" gerontology.

2. In parallel to Laslett, American social psychologist Bernice Neugarten stressed the idea of an "age-irrelevant" society. She introduced new demographic terminology such as the "young-old" and the "old-old" (1974, 1982). While Laslett and Neugarten invented new terms to highlight the positive aspects of aging and reframe the relationships between social time and personal experience, both were criticized for undertheorizing the last stages of life or the "Fourth Age" which has continued to be treated as a time of decline, loss, and finality (Gilleard and Higgs 2010). Gerontologist Linda George comments that the popularity of the term "third age" overwhelms its validity, hence "I doubt that it will make much difference whether or not the Third Age is an empirically verifiable new life stage" (2011, 249).

3. The Moondog Coronation Ball (and riot) in Cleveland in 1952 is considered the first "rock concert." Elvis Presley's "That's All Right" and Bill Haley and His Comet's "Rock Around the Clock" are considered the first rock hits in 1954 (Melina 2008). However, the history of rock and roll is usually a white history with Afro-American "cross-over" successes (as in cross-over to white audiences). While Presley pioneered the cross-over as a white musician, critics maintain that he, like other white musicians, stole Afro-American music and re-created it as their own. Similarly, the British "invasion" bands of the 1960s including The Beatles, The Rolling Stones, The Yardbirds, The Who, and The Animals all had early hits with covers of songs by Afro-American artists.

4. See the illuminating documentary series *Metal Evolution* (2011) by anthropological filmmaker Sam Dunn on how music can be represented as a form of evolution, with various "families" and "trees" that include twenty-six heavy metal subgenres.

5. Even as original bands disappear, the tribute industry flourishes with acts big and small representing every classic act in history. There are hundreds of Elvis Presley and Beatles tribute acts and some bands, such as Judas Priest, Kiss, Journey, and YES, actually recruited tribute band musicians to join rebooted versions of the original bands. As with the original bands, there are also biographies of tribute bands, such as Martin Dimery's entertaining *Being John Lennon* (2002) and Steven Kurutz's touching *Like a Rolling Stone* (2008). Tribute bands can be creative alternatives to the originals; for example, the quirky Dread Zeppelin interprets Led Zeppelin songs in good reggae versions sung by an Elvis impersonator.

6. A good part of this classic rock elitism derives from a general critical condemnation of recent metal and rap subgenres for being unmusical, violent, and psychologically damaging. This view is also supported by studies of adolescence that correlate such music with antisocial behavior, school failure, and drug abuse. For example, one study claims that it provides "evidence that an early preference for different types of noisy, rebellious, non-mainstream music genres is a strong predictor of concurrent and later minor delinquency" (ter Bogt, Keijsers, and Meeus 2013, 7). However, what connects deviant music to deviant behavior is not simply the music itself, but its alignment to impoverished, violent, leaderless, and neglected environments.

7. A popular example of life narration through musical biography is the book *High Fidelity* (1995) by Nick Hornby, made into a film directed by Stephen Frears (2000). While *High Fidelity* is a humorous take on the failings of the male obsession with music, *I Think I Love You*, by Allison Pearson (2011) is an equally poignant story of a girls' world of musical fandom.

8. The marvels of modern technology can help bond the generations as this video of Led Zeppelin demonstrates, where Jason Bonham performs a drum solo with his late father John Bonham: www.youtube.com/watch?v=4sHLt6B_dfo.

9. The literature on women and rock music is beyond the scope of this chapter to encompass, spanning ethnographic studies (Jones 1998), aging female artists (Jennings and Gardner 2012), and the alternative "queering" of mainstream rock by lesbian feminist groups (Halberstam 2007). The sexism and misogyny embedded in many rock musical genres have not gone unchallenged.

Chapter Nine

"The Long Strange Trip" Continues

Aging Deadheads

Rebecca G. Adams and Justin T. Harmon

The community surrounding the Grateful Dead, a San Francisco–based psychedelic rock band that had played together for thirty years when its lead guitarist Jerry Garcia died in 1995, still persists. For many Deadheads, as these fans are called, membership in this community has been a major component of their identity and following the band from place to place had provided structure and meaning to their everyday lives. Many older Deadheads continue to participate not only via online, recorded, and print media but also by attending performances of bands including surviving members of the Grateful Dead, cover bands, and other jam bands. This chapter examines the challenges to identity maintenance and community participation faced by Deadheads as they age, the ways in which the community has addressed the aging of its population, and how fans have adapted the ways in which they participate in the community to allow continuity in their identity as Deadheads.

THEORETICAL PERSPECTIVE

Since Havighurst and Albrecht's (1953) original statement of Activity Theory in their book, *Old People,* and especially since Havighurst (1961) published his influential editorial in the first issue of *The Gerontologist,* aging scholars have studied what Havighurst called "successful aging"—the "maintenance of the level and range of activities that characterize a person in his [*sic*] prime of life with a minimum downward adjustment" (10). Although early debates focused on whether continued involvement in middle-aged activities was important for well-being in later life as Havighurst had argued or, in contrast, whether disengagement from society led to well-being during old age as Cumming and Henry (1961) had observed, gerontologists since the 1980s have emphasized the importance of continuity for successful aging (Adams and Taylor forthcoming; Atchley 1989; Rowe and Kahn 1987).

Atchley (1989) described "continuity" as "a grand adaptive strategy that is promoted by both individual preference and social approval" (183). He argued that

> in making adaptive choices, middle-aged and older adults attempt to preserve and maintain existing internal and external structures; and they prefer to accomplish this objective by using strategies tied to their past experiences of themselves and their social world. Change is linked to the person's perceived past, producing continuity in inner psychological characteristics as well as in social behavior and in social circumstances. (183)

This distinction between "inner psychological characteristics" and "social behavior in social circumstances" is relevant here, because some Deadheads continue to identify with the community even though they no longer attend live performances. These fans sometimes interact with other members of the community outside of shows (i.e., online or elsewhere) or lead "invisible lives" (Unruh 1983) as Deadheads through consumption of recorded or print media. So here we focus on the challenges posed by the increasing difficulty of attending live performances but also acknowledge that aging Deadheads may also experience decreasing opportunities to participate remotely in the community.

Gerontologists since Atchley (1989) have emphasized that as the relationship between the person and the environment and the goodness of fit between them changes with age, adaptation becomes important to successful aging (Adams and Taylor forthcoming). Goodness of fit is sometimes achieved through modifications to the environment (Wahl, Fänge, Oswald, Gitlin, and Iwarsson 2009), adaptation of the individual (Baltes and Lang 1997), or the older adult's identification of and relocation to new environments more suitable for an aging individual (Kahana, Lovegreen, Kahana, and Kahana 2003). In this chapter we conclude by discussing the ways in which goodness of fit between the older Deadhead and the Deadhead community is facilitated by an existing infrastructure and has been improved by recent changes to the show environment, through changes in Deadhead behavior, and by older Deadheads "relocating" to an area where it is more convenient to attend shows, to venues set up to accommodate aging fans, or to online communities. We conclude by discussing how some Deadheads continue to identify with the community although they no longer interact with other members.

THE DEADHEAD COMMUNITY PROJECT

The data on aging Deadheads were collected as part of the Deadhead Community project, 1987–present (Adams 1998). The data consist of a 1987 parking lot survey of Deadheads ($N = 286$), observations at ninety-one Grateful Dead shows and nine Jerry Garcia Band concerts (1989–1995) by Adams, online conversations starting in 1989 among members of the Usenet users group rec.music.gdead, eighty-four observations of shows, and seventy-seven open-ended interviews by twenty-one students in that same year, 177 responses to three mailed questionnaires with open-ended questions (1990–1996), and interviews with Deadheads with identifiable roles within the community and key members of the Grateful Dead organization. Between Garcia's death in August of 1995 and May of 1997, Adams received 150 letters describing Deadhead reactions to his death (Adams, Ernstes, and Lucey 2014). In 1998, the Grateful Dead organization collected responses to a self-administered questionnaire during their twenty-two-venue national Furthur Festival tour and hired Adams to analyze the data ($N = 6,020$) (Adams 2012 [2010]). Since that time she has continued to attend performances by Grateful Dead survivors, performances of jam bands, and other Deadhead gatherings, and the second author of this chapter, Harmon, has done so as well. Throughout this research process, Adams has also collected artifacts, photos, videos, recordings of performances, and Deadhead and mainstream media. Although the project was not designed to examine the effects of aging on fan identity and community participation, ample information on older Deadheads are included in these data to allow for preliminary analysis.

THE DEADHEAD COMMUNITY

The Deadhead community is long-lasting, distributed, and large. Its roots are in the hippie culture that grew up in the Western United States during the 1960s. The Grateful Dead were the "house band" for the Acid Tests, public psychedelic celebrations held in 1965 and 1966 before LSD became illegal. By late 1966, the Grateful Dead were headquartered in San Francisco, California, at 710 Ashbury, near its intersection with Haight Street, the symbolic heart of the hippie community (Adams and Rosen-Grandon 2002; for more detailed histories of the Grateful Dead, see Greenfield 1996; Lesh 2006; McNally 2003; Troy 1991).

The community continued to spread and grow in size after its inception in the 1960s. By 1995, when Garcia died, Deadheads lived throughout the United States and in many other countries as well, which is not surprising because during its career, the band played at least once in forty-five states and thirteen foreign countries (Scott, Dolgushkin, and Nixon 1997). Based on information provided by Grateful Dead Productions during the summer of 1998, a conservative estimate of the number of Deadheads at that time is more than a half million (Adams and Rosen-Grandon 2002).

The Deadhead community is not only remarkable among music communities because of the length of time it has survived, how geographically dispersed it is, and how large it is, more relevant here is the length and intensity of involvement of individual fans (Adams 2012 [2010]). On the average, the fans who Grateful Dead Productions surveyed in 1998 saw their first show in 1984 or 1985, with 50 percent of them having seen their first show at least eleven years previously. The average Deadhead had traveled 1,223 miles to attend a show and had attended sixty-one concerts.

Deadheads did not attend shows merely for entertainment or to socialize with like-minded people. Many of them reported having spiritual experiences at shows, which provided them with an additional motivation to attend (Sutton 2000) and contributed to community solidarity. Although the spiritual experiences of Deadheads varied widely and included feelings of déjà vu, out-of-body experiences, connecting with a higher power, and living through the cycle of death and rebirth, the most commonly mentioned experiences were inner and outer connectedness—self-revelation and unity with others (Adams 1991). Although dancing and drugs surely contributed to these experiences for some Deadheads, others attributed their occurrences, at least in part, to the power and trajectory of the music (Goodenough 1999; Hartley 2000). "Getting it" is an expression Deadheads use to describe the process of learning to perceive shows as spiritual experiences and to understand "these spiritual experiences as inseparable from the music, the scene, and a cooperative mode of everyday existence" (Adams quoted in Shenk and Silberman 1994, 106).

The feelings of unity and empathy Deadheads experienced at shows often were extended to the band. Some Deadheads claim that the band was psychically "connected" to the audience or that the audience "controlled" the band (Carr 1999). These Deadheads believe that they influenced the selection of songs, the way they were played, and thus the trajectory of the music. Lyricist John Barlow confirmed Deadhead beliefs that band members did not know what they were going to play before a performance but were rather guided by "the groupmind" in selecting songs while they were on stage (Shenk and Silberman 1994, 127). Thus by having spiritual experiences at many shows over a long period of time, Deadheads developed feelings of closeness, a high level of commitment to the band, and a high level of identification with the community.

COMMUNITY EFFORTS TO PRESERVE CONTINUITY

Deadheads never relied exclusively on interaction at shows to maintain their community, even when the majority of the audience was young and able to attend live performances more easily. Even before Garcia died, Deadheads kept in touch between the Grateful Dead's performances so they would know when tickets were available, to trade tapes of live performances, by attending performances of cover bands, attending Deadhead parties, interacting via the Internet, and reading the Deadhead print media. By wearing tie-dye and subsequent to its popularization, more exclusively used in-group symbols such as the Skull and Lightning Bolt (known as a "Steal-Your-Face" or "Stealie"), Skeleton and Roses, or Dancing Bear, Deadheads were able to recognize each other as they lived their mainstream lives. Although these activities were not consciously designed to maintain Deadhead identity and community between shows, they served this purpose (Adams 1992; Barnes 2011).

Garcia's death represented a threat to community solidarity and challenged Deadheads to rethink their identities and lives as fans. Although Deadheads lamented Garcia's passing and celebrated his inherent value as a human being, many of them, even in the early stages of mourning, also expressed their concerns about how his death would affect their own way of life, identity, and community (Adams, Ernstes, and Lucey 2014). Fortunately for Deadheads, however, because an infrastructure for maintaining contact between shows already existed, they did not have to start from scratch in developing mechanisms to achieve continuity. After his death, they continued to listen to recordings of Garcia's music; organized and participated in Deadhead subgroups and networks; planned and attended local annual celebrations; established and participated in sometimes more frequent local gatherings; connected with other Deadheads on the Internet; attended performances by or themselves played in cover bands, other jam bands, or bands including one or more of the remaining members of the Grateful Dead; and traveled to annual festivals outside of their local areas. Far from being passive consumers, they have actively participated in the creation of opportunities to enjoy music and other community activities. For example, even immediately after his death Deadheads have already begun to help establish annual festivals that now attract national audiences. One consequence of Garcia's death was thus the strengthening of this infrastructure—locally, nationally, and virtually. This infrastructure is still in place to facilitate the continued involvement and identification of aging fans.

THE AGING OF THE DEADHEAD COMMUNITY

Grateful Dead Productions surveyed 6,020 people attending the shows that were part of the 1998 Furthur Festival Tour (Adams 2012 [2010]). These data represent the largest and probably the most geographically dispersed sample of Deadheads ever studied systematically. Furthermore, given that they were collected after Garcia passed away, they do not include the Deadheads who permanently disengaged from the community in response to his death and thus are more likely to be predictive of current community demographics. Assuming these data accurately represent the age distribution of Deadheads in 1998 and assuming that this distribution has not been greatly affected by attrition and recruitment, it is possible to project that, fifteen years later, the average age of Deadheads is now approximately forty-seven years and the range in ages is now from twenty-five years through seventy-seven years. Comparisons of these 1998 data and the projected 1998 ages of Deadheads who participated in older, smaller studies suggest that there is some attrition from shows as fans age (Adams 2012 [2010]). Although 2.9 percent of the 1998 respondents were more than forty-nine years old, it is probable that fifteen years later, in 2013, that a lower percentage of those still actively attending live performances of the bands in which the remaining members of the Grateful Dead perform are sixty-five years old or older. The next youngest cohort of Deadheads, who were between forty and forty-nine years old in 1998 and would now be between fifty-five and sixty-four years old, was much larger (21.5 percent) however, so the number of fans facing the challenges of aging will soon increase.

CHALLENGES OF MAINTAINING
A DEADHEAD IDENTITY

Although continuity is desirable in old age, it is also challenging to achieve. Immediately after retirement some older adults participate more fully in the activities that they have enjoyed earlier in life (Holloway 2007; Nimrod and Kleiber 2007), but with the physical, social, and financial constraints imposed by aging, it eventually becomes necessary to prioritize and focus on the activities most vital to well-being (Kleiber, McGuire, Aybar-Damali, and Norman 2008), to preserve involvement in the most significant leisure pursuits (Lang, Rieckmann, and Bates 2002), and to pursue meaningful relationships rather than superficial social interactions (Tornstam 2005). For Deadheads, who consider participating in their community important for their physical, emotional, social, and spiritual health (Adams and Rosen-Grandon 2002), attendance at shows remains an important priority during old age. An increased focus on spirituality often accompanies these age-related changes

(Atchley 2009), presumably making continued involvement in shows even more important for older Deadheads than for younger ones. Although recent observations suggest it less true for older Deadheads, some fans are also dependent on shows for their financial health because they derive income from selling food, clothing, or drugs in the parking lot before and after shows (Sheptoski 2000). Similar to the aging punk rockers that Bennett (2013) studied, music is intertwined with Deadhead lives.

Overcoming barriers to attend shows is not a new experience for aging Deadheads. Deadheads of all ages experience tribal stigma (Goffman 1963) due to their musical taste, their assumed use or approval of use of psychedelic drugs, and the way they dress. Due to the association of these "hippie" attitudes and behaviors with youth, this stigma is particularly salient for midlife and older Deadheads. Deadheads struggle to carve out time from their mainstream lives to go to shows because those surrounding them do not necessarily value or even tolerate their involvement. Married Deadheads, especially those married to non-Deadheads and those with children, face the same problems all couples face when they do not share leisure interests, but because the Deadhead lifestyle is costly both in terms of time and money, sometimes involves participation in illegal activity (i.e., drug possession and use), and involves noncouple socializing, the challenges posed to participation are greater than those for participation in more acceptable activities (Adams and Rosen-Grandon 2002).

Despite the estimated age distribution reported earlier, the Deadhead community is still a relatively young community, with most of its older adults still in the "third age," the period between active earning and deep old age (Holloway 2007). Although some Deadheads are beginning to experience the physical and mental constraints associated with aging, some members of the community who are leading-edge baby boomers are currently experiencing an at least temporary lessening of the constraints on participation imposed by midlife career and family responsibilities. Like other adults in the third age, Deadheads in this cohort are inclined to travel now more than they probably will later (Kelly, Steinkamp, and Kelly 1987). Although Deadheads (and hippies in general) are often stereotyped as slackers (Paterline 2000), the vast majority of Deadheads eventually obtain college degrees or finish graduate school and become professionals or fill white-collar positions (Adams 2003). In retirement then, they have the resources to attend live performances and enough leisure time to go "on tour," in some cases for the first time in their lives. Even older adults with a limited fixed income sometimes make sacrifices in other areas to meet their social needs (Roalf, Mitchell, Harbaugh, and Janowsky 2012), and Deadheads on fixed incomes are not an exception.

Some older Deadheads are not so fortunate, however, and are physically challenged in ways that make it difficult or impossible for them to attend shows. Ironically some of these physical constraints result from the accumulated effects of past participation in the community (e.g., wear and tear on joints and muscles from standing and dancing, physical effects of prolonged drug or alcohol use, hearing issues resulting from exposure to loud music). Whatever their causes, however, the physical changes that often accompany aging, such as decreased physical mobility (Hillsdon, Brunner, Guralnick, and Marmot 2005), increased risk of falling (Merom et al. 2013), decreased energy levels and ability to go without sleep (Venn, Meadows, and Arbor 2013), and hearing impairment (Walling and Dickson 2012), sometimes interfere with the ability of older Deadheads to travel to shows and to participate fully once there.

DEADHEAD-ENVIRONMENT FIT

The Show Infrastructure

Fortunately for aging Deadheads, just as an infrastructure already existed to facilitate the continuation of the community when it was endangered by the death of Garcia, the Deadhead community has traditionally had mechanisms in place to support its age diversity and inclusiveness. Although venues vary in how automatically accommodating they are, Deadheads have a history of active advocacy when necessary. All public venues are technically required to be compliant with the Americans with Disabilities Act of 1990 (as subsequently amended) which requires the provision of full and equal access to goods, services, facilities, and accommodations. In the Grateful Dead's later years it was therefore possible to navigate a show in a wheelchair and a spot was always reserved for the "Wheel Chair guys," as Deadheads called them. In addition, the Grateful Dead often reserved space, known as the Deafzone, for deaf Deadheads, who were known as the Grateful Deaf (Ladd 1990, 1996). Although people who develop hearing impairments as they age do not usually learn sign language and therefore would not benefit from sitting in this section, its existence does illustrate a commitment to adapt the concert context to accommodate a wide variety of participants.

The Grateful Dead were also pioneers in offering medical assistance at rock 'n' roll concerts. In 1972, Bill Graham, the Grateful Dead's promoter, asked the Haight Ashbury Free Clinics to staff a medical care tent at his Grateful Dead and Led Zeppelin outdoor events. Rock Med is still in operation and setting the standard in nonjudgmental event medicine (Rock Med, n.d.). Not all venues have medical staffs as extensive as provided at venues served by Rock Med and not all medical staff have the same nonjudgmental philosophy, but emergency medical care is generally available at public venues.

In addition to these occasionally officially sanctioned aspects of the infrastructure, Deadhead culture also has characteristics that should be supportive of continuity in participation with aging. Not only do Deadheads respect "old hippies" as those who experienced a romanticized past and have survived a lifetime of stigma and discrimination, they believe that "what goes around comes around," which encourages them to treat each other well. Furthermore, status within the Deadhead community is enhanced through sharing resources. A relatively new custom of "pinning" of fellow Deadheads in response to acts of kindness is a visible representation of a long-standing community norm. Affluent Deadheads have always supported younger Deadheads currently on tour by shopping in the parking lot, "miracle-ing them" with free tickets, or sometimes offering them places to sleep, but recent observations suggest that intergenerational transfers are becoming even more common now that the population is aging. These intergenerational transfers of resources include direct ones such as the older Deadheads buying food, clothing, or drugs from younger ones, but also indirect ones such as random acts of kindness that Deadheads believe affect their Karma. For example, one young woman who has been touring the last few years with Dark Star Orchestra (the leading Dead cover band) and then Furthur (including Phil Lesh and Bob Weir, original members of the Grateful Dead) often watched over an older Deadhead with breathing problems as he danced at shows. At a recent Furthur show, an older Deadhead who had heard of her kindness gave her two tickets to a sold-out show for her and her boyfriend. When the person who had told him the story thanked him for his spontaneous gift to her young friend, he simply said "it seemed like it was the right thing to do." This tendency of the young and old to support each other within this community bodes well for the continued involvement of older fans.

The increase in the number of festivals allows affluent older Deadheads more options for hearing multiple bands perform over a series of days without traveling from place to place. VIP tickets ensure easy access to the venue and comfortable priority seating with good sound and views of the stage, access to nicer bathroom facilities, and shorter lines for food and drinks. These tickets can sometimes be combined with hotel packages, complete with shuttle service. Some festivals also or alternatively supplement VIP tickets with onsite cabins, already setup rent-a-tents complete with beds, or VIP RV camping. These festivals often take place in the same place year after year, so improvements are made overtime and the festival grounds become easier to navigate as a result (e.g., Bonnaroo and Electric Forest).

Deadhead Behavioral Changes

Deadheads also tend to modify their behavior as they age. Although retirement frees some Deadheads up to attend more shows than previously, with advanced age some find themselves unable to attend as many shows. Many of them travel by air rather than by driving or allocate more time to go to a live performance than they would have when they were younger. They sometimes travel at a more leisurely pace, arrive earlier, stay later, or "take off" or "take it easy" for a night during a festival or run of shows. Rather than "doing" a whole tour, some older Deadheads do a minitour in a geographically defined area. They may consciously select shows to attend that are easy to navigate or set up to accommodate Deadheads of all ages. Once they are in the show environment, older Deadheads are less likely to move from place to place than younger Deadheads. Even if they like to immerse themselves in the fray with the rest of the crowd occasionally, they tend to establish a "home" a distance from the stage where the sound is not too loud and where it is possible to sit down comfortably when necessary. They tend to wear shoes, presumably to protect their feet and to enhance their balance, rather than going barefoot the way many younger Deadheads do. They may cut back on how much of the show they remain standing or dancing. To prevent hearing damage, they wear earplugs, sometimes the type designed for musicians that make it possible to hear the music while wearing them. Some older Deadheads try to get more sleep while on tour than they did when they were young; as one older Deadhead mentioned recently, he sleeps at night now instead of "raging until dawn."

Deadhead Relocation

For Deadheads, relocation to a new environment to improve person-environment fit can mean moving to a location where it is more convenient to attend shows, selecting venues designed for all-age access, or participating in the community only via online interaction (i.e., "moving" to a virtual environment). Some Deadheads relocated to San Francisco years ago to be closer to where the band members have always lived and given the most performances. With the development of bassist Phil Lesh's Terrapin Crossroads in San Rafael and rhythm guitarist Bob Weir's Sweetwater Music Hall in Mill Valley, San Francisco remains a retirement destination for Deadheads, but other areas of the country where music is easily available also attract them. Due to the common use of marijuana by older adults (Benyon 2009), the recent legalization of marijuana in some states and not in others could affect some Deadheads' retirement destination decisions as well. Recently Phil Lesh announced a deal with promoter Peter Shapiro to play multiple concerts at his New York venues (the Brooklyn Bowl in Williamsburg, New York, and the Capitol Theater in Porchester, New York) as well as the Lockn' Festival Shapiro sponsors in Arrington, Virginia (Sisario 2013; www.thecapitoltheatre.com). This decision to perform multiple shows in a few locations, made by Lesh in deference to his own aging, will provide an opportunity for older Deadheads to attend multiple shows without traveling in between them, whether as visitors to the area or as local residents.

Some older Deadheads do not choose to live near or are not able to relocate to live near venues where the remaining members of the Grateful Dead, cover bands, or other jam bands play regularly. For these Deadheads who choose retirement destinations for other reasons or decide to age in place, person-environment fit can be improved by selecting shows to attend based on how well the venue is set up to accommodate aging fans. Challenges to be considered include loss of hearing and eyesight, physical impairments, bodily needs, and decline in cognitive functioning. Strategies to increase a safer and more welcoming environment for the aging fan include decreasing background noise, speaking (or singing) more clearly and slowly, providing physical assistance, and displaying easy-to-read signs for restrooms and refreshments (Barba and Tesh 2011). Some venues are easier to adapt to the needs of older adults than others because they have better acoustics, are better lit, include seating, are easier to navigate, and have more accessible facilities. Of course, not all of these features will be important for all older Deadheads—it depends not only on how they are aging but what is important for their enjoyment of shows, for example, sound quality, seeing the band, or being able to dance (Adams 1999).

Not all older Deadheads can continue to attend shows no matter how much they would like to do so or how conveniently they are located and set up. Fortunately, however, Deadheads were Internet pioneers (Hoffman and Cosgrove 1990), participating in a Usenet group, rec.music.gdead, and a virtual community, the Well (the Whole Earth 'Lectronic Link), and other bulletin boards, chat rooms, interactive web sites, and social networking sites long before such activities became common (Rheingold 1991; Smith and Kolluck 1999). As long as they have access to a computer and retain the ability to log on and use it, older fans can choose one or more of many virtual Deadhead communities to join.

Invisible Deadhead Lives

The Grateful Dead and other bands have left a rich recorded legacy of music. Even older Deadheads who can no longer attend shows and do not participate in their community interactively online can continue to lead what Unruh (1983) called "invisible lives" as Deadheads by "listening to the music play" (Hunter 1990, 84) and, at least if they remain somewhat autonomous, by maintaining a hippie lifestyle at home. Although most Deadheads have purchased or downloaded ample numbers of Grateful Dead and related shows (Bradley 2007), some Deadheads also listen to music played on the radio programs such as *The Grateful Dead Hour* and *Tales from the Golden Road*, all with the realization that tens of thousands of other fans are participating in these same events. In similar ways, Deadheads can maintain their identity by reading Deadhead print media, such as *Relix* magazine or some of the many books and articles about the Grateful Dead and Deadheads, many of which are cited in this chapter. These Deadheads with invisible lives may wish to continue other behaviors sometimes associated with a hippie lifestyle such as illegal substance use, but this could be difficult for them to achieve unless they maintain autonomy and control over their living environment.

CONCLUSION

For more than half a century, gerontologists have stressed the importance of continuity in activities and identity for successful aging (Adams and Taylor forthcoming; Nimrod and Kleiber 2007). Attending live performances by the remaining members of the Grateful Dead, cover bands, or other jam bands is important to the well-being of Deadheads of all ages and provides meaning to their lives. With aging, physical, cognitive, and emotional challenges naturally occur, and participation in their community sometimes becomes more challenging for older Deadheads.

Adams was inspired to write this chapter after an experience she and her partner had at the Allgood Music Festival in 2012. At the ages of fifty-nine and sixty years, she and her husband were among the youngest people on the hotel shuttle leaving Legend Valley in Thornville, Ohio, sometime after one in the morning. A young woman standing at the front of the bus cautioned occupants to remain awake so they did not miss their stops and end up in Columbus with no place to stay. At that moment, Adams saw her future flash before her and began to problematize her own aging. This chapter represents her attempt, in collaboration with Harmon, to explore whether it is likely to be possible to continue participating in this community as she grows older.

Continuity is more achievable when the fit between the person and environment is good. Sometimes this goodness of fit can be achieved by modifying the environment in which the older adult ages (Wahl, Fänge, Oswald, Gitlin, and Iwarsson 2009). Fortunately for older Deadheads, the show infrastructure that is already in place is fairly accommodating and recent changes to the show environment have improved it further. Other times this goodness of fit is improved through the adaption of the aging individual (Baltes and Lange 1997). For aging Deadheads, this sometimes means attending fewer shows, perhaps closer to home, taking precautions to protect their physical well-being, and participating in them less strenuously. Finally, goodness of fit can be improved by the location of an aging individual to a more suitable environment (Kahana, Lovegreen, Kahana, and Kahana 2003). For some Deadheads "relocation" means moving to areas of the United States where it is more convenient to attend shows, attending shows in venues designed for all-age access, or participating in the community online. Even Deadheads who cannot continue to interact with other members of the community can maintain their identity by staying in touch through the Deadhead media and by listening to recorded music. After exploring the possibilities, Adams is now feeling better about her future and the future of other Deadheads.

Deadheads are not, however, the only older adults who benefit from listening to music (Coffman 2002) or derive their identities from it (De Nora 2000). Music has been linked to well-being in numerous ways, including as a conduit for spirituality and increased cognitive maintenance (Perkins and Williamson 2013) and as the most frequent trigger of peak experiences integral to self-image, esteem, and the creation of meaning in one's life (Schäfer, Smukalla, and Oelker 2013). Research on the effects of music involvement for seniors has shown that it can be very beneficial to maintaining a sense of belonging and improving depressive symptoms that might coincide with other impairments that come with the aging process (Cooke, Moyle, Shum, Harrison, and Murfield 2010). Involvement in music has also been shown to mediate physical symptoms through increased vitality, as well as to provide structure to life and routine events and activities to anticipate (Creech, Hallam, McQueen, and Varvarigou 2013).

Social norms dictate that old people should act their age, and unfortunately these ageist expectations lead older adults to disassociate themselves from the activities they love (North and Fiske 2013). Despite the evidence of age-related schisms in our society, however, older adults are commonly open to interacting with youth as a manner of sharing valuable life experience and knowledge (Sedgley, Morgan, and Pritchard 2007). Music scenes not only provide the opportunity for the aging individual to "play" but also serve as safe places for shared intergenerational experiences (Yarnal 2006). Fortunately for aging Deadheads, the surviving members of the Grateful Dead and other like-minded musicians have worked with members of the Deadhead and larger jamband communities to provide safe, age-diverse, nonjudgmental spaces to support the continued involvement of community elders. To paraphrase the Grateful Dead, it is no longer just "the kids" who "dance and shake their bones" (Barlow 1987); so do those whose hair has more than "a touch of grey" (Hunter 1990, 228).

NOTES

The title of this chapter references Robert Hunter, *A Box of Rain: Collected Lyrics of Robert Hunter* (New York: Penguin, 1990), 230.

Lyrics to Grateful Dead compositions © copyright Ice Nine Publishing Company. Used with permission.

V

Fandom

Chapter Ten

A Life Course
Perspective on Fandom

C. Lee Harrington and Denise D. Bielby

A forty-two-year-old man who has watched the US soap opera *The Young and the Restless* (CBS) since he was eight remarks, "Genoa City [the show's fictional setting] has been the most stable 'home' of my adult life." A fifty-year-old woman who has watched the US serial *General Hospital* (ABC) since early childhood muses, "What I have learned about myself over years of viewing is that my perception of which characters I love and why has grown and changed with my life experience." A fan of the US soap *As the World Turns* (CBS) for the past fifty-one years, who has been watching since she was a teenager, explains, "I would not have been a different person without soaps, but I am a richer person because of them." In this chapter we explore a life course perspective on fandom with particular emphasis on fandom and adult development. While there is growing interest in issues of age and aging within fan studies and within media studies more broadly, there is a tendency in this literature to discuss aging and the life course atheoretically, ignoring a rich body of scholarship in gerontology, sociology, psychology, and human development that examines how lives unfold over time. Our goal in this manuscript is to make *explicit* what is typically rendered *implicit* in fan studies by drawing directly on life course perspectives to enrich our understanding of long-term and later life fandom, and to suggest ways that fan studies might more fully account for fandom over time. Given rapid processes of global aging currently underway and thus rapidly changing demographics of media audiences worldwide, it is especially timely to bring together two bodies of literature that rarely inform one another: fan studies and life course scholarship.

In the below section we discuss life course and the media, followed by a section in which we elaborate on the conceptual gaps in fan studies' approach to issues of age and aging. In the third section we shed light on a variety of life course issues in fandom, demonstrating how explicit attention to issues of age, aging, and human development can offer new insights into fans' identities, practices, and interpretive capacities. We conclude with a discussion of the utility of life course perspectives to future fan scholarship.

LIFE COURSE AND MEDIA

In simplest terms, understanding the life course is about "understanding lives through time" (Fry 2003, 271). Life course scholars are interested in the social and historical changes that impact a particular generation at a particular point in time and come to "govern the manner in which members of that generation make sense of a presently remembered past, experienced present, and anticipated future" (Cohler and Hostetler 2003, 557). From this approach, based in the social sciences, the way our individual lives unfold is shaped by both internal psychological and external social processes.[1] Scholarship on the life course occurs in many parts of the academy and has resulted in multiple approaches rather than a single integrated theory. Various perspectives share focus on issues of time and timing, intersections of social context and personal biography, interdependent or linked lives, and the importance of human agency (George 2003, 672).

Most contemporary perspectives conceptualize the life course through general patterns of stability and transition, not evolutionary or hierarchical sequences or stages. Since life journeys do not always follow expectable paths—"there is no career or script to follow at every turn" (Fry 2003, 286)—the challenge for scholars is to "simultaneously do justice to long-term patterns of change and stability and to the heterogeneity of those patterns" (George 2003, 675). Though unscripted, different life phases tend to be marked by unique developmental opportunities and our engagement with those opportunities helps shape our maturation from infancy through childhood, adolescence, adulthood, and late(r) life. Moreover, each individual life course is guided by culturally and historically bound ideals of how lives "should" unfold, offering normative pathways against which we assess and make meaning of our personal trajectories. These normative ideals are currently undergoing significant transition in the United States, as will be discussed in the conclusion, but continue to offer a benchmark against which we understand our lived experiences.

Popular media are, of course, thoroughly implicated in life course processes and transitions, offering representations of normatively appropriate age-based identities and activities (and tantalizingly nonnormative ones), producing so-called television, computer, and Facebook generations and thus redefining generational divides, radically altering expectations for how publicly lives can or should be lived, and transforming relatively nonmediated lives in earlier historical eras into thoroughly mediated ones today. Media texts and technologies help unite cohorts, define generations and cross-generational differences, and give structure and meaning to our lives as they unfold. For example, when J. K. Rowling published the seventh and final Harry Potter book in July 2007, critics mourned not just the end of the series but the end of a life stage:

> The sadness that many readers will experience . . . has nothing to do with the fate of the characters and everything to do with . . . the end of childhood. The readers who have grown up with this series—who have read it, as it were, in real time as it unfolds—are themselves at that end. Saying goodbye to Harry is like saying goodbye to a piece of themselves. (Jones 2007)

Similarly, the fortieth anniversary of the Woodstock concert in August 2009 presented an opportunity to revisit the intersections between generational and national identities (the so-called Woodstock Nation), the September 2009 cancellation of the US soap *Guiding Light* (CBS) after seventy-two years of storytelling on radio and television was seen by many as the end of an institution (as one journalist put it, it's "like your old high school being demolished"),[2] and the high-profile celebrity deaths throughout the summer of 2009 (Michael Jackson, Farrah Fawcett, Ted Kennedy, Walter Cronkite, Patrick Swayze, Ed McMahon, etc.) caused baby boomers to

> turn to the obituaries first, to face not merely their own mortality or ponder their legacies, but to witness the passing of legends who defined them as a tribe, bequeathing through music, culture, news and politics a kind of generational badge that has begun to fray. (Kershaw 2009)

Over the past thirty years fan scholars have engaged with a wide variety of life course *issues* but have rarely utilized life course *theories* to help ground their analyses. Our already rich understanding of media fans' identities, practices, and interpretive capacities can be enhanced, we argue, through a more explicit consideration of the various mechanisms and social processes that shape life course development.[3] The opening quotations from soap opera fans echo prior scholarship in suggesting fundamental changes in fan experiences over time—we aim to explore such changes from a life course/life span approach.

FAN STUDIES AND LIFE COURSE THEORY

We begin by clarifying what we are *not* arguing in this manuscript. First, we are not implying that fan studies scholars have wholly ignored issues of *age* or *aging* in prior work. The centrality of fandom in (pre)adolescent explorations of gender identity and romantic/sexual fantasy has been well documented (e.g., Ehrenreich, Hess, and Jacobs 1992; Frith 1990; Kuhn 2002; Williams 1980), though as Matt Hills (2005, 804) notes, the larger cultural equation of fandom with adolescence remains overly rigid: "This commonsense notion of fandom as an 'all-consuming' stage in the life course that will later be abandoned, or only nostalgically revisited, finds its stereotypes in the 'hysterical' tweenage or teenage female fan of a pop band or male actor." While scholarly interest in teen fandom continues—see Melanie Lowe's recent (2004) study of Britney Spears fans, for example—there is a growing body of literature that focuses on fandom among older adults (Bennett 2006; Stevenson 2009; Vroomen 2004) and on the impact of generational affiliation on the formation of interpretive communities (e.g., Brooker 2002). In the context of television fandom, Christine Scodari explores the politics of age and aging through separate studies focusing on power dynamics among younger vs. older female fans online (1998), and gender, age, and romantic fantasy in an analysis of a May–December romance on the now-defunct US soap *Another World* (CBS) (2004). Other media scholars examining older adults' fannish engagement with television in different industrial, historical and institutional contexts include John Tulloch (1989), Elizabeth Riggs (1998), and C. Lee Harrington and Denise Brothers (2011).

Second, we do not mean to imply that prior scholars have ignored larger issues of *process*, per se. For example, our own prior work (Harrington and Bielby 1995) investigates how people enter into soap opera fandom and construct and maintain fan-based identities. Melissa Scardaville (2005) examines how fans enter into media-based activism and how the politics of fandom shape subsequent activist experiences. Hills (2005) considers the cyclical nature of fandom, where fan-consumers move from one fan object to another. Paul Booth (2008) analyzes MySpace profiles that fans create for media characters, arguing that media transformation engenders fundamental changes in identity formation and thus requires change in the study of audiences (see also Grodin and Lindlof 1996; Sandvoss 2005a). Moreover, larger issues of process in fandom itself have been studied, including the historical trajectory of US soap fandom since the early 1900s (Ford 2008), the emergence and maintenance of community in online fandom (Baym 2000), the explosion in fan fiction online (Hellekson and Busse 2006), and the mainstreaming of fandom in the late twentieth and twenty-first centuries (Gray, Sandvoss, and Harrington 2007).

Third, we are not suggesting that scholars have ignored issues of *auto-biography* in fan studies, particularly the crucial role of memory in shaping self-narratives. In her study of 1930s filmgoing, Annette Kuhn employs an ethnohistorical approach grounded in psychological theories of memory and narrative construction to explore how "personal and collective memory meet in stories of cinema and cinemagoing" (2002, 1). Through interviews with members of Britain's "first movie-made generation," Kuhn explores how this generation managed the transition from childhood to adulthood through cine-magoing, and how movie-based memories formed early in life are situated in self-narratives and sustained through current relationships. A decade later, Carol Williams (1980) explores memory and cinemagoing in the United States in the 1940s, focusing on her own childhood and adolescent experiences with movies as an agent of socialization into romance, sexuality, and parenthood, and as a central element in her identity construction. Similarly, Bailey (2005) investigates Kiss fans' autobiographical narratives of their involvement with the band—their "Kisstories"—as "narratives of self-hood" sustained through "the present reality of maintaining one's devotion to the band" (146). In the broader context of national identity, Cornel Sandvoss (2008) examines the decades-long Eurovision Song Contest as an "object of retained childhood media consumption" (190), exploring how the televised contest offers long-term viewers an affective space of personal and collective belonging.

Finally, and relatedly, we are not arguing that fan studies have failed to engage with the role of the media in *self/identity construction* and *self-transformation* over time. This has been a central and powerful theme in fan studies over the past twenty years, from Daniel Cavicchi's (1998) richly nuanced account of how Bruce Springsteen's music transforms his fans, to Hills's (2005) theorization of fan identities as shaped differently by the entering *and* leaving of fandoms, to Sandvoss's (2005a) conceptualization of fandom as a form of narcissistic self-reflection, to Nick Stevenson's (2009) study of David Bowie's impact on fans' construction and negotiation of masculine identity. Analytically and experientially, these issues are of course inseparable—aging, time, process, memory, identity construction, and the formation and reformation of autobiographical narratives all implicate and inform one another—and there are any number of compelling theoretical frameworks through which to explore them in fan studies, including narrative and memory theory (Kuhn), Mead and the neo-Meadian tradition (Bailey), psychoanalysis (Hills), social psychology (Sandvoss), William James and the psychology of religion (Cavicchi), and so on.

But what is missing from contemporary fan studies, we argue, is *explicit* consideration of life course perspectives that can help clarify and deepen our understanding of fans' sustained engagement with media objects over time and the transformations of fandom in later life. We find surprisingly little engagement with aging and/or life course theory in fan studies. For example, Cavicchi (1998) includes several paragraphs on developmental theory in his study of Springsteen fans but goes on to discuss life course processes in quite generalized terms. Hills (2002, 2007) and Sandvoss (2005, 2008) are engaged in an ongoing debate about the meaning of adults' retained attachments to childhood transitional objects but do not consider theories of adult development in their dialogue. Scodari (2004) describes life course approaches briefly in *Serial Monogamy* but does not fully utilize them in her analysis. Will Brooker (2002) offers a compelling analysis of the impact of generation on consumption and interpretation of the *Star Wars* text but includes no scholarly literature on generational theory. Finally, Kuhn's (2002) examination of how cinema-based memories shape self-narratives over time includes minimal discussion of aging and later life per se. In an epilogue which summarizes the major contributions of her study, Kuhn includes a section titled "Aging" which reads in its entirety, "The content and the discursive registers of the cinema memory-stories of the 1930s generation throw light on the cultural as well as the psychical processes involved in ageing" (237). While the life stage of adolescence has been explored theoretically by fan scholars, the overall aging process has been relatively neglected.

Our intent in this manuscript is not to criticize our colleagues for their choice of analytic frameworks but to highlight the utility of a life course perspective to fan studies. Given changing demographics of media audiences and the undertheorization of older adults throughout media/fan studies, we are particularly interested in exploring how life course theory might expand our understanding of adult and later-life fandom. In the next section we demonstrate the value of this approach through a synthesis that explicates life course issues in prior fan scholarship. In the concluding section we discuss implications of a life course perspective for future fan studies.

LIFE COURSE ISSUES IN FANDOM

In this section we suggest that fan identities, practices, and interpretive capacities have more age-related structure than has previously been addressed within fan studies. We discuss four age-based issues that have received varying attention from fan scholars—fandom and life milestones, changes in the fan (self) over time, age norms within fandom, and changes in the fan object over time—and illustrate how a life course perspective sheds new light on these issues and raises a new set of research questions for future fan scholarship. Throughout the remainder of this manuscript we foreground scholarship on age and aging to illuminate new ways of thinking about fans and fandoms over time. Due to space restrictions this synthesis moves fairly quickly, but points to numerous ways that an explicit life course perspective can be beneficial to fan studies.

Fandom and Life Milestones

Life course scholars explore how lives unfold by examining the factors that disrupt or interrupt the stability of our journeys—in other words, the factors that cause our current path to shift direction. Scholars agree that stability in the life trajectory can be interrupted by *physiological changes* (e.g., puberty or menopause), age-graded *life transitions* (e.g., graduating from high school), or *turning points* "in which a person has undergone a major transformation in views about the self, commitments to important relationships, or involvement in significant life roles" (Wetherington, Cooper, and Holmes 1997, 216). In terms of physiological changes, fan scholars have been most interested in the role of fandom in puberty—less in terms of bodily changes associated with puberty (e.g., development of secondary sex characteristics) than in adolescents' engagement with fan objects to help make meaning of their changing bodies, and to help explore their emergent sense of self and overall independence:

> For the 1930s generation, cinema provided a safe space for challenges to adult rules . . . for assertions of independence from parents, teachers and other authority figures [and for] adolescent explorations of love, romance and sex (Kuhn 2002, 62, 181).
>
> I saw *A New Hope* back when it was simply *Star Wars* in '77, and was hooked. I think it was the scene with Luke gazing at the setting suns that nailed me through the heart. As a young teenager, just beginning to explore the boundaries of my life and the possibilities ahead, I knew exactly what young Luke was thinking and feeling. . . . I have invested a great deal of emotional energy in the [*Star Wars*] saga and entrusted part of my "inner child" to [it]. (thirty-five-year-old female fan quoted in Brooker [2002, 85]; ellipses in original)

Analytic focus in this body of fan scholarship is primarily on issues of identity—the intersections of fan identity, gender identity, and sexual identity (orientation)—and secondarily on how specific adolescent fan practices enable identity acquisition and/or modification. Other physiological changes that might alter the trajectory of the life course—particularly those associated with aging and later life, such as changes in bone density and cognitive functioning, decline in sexual arousal and response patterns, changes in physical appearance (waistlines, skin elasticity, hair texture/amount/color), and so on—are relatively unexplored in fan studies. There is emergent evidence that fan practices are altered over time due to bodily constraints. For example, in his study of punk fans, Andy Bennett (2006) observes older fans' relief at being "honourably discharged from the excesses of the mosh pit" (228) due to their age and privileged status in the punk community. Explains one fan, "It does get difficult now to go to gigs and stay at the front all the time, an' rock around all the time. . . . I can't do it no more. [My] body's sayin', 'it's time to slow down . . . you've 'ad your fun'" (228). Others describe changes in their physical expression of fandom over time, from the "visual shock tactics" (226) of their youthful punk appearance (pink Mohawks, multiple piercings) to a more subtle punk aesthetic in later life that can translate more easily to employment and more formalized social settings. Music fans in several different studies say they "paid their dues" in their youth and do not feel as accountable to the aesthetic, bodily, and/or performative aspects of fandom as they did in their youth (Bennett 2006; Cavicchi 1998).

If the impact of the aging *body* on fan identities and practices is relatively unexplored in fan studies, we know even less about the impact of the aging *mind*. Brooker (2002) offers a fascinating discussion of how age can shape *Star Wars'* fans' textual readings by positioning them "in a specific interpretive community giving them a different perspective to fans of another generation" (223). While older fans make a clear distinction between the original *Star Wars* trilogy and its prequels due to the sixteen-year gap between the trilogy's conclusion and the prequels' launch (which was also a meaningful gap in their own lives; see below), younger fans see both the original trilogy and the prequels as part of the same six-part story. Moreover, younger fans are more likely to have seen the six films "in order" (beginning with the first prequel, ending with the last of the original trilogy), whereas older fans saw the original trilogy first followed by the prequels. Younger viewers thus saw/read/consumed a very different *Star Wars* text than did long-term fans—knowing much sooner, for example, that Darth Vader is Luke Skywalker's father (a vitally central story element in the overall narrative). Subsequent generations of fans can thus experience the "same" cultural text in very different ways.

However, Brooker's discussion of the impact of age on membership in interpretive communities does not quite capture the aspect of the aging mind that most interests life course scholars—changes in cognitive capacity. Research on media engagement and cognitive functioning in older adults is situated outside of media/fan studies and reveals a lingering assumption that media consumption is a passive experience. For example, Heather A. Lindstrom and her colleagues (2005)[4] found that TV viewing is associated with a greater likelihood of developing Alzheimer's disease. Using a life history approach to question adults in midlife (forty to fifty-nine) about a range of leisure activities, the authors conclude that "time spent on television viewing may reflect a desire to avoid more stimulating activities and may be indicative of a mentally inactive lifestyle" (163). The authors divided the activities into four categories—television viewing, social activities, intellectual activities, and physical activities—thus seemingly obviating the possibility that

TV watching can be intellectually stimulating or social. In a more genre-specific approach, Joshua Fogel and Michelle Carlson (2006)[5] focus on talk shows and soap operas in their research on adults seventy to seventy-nine years old, finding that both genres "were at least four times as likely to be associated with clinical impairment for . . . various cognitive outcomes" related to attention and memory (229). While the authors note that it is unclear whether watching these genres "is a *risk factor* or a *marker* of possible cognitive impairment" (231; emphasis added), they conclude with a policy recommendation: clinicians should ask questions about favorite TV shows when conducting screenings for cognitive impairment or dementia in older adults, and "For those patients who respond with a choice of either talk shows or soap operas, more attention by the clinician should be placed on cognitive screening at that clinical interview and also during future clinical interviews" (232). In contrast, and offering more encouraging news from a media studies perspective, Paolo Ghisletta and his colleagues (Ghisletta, Bickel, and Lovden 2006)[6] examine sixteen different activities in relation to performance in two cognitive abilities among adults aged eighty to eighty-five, concluding that higher engagement in media and leisure activities tends to slow down cognitive decline; indeed, engagement with these activities was more cognitively challenging to older adults than were religious, social, manual, or physical activities.[7] While it is difficult to assess the applicability of these specific research findings to fan studies, it is clear that age-related changes in cognitive functioning do occur, they may alter fans' engagement with media texts, and they thus may transform fandom over time. Suffice it to say, this area of research is wide open in fan studies.

In addition to physiological changes, the other types of interruptions to life course stability noted by life course scholars (age-graded life transitions and major life turning points) impact fandom as well. For example, age-graded life transitions significantly alter fan identities and practices—reaching the legal age to drive opens up new possibilities for attending formal fan events, school-to-work and nonparent-to-parent transitions constrain the time one has to devote to fandom (Vroomen 2004), and retirement from paid labor allows for new time investments in personal interests (Riggs 1998). Additionally, fandom itself (that is, entering or "finding" fandom) is typically experienced as a major turning point that profoundly reshapes one's identity, daily activities, and life trajectory. Indeed, becoming-a-fan narratives are central to fan studies—fans' stories of encountering media texts that resonate with them in such deeply personal ways that a fundamental transformation of the self occurs: "becoming a fan is, for most fans, a milestone in their lives in which 'everything changed'; they tend to think of themselves in terms of being a fan and not being a fan" (Cavicchi 1998, 153). Long-term fandom also provides structure to life narratives, as fans employ specific cultural texts to segment or divide their lives into different periods:

> Many fans to whom I spoke . . . were able to go through all of Springsteen's
> albums and, as if they were looking at a photo album, discuss where they were
> and what they were doing at the time such albums came out. Others just as
> readily listed all the Springsteen concerts they had been to over the years and
> talked about the circumstances of their lives around each one. (Cavicchi 1998,
> 154; emphasis deleted)

Becoming a fan thus redirects the life course, gives new meaning, structure, and purpose to specific life stages, and marks periods of one's personal past—hallmarks of a major turning point according to life course scholars.

We have discussed above how a life course perspective on how lives unfold over time can help illuminate findings in prior fan studies. Below we explore how fandom is shaped over time by modifications in the self and how research findings in this area of fan studies may also be enriched through consideration of a life course perspective. Again, we foreground the discussion with life course scholarship.

The Aging Self

Life course scholars agree that while there are continuities in the self (personality coherence) from infancy to adulthood (Caspi 2000), the self changes in reasonably predictable ways due to life course disruptions and to the concomitant developmental challenges/opportunities associated with each life phase. In Kay Deux's (1991) formulation, long-term identity changes can transpire in the *characteristics* associated with an identity, a shift in the *salience hierarchy* of an identity, or the outright *gain* or *loss* of an identity. In the context of fandom, scholars have documented changes in the characteristics associated with fan identity over time—for example, from the shameful impact of the loser/lunatic stereotype in existence through much of twentieth-century fandom (Harrington and Bielby 1995; Jenkins 1992; Jensen 1992) to the contemporary mainstreaming of fandom as a widespread affective stance on modern life. One might describe this as a general historical shift from fandom treated as a "bad" characteristic to fandom treated as a "good" characteristic (see Gray, Sandvoss, and Harrington 2007). Fan identity can also shift place in one's salience hierarchy due to the emergence of competing priorities and identities (as parent, grandparent, employee), shifting patterns of interest/disinterest in the fan object (Cavicchi 1998; Hills 2005), and the relative influence of age norms (see below). As noted above and as discussed in the following section, the fan identity is always acquired (one is not born a fan) and becoming-a-fan narratives are replete in fan studies. At the same time, one's fan identity is elective and thus can be abandoned at any point—and as particular fan objects are acquired and then discarded, the nature of one's fan identity shifts (see Hills's [2005] discussion of cyclical fandom).

The self also changes due to general processes of human development. While many developmental theories only address childhood and/or adolescence, adulthood, and late(r) life are also strategic sites for self-examination and the very process of getting old "poses challenges, and perhaps threats, to the self" (George 1998, 139). One of the most well-known models of psychosocial development over the life course is that proposed by Erik Erikson in the 1950s (Erikson 1959).[8] Erikson believed there are eight phases of life, beginning at birth and ending at death, through which a healthy human matures. At each phase, people experience a distinct conflict or challenge that represents a turning point for development—an opportunity for personal growth or failure. Of particular interest to us here are the three phases of adulthood—young adulthood (approximately eighteen to thirty-five), middle adulthood (thirty-five to sixty-five), and older adulthood (sixty-five and older)—and the relevance to fandom of the challenge presented in each phase. Erikson posited that the challenge of young adulthood is to forge intimate bonds or risk isolation (intimacy vs. isolation); the challenge of midadulthood is to contribute to the betterment of the world through transmission of core values or culture, or to risk stagnation (generativity vs. stagnation); and the challenge of late life is to come to terms with life's accomplishments and thus achieve wisdom, or die with bitterness and regret (integrity vs. despair).

While we have hesitations about subscribing to a sequential model, we believe the challenges Erikson identifies are potentially useful to fan scholars. The intimacy versus isolation challenge of early adulthood is implicit in numerous fan studies that examine the emotional authenticity and/or social ("real life") implications of adult fans' attachments to media objects. See the large literature on parasociality in media psychology, for example, or early historical analyses of fandom that assumed fan attachments merely compensated for loneliness or social isolation. Here, the adult fan would "fail" the developmental challenge because emotional intimacy with cultural objects was long perceived by scholars as "fake." In contrast, evidence of successful negotiation of the developmental challenge of midadulthood (generativity vs. stagnation) is evidenced in the various mentoring practices of aging fans. For example, Brooker (2002) notes that adult fan apprenticeship is central to introducing younger persons to the *Star Wars* saga, Harrington and Bielby (1995) articulate the grandparent-to-parent-to-grandchild viewing model traditional in soap fandom, and Bennett (2006) describes how older punk fans adopt the role of 'informed educators' of younger fans, sharing personal history of classic punk performances and positioning themselves "as playing an important part in preserving the punk aesthetic and passing this on to the next generation" (229). Finally, evidence of the developmental conflict associated with late life (integrity vs. despair) can be seen in the contemplative dimension of older adults' positioning of fandom in their life course:

when older punks discussed their continuing attachment and loyalty to the scene, it was clear that they were viewing this attachment *through a specifically altered lens* which facilitated their being among a crowd of people who were in most cases fifteen to twenty years their junior, and in some cases more junior still. (Bennett 2006, 228; emphasis added)

Springsteen fans [use] both their abstract knowledge of the progress of Springsteen's music over time and their concrete memories of listening to the music to *think about and cohere* who they are and who they have been. (Cavicchi 1998, 152; emphasis added)

I was seven when *Star Wars* came out, and so grew up with the trilogy, and it probably saved my life. As a teen, my mother died young and unexpectedly of cancer, and my stepfather was abusive, and being an only child, *Star Wars* was my distraction, my escape, my addiction and my dreams, all wrapped up into one. As an adult, I have continued to be a fan, and it holds both the same appeal for me that it did when I was young, and an *added meaning for all that it represents of the life I escaped* when I immersed myself in that universe. (quoted in Brooker [2002, 11]; emphasis added)

Here, fans' reflection of their fandom across time—and their own aging selves within fandom—results in a gradual repositioning of their place in various fan communities.

In the above discussion we adopted a life course perspective in considering how long-term changes in identity transpire and how those changes might impact fan identity. Below, we explore the age appropriateness of fandom in later life and age-based role modeling within fan communities, suggesting ways that life course scholarship on age norms can enrich our understandings of older fans' identities and practices.

Changing Age Norms

As has been well documented by life course scholars, age norms—the benchmark against which we evaluate ourselves and are evaluated by others to be age appropriate or age inappropriate—change over time. Age norms change for us as individuals (what is age appropriate for me at fifteen is different than at forty-five), they change historically (what is considered age appropriate for a fifteen-year-old today is different than for a fifteen-year-old in 1920 or 1950 or 1990), and their overall impact changes over time (our adherence to age norms is more powerful in some life phases than in others). Within fan studies, age norms faced by individuals have received the most attention, with adult popular music fans perhaps subject to the greatest accountability by both scholars and nonscholars. Until recently, scholars ridiculed older adults' participation in music fandom as age inappropriate at best and "arrested development" at worst (Calcutt 1998, 6). As Laura Vroomen (2004) explains:

> Involvement in music-based subcultures and scenes has often been character- ized as an attempt to delay adult responsibilities, as a way of resisting "social ageing." . . . There is a [scholarly] assumption that intense popular-music investments cannot be carried over into adult life. (2004, 243)

This "pathological" scholarly discourse (to use Bennett's [2006] term) is echoed by adult music fans' everyday experiences of being held accountable for their tastes. Steve Bailey (2005) interviewed fans of the rock band Kiss, many of whom became fans at a very young age (between five and eleven years old) in the 1970s, and who describe struggling with their adult fan identity in light of a musical culture that has long reviled Kiss as well as "a wider culture that tends to hold music beloved by children in extremely low regard" (2005, 109–10). As such, "the world of Kiss fans is marked by a particularly intense set of 'self-esteem' discourses" (Bailey 2005, 105). Simi- larly, most older Kate Bush fans are hesitant to express their fandom in public due to concerns about age norms: "many of the fans who were in their thirties and forties . . . felt a certain ambivalence about their popular music investments and questioned what is 'right and proper' to listen to at a particu- lar age" (Vroomen 2004, 242). One fortyish fan explains her eclectic appreci- ation of both Kate Bush and the Spice Girls as follows:

> I find myself in regular arguments with people (only adults) about the talents of the Spice Girls and the appropriateness of someone my age liking them. I accuse them of being dull and trapped in the adult mentality of sticking with what's safe and known to be OK within the social circle. I think liking the Spice Girls is probably extreme in terms of age difference. (quoted in Vroo- men 2004, 242)

Our own prior work on soap opera fans (Harrington and Bielby 1995) echoes these findings. In our study, many adult soap viewers were adamant about keeping their fandom concealed from coworkers, neighbors, and even family members, due both to age considerations (what is acceptable for adults) and to the genre in question (the low social value of soaps). So while the last two decades have witnessed the general mainstreaming of fandom, as noted earli- er, there continue to be disparities in how fans experience and express their fandom in public—and those disparities are shaped in part by age norms.

Age norms are also relevant within adult fandom in terms of the *role modeling* for later life provided by aging actors, singers, musicians, and fictional characters. Writing about long-term David Bowie fans, Nick Ste- venson (2009) explains that

> Bowie has encoded the possibility of reinventing yourself and handling change over a long career. Bowie for the fans is representative of change and the passing of time. . . . Bowie is valued precisely because he can positively respond to change, and has done so in a way that is seen to be "appropriate" for a man at his stage of life. He offers a model for how to grow old without shutting out new ideas and influences. . . . Bowie is valued as someone who could help you respond to change in your own life. (86)

Interestingly, as long-term fans make sense of aging through the model provided by aging celebrities, those celebrities must negotiate their own aging process in tandem with their construction or embodiment of an aging cultural text (Harrington and Brothers 2010). For example, actress Kassie DePaiva claims that her years playing Blair on the US soap *One Life to Live* (ABC) have accelerated her own physical aging:

> Blair wears me out! I'm not joking. . . . No wonder where these wrinkles came from. It's not my life. It's from putting on her shoes every day because she's sad. There's something really broken in her. (Sloane 2007, 39)

As such, media performances that might provide one kind of age-based role modeling for fans might generate very different age-based outcomes for performers, both positive and negative.

In the above discussion we employed the life course concept of age norms as a way to bring together a number of disparate findings within prior fan studies. In particular, our discussion points to the importance of attention to changes in age norms for understanding the suitability or relevance of fandom in individuals' lives. While age norms clearly operate within fandom, it is less clear how they fluctuate over time and in the context of the changing cultural status of fandom writ broadly, as well as fairly radical changes in the structure of the life course (see conclusion). Below we explore how a life course approach might shed light on the impact of changing *texts* on fandom—just as fans change over time, so do the cultural texts that engage them.

Changing Fan Objects

We are interested here in how a life course perspective might aid our understanding of how *fan objects* themselves change over time, many undergoing "profound transformations during their lifetime" (Sandvoss 2005a, 110). From the first Harry Potter novel to the last, from one James Bond movie to the next, from the many incarnations of Batman and Superman, and across the seventy-two-year run of the US serial *Guiding Light*, fan texts age as fans do—unpredictably. Our own ongoing fascination with US soap operas is based in part on the diachronic relationship between soap narratives and viewers, such that there is a long history of soap storytelling intimately intertwined with a viewer's history of reading soaps: "Soap opera narratives are built around 'historical' characters, in the sense that those characters themselves have both personal histories and memories of a social past—both of which are shared with and relied upon by viewers" (Allen 2004). In many ways, soap fans' experiences are comparable to those of music fans, movie franchise fans, serialized novel fans, celebrity/star fans, and others faithful to a singular fan object over a long period of time. They may be different, however, in that the delivery of the US soap opera narrative (five days per week, fifty-two weeks per year, 130 to 260 hours of original programming per year, no broadcast network repeats, and airing for decades) results in the histories and memories of soap characters, communities, and viewers unfolding in a comparable (daily) temporal framework. As such, soap viewers may be at the far end of a continuum in terms of the complexity of adult development and long-term fandom.

It is a complicated task, however, to assess the interactions between self-unfolding-across-time and fan-object-unfolding-across-time—and we emphasize that even when fan objects do *not* seem to develop over time the way that soap operas do (such as original song lyrics or movie dialogue, or the outcome of sporting events), their meaning is always different because the *fan* has changed. Both Williams (1980) and Kuhn (2002) examine movie fans' memories of favorite films in later life, finding that fans' selective memory of scenes and characters reflects who they were at earlier life stages. Similarly, the *General Hospital* fan quoted at the opening of this manuscript says that as she has changed over time, so has her understanding of specific characters. Cavicchi (1998) explains the changing meanings of specific Springsteen songs across fans' personal life trajectories as follows:

> Fans are consciously engaged with the ways in which Springsteen's music works to shape their experiences and perceptions. . . . [Fans'] study of Springsteen's music and the ways in which they use the music to make sense of the world around them both fit together to form a complex kind of listening: while fans interpret Springsteen's music in terms of their experiences, the music works to influence and shape their experiences. . . . Listening involves creating associations between the music and experience; in fandom, the two become so entangled that it is difficult to locate the music's meaning without talking about fans' personal lives. (109, 110, 134–35)

Drawing on work by Cavicchi and other fan scholars (including his own prior [2003] work on football fans), Sandvoss (2005a) offers a compelling argument for the social psychological basis of fandom, suggesting that fan objects come to form "part of the self, and hence function as its extension" (100) rather than being a mere possession. Fans' narcissistic relationships with cultural objects, in which fans "superimpose attributes of the self, their beliefs and value systems, and, ultimately, their sense of self on the object of fandom" (104), become gradually more complicated as the relationship between self and fan text develops. Over time, then, "the object of fandom . . . becomes a narrative focal point in the construction of life narratives and identities" (111). To make a comparable analysis to that of Harrington and Brothers (2010) in their study of long-term soap opera actors and the aging process, we might say that long-term fans' *existence* is gradually transformed into *texistence*—the self unfolds over time in ongoing dialogue with the media object that helps define and sustain it.[9] As one long-term music fan succinctly put it, "[Now] I think in Springsteen" (Cavicchi 1998, 109). Our observations here point to a rich potential research trajectory for fan scholars focusing on, for example, how texts age from a life course perspective (life course analysis of a media text) and how life course approaches might illuminate the duality of self-aging and text-aging.

In this section of the manuscript we have synthesized a variety of age-related issues discussed in prior fan studies—fandom and life milestones, age norms, changes in the self over time, and changes in fan object over time—suggesting that a life course approach can deepen our understanding of the impact of aging on fandom by offering a more systematic view of the disparate findings on continuity and change in fans, in texts, and in the intersection of the two. We emphasize that each of these issues warrants more in-depth research by fan scholars who explicitly engage with life course theory.

CONCLUSION

Our goal in this manuscript has been to explicate the value of a life course perspective for fan studies. Through a synthesis of life course issues in prior fan studies with particular focus on the age-related structure implicit in fan identities, practices, and interpretive capacities, we have aimed to make explicit the rich developmental issues raised by long-term fandom. Our focus has been on adult and late(r) life fandom, since adult fans remain undertheorized and understudied by media scholars. As we have suggested in our analysis, a key element of the "storying" of media fans' lives is the integration and revisiting/revising of media texts with our own self-constructions over time (Sandvoss 2005b) such that those texts inform our aging process—both *who* we (continue to) become as we grow older and indeed *how* it is that we grow older. Media fans' life narratives might thus be said to comprise complex interactions between our "real" life (our biography), our autobiography (our storying of our life), and the media texts which help construct, give meaning to, and guide the relationship between the two—and that age along with us.

The interplay between these elements may be experienced differently by long-term fans of a singular fan object than by cyclical fans (Hills 2005), and differently based on genre of fan object. Kuhn (2002) was surprised in her interviews with elder cinemagoers that people were unable to recall basic information about much-loved movie characters or plots, but could remember vividly certain aspects of place: where the theater was located, what concessions were sold and how much they cost, where they liked to sit, and so on. In contrast, some music fans report such deep engagement with song lyrics that those lyrics serve as instructional guides for their own approach to life: "fans talked about using Springsteen songs to come to conclusions about the potential circumstances of their lives, to map out where their current life course might take them and whether they wanted to go there" (Cavicchi 1998, 129). One of the most compelling themes that run through research on long-term fans is the extent to which fan objects serve as touchstones or "lifelines" as fans age. Consider the quotation that opened this manuscript from the male soap fan who reports that the fictional setting of CBS' *The Young and the Restless* has been the "most stable home" of his adult life (see also Sandvoss 2008; Schimmel, Harrington, and Bielby 2007). Or the fan who says her favorite Springsteen song "gives meaning to my life. . . . It gives me hope when all of my hope is gone" (Cavicchi 1998, 128). Or the European Song Contest fan who has been watching the show for "as long as [she] can remember" and "can't imagine [her] life without it!" (Sandvoss 2008, 192). Or the Bowie fans whose connection to the singer "acted as a relatively permanent anchor" through their life journeys (Stevenson 2009, 85). From a life course perspective, this emotional anchoring is crucial in an era characterized by the rapid dismantling of normative adult life, as has been observed by human development scholars. Rick Settersten (2007), for example, documents in particular the dissolution of traditional timetables for life transitions, the increasing lack of synchrony among age-related roles, and the growing absence of clear life scripts:

> In the matter of just a few decades . . . the straight and narrow road into and through adulthood has all but disappeared. Roles, responsibilities, and expectations have been shattered, leaving a brand new world to navigate. . . . The social scripts that once signaled a single right time and order for all of life's transitions have dissipated. . . . The whole life course has undergone some dramatic changes. (2007, 250)

We suggest that as normative adult life destabilizes, cultural objects are increasingly providing a reference point for navigating the trajectory through adulthood and later life, and that fan studies scholars should be more attuned to the intersection between the two. The mainstreaming of fandom in the late twentieth and twenty-first centuries as articulated by Gray, Sandvoss, and Harrington (2007) is thus in part a *result* of this radical restructuring of normative adulthood. Just as the "ambiguity of adult life today brings brand new freedom and flexibility to live life in greater accordance with one's interests and wishes than in the past" (Settersten 2007, 244), so have "the particular and conspicuous patterns of fan consumption and the specific forms of social interaction that take place between fans . . . become an ever more integral part of everyday life in modern societies" (Gray, Sandvoss, and Harrington 2007, 9). We agree with Gray and his colleagues that challenges to life in the twenty-first century are increasingly mediated through fannish relations, and suggest that rapid global aging partly *accounts for* and *contributes to* this transformation.

A number of intriguing new research questions emerge when we take a life course perspective on fandom. Fan scholars might study the impact of changes in cognitive capacities on fandom over time, a comparative study of age norms in different fan communities, a longitudinal study of the impact of age-graded life transitions on fan identities and practices, a life course analysis of a specific cultural text, or the ways in which different cultural forms shape the kind of long-term interaction between fans and cultural objects. Our analysis might also prove useful to scholars of human development who have only recently begun exploring the impact of *fictional* narratives on relationship networks over time (Harrington and Brothers 2010). We have argued elsewhere (Schimmel, Harrington, and Bielby 2007) that fan studies would benefit from greater engagement with scholarship produced in other areas of the academy, and certainly current literature in gerontology, human development, and the sociology and psychology of aging is crucial to our full understanding of adult and later life fandom. Dramatic social trends unfolding relationally—the aging of the global population and global media audiences, the dissolution of normative adulthood, and the profound changes in the public recognition and evaluation of fandom over the past twenty years—render a life course perspective on fandom both timely and important.

NOTES

This chapter is reprinted from the *International Journal of Cultural Studies* (2010, Volume 13, Number 5) Courtesy of Sage Publications Ltd.

The quotations for this chapter were collected as part of a separate project on long-term soap opera actors and viewers. For project details see Harrington and Brothers (2010; 2011).

1. Psychologists tend to use a terminology of "life span" whereas sociologists refer to the "life course." Life span refers to the entire span of an individual's life (e.g., human development models). Life course refers to the age-structured sequence of roles, opportunities, and experiences that an individual moves in and out of, and that are influenced by macrostructural forces as well as human agency. Both psychologists and sociologists are interested in understanding the processes through which lives transform over time.

2. From the *Wall Street Journal* online ("A Veteran TV Soap Opera Executive on Why 'Guiding Light' Burned Out After Seventy-Two Years," WSJ Staff, August 14, 2008, www. blogs.wsj.com, no author).

3. While absent in fan studies proper, developmental perspectives have been utilized elsewhere in media studies. For example, see Young's (2000) analysis of the importance of film in everyday life.

4. This research team is located in the areas of neurology, memory and aging, neurogeriatrics, nutrition, epidemiology, and biostatistics.

5. The authors are located in the fields of economics and mental health.

6. The authors work in the fields of sociology, psychology, social medicine, and econometrics.

7. However, we find it interesting that the broad category of "social" includes cinema, theater, and music, which implies that these are fundamentally different types of activities (i.e., *not* media activities) and that television is by definition nonsocial.

8. Erikson's theory is not uncontroversial, in part because it posits a sequential, hierarchical model of human maturation with successful negotiation of each stage calling on skills acquired in prior stages.

9. The term *texistence* is borrowed from Randall and McKim (2004) with slightly altered meaning (Harrington and Brothers 2011).

Chapter Eleven

Breaking Dusk

Fandom, Gender/Age Intersectionality, and the "Twilight Moms"

Christine Scodari

Aging, ultimately, is the greatest evil in the *Twilight* world.

—Monica Dufault (2011)

If these were forty-year-old men screaming for seventeen-year-old girls, someone would call the police.

—Slogan from a viral anti-*Twilight* Moms poster

Informed by media/cultural, fan, aging, and gender studies, this chapter investigates "*Twilight* Moms," the adult female fans of the *Twilight* series of YA (Young Adult) novels authored by Stephenie Meyer (2005, 2006, 2007, 2008a) and their film versions, through qualitative, empirical analysis of interactions on their foundational fan site, TwilightMOMS.com, and other Internet content.[1] For those who may yet be unfamiliar with *Twilight*, it centers on Bella Swan, an awkward high-schooler who moves in with her father, a lawman in Forks, Washington, while her mother travels with her baseball-playing husband. There she falls for classmate Edward Cullen, who confesses that he and everyone in his deceptively youthful but genetically unrelated "family" are vampires sworn to resist human bloodlust. Where Bella is concerned, Edward's struggle with this temptation becomes a metaphor for the couple's mutual virginity and sexual abstinence until such time as they marry in the controversial final installment, *Breaking Dawn* (Meyer 2008a).

This analysis interrogates fan practices at the gender/age intersection, primarily regarding the Edward/Bella relationship and *Breaking Dawn* (Meyer 2008a), which was adapted for the big screen in Bill Condon's *The Twilight Saga—Breaking Dawn, Part 1* (2011) and *Part 2* (2012). It considers whether "*Twi*Moms" idolize *Twilight's* young male characters and/or their portrayers as implied by the slogan in the epigraph, and whether their readings and investments reflect traditional gender roles, the gender/age double standard, and/or a hypercritical posture toward female personae. It questions whether nostalgic reminiscence motivates their fandom, thereby mobilizing a hegemonic stereotype of aging women. Ultimately, it establishes whether these fans confront and/or reproduce a gendered and aged politics of fantasy in which unequal access to emancipatory representations and empowered identities prevails.

GENDER, AGE, AND MEDIA CULTURES

Theories of intersectionality were cultivated by feminists of color such as Patricia Hill Collins (2000) and Kimberlé Crenshaw (1993). Argues Hill Collins: "Intersectionality refers to particular forms of intersecting oppressions, for example intersections of race and gender, or of sexuality and nation," which "work together in producing injustice" (2000, 21). Similarly, in discussing rappers 2 Live Crew and their 1990 obscenity case involving sexist lyrics, Crenshaw (1993) notes that commentators who defended the rappers on the basis of African American culture neglected the pivotal intertwining of race with gender.

Age and gender coalesce to generate inequity, forming a cultural double standard that constructs midlife women as "over the hill" and men of similar vintage as "in their prime." In media, this produces greater visibility for male characters and/or performers in midlife (and beyond) than for their female counterparts. The double standard extends to the fashioning of romantic duos, as creators are less likely to depict a woman ten years older than her casual lover than to seriously pair a fifty-year-old male protagonist with a female character twenty years younger. The poster slogan in the epigraph, which invites comparison between *Twi*Moms' idolization of the films' young male actors and forty-year-old men lusting after teen ingénues, appears apt. Robert Pattinson, who portrays Edward in the movies, the object of most such adulation, was twenty to twenty-four years old during the course of filming. Increase the younger age by a few years, however, and an *actual* older man/younger woman coupling would be culturally acceptable while the reverse would still be disparaged. In her book on aging women, *In Full Flower*, historian Lois Banner (1993) writes:

The term "gigolo" . . . refers to a younger man who services an older woman sexually for pay. There is no similar term for a young woman prostitute with an aging man. The disparity in terminology indicates . . . that the young woman/older man relationship is so usual that it does not require semantic notice. (12–13)

A term signifying a predator, "cougar," is now used for an older woman involved with a younger man, despite the mainstreaming of such romances between celebrities. However, there is no equivalent, or any label at all, deemed necessary to reference an older man in the reverse case.

Banner (1993), those contributing to Kathleen Woodard's collection, *Figuring Age* (1999), and other scholars consult texts of media, literature, history, sociology, and celebrity icons in situating aging women and the status of gender and aging inquiry. Banner (1993) dissects Billy Wilder's 1950 film, *Sunset Boulevard*, depicting the descent of an aging Hollywood "actress." Wearing (2007) considers Nancy Meyers's 2003 film *Something's Gotta Give* and makeover reality series in her appraisal of older women in postfeminist culture.

However, recent qualitative studies pinpointing the age/gender nexus in analyses of popular media *users* are few. Riggs's 1998 volume, *Mature Audiences,* assesses television's older viewers, highlighting seniors. She connects gender and age in a chapter about senior women's ritual viewing of *Murder She Wrote* (CBS 1984–1996), declaring it a repository of "conservatively portrayed comfortable social messages" that arouse devotion from such elders (54). Harrington and Bielby, in the previous chapter, do not highlight gender in assessing works on fandom and aging throughout the life span. Harrington and Brothers (2011) employ interviews of experts and veteran actors and surveys of longtime viewers of the women's genre of soap opera without problematizing the gender/age juncture. Bennett's (2006) study of older punk fans demonstrates that they engage in cultural practices that validate their place in the otherwise youthful punk scene (219). He acknowledges the critique that studies of cultural practices often generalize to an entire class and/or age group based only on male subjects. Yet, his subjects are male—a specificity not indicated by the generalizing "older generation of fans" reference in his title.

Other contributions emerge from the interdisciplinary field of aging studies. Emma Domínguez-Rué (2012) recognizes the significance of the gender/age intersection:

In the same way that many aspects of gender cannot be understood aside from their relationship to race, class, culture, nationality and/or sexuality, the interactions between gender and aging constitute an interesting field for academic research, without which we cannot gain full insight into the complex and multi-faceted nature of gender studies. (428)

In reviewing the gender- and age-related scholarship of Carolyn Gold Heilbrun (1926–2003) in conjunction with facets of her mystery novels written under the pseudonym Amanda Cross, Dominguez-Rué argues that the series was able to reach a larger audience of readers "who might not have read her nonfiction, but who were perhaps finding it difficult to reach fulfillment as women under patriarchy, especially upon reaching middle age" (428). She does not, however, empirically examine such readers. In a gerontological offering by Richards, Warren, and Gott (2012), images of aging women created by older female subjects are scrutinized. While their images challenged the "'heroes of ageing'/'bodily decline' binary," they reproduced cultural stereotypes of such women as linked to melancholy, nostalgia, and the carnivalesque (65).

My virtual ethnographies of Nancy Meyers's 2003 film *Something's Gotta Give* (Scodari and Mulvaney 2005) and soap opera (Scodari 2004) address the neglected panoply of issues. The former explores Internet responses to this film starring Diane Keaton, Jack Nicholson, and Keanu Reeves. Meyers is known for bucking hegemony in featuring middle-aged women as romantic heroines. The essay inspects gender- and age-related online commentary in terms of the acceptability of older heroines in general and, specifically, of Meyers's choice to have Keaton's character prefer the derisive, aging Lothario played by Nicholson to a fervent younger suitor portrayed by Reeves. The second study (Scodari 2004) assesses portrayals of older women in daytime dramas, cyberfan commentary, and creator choices, highlighting a case study of an older woman/younger man romance on the soap opera *Another World* (NBC 1964–1999). It argues that the myth that older women should only relate nostalgically to popular media denies them currency—a sense of present and future possibilities.

GENDER, AGE, AND *TWILIGHT*

Academic essays and Internet blogs negotiate issues around gender and/or age in the *Twilight* series and allow us to determine, in general, the relevant points of contention before exploring the engagements of *Twi*Moms. One overarching question is whether the extended narrative can be considered feminist. Most scholars respond in the negative. Platt (2010) gauges the sexual politics of the saga as "decidedly conservative" (80), Hawes (2010) notes that the novels "depict gender roles that reflect the rigid social mores of a few centuries ago" (174), and Groper (2011) dissects the series' postfeminism. Nicol (2011) compares *Twilight's* Bella to Buffy of *Buffy the Vampire Slayer* (WB 1997–2001; UPN 2001–2003) and concludes that both stories offer a "masterplot of romantic love . . . providing young women a socially sanctioned space in which to explore their sexual desires," even as this space is "illusory" (3384–90). Dietz (2011), a Mormon herself, identifies author Meyer's Mormonism as a source of the series' patriarchal conservatism—a conclusion echoed by both Toscano (2010) and Schwartzman (2010)—especially insofar as the saga valorizes abstinence outside of marriage, marriage, and family. Others unpack patriarchal constructions of heteronormativity (Donnelly 2011; Kane 2010) and Edward's masculinity (Miller 2011).

Exchanges on blogs and online news sites exhibit more variance. On her website, Meyer (2008b) defends *Breaking Dawn* (2008a), in which Bella's first momentous choice is to marry Edward while still a teen, and her second is to risk death rather than end her unexpected, unstable hybrid pregnancy: "In my own *opinion* (key word), the foundation of feminism is this: being able to choose." Similarly, screenwriter Melissa Rosenberg states in an interview: "We are fighting for choice and she makes choices. She makes choices that I wouldn't have made. . . . My objective has always been to make Bella a very strong character. . . . But people see what they want to see" (Cornet 2011). Her interviewer concurs, questioning the "lens with which we all choose to view feminism": "Is a woman strong and capable if she chooses to forgo a family in favor of her work, and weak if she chooses the opposite?" (Cornet 2011). In an online rejoinder to Meyer's (2008b) pronouncement of "choice" as the feminist ideal, *The Guardian*'s David Cox (2010), echoing other critics, writes: "This seems to imply that anything a woman does is a feminist act, unless she's performing it because someone's put a gun to her head. I don't know if this is all that feminism amounts to, but then I'm only a man."

Other views, some from an ostensibly feminist standpoint, emerge. In reply to a blog entry interrogating Bella's choice to endure her pregnancy, a poster wonders:

> Does anyone else suspect . . . that the *Twilight* series is secretly a feminist work, by showing what a bad idea it is to get married young, how abusive relationships are harmful, and by making pregnancy and childbirth look even more unpleasant than they really are? (Newitz 2011)

Protesting contrasts between Bella and Katniss Everdeen, the bow and arrow wielding heroine of *Hunger Games* (2008), the first of three novels in Suzanne Collins's dystopian, YA series of the same designation, Berlatsky (2011) asserts that Bella's femininity equals strength:

> She turns into a vampire who has the physical and magical wherewithal to save her entire family from death. . . . Katniss, conversely, finds that what she desired all along was domestic bliss with her nice-guy suitor and a bunch of kids running around the cottage.

Rosenberg (2011) takes exception to Berlatsky's (2011) lecture on the definition and virtues of femininity, and elicits the following retort challenging the feminist critique of *Twilight*:

> It's a critique that zeroes in on Bella. Bella isn't the right sort of girl; she doesn't make the right sort of choices; she's bad for girls. Not EDWARD is bad as a romantic lead, or even that Stephenie Meyer's worldview is limited. (Rosenberg 2011)

This is vital to consider, as many of my fan studies observe women who view male personae/characters as fantasy objects to be hypercritical of any female persona/character who was, is, or could be paired with their idol (Scodari 2003, 2004, 2007, 2008, 2012; Scodari and Felder 2000). *Twilight* is twice as ripe for this, since Kristen Stewart, who portrays Bella, has also been romantically linked with Robert Pattinson offscreen.

Scholarship addresses age representation in the *Twilight* saga more than blogs and news sites. Dufault (2011), quoted in the epigraph, focuses on Bella's predicament regarding age and on the fact that the ultimate villains in the saga are the murderous, ancient vampires called the "Volturi." She invokes a scene from the first chapter of the second book, *New Moon* (Meyer 2006), in which Bella describes a dream about her late grandmother, but soon realizes that she has conjured up an image of her older self out of fear of losing Edward once she ages.

Benning (2011) takes a different tack, seeking to account for age diversity among fans. She focuses on the "coming of age of Bella and her ever-present fear of age and death" (1232–33). She, too, dissects Bella's dream, but suggests that it also emerges from a generalized anxiety about aging. She observes that only Bella's grandmother has undergone a lifetime of biological aging and that the cultural obsession with and commercialization of youth are implicated in these representations. She recognizes that "mental" maturity exists among the Volturi, the ancient but physically youthful vampire villains of *Twilight*, who draw upon "centuries of experience" in wielding their power (1311–12).

Dufault (2011) and Benning (2011) allude to Bella's unease about remaining attractive to Edward, but fail to grasp that age cannot be fully unpacked without inspecting the gender/age intersection at play in the saga. While Edward professes his undying (or undead?) love for Bella whatever their biological differences portend, and fans take this as a measure of his devotion, their desire to follow the romance forward to such an outcome is debatable. Also, would this issue be as problematic if the genders were reversed? In what follows, the views of *Twilight* Moms are explored with the gender/age intersection in mind.

*TWI*MOMS WEIGH IN

*Twi*Moms are subjects in both Leogrande's (2010) quantitative survey of mother and daughter *Twilight* fans and the quantitative survey and focus group analysis of Behm-Morawitz, Click, and Aubrey (2010), which assesses, compares, and contrasts the gender-related attitudes of younger and older *Twilight* fans. Leogrande (2010) chronicles that "older" devotee Lisa Hanson formed TwilightMOMs.com out of a small group on MySpace, and that it mushroomed to 25,000 members by 2009.[2] Her research reveals *Twi*Moms' belief that "the books helped forge or deepen their connections with their teenage daughters" (158–59), allowing entry points through which they might discuss sensitive issues such as sex. Behm-Morawitz, Click, and Aubrey's (2010) investigation demonstrates that adult fans identifying as feminist were less immersed in the series and more disappointed with *Twilight's* "old-fashioned" themes than their younger and/or nonfeminist counterparts. Feminist teens and adults were less likely to choose Edward and Bella as their favorite couple, and adults who preferred this romance were more dissatisfied with their own relationships. The authors assert that desiring fantasy escape from real life via Bella and Edward is a possible explanation.

On the TwilightMOMS.com forums, gender- and/or age-related issues are deliberated in many discussion threads, including those in the "Edward" and "Bella" forums, and in those forums, and topics within forums, specifically devoted to *Breaking Dawn (BD)* (Meyer 2008a). The upcoming fan remarks appeared between 2008 and 2012.

In addition to Bella marrying and persisting with her life-threatening pregnancy, another *BD* issue was Edward's choice to transform Bella into a vampire while she was delirious and near death on account of her pregnancy, hoping that the vampire's regenerative powers would save her. It worked, but some *Twi*Moms felt that her metamorphosis altered the dynamic of the relationship. Several saw the change as positive: "I loved the new Bella as a vampire. She is stronger, more sure of herself and beautiful. . . . Finally their life together had come into complete balance." More invoked the realities of aging, expressing that *BD* showed that relationships grow over time: "First love is overwhelming, intense, etc. As relationships mature and life continues we become involved in families, life. . . . It doesn't mean you love any less, I think you love more as a relationship matures." Age was more pivotal in this sentiment: "A story has to keep moving forward and the characters need to grow. At fifty-four, I can look back over my life and see what changes have taken place, and, for me, I am much more comfortable with myself now. . . . To have those vampire abilities would be incredible! Not to mention that antiaging thing; now THERE's a perk!!"

However, other statements coalesced around the view that Bella becoming a vampire, or how it occurred, undermined romantic tension. One poster wrote: "It's not the same teenagers in love, sneaking around, [excitement] and angsty love. Which is kinda sad—that's the best kind to swoon over!" Another lamented: "I would have been happier if that love had extended to the unborn child; instead it nearly drove them apart. . . . I was almost mad at Bella being so callous about how much she was hurting Edward by putting her life in danger."

The preceding post lends credence to the blog respondent's concern (Rosenberg 2011) that the critique of *Twilight* focused suspiciously on Bella's deficiencies. On TwilightMOMS.com, this occurred in deference to Edward. Some preferred Bella to remain vulnerable: "I liked her better as human Bella. I liked how she seemed fragile and it really made the books funny to me how Edward was always trying not to 'break' her." A like-minded fan added: "The element of danger had vanished. I felt that after she became a vampire. . . . The need for Edward to protect Bella was over." It is telling that as of January 2013 the "Bella" forum contained 6,522 posts while the "Edward" forum had more than double that number. Criticisms of Edward were met with terse, telling pushback. When a poster admitted that she wanted to slap Edward when he stridently declared "she's mine!" regarding Bella, one respondent wondered: "Why? Just curious, what is wrong with belonging to someone?" A second confessed that it was a "major turn on" for her, while a third followed suit: "I don't know why but I loved it when he said that. . . . I would have taken him right there, it was HOT!!!!"

In a number of threads, fans found validation in Bella and Edward's romance for their own, mostly traditional life choices. In response to a query asking whether "happily ever after" is real, a discussant wrote:

> I've found it in my life. But it's messy and imperfect, just like I'm sure Bella and Edward's "happily ever after" will be. . . . That is what my marriage is all about . . . unwavering commitment to my husband, even if I don't feel like it that day.

After stating that her own relationship was shaky, a second *Twi*Mom insisted: "I have seen couples who have made it last forever. Couples who age together and who die in their old age virtually at the same time. They just cannot go on without each other." Still another remarked, referring to the third in the *Twilight* triangle, the werewolf Jacob Black, whose love for Bella helped spawn the "Team Edward" vs. "Team Jacob" rivalry among fans:

> The first three books have mirrored my life with eerie accuracy. . . . I never really dated for fun. To me, the point was to find my HEA [happily ever after]. . . . I found my DH [dear husband] at fifteen, married at seventeen. I had a Jacob, wishing I could have some brotherly claim on him so I could love him without complication.

Such comments buttress Behm-Morawitz, Click, and Aubrey's (2010) claim that older fans crave fantasy escape from real life via Bella and Edward. On the one hand, the saga seems to rubber stamp conservative choices for women. On the other, it allows older fans, a number of whom indicated that they married quite young, to replay, in compensatory fashion, the excitement they once experienced within the traditional paradigm.

Age and gender fused in commentary as *Twi*Moms debated whether *BD* is appreciated differently by younger vs. older fans. One said she understood why teens couldn't relate: "Most [don't] even think about motherhood yet. Being pregnant I think is what really made me love this book. I felt in touch with [Bella] and her feelings of motherhood and marriage." Another post, however, recognized an age division regarding the book while disagreeing with other *Twi*Moms:

> Actually there was a pretty nasty thread on one of the young sites . . . on how this book was written by SM [Stephenie Meyer] to please us, the TMs [*Twi*Moms]. And it got pretty well [received]. Well I am a TM and was less than thrilled Bella was getting married/having children/changing at eighteen.

Some found the notion that Meyer targeted *BD* to older fans commonsensical: "We can better relate to Bella's feelings and her transformation to a woman and mother. In fact, I think adults relate these books and experience these books in an entirely different way than YAs do." A final insight bolstered the theory that nostalgic reminiscence motivates *Twi*Moms' love of the series:

> I've been married eighteen years, [I'm] thirty-seven with three kids and these books have really helped me remember my first love and the feelings I had when I first met my hubby. . . . I think these books really help us remember not to forget the romance in our lives.

Neither Benning (2011) nor Dufault (2011) problematize Bella and Edward's emotional, experiential, and intellectual age incompatibility. Edward's physical vs. emotional/experiential age was negotiated by *Twi*Moms in a thread addressing the query, "Do Vampires Mentally and Emotionally Age?" One discussant offered the following after witnessing many exchanges in which the youthfulness of *Twilight's* vampires was assumed: "Although their bodies are frozen at a certain point in time, their life experience should demonstrate an 'age' far beyond what their external appearance reflects. Don't we learn things and mature simply by an accumulation of life experiences?" Some discussants were keen to justify their investment in teen Edward:

> When you are of a species where personal and emotional changes are so absolute and infrequent (like falling in love), I don't think there's the same

kind of emotional growth that we have. Edward for instance. Unlike some people, I totally see him as a long time seventeen-year-old boy.

In similar vein, a poster quoted Meyer writing Edward's dialogue from *Eclipse* (2007):

> You think of me as a . . . living stone—hard and cold. That's true. We are set the way we are, and it is very rare to experience a real change. When that happens, as when Bella entered my life, it is a permanent change. (Twilight-MOMS.com)

Meyer avoids complicating Edward's age identity, while Anne Rice's vampire series, *The Vampire Chronicles* (1976–2003), creates great drama out of the age paradox. Her vampire character Claudia, who appears most pertinently in the first novel, *Interview with the Vampire* (Rice 1976), turns as a prepubescent girl but otherwise matures, only to agonize over her inability to experience relationships as an embodied adult. *Twilight*'s YA designation and the desire for readers to idealize its featured romance precludes, perhaps, making literary hay out of such a predicament.

This quandary was also deliberated in a thread entitled, "The 100 Year Old Virgin":

> [Isn't] it just a bit creepy when you think about it for Edward who is close to one hundred years old to be smitten with a seventeen-year-old? I know he looks the part of someone much younger but still has the life experience of his age.

A tongue-in-cheek reply assuming a gender/age double standard followed:

> I don't think it's too creepy [because] he's seventeen in a lot of ways. BUT I think you are onto something—like Stephenie Meyer should rework the story and target senior citizens the next time around by having Edward fall in love [with] an eighty-year-old grandma.

One poster praised Edward for loving Bella "despite" her youth, while another nodded to the double standard and hinted that *Twi*Moms would rather not envision Edward with Bella in her declining years: "I'd rather not imagine my lovely Edward considering 'older' women. . . . Though I guess he was willing to stay with Bella until she looked old, but that's gradual and not so ummm obvious in the beginning." Some cheeky responses evoked the double standard in claiming Edward as a fantasy object: "Edward is MUCH too old for Bella. He should be with someone more mature . . . like me"; "Okay, don't tell anyone, but I am a grandmom of four, and I still am quite able to appreciate the beauty of a young man"; "You go girl! I too, while not a grandma, am on the older end of the TMs spectrum. Looking at fine young men is what keeps us young [winking]"; and "Edward is 'My brand of Ensure.'"

CONCLUSION

*Twi*Moms' devotion to Edward suggests that they regard him and, perhaps, the persona of Robert Pattinson, as fantasy objects. This indicates what Stuart Hall (1980) termed a preferred reading—in this case, one consistent with patriarchal norms—even if *Twi*Moms are not preferred, YA readers. However, the key word is "fantasy." While middle-aged men might not ogle twenty-year-old starlets based on their fictional roles, it could be because this brand of fandom isn't their thing. Certainly, they otherwise direct their gaze at young women, and without the police being called.

The politics of fantasy is simply this: Under the right conditions, it is empowering. In my dissection of fan reactions to the older woman/younger man soap opera romance (Scodari 2004), I argue that whether such a relationship could, or should, be sustainable in reality is beside the point. Instead, we might ask if empowering, otherwise innocuous cultural fantasies are as accessible to aging women as they are to aging men. Their function—in this case, whether they offer coping strategies respective to age/gender hegemony—is more crucial. While diversity exists among *Twi*Moms, the study reveals a nucleus of fans representing and advocating traditional gender norms that lionizes the Bella/Edward coupling. This punctuates Behm-Morawitz, Click, and Aubrey's (2010) claim that older women use *Twilight*, and chiefly its central romance, as fantasy escape from routine existence. Here, the commentary of *Twi*Moms reconnecting with young love and/or new motherhood via this narrative renders nostalgic reminiscence a key enticement.

Gerontological researchers assert the advantages of embracing the present rather than the past. Markus Schafer and Tetyana Shippee (2010) find that aging women who *feel* old experience diminution of vigor and Becca Levy (2009) argues that seniors' internalization of "stereotyped embodiment" has comparable effects. In *Counterclockwise*, Ellen Langer (2009) demonstrates that elders who focus on new possibilities live longer. As posited elsewhere (Richards, Warren, and Gott 2012; Scodari 2004), nostalgia represents a preferred, hegemonic reading, disaffirms currency, and fossilizes readers in the stone of recollected youth. It is no surprise, then, that *Twi*Moms lionize *Twilight's* similarly frozen vampires. Even Edward and Bella's daughter, the hybrid Renesmee, undergoes accelerated aging for seven years, at which point her body remains seventeen. Additionally, the shape-shifting of Jacob, who "imprints" on Renesmee as his future mate, preserves his youthful physicality.

Also evident are the gender/age double standard and fans' hypercriticism of female characters linked to male fantasy objects. This core of *Twi*Moms regarded Edward's possessive attitude positively and would surely reproach Bella, as they did a couple of fans, if she questioned it. Bella's baby dilemma was also viewed primarily from Edward's perspective. Moreover, the only older woman/younger man liaison sanctioned by these fans is one in which Edward serves as their (tongue-in-cheek) fantasy object. However, Edward's readiness to squire human Bella into her dotage only speaks to his admirable character, not to *Twi*Moms hoping to witness such an endgame or valuing the experience and wisdom that comes with age. These stances also reflect a preferred, patriarchal reading.

Fan sentiments reveal that traditional mores still lead some to secure their "HEA" before fully exploring their talents and identities, spurring them to seek fantasy escape from and validation for their choices as dusk breaks in their lives. Whether they might contest this in other formats is a question for future investigators. However, this study reasserts the need for cultural equipment for living that offers aging women a sense of currency, and nudges them beyond nostalgic reminiscence to cultivate a sense of present and future possibility that could also enhance their longevity.

NOTES

1. TwilightMOMS.com data were identified by scanning forum topics for pertinent issues. Using the resulting key terms, TwilightMOMS.com (website dismantled) forums, blogs, and news sites were then searched via Google.com. So as to cushion the privacy of forum posters and blog/news site respondents, their names and posting dates are not cited. News site articles and blogger entries are, however, cited in full.

2. While it is unknown whether she ever frequented TwilightMoms.com, perhaps the best known *Twi*Mom is E. L. James, author of the erotic bestseller *Fifty Shades of Grey* (2011), who developed the idea out of *Twlight* fan fiction she authored (Keegan and Sperling 2012).

VI

Gender and Sexuality

Chapter Twelve

"Let's Do It Like Grown-Ups"

A Filmic Mènage *of Age, Gender, and Sexuality*

Leni Marshall and Aagje Swinnen

In the humanities, gender studies is the foundation of much of age studies scholarship, so analyses of age, gender, and sexuality evolved intersectionally from their conception. To make age studies concepts accessible and to demonstrate their applicability, frequently, scholars use media representations' myriad examples of ageist stereotypes and exemplars of resistance to ageism.

Critics including Wearing (2007, 2012) and Woodward (1999, 2006) consider the fraught visibility/invisibility of the aged female body in media, calling for attention to its important but infrequent presence. The twenty-first century has brought a proliferation of movies about older people, especially romances targeted at women of a certain age. Many of these films challenge historical narratives of older women's sexual agency as "deviance," giving a "liberatory nod and affirmation," particularly for white, middle-class, single women (Tally 2006, 51; see also Dolan and Tincknell 2012; Hant 2007; Holmlund 2002; King 2010; Krainitzki 2011; and Wearing 2007, 2012). Most age studies analyses of film focus on productions that continue the careers of well-known stars. Internationally, somewhat less-mainstream recent movies, with lesser-known female actors, seem more accepting in their depictions of time-ripened, sexually active, female bodies, offering new, potentially disruptive representations.

Many age studies analyses employ some media studies concepts, but few researchers engage with detailed, specific tools within media studies to create a deeper understanding of films as reflections and vehicles of cultural age ideologies. In employing such an approach, this chapter expands on the work of scholars such as Kaplan (2010), Chivers (2011), Cohen-Shalev (2012),

Wearing (2007, 2012), and Wohlmann (2014). Understandings of filmic representations of cultural ideas about the intersections of age, gender, and sexuality entail considering how movies portray elder women as subjects that can advance or refuse participation in scripts of love and sexuality. Incorporating a broad range of film narratology tools, including considerations of the narrative impact of mise-en-scène, cinematography, sound, and editing choices, enriches explorations of age ideology in film.

This chapter explores contemporary filmic portrayals of visibly aged women's bodies, the connection between sexual activity and rejuvenation, expressions of sexual agency, and narrative revisions and restrictions. Three twenty-first-century films serve as the foundation for these observations: the British *The Mother* (Michell 2003), the German *Wolke 9* (Dresen 2008), and the Belgian/Australian *Innocence* (Cox 2000). Each film features an older woman in a heterosexual marriage who then begins a new sexual relationship, disrupting her apparent narrative stagnation and emphasizing the transformative possibilities of new sexual engagements; the similar plots invite a comparative approach. In *The Mother*, May (Anne Reid, at 68) is widowed and has an affair with Darren, her daughter's lover, who is half her age, which results in May's eviction from the family. In *Wolke 9*, Inge (Ursula Werner, at 65) has an affair with a widower, Karl; when she leaves Werner, her husband of thirty years, for Karl, Werner commits suicide. In *Innocence*, the widowed Andreas and the still-married Claire (Julia Blake, at 64) rekindle an old love, a situation resolved by her death.

In each movie, the main character is a woman visually coded as "old"—as a grandmother rather than a mother. Reviewers have praised these films for their courage in presenting such subject matter (e.g., Haynes 2001), but narratives of women's self-discovery through sexual exploration is not a new genre. These films' innovations lie in the protagonists' ages, the visibility of chronologically gifted bodies, the coding of such bodies as sexual, and the aged characters' attempts to rescript traditional cultural narratives. Thus, these movies are useful means of exploring the current boundaries of social acceptance for old women's bodies and agency.

"WILL YOU TOUCH ME?"
SEXUAL AGENCY OF OLDER WOMEN

Discussions of cultural production of women's sexuality should explore ways in which society creates and displays sexual agency. In traditional narratives, usually "the old woman" holds one of two roles: a metaphorical emblem of the past (Beugnet 2006), or a helper or opponent to the protagonist (Bazzini et al. 1997; Lauzen and Dozier 2005b), and their agency furthers the narrative of central, usually younger, characters. Through the aged protagonists' agency, expressed in actions, gaze, and voice, *Wolke 9, The Mother*, and *Innocence* display a level of sexual engagement that even many younger filmic counterparts would not have held in movies fifty years ago. [1]

Actions

Often, media portrayals of aged female sexual agents figure them as predatory "cougars" or as comedic figures (e.g., *Golden Girls*; Bildgårdt 2000), reinforcing their social exclusion and restricting older women's ability to act even as objects of desire. Our films can help people who are inexperienced at living into old age appreciate older women's experiences of sexual desire (Swinnen 2010).

The sexual agency of the protagonists in these three films counters stereotypes of chronologically endowed women as sexually uninterested and uninteresting. Two of the protagonists initiate sexual contact: in *The Mother,* this happens when May kisses Darren, and in *Wolke 9*, Inge seduces Karl as she is fitting his altered pants for him. In all three movies, the initial sexual activities are followed by a demonstration of control over the liaison, a rejection. May shies away from Darren's kiss, Inge sends Karl away, and Claire writes to Andreas that they should not meet again. Scenes of the women's masturbation presage their next encounter with the men: Inge in the tub and Claire on the sofa. The women deepen the relationships: May invites Darren into the spare room and asks him to touch her; Inge goes to spend the day with Karl and necks with him; Claire agrees to see Andreas and has sex with him. Their new lovers respond positively to these sexual and emotional desires.

The Gaze

Kathleen Woodward (2006) developed a concept similar to "the male gaze" (Mulvey 1975; 1992), but focused on age difference, theorizing that "the youthful structure of the look" constructs the subject of the erotic gaze as young as well as female. Our films disrupt both configurations. For example, May objectifies Darren, encouraging viewers' enjoyment of his topless virility. Her sketches reflect and deepen the objectification. In *Wolke 9*'s opening sequence, the camera follows Inge's gaze, viewers enjoy her sexual interest; once Karl mirrors her pleasured gaze, the audience is engaged in a three-way experience of sexual desire. In film, the multiple perspectives demonstrate a variety of agencies and visual representations of chronologically endowed bodies' desirability, offering viewers alternatives to the male-gendered and youth-aged gaze.

Voice

In our movies, as in most filmic narratives, women rarely articulate sexual desires. For example, speaking to Andreas about sex, Claire highlights chronology rather than desire: "If we are going to do this, let's do it like grownups." The exception, May, uses explicit, although not particularly erotic, language: "Will you touch me?" May partially negates this agency, calling her body undesirable, a "lump" close to death. Such verbalizations express the tension between the women's newfound voices and traditional social scripts.

Utterances of pleasure during intercourse are another significant form of protagonists' vocalizations. As detailed below, in sex scenes, filmic devices such as filters, lighting, and interior design veil the aged bodies. That separation is in tension with the connections the narratives create between viewers and the older women's pleasures. Auditory expressionism reengages the audience; the volume increases during sex scenes, foregrounding protagonists' orgiastic noises. This audioeroticism contrasts with traditional postcode Hollywood soundtracks, which "had little interest in the specificity of female pleasure" (Williams 2008, 170). The soundtracks reinforce the women's sexual agency even while (re)producing women's pleasure as an erotic element for auditory consumption.

A VEILED CONUNDRUM:
THE VISIBILITY OF OLDER FEMALE SEXUAL BODIES

Advanced age creates a unique cultural location in many societies. Unless they die first, all individuals advance into this category of Otherness, yet ageism is prevalent, with media medicalizing visible elderhood as unattractive, even aberrant (e.g., Marshall and Katz 2012). The desire for youth is "naturalized," paradoxically feeding a multibillion-dollar antiaging industry (Chambers 2012; Clarke 2010; Gullette 2004; Katz and Marshall 2003). Even people with chronologically enriched physiques are other aged. Other aged bodies, riddling social visibility and agency with complexity.[2] The "double standard of aging," through which visible age Others women at younger ages than it does men (Sontag 1972), creates additional complications. Our movies reflect these complexities, advancing the visibility and agency of older women while simultaneously demarcating the limits of acceptability, unveiling and then reveiling time's inscription on sexual female bodies.

One way in which movies accomplish this is by manipulating viewers' sense of relative distance to the women's bodies before showing sexual encounters. For example, in *Wolke 9*'s opening scenes, the camera alternates between medium shots, close-ups, and extreme close-ups of Inge's body and face, leading viewers to appreciate her visible ageness as ordinary and acceptable. The camera's distance from Inge's sexually active body is then a relatively large separation. *Innocence* accomplishes this dual purpose with editing that creates and disrupts narrative connections viewers experience as they see the older and younger versions of the two main characters. In the tension between temporal continuity and discontinuity, the greater visibility of the young lovers' bodies (e.g., Claire's breasts) and relative invisibility of their older bodies induce viewers to understand both the connections and the distance between past and present (Holmlund 2002, 87), coercing viewers into appreciating older bodies' desirability. In these ways, the filmic techniques teach the viewers about acceptable levels of visibility for time-ripened women's bodies.

Even while moving viewers toward greater levels of comfort with aged, sexually active female bodies at some distance, the films disrupt these views, unsettling and blurring viewers' perceptions through techniques that include backlighting, overexposure, and filters, as well as elements of the mise-en-scène, such as the settings' colors, props, and fabric placement. Through these interventions, directors disconnect the viewers from a sometimes hyperrealistic gaze. The wrinkles, pores, and age spots fade away, particularly from women engaged in sexual acts. For example, as Kaplan explains, *The Mother*'s director "refrains from shooting [May's] naked body in full light, softening the scene rather through careful lighting and . . . grey/white colours" (39). In *Wolke 9*, camera distance, backlighting, and overexposure significantly blur the background; in their first sexual encounter, Karl and Inge float in white clouds, the contrast between bodies and background disconnecting them from earthly experience.

The aged male sexual body is less filtered than the female's is. For instance, during sexual encounters, viewers see Karl's age spots and an extreme close-up of his face; in contrast, Inge's visible parts (her curvaceous hips, her firm ass, and a glimpse of pubic hair) minimize the markings of age. Viewers see Karl's full frontal nudity near the beginning of the film. Later, Inge stands nude before a mirror in a dim hallway, but viewers must piece together mirrored parts with parts visible in her stance. Even in films that develop appreciation for women's time-ripened bodies, the double standard of aging is present. In each movie's depictions of aged female corporeality, the texts simultaneously reflect and resist sexually active aged women's marginality.

AESTHETICS OF REJUVENATION:
SEX AND TIME TRAVEL

Many narratives present the biological changes of aging as "natural," outside of the social realm. In media, however, often agency and sexuality visibly impact people's bodies, challenging the "naturalness" of age's impact. In film, for instance, heteronormative sexuality may "rejuvenate" women's bodies.[3] Our observations build on the work of scholars such as Holmlund (2002), Tally (2006), and Wearing (2007), who posit that in pop culture, older women's visible rejuvenation is both "necessary because in complex ways the aging body is pathologized and disavowed; [yet] impossible because . . . deference to quite rigid demarcations of the appropriate, the decorous, and the 'natural' still" apply (Wearing 2007, 278). These scholars focus mainly on mainstream movies featuring stars, including Judy Dench, Diane Keaton, Helen Mirren, Susan Sarandon, and Meryl Streep.[4] The films' social frameworks include the audience's knowledge of stars' private lives, appreciation of stars' decades-long careers, and ability to relate to the movies' characters (Tally 2006, 40). When this combination works, its impact is significant. For example, one viewer says that seeing *Something's Gotta Give* "gave me amazing hope that I was going to remain vital, sexy and . . . desirable for my accomplishments to men of all different ages, statuses and backgrounds. It was everything that the image of the woman past her prime isn't" (e.g., Merkin 2009). Our films' female protagonists were not icons of youthful beauty. Nonetheless, the films connect older women's sexual agency with signs of youth.

The mise-en-scène elements that signify characters' rejuvenation include the choice of the actors' and the characters' clothing, hairstyle, and acting style. In our films, the actors are approximately the age of their characters but have relatively youthful appearances, conforming to Bildgårdt's observation that in film, sexually active elderly people look younger (2000, 174). Werner and Reid have stereotypically mature body types, although Werner has a particularly firm backside, featured when she is naked onscreen; Reid's few facial wrinkles become noticeably less pronounced as her character becomes involved with Darren; Blake's relatively youthful face and trim figure contrast with her chronological age and white hair. As the sexual relationships deepen, the characters' clothing and hairstyle are further youth-enized. May's beige, shapeless clothes are supplanted by whites and colors in more flattering and more revealing designs; her hair becomes curlier and lighter in color. A hastier "do" and less formal wardrobe replace Claire's pinned-up coiffure and quasi-Victorian apparel. The acting styles mirror these changes: Reid's and Werner's characters become more energetic after pairing with their lovers, engaging in more stereotypically "girly" behavior, casting sidelong glances, flashing flirtatious smiles, flushing with excitement, and giggling more. Cinematographic choices further reinforce the evidence of rejuvenation in the mise-en-scène.

The specifics of setting, lighting, framing, and sound provide additional revitalization, with views of confined domesticity involving the husbands contrasting with the energy and expanses of the scenes featuring the lovers. In May's home, viewers see few windows, and room size is curtailed as the camera does not give full-height shots. Camera shots in Inge and Werner's apartment often are double-framed, underscoring Inge's sense of separation and restriction. Claire interacts with John only indoors; he limits activity with her because of her "heart problems." These indoor scenes contrast with the scenes that include the women's lovers and with the lovers' relative youthful demeanors and activities. Karl and Inge go skinny-dipping, bicycling, dancing, and running through the rain, with the camera emphasizing movements within the frame, and the brighter lighting of the outdoors reflects her emotional state. Claire and Andreas have outdoor trysts; Darren and May most often meet in an unfinished greenhouse. The sounds of the outdoors connect the characters with freedom and life, further signified by the green spaces and, often, a springlike atmosphere. Viewers may experience these changes as positive even as they note the narratives reinforcing associations of lovability and sexual desirability with youthfulness.

The filmic sexual encounters further reconsider associations of sexual functionality, erotic engagement, and emotional intimacy. Viagra is not mentioned, a difference from more mainstream films such as *The Best Exotic Marigold Hotel* and *Something's Gotta Give* (e.g., Dolan [forthcoming]; Wearing 2007). Instead, the absence of an erection in *Wolke 9* does not constrain Karl and Inge's relationship or interrupt their desire for each other's companionship. It leads instead to increased emotional connection through shared humor,[5] further indicating that the affair is not just about sex. Inge and Werner's enjoyable physical engagements do not fulfill her desire for emotional intimacy. Similarly, John and Claire haven't had sex in twenty years, perhaps a hyperclichéd depiction of empty nesters unable to reconnect after the man retires. Claire's initial willingness to have sex with Andreas is, in part, because he, unlike John, displays emotional vulnerability. May and Toots's marriage is equivalent to Claire and John's. Initially, May's relationship with Darren foregrounds physical desire, but it ends in part because she wants more emotional commitment; May's evening with Bruce is distasteful in part because he treats her as a sexual object rather than as an emotional equal. These women experience rejuvenating effects through emotional connection as much as through sexual activity.

The movies code the women's rejuvenations as positive, but the ageist dialogue of their family members suggests the changes are problematic, potentially pathological childishness and mental infirmity. The visuals do not validate the family members' concerns. Viewers can appreciate Inge's explanation—"This could happen at any age. You say I'm being childish. Is it childish to change one's mind?"—as a contrast to Werner's observations, "I thought you had the air of a young girl; now I know why," and his accusations that she is crazy. Claire says to John: "Funny how I am being watched and not believed, like I'm a sixteen-year-old girl." Andreas, after professing to his daughter his newfound love, says, "You're a wonderful child"; her positive retort includes the affectionate infantilism, "You're a wonderful child too." These responses parallel traditional narratives and historical realities: women who resisted normative scripts of sexuality and agency faced social estrangement and accusations of cognitive instability (e.g., the madwoman in the attic). Even as the protagonists and viewers experience the new relationships as freeing, other characters' responses pressure the women to conform to traditional narratives.

NOT "TOO OLD TO RUIN OUR LIVES": LIBERATION AND PUNISHMENT

Many cultures' love and sexual scripts are gendered and aged. Viewers may have experience with the tensions among competing definitions of love as a commitment and an avenue of self-development (e.g., Harrington and Bielby 1991; Tally 2006). In our films, the protagonists' long-standing roles as wives and mothers indicate the women's commitment to and awareness of conventional age and gender scripts. This cognizance complicates their potential to effect narrative change through self-development. As Claire says to Andreas, "We're too old to ruin our lives and hurt the people that love us." Nonetheless, in their efforts to alter their lives, the women break rules about proper mothering (e.g., May seduces her daughter's lover), proper grief (May does not shed tears for Toots), proper heteronormative monogamy (Inge and Claire cheat on their husbands; May is another "other woman" for the married Darren), and proper sexuality (the older women initiate sex; May seduces a younger man). Their expressions of agency, including sexual agency, create narrative disruptions. To support the narratives, the authors depict chronologically endowed women in social positions more usual for aged men: the women's only emotional connections are with their families and sexual partners, so they lack role models and social support.[6]

In these movies, thinking of the women as having, or even wanting, sexual agency is so far from normative that the women's transgressions are literally unheard of. When Inge tells Werner about Karl, he asks her to repeat herself ("say that again"). John experiences Claire's admission of infidelity as gibberish ("what are you trying say?"), as falsehood ("I don't believe you"), as humor, and after comprehending her message, as a pathological symptom of depression. The children respond similarly. May's son initially frames his mother's sexually explicit sketches as imaginative ("She wouldn't do that"). Inge's daughter responds positively, but her first words are of surprise and disbelief. The underlying message remains that new romance in later life is beyond comprehension. This lack of gerontological literacy in people of all ages can add to seniors' feelings of isolation.

Cultural critics (e.g., Gullette 1988; Rooke 1988; Waxman 1990) introduced age as another category of cultural and literary analysis with which one can explore depictions of resistance to restrictive options. Their scholarship focuses on genres—the midlife progress novel, *Reifungsroman* and *Vollendungsroman*—in which time-ripened female characters journey toward self-knowledge, demonstrating the transformative potential of late-life development. *Wolke 9*, *Innocence*, and *The Mother* seem to echo such narratives. In each case, the audience may appreciate the liberatory effect of the protagonist's choices. However, the women's newfound sexual roles are paired with a return to the punitive dynamics of conventional romances, scripts that have limited options for narrative closure: euphoric endings, in which heteronormative coupling leads to social reintegration, and dysphoric narratives, which end with death disciplining transgressive agency (Miller 1980). Although twenty-first-century narratives somewhat modify the punitive dynamics, the plots reinscribe narrative boundaries for older women's agency, leading these authors to wonder how much the films reflect or support cultural change.

For example, in *The Mother*, Toots's death displaces May from her narrative role and her home. Her sexual encounters take place in the spare room and unfinished greenhouse, marginal locations. When May's daughter, Paula, discovers May and Darren's relationship, Paula schedules a date for May with an age-equivalent man who, in effect, rapes her.[7] In the end, May, now an unwelcome outsider to her family, embarks on a journey to unknown places. The story creates a potential for future happiness, yet it punishes May's sexual agency.

In *Wolke 9*, the death of the woman is displaced onto Werner, who commits suicide. Inge's punishment is her overwhelming guilt. At the funeral, she is immobile, mum for the first time in the movie. The film's ending echoes its start—Inge walks upstairs to Karl—yet heavy steps, dark clothes, and a devastated facial expression replace the opening's bright vitality. In this final scene, Inge and Karl connect intimately, but not sexually, suggesting that she might eventually return to happiness despite the terrible guilt. Inge's possibilities for happiness, however, remain within the boundaries of a heteronormative narrative.

Innocence's Claire seems to be the movie's central character, but the film's plot more cohesively supports the storyline in which Andreas accepts his mortality. Notably, their sexual relationship is rekindled when Andreas invites Claire to witness the relocation of his wife's remains. Claire arrives as the skull, a symbol of vanitas, is disinterred. Andreas, trying to overcome his grief and sense of life's meaninglessness, asks Claire for sex. Their deepening relationship and her renewed sexual activity fulfill his needs as much as they do hers. For Andreas, "Real love never dies," sexual consummation is sanctity, and love extends life beyond the grave. Near the film's conclusion, with Andreas playing "Amazing Grace" on a church organ, Claire dances with her arms raised high, surrounded by light—a symbol of liberation and a gesture of benediction at the moment of her death. Claire's last words to Andreas are, "I love you dearly. You're my life." His anxieties and her "heart problems" are resolved, and her agency is dissolved, by her death. Claire's corporeal death supports enlightenment and connection for John and Andreas, leaving them even more "alive." Classical tropes—eros, thanatos, and momento mori[8]—further the connections to traditional scripts, again casting doubt on the film's potential as an agent of change despite Claire's seemingly liberatory narrative.

As with the three films' unrealistic depictions of women's social connections beyond the family, the films' portrayals also belie the reality that elder women engage in a diversity of nontraditional romantic and erotic options (Connidis 2006; Hislop and Arber 2006). Instead, the plots support some of the same narrative elements that the movies appear to undermine.

CONCLUSION: A NEW EROTICS OF DESIRE

All three of these films seem to convey new and liberating possibilities in which chronologically endowed women express sexual agency and alter their life narratives. However, interdisciplinary analysis combining media studies and age studies methodologies demonstrates ways in which these texts reinforce ideological conventions. The protagonists gain some freedom as sexual agents, yet are punished for transgressing traditional scripts. Moreover, the women's "transformations" support male characters' abilities to enact virility, overcome fears of mortality, and/or develop emotionally.

Each of the female characters abandons a narrative she has upheld for decades and finds fulfillment through a sexual relationship with a more active, engaged, and sensitive partner. The women's actions indicate their belief that the changes are worthwhile, despite the damage to their families. In Western cultures, many people fear growing old and believe they are more active and engaged than others in their cohort (e.g., Lamb 2014). Accordingly, male viewers across the age spectrum are more likely to identify with the new lovers than with the abandoned husbands, and the new lovers are not narratively disciplined. Thus, to some degree, these films are scripts of male fantasy fulfillment, reassuring men that they will be sexually competent and desirable in old age. Perhaps it is no coincidence that the authors and directors of these films all are men.

These films' plots reinscribe the connections between relative youthfulness and sexual desirability for women as well as for men. Most Western cultures connect "successful" aging to consumerism, so that people literally buy in to the need for products and services designed to hide signs of aging. A youthful appearance's value connects to a heteronormative standard of attraction (e.g., Gilleard and Higgs 2013). In these films, the protagonists' bodies associate sexual engagement with youthful appearance; sexual activity becomes the "product" (or perhaps the service?) connecting aged women to youthful appearance and performance, transformations instrumental to the men's narrative development. The women achieve these changes by rejecting traditional roles, actions punished via rejection by a lover, ejection from the family unit, and at the most extreme, death.[9] Thus, the movies are limiting in their representations of the possibilities for older women who claim agency and attempt to live for themselves, rather than for others.

Although the plot innovations are restrictive, the women's onscreen corporal visibility is innovative and subversive. These movies show sexual desire and activity in visibly time-ripened female bodies. Although the movies veil older bodies' sexual performances, nonetheless, they display elders' sexual agency in ways that most cinematic representations have not. The lighting, sound, and editing in these films' sex scenes are similar to those with more traditional-aged actors, an approach that portrays aged women's bodies as similarly sexually desirable. Even as the films persist in connecting relative youth with desirability, they offer innovative displays of gendered, aged, eroticized bodies.

These movies gesture toward means of appreciating and desiring ripened bodies. Most viewers do not yet envision older bodies' aesthetics as desirable; to theorize and appreciate chronologically enriched physiques as attractive, we need a new aesthetics of old age that expands the means by which viewers associate aged bodies with erotic desire (Bruggeman and Smelik 2010, 268). We argue that the combined analytical capacities of media studies and age studies can lead to *a new erotics of desire*, one that combines new aesthetics of desire with innovative narrative options.

Constructing new kinds of aesthetic and narrative erotics requires a revisioning of the valuative strictures of the gaze. Critical engagements with the concept of the gaze begin by privileging the visual, moving beyond that to encompass a wider range of intellectual as well as aesthetic perceptions. Our analysis points to the possibility of a new erotics of desire that reduces the primacy of aesthetics in the formation of erogeneity. A cohesive theorization of those possibilities is a topic for another article.

For the union of media and age studies, we eagerly anticipate a continuation of the recent trend: an increase in the number of movies that portray late life intimacy for an increasingly diverse range of sexually active, gendered aging bodies. We look forward to seeing how movies demonstrate and reflect the variety of ways in which people aging into old age perform desire and desirability, pleasing viewers as the characters please themselves. In this way, films can continue the tradition of cultural production and subversion as well as that of repressive replication, expanding the narrative diversity and the visual representations of possibilities for aged, gendered sexual agency.

NOTES

This article is a collaborative effort by members of the European Network in Aging Studies (ENAS) and the North American Network in Aging Studies (NANAS). The authors thank The Netherlands Organization for Scientific Research for supporting this partnership through the Internationalization in the Humanities program (project title: "Live to Be a Hundred: Cultural Narratives of Longevity").

1. Exceptions include *La Veuve Couderc* (1971), discussed in Leahy (2006).

2. Our examples are women in their sixties, but the concepts apply across the life span.

3. Analyses of younger women's heteronormative sex/rejuvenation connections in film include Addison (2010) and Wohlmann (2014, 73–86). In film, men's successful aging includes youthful performance and sexual functionality (Calasanti 2009, 481); also Calasanti and King (2005), Chivers (2011), Cohen-Shalev (2012), Gravagne (2013), Holmlund (2002), King (2010), and Marshall and Katz (2005).

4. Analyses of the tension between aging and star personae include Dolan (2012), Feasy (2012), Krainitzki (2011), Leahy (2006), Salzberg (2012), Tincknell (2011), and Wearing (2012).

5. Further discussions of Viagra: Marshall and Katz (2005, 2012); Calasanti and King (2005).

6. Usually, old married men's social connections are through their wives; old women tend to have more social connections than do old men (Thorsheim and Roberts 1995).

7. Kaplan suggested this reading in early drafts of her article.

8. Andreas's disjointed "momento mori" nightmare references Borg's in *Wild Strawberries,* reminding the protagonist of his mortality and offering him a possibility of resolution. Andreas's dream connects Claire's narrative deviance to death.

9. More mainstream films (e.g., *Something's Gotta Give*) tend to feature unmarried protagonists whose developing heteronormative relationships do not necessitate disciplining.

Chapter Thirteen

Sexualizing the Third Age

Barbara L. Marshall

Sexy secrets: Men on Fire. . . . We reveal the 21 HOTTEST GUYS on the planet
Sex and dating: 18 expert tips
Instantly LOOK BETTER
Boost your SELF ESTEEM
And have GREAT SEX
Sex, Beauty: Secrets from supermodels

Here's a quick quiz: which of the above juicy tag lines were lifted from the covers of magazines aimed at adults at midlife and beyond? The answer: all of them.[1] Drawing on both aging studies and feminist media studies, this chapter provides an analysis of *Zoomer* magazine—a Canadian magazine aimed at the forty-five and older demographic—to demonstrate the extent to which the performance of gendered heterosexuality is now considered an indicator of "successful" aging. While these new representations may suggest a positive trend, reversing earlier tendencies to portray older people as both undesiring and undesirable, I suggest that they may also act to discipline sexuality in later life.

I first sketch out what I mean by the "sexualization of the third age," and then describe media products like *Zoomer* and the role they play in providing cultural resources for identity formation, including those which illustrate gendered, heteronormative, and consumption-based forms of sexual agency in mid- to later life. I argue that we (at least those of us in the media-saturated consumer societies of the West) are living in a time of "postageist ageism," where antiageist sentiments are embraced at the same time as old age is constructed as something to be resisted at all costs, and that an important component of this is the reentrenching and renaturalization of sex and gender difference.

THE RECONSTRUCTION OF SEXUAL
LIFE COURSES AND THE "THIRD AGE"

As I've recounted elsewhere (Marshall 2012) common wisdom of the nine-teenth and early twentieth centuries often praised the benefits of a postsexual life. Aging individuals were counseled to accept and even welcome the wan-ing of their sexual desire and capacities. Sexuality was linked to reproduction for both men and women, and the post-reproductive years were seen as marking entry into a more androgynous stage of life. Sexual retirement—like retirement more generally—was folded into cultural narratives of life course transitions. However, it is now widely accepted that life courses are not what they used to be,[2] and sexual life courses are no exception. No longer neatly divided by the conventional, usually chronological, markers of childhood, adulthood and old age, contemporary life courses are now viewed as more individualized and open to reconstruction through choices about work, lei-sure, and consumption. In cultural gerontology, the concept of the "Third Age"—first proposed by British historian Peter Laslett (1987) to describe what Bernice Neugarten (1974) in the United States had earlier described as the "young old"—has gained widespread currency as describing a positive and activity-laden view of later life tied to both demographic shifts and generational cultures. Those entering the third age are to have an expectation of a significant period of good health, activity, mobility, and appetite for new and life-enriching experiences. The idea of the third age is not so much a stage of life as a cultural field (Gilleard and Higgs 2011) which has opened up the flexible demarcation of life stages to the imagination of cultural entre-preneurs and marketers (Katz 2005). It is a "generationally saturated social terrain on which aging occurs" (Higgs and Jones 2008, 26).

Linked to, though not defined by, the "baby boomers" whose "genera-tional habitus" (Gilleard and Higgs 2005, 70) has been shaped by expecta-tions of consumption, individuality, self-expression, and the erosion of tradi-tional anchors of identity, the third age is a cultural field and arena of prac-tice. This terrain is centrally defined by a rejection of that which is identified as "old," with its connotations of infirmity, dependency, and lack of agency. Gilleard and Higgs (2010, 121–22) characterize this agency-less "fourth age" as a "kind of social or cultural 'black hole' that exercises a powerful gravita-tional pull upon the surrounding field of aging." Sexuality is now central to this package. As Stephen Katz and I have argued elsewhere (Katz and Mar-shall 2003), active sexuality—narrowly understood as the ability to perform heterosexual intercourse—has become a key indicator of positive and suc-cessful aging. Waning sexual capacities that were once associated with "nor-mal" bodily aging are now pathologized as sexual dysfunctions that require correction. While a considerable literature has emerged critiquing the post-Viagra pharmaceuticalization of sexuality (Marshall 2010) the focus on medicalization may underplay the role of popular resources such as magazines and other texts which speak to a more diverse framework for defining and addressing sexual expectations and discontents (Angel 2012).

There is good reason to look at the ways in which sexuality has become central to cultural representations of aging. As sexiness is added to the list of active, third-age capacities, an ability to meet certain standards of sexual function and appearance becomes part of the boundary work needed to sustain the distinction between the third and fourth ages. In other words, as "sexiness" becomes an important means of distinguishing oneself as *not* old, the third age has become increasingly sexualized. New representations of sexy middle-aged and older adults are displacing what earlier observers have criticized as unflattering, asexual, or blatantly absent representations of older bodies (Walz 2002). This new vision of aging offers a particular kind of cultural imagery around which consumer marketing has rallied, with an explosion of new demographic descriptors such as "boomers," "third agers," and in Canada, "Zoomers." It is to the latter that I now turn.

INTRODUCING THE "ZOOMER"

In 2008, Canadian media mogul Moses Znaimer (best known for spearheading youth-oriented television channels such as the MTV-like *MuchMusic*) brought us the "Zoomer." Described as a "boomer with zip," Znaimer swiftly popularized the term "Zoomer" to define the baby boom generation, took over CARP—formerly known as the Canadian Association for Retired Persons, now reinvented as an "advocacy association for the forty-five plus"—and assembled a full suite of media products (including print, TV, radio and websites). At its center is the glossy *Zoomer* lifestyle magazine which lays claim to being the "largest paid circulation magazine in Canada for the mature market."[3] Like *Cosmopolitan* magazine's "Cosmo girl," the "Zoomer" is presented as an aspirational identity. The initial media release[4] featured a picture of Znaimer as the prototypical Zoomer, with captions referring to various parts of him indicating "the body of a sixty-five year old," "the mind of a forty-five year old," "the libido of a twenty-five year old" and "the heart of a teenager." Perhaps most significant, however, is the caption closest to his trouser pocket, where presumably his wallet is kept: "Zoomers control 77 percent of all Canadian wealth." As one executive of *Zoomer Media* put it, "for the Zoomer there is no *retirement*, there is only engagement: more experiences, more discovery . . . more spending!" (Cravit 2008, 26).

Journalist Mireille Silcoff describes *Zoomer* magazine's construction of this consumer thus:

> The magazine promotes a new kind of archetypal ideal. It is a person, say, seventy-three, who goes footloose in five-inch Jimmy Choo stilettos. A person

who can toss back a large late dinner of steak and bold Shiraz after a full, extremely hip day of dieting, ab crunching, "chilling," Pilates, hardcore jogging, subtle cosmetic surgery, not looking one's age, shopping without dropping, and engaging in various non-old person modes of "getting your game on," including the super hot sex of one's twenties. (Silcoff 2010)

To be sure, Silcoff is exaggerating for effect here, but the "archetypal ideal" she sketches taps into a range of recent shifts in the representation and cultural expectations of aging bodies and identities, particularly as these incorporate expectations about continued sexual vitality.

Zoomer magazine is not alone here—similar products in the United States (such as *AARP Magazine*), the United Kingdom (such as *Saga*), and elsewhere deploy similar imagery and strategies, such as the profiling of successfully aging celebrities, to connect with, sell to, and shape changing representations of this demographic. Relatively little attention has been paid to this genre in either media studies or aging studies however, especially when compared to the attention given to popular media aimed at other age groups. It is taken for granted in contemporary scholarship that consumer-media culture "has established itself as one of the most powerful influences over identity formation for children and young people," providing important and influential resources for self-fashioning (Brookes and Kelly 2009, 599). Given that the extension of capacities for reflexive self-fashioning to those in later life is one of the hallmarks of the revision of life courses in "post," "late," "liquid," or "second" modernity that conceptualizations of the third age seek to capture (Gilleard and Higgs 2013), it seems appropriate that more attention is directed to the cultural resources on offer in mid- and late life. Thus, the mediatized third-ager or Zoomer might be seen as akin to other constructions such as the "tween" in that it is a particular construction of consumer media culture, offering resources that pose both possibilities and limits for imagining the self, body, and sexuality (Brookes and Kelly 2009).

Hepworth and Featherstone's *Surviving Middle Age* (1982) was important in mapping midlife as a significant cultural space and in recognizing the critical role played by the media in generating new images of aging which promoted "looking good" and "ageing slowly." Subsequent research has noted a further shift in print media toward a "pro-active Third Age awareness" (Blaikie 1999, 101). Magazines such as *Zoomer* might be viewed as a further step in this shift, located at the heart of what Patricia Cohen (2012, 161) has described as a "midlife industrial complex." Lying at "the intersection of self-improvement and mass consumption," the midlife industrial complex incorporates both a "massive industrial network that manufactures and sells products and procedures" and the production of anxiety about midlife decline (Cohen 2012, 165). Paradoxically, the extension of life spans seems to have been accompanied by increased anxiety about aging, with younger entry points into cultural decline narratives (Gullette 1998). Middle age is, as Gullette (2011, 126) suggests, a "floating signifier, floating youthward." Katz (2005, 190) noted that the so-called ageless senior's market was usually pegged at fifty-five and older, but as the work of *not* becoming (or appearing or acting) old intensifies, this has shifted downward, as suggested by the expansive demographic of "Zoomers." In the first two years of publication, the masthead identified the magazine as aimed at "men and women 45+." By the third year of publication, this changed to "for 40s, 50s, 60s, 70s, 80s, plus," and in the current and sixth year of publication, reference to age on the cover has been dropped altogether. Presumably "Zoomer" has become enough of a brand identity that one should know when one is one, as indicated by the cover tag line describing each month's cover celebrity (He's one! She's one!) and reinforcing the desirableness of aspiring to this identity.

ZOOMER AND THE CONSTRUCTION OF "THIRD AGE" SEXUALITY

Sexuality—and specifically heterosexuality—has been central in defining the Zoomer identity from the outset. From Znaimer's "libido of a twenty-five year old" in that original launch pastiche through the regular references to getting it, doing it, and talking about it, sex is central to *Zoomer*'s vision of aging "successfully." An editorial in the first issue (October 2008, 12) declares: "We see this time not as 'the end' but as a new and exciting stage in life. And yes, we want romance and expect to continue with the joys of sex. We like to keep up to date with the latest ways to keep ourselves in good shape and looking and feeling good. . . . As a generation we've never conformed and we refuse to start falling into line with stereotypes that no longer apply."

Presumably the stereotypes decried here are those that suggest the negation of sex with age. However, other stereotypes—such as the emphasis on romance, and distinctly gendered and heterosexual forms of sexual expression and representation—seem less open to rejection. In what follows, I identify three themes: (1) sexuality as central to the "not old," generationally linked "Zoomer philosophy"; (2) the "sex as health" discourse; and (3) the location of sexuality in gendered, heterosexual relationships.

Sexuality and the Zoomer Philosophy

In the first anniversary issue (October 2009) a new editorial column was launched—"The Zoomer Philosophy." It is no coincidence that much of the Zoomer identity seems reminiscent of earlier popular-magazine identity constructions like the *Playboy* and the *Cosmo* girl. Znaimer explicitly modeled his monthly "Zoomer Philosophy" columns after Hefner's "Playboy philosophy" (which published twenty-five installments between 1962 and 1965). On Znaimer's account, just as Hefner took on what he considered to be the "last taboo of his day—sex," the Zoomer philosophy seeks to shatter the taboos around age and aging:

> Aging is sex for the new millennium, the topic we don't discuss openly, the thing that happens to other people behind closed doors. In deference to this last taboo, people of age have been denied their right (our right!) in the popular mindset to sensuality, to adventure, to any unconventionality that can't be smiled at fondly by a condescending universe. . . . It's time to create a new story for ourselves, to invent a New Old, a new word for Boomers with Zip— and a new philosophy to go with it. (October 2009, 14–15)

Sex is central to the Zoomer identity—"part and parcel of keeping the zoom in Zoomer" (Winter 2009, 17). Sex involves what Znaimer considers "the Life Force at its best: curiosity and hope in the pursuit of novelty and pleasure—sensual, romantic, relational—at a time when we need it most; and when we may be uniquely positioned to enjoy it without the usual baggage" (July/August 2013, 10). That Zoomers "do it" is frequently underscored by factoid insets throughout the magazine that cite statistics on, for example, the frequency of sexual activity among older people (e.g., April 2009, Summer 2010), their preferred time of day for sex (March 2011), or how many use vibrators (March 2012).

Features by other writers also stress a certain attitude toward sexuality as linking the Zoomer identity to the "generational habitus" of those who came of age in the 1960s. For example, Leanne Delap's regular column on sex recently focused on the continuing influence of the "summer of love" on some participants' views on sexuality today: "We walked around flashing peace signs at each other and hooked up without hitches. . . . My world view was formed in the sixties and it is still a part of me" (July/August 2013, 21). The Zoomer philosophy suggests that Zoomers "enjoy sex more" (October 2010, 13) and perhaps even do it better than younger folk: "Without the pressure of procreation . . . sex for older people is a potentially purer, more advanced expression of human beings' attraction for each other" (Winter 2009, 17).

The Zoomer philosophy embodies the contradictions of growing older in antiaging cultures, acknowledging that "we live in an image-dominated, youth-oriented culture": "Unless we look sexy, the equation runs, we don't feel sexy and if we don't feel sexy, we can't imagine anyone being interested in us. Wrinkles and extra flesh, we've been drilled to believe, do not a sexy look create. As a result, we risk being turned off not by any potential partner but by ourselves. . . . So ultimately the greatest gift we can give ourselves as we age is the gift of true liberation" (Winter 2009, 17). At the same time, every issue of the magazine is replete with images, advertisements, and feature articles advising how to get rid of those wrinkles and extra flesh so that we do look and feel sexy. The philosophy continues: "What more could any of us ask, from sex or any other pleasure, as we approach eternity? To indulge or abstain according to our inclination—and to laugh along the way" (Winter 2009, 17). Yet, as the next theme illustrates, sex is not treated as equivalent to "any other pleasure," and abstinence is portrayed as an outright danger to health and well-being.

The Discourse of "Sex as Health"

It is now widely asserted—by urologists, sexologists, gerontologists, and psychologists—that the maintenance of sexual activity is healthy and beneficial for older people (Marshall 2011). Popular media has been quick to pick up on this, arguing that maintenance of sexual function is both a benefit of a healthy lifestyle and a compelling reason for that lifestyle. As the "Zoomer Philosophy" puts it, sex is "simultaneously a result of good health, a motivator of good health, and a metaphor for good health" (Winter 2009, 17). *Zoomer*'s treatment of sexuality falls squarely within what has been called the "sex as health" discourse (Gupta 2011), and illustrates a largely biomedical framing of risks and interventions related to sexuality and aging.

Central to *Zoomer*'s coverage of health issues is the promotion of research suggesting a link between frequent sexual activity and overall health in later life. Regular sexual activity, we are told, "can statistically improve a person's sense of smell, resistance to heart disease, and ability (i.e., willingness) to lose weight and stay fit; reduce their susceptibility to depression, chronic pain, colds and the flu; and give them better bladder control and teeth" (Winter 2009, 17). Other research is cited suggesting that regular orgasms for men can lower their mortality rate, and that "regular sexual activity for women can ease back pain and, yes, cure headaches" (Summer 2013, 10). Another study cited suggested that men who ejaculate at least three times a week have fewer prostate problems (September 2010). A feature article in the Winter 2009 special issue highlighting sex delineated "10 feel-better reasons to just do it" (p. 72) and reiterated many of the health claims purported to accrue from regular sex, including improved immune systems, lower cancer risk, better cardiovascular health, and incontinence prevention. A short feature entitled "The Love Drug" emphasizes the benefits to brain health that regular sexual activity offers (September 2009, 52). A themed issue on longevity cites continued sexual activity among the top dozen things you need to do if you want to live to one hundred (June 2011). Readers are also instructed that improving their general health will have benefits for their libido (June 2010).

It is readily acknowledged that there are physical changes associated with aging that may present challenges with respect to sexuality. The ability to perform penile-vaginal intercourse is explicitly the measure of (hetero)sexual functionality and biomedical intervention is normalized as a way to achieve this goal: "for those experiencing an issue in the bedroom, there are two important things to keep in mind: sexual problems are common, and treatments are readily available" (September 2010, 24). The two most commonly described problems are vaginal dryness/lack of lubrication in women and erectile dysfunction in men (both of which are problematized as interfering with intercourse), and a range of remedies are recommended (November 2008; April 2011; October 2011). Difficulties in performing intercourse (and recommended remedies) are also discussed in relation to other issues such as prostate cancer (November 2011), arthritis and mobility issues (October 2008; Winter 2008), and pain (September 2011; Winter 2012). Readers are encouraged to nurture their sexuality by "finding doctors and clinics that will assume that you will want to continue enjoying a healthy and active sex life and will help you to make medical decisions accordingly" (Winter 2009, 76), and these might include hormone replacement for both men and women (April 2009; June 2009; November 2011; June 2013).

Again, we find contradictory elements in this theme. While age-related bodily changes are addressed and openness to doing things differently as we age is expressed, the overriding message is one of opportunities for rehabilitation to permit the ongoing performance of penile-vaginal intercourse, all in the name of "health." *Zoomer*'s sex advice is a good example of the manner in which health has become the "cultural/discursive home for sex" (Segal 2012, 376).

Sexuality, Gender, Dating, and Relationships

In addition to bodily change, the Zoomer philosophy acknowledges a host of changes in lifestyle and relationships that define mid- and later life. While this includes acknowledgement of changes for long-term heterosexual couples (Winter 2009), frequently addressed is the fact that increasing numbers of older adults are dating, usually after becoming single through widowhood or marriage breakdown. Analogies are frequently made to adolescence and to dating in high school. For example the Zoomer philosophy recently focused on what Znaimer calls the "second great age of dating" where "people of our demographic are actively involved in 'mating, dating, and relating' that can be every bit as comprehensive as their first adolescence" (Summer 2013, 10). As Wearing has noted, contemporary representations of aging articulate a clear relationship between youthfulness and "rejuvenation" with "highly conventional" representations of gender and sexuality (Wearing 2007, 305).[5]

Numerous features address the "rules of the game" (October 2008, 36–37), including legal advice for men hooking up with younger women (September 2009), speed dating for older adults (March 2010), the ins and outs of online dating (May 2010), May–December relationships (November 2010), and meeting the parents of a younger lover (May 2010). Contemporary phenomena are addressed, such as multiple marriages (June 2013), casual sex with friends and acquaintances ("friends with [retirement] benefits") (Winter 2010, 16), advice to younger Zoomers on how to handle their elderly parents' dating (April 2012), remarriage to a younger spouse (April 2009), and fathering children in later life (June 2010).

One topic which has received fairly little attention in *Zoomer* (in only two articles) is sexually transmitted infections, despite evidence that this is a not-uncommon problem for older adults. In one article, a general piece on reentering the dating world, readers are encouraged to be "proactive in protecting themselves" and to "educate themselves about safe sex practices and ask questions about their partner's sexual health" (Winter 2009, 76). As research with younger people has shown, however, the assumption that sexual partners will experience the sort of equality and openness of communication that allows this has proven to be a dubious strategy (Holland, Ramazanoglu, and Sharpe 2004).

The assumption of heterosexuality on the part of its readership is underscored by the one feature that explicitly addressed same-sex sexuality[6] ("Same Sex Sizzle" in the Winter 2009, 75, sex-themed issue). After a brief introduction establishing that gays and lesbians, like everyone else, "can find love at any age" the tone of the article moves on to suggest that "we" (read heterosexuals) can "learn a thing or two from the LGBT set" (go to the gym to get buff, use sex toys, act out fantasies, try a threesome, . . . , p. 75). Besides reiterating some tired stereotypes of gay hedonism, this advice echoes the imperative to constant novelty and change given to modern lovers of all ages. As Jackson and Scott (2004, 243) note "a routinized sex life is to be avoided, and recipes for such avoidance are the stock in trade of advice manuals." This directive is reflected in other features that suggest how to have better, more interesting sex, including seeking sex therapy (April 2009), learning how to communicate your sexual desires to your lover (September 2009), keeping passion alive (May 2009), cooking food with aphrodisiac properties (November 2008), and incorporating sex toys into your sexual repertoire (March 2012). While the advice is ostensibly pitched at all readers, it closely replicates the sex advice dispensed in magazines pitched at younger women, and research suggests that it is women who will bear the brunt of what Cacchioni (2007, 299) calls the "labour of love."

SEXY SENIORS AND POSTAGEIST AGEISM

Sexuality—as central to the "life force" that defines vitality in later life, as a metaphor for health, and as central to a matrix of assumptions about gender and relationships—suffuses the content of the growing genre of media designed for a "mature market." But as Gullete (2011, 126) suggests, the "still doing it" mantra doesn't necessarily translate into a useful progress narrative.

While the new celebration of "sexy seniors" is, in many ways, a development to be applauded, recognizing as it does a capacity for pleasure and intimacy which does not end with the flush of youth, the alternatives of an asexual old age and the "sexy oldie" discourse do not provide much of a range of positions, nor do they resonate with what qualitative research suggests about older peoples' experiences (Gott and Hinchcliff 2003; Kleinplatz et al. 2009). The conflation of "sexy" and "empowered" that has been subjected to such robust critique elsewhere (see e.g., Jackson, Vares, and Gill 2013) deserves more scrutiny as it has emerged in relation to older people. As Linn Sandberg argues, the new discourses of lifelong sexual vigor, claiming to release us from the limits of previous conceptions of an asexual old age, may in fact function as yet "another 'will to truth' on later life sexuality" (Sandberg 2011, 29).

While the discourse and imagery of the third age, exemplified by cultural products such as *Zoomer*, may be criticized for grounding new forms of ageism premised on a continuing dichotomy between "good" and "bad" aging (Holstein 2011), this is more complex than simply old, ageist wine in new, third age bottles. While youthful standards of gendered sexuality continue to ground successful aging identities, these are not unequivocal emulations of youth. Alongside the rhetoric of agelessness is a "sort of praise for the charisma of aging" (Lumme-Sandt 2011, 50). A space is thus created for the development of contradiction-laden identities for aging, where conventional (and traditionally stigmatized) signifiers of old age may be *re*signified. At the same time, in its commercialized versions, this resignification is still largely premised on a fear of aging, rather than its celebration. Building on critiques of postfeminism in the media, I call this "postageist ageism" and suggest that it now provides a prominent and troubling narrative of aging in media-saturated consumer culture.

Critiques of postfeminism have explored sexualized figures in advertising, the absorption of feminist iconography and discourse by consumer culture, and what have been called the "technologies of sexiness" (Evans, Riley, and Shankar 2010, 114) that are on offer to young women as they construct their sexual agency. Critics have pointed out that the postfeminist sexualization of culture has been a double-edged sword, making available new forms of sexual agency, but also new forms of discipline. Yet the focus of these critiques has been squarely on young women—as if once sexual subjectivities are formed sometime in youth or early adulthood, its job done.[7] The new discourse of "sexy seniors" suggests that we might extend the critique. In the same way that postfeminism both articulates and expresses feminist ideas at the same time that it disavows them, antiageist sentiments are embraced at the same time as old age is constructed as something to be resisted. Gill's (2007) observations about women in postfeminist culture—"on the one hand, presented as 'active, desiring social subjects'" (152) but on the other hand "subject to a level of scrutiny and hostile surveillance that has no historical precedent" (163)—might just as easily be made of older people (and especially older women) in postageist media cultures. Thus, to view media products like *Zoomer* as unambiguously antiageist is akin to treating *Cosmopolitan* as the vanguard of feminism.

Postageist ageism can only make sense in a culture where consumption and lifestyle choices increasingly frame age and gender-related identities and where age and gender are viewed as the bodily properties of individuals rather than as culturally mediated and historically fluid categories. Antiaging culture, with its reimagination of life courses, has not so much released aging individuals from restrictive chronological identities as it has relocated them. The self-reliant, healthy, sexy, and distinctly gendered third ager comprises a subject position which is dynamic, historically located, and dependent on cultural resources.

CONCLUSION

The cover of the Summer 2013 edition of *Zoomer* features Pamela Anderson in a classic pinup pose on the beach. At forty-six, the choice of actress and former centerfold model Anderson as cover celebrity highlights some of the contradictions of sexualization in the era of postageist ageism. She is presented as illustrative of the need to fight back against ageism in popular culture ("There just aren't that many starring roles for a woman of Pamela's age," fifty) and a shining exemplar of just how sexy aging can be ("I don't want to do that chasing youth thing," she says). Still, her celebrity is appearance based, and she portrays the kind of blond, slim-but-for-the-boobs stereotype of youthful feminine sexuality that retains a powerful hold on the cultural imagination. The fact that she's only forty-six plays up the extent to which awareness of—and anxiety about—the potential impact of aging on sexuality and sexual desirability has been downloaded to ever younger age groups. Despite the rhetoric of positive aging, "decline"—particularly sexual decline—is something to be constantly vigilant against.

The "new aging" stresses choice and agency in the fashioning of self, and this includes appropriately gendered and sexualized selves as particular manifestations of sexiness are folded into the work integral to "successful" aging. Despite the appealing and positive discourse on empowerment and agency that surrounds sexual aging, the contemporary sexualization of aging bodies intensifies the sense in which performing gender becomes a lifelong project for both men and women. In addition to mapping out the production and dissemination of such discourses and images, aging studies, media studies, and feminist studies all have important roles to play in critically exploring how aging individuals negotiate the new sexual landscape of the third age, engaging with, negotiating, modifying, and/or refusing its expectations and resources.

NOTES

I would like to thank the Social Science and Humanities Research Council of Canada for financial support and Danielle McIsaac for her excellent research assistance.

1. They are from, respectively, *AARP* magazine, June/July 2012, and *Zoomer* magazine issues from May, June, and November 2010. The last cover line originally read "Age, sex, beauty: Secrets from *Zoomer* supermodels."

2. My understanding of the concept of the "life course" draws from Stephen Katz's elaboration of the "postmodern life course" as "characterized by a number of overlapping, often disparate conditions associated with the blurring of traditional chronological boundaries" (Katz 2005, 32), and associated with a range of political, economic, and cultural shifts. See also Katz (2010).

3. According to the Zoomermedia.com website, average issue readership is 512,000.

4. This may be viewed online through Moses Znaimer's website at www.mosesznaimer. com/.

5. While Wearing focuses on the connections between rejuvenation and the reassertion of conventional forms of femininity here (in an analysis of films) I think her insights can be extended to the representation of gender more generally.

6. Only one other article mentioning same-sex relationships was noted—a feature on fashion designer Wayne Clark on "the struggles of aging in youth-obsessed gay culture" (September 2009).

7. Exceptions to the focus on younger women include Garde-Hansen (2012), Hine (2011), Tincknell (2012), and Wearing (2007).

VII

Social/New Media

Chapter Fourteen

Learning New Tricks

The Use of Social Media in Later Life

Kelly Quinn

The ubiquity of social media has made it a topic for popular debate as well as a subject of serious study. Widely used by youth and young adults, scholarly researchers have pursued an understanding of these media forms not only as mechanisms for communication, but also as cultural icons and sites of identity performance. But perhaps because they are so widely used by youth and young adults, research has been heavily weighted toward the way they are used and interpreted by young people. While recent reports demonstrate very large increases in social media use by older adults over the past several years, they also point out that participation in most social media platforms by adults at older ages lags that of youth and young adults by a considerable degree (Duggan and Brenner 2013; Ofcom 2013). What is becoming clear, however, is that patterns of social media use, and the specific platforms employed, often differ between younger and older users, making the study of older adult use of social media an important emerging area of study. This chapter highlights the significant questions that have been the focus of research on social media use at older ages to date, and the predominant theoretical frameworks that have guided this research. It then suggests important next steps for scholars to consider based on developing questions, existing research limitations, and emergent findings.

Social media platforms provide a digital representation of an individual's social network, making them at once visible and tangible. They are defined as "networked communication platforms in which participants: (1) have a uniquely identifiable profile that consists of user-supplied content, content provided by other users, and/or system-level data; (2) can publicly articulate connections that can be viewed and traversed by others; and (3) can con-

sume, produce, and/or interact with streams of user-generated content provided by their connections on the site" (Ellison and boyd 2013, 158). These
communication technologies specifically include social network sites, such
as LinkedIn, MySpace, and Facebook, and microblogging platforms, such as
Twitter. The definition also encompasses online communities, such as Seni-
orNet and GreyPath, content-sharing sites such as YouTube, and discussion
boards such as those found on AARP.org. Networks that are represented
through these media are distinct from social networks: social media map
one's social network, but can only embody the connections that are represented within it. Given the high adoption rates of platforms such as Facebook
for younger persons, the network mapped by social media often represents a
large proportion of the social network. For older adults, however, the overlap
between these two network forms may be significantly less due to lower
usage rates among earlier birth cohorts.

CRITICAL QUESTIONS:
OLDER ADULTS AND SOCIAL MEDIA

Amidst the growing popularity of social media, there are three key focal
points related to the academic discourse on social media and older adults, and
these reflect an optimistic stance toward their impact on later life stages. The
first cluster of research studies concerns the social media usage gap between
youth and young adults and those at older ages. Numerous studies have
detailed the marked differences in Internet and social media use between
younger and older users in the United States and Europe (e.g., Duggan and
Brenner 2013; European Commission 2012; Ofcom 2013). As societies and
governments have become increasingly reliant on the Internet as a primary
communication medium for shopping, banking, and access to government
services, increased efforts toward digital inclusion have emphasized understanding potential barriers to its use (e.g., Braun 2013; Xie et al. 2012) as a
means of increasing engagement levels.

A second, and related, nexus of research has emerged around older adults
who actively engage in social media and the Internet. It has become increasingly apparent that older adults who adopt social media do so in ways that
differ from youth and young adults, not only in the platforms that are selected
but also in how those platforms are employed (e.g., Arjan, Pfeil, and Zaphiris
2008; Quinn 2013; Zickuhr 2010). Understanding these differences is an
important avenue for policy makers and social media designers alike, in
efforts to appeal to a wider, but older, user base.

Finally, social media are often seen as a low cost/low barrier means of
staying connected. Studies of young adult populations suggest that users are
more socially connected and less lonely than nonusers (Lee, Lee, and Kwon

2011; Lee, Noh, and Koo 2013) and that social media use is related to social capital formation (e.g., Ellison, Steinfield, and Lampe 2007). Given the strong relationship between the quantity and quality of social ties and life quality (e.g., Cherry et al. 2013; Smith and Christakis 2008; Wilhelmson et al. 2005), scholars have sought answers as to whether similar benefits extend to older adults and how use of social media may relate to sociality, social connectedness, and life quality.

These active research efforts and associated findings can be grouped into three broadly related categories: barriers to use; generational characteristics; and sociality and social well-being. Thus, the following sections examine what research has to say about why many older adults do not engage in social media, how older adults' social media use differs from youth and young adults, and how the use of social media relates to social well-being.

Why Don't Older Adults Use Social Media?

Recent reports have indicated that older adults are one of the fastest growing segments of social media users (Madden 2010), yet despite this growth, overall adoption of social media platforms remains at levels significantly below that of younger persons (Duggan and Brenner 2013). Given the overall popularity of these communication media, social scientists have aggressively pursued an understanding of these slower adoption rates and, consequently, a central theme to studies on older adults and social media use relates to factors that have hindered participation. Studies tend to revolve around three obstacles: the physical and cognitive changes associated with aging; attitudes related to privacy and security; and a general lack of interest in the underlying technologies.

Despite that today's older adults are healthier and better educated than previous generations, the physical and cognitive changes coincident with aging may present barriers to Internet and social media use. Vision function decreases with age, specifically in the areas of visual acuity, color perception, and contrast discrimination (Rubin et al. 1997). This may cause some older adults to have difficulties in the perception or comprehension of visual information on a screen (Charness and Holley 2004; Czaja 2005). Declines in response times, coordination, and in the ability to maintain continuous movements at older ages may make use of input devices, such as a keyboard or mouse, more difficult (Rogers et al. 2005). Cognitive function may deteriorate at older ages as well. Fluid intelligence, which involves processes such as working memory and perceptual speed, declines with age (Czaja et al. 2006; Czaja and Lee 2006) and is important to the acquisition of new skills (Czaja and Lee 2006), retrieving information, and working in interactive, web-based environments (Sharit et al. 2008).

Several studies have suggested that older adults resist the use of social media because of concerns about privacy and security (Brandtzæg, Lüders, and Skjetne 2010; Braun 2013; Gibson et al. 2010; Lehtinen, Näsänen, and Sarvas 2009), and concerns are often fueled by media reports (Gibson et al. 2010). Older adults are cautious about providing personal information online, and worry about identity theft has kept some from using specific online services (Gatto and Tak 2008; Gibson et al. 2010). Some older adults perceive that social media providers do not protect individual privacy (Lampe, Vitak, and Ellison 2013; Xie et al. 2012), and this may lead to nonuse or preempt certain online interactions between users (Lehtinen, Näsänen, and Sarvas 2009). Further, older adults often find privacy controls on social network sites difficult to navigate and implement (Brandtzæg, Lüders, and Skjetne 2010), fueling their concerns about being able to protect their privacy when using these platforms. While there are few significant differences in the privacy concerns of older and younger adults or in the engagement of privacy controls (Hoofnagle et al. 2010; Madden 2012), younger adult users appear more confident in their use of privacy enhancing strategies to protect their privacy (Brandtzæg, Lüders, and Skjetne 2010; Madden 2012).

Several studies of Internet nonuse have highlighted that lower levels of engagement may result from preference, due to a lack of relevance to everyday living (Hakkarainen 2012; Sundar et al. 2011; Lampe, Vitak, and Ellison 2013). These studies offer some evidence that factors other than skills or literacy may be involved in the disparities between younger and older users, and possibly reflect differences in values, interaction styles, or entrenched patterns of communication with existing relationships (Gibson et al. 2010; Lampe, Vitak, and Ellison 2013; Lehtinen, Näsänen, and Sarvas 2009).

More recent studies suggest that midlife and older adults who do not use social media often fail to perceive benefits of social media applications (Braun 2013; Lampe, Vitak, and Ellison 2013; Lehtinen, Näsänen, and Sarvas 2009). Perception of benefit has been found to be a strong motivator for technology use by older adults (Czaja et al. 2006; Melenhorst, Rogers, and Bohuis 2006), and social media appears to be no exception. Those older adults who perceive higher benefits of participation are more likely to indicate they will attempt to use social media (Braun 2013), but often need clarification on how these media platforms differ from other communication technologies such as email (Braun 2013; Xie et al. 2012). Nonusers have indicated that connection with children or grandchildren may be an important reason to consider using social media (Sundar et al. 2011), and several studies have demonstrated the importance of providing instructional support to engender social media participation (Gibson et al. 2010; Xie et al. 2012). Finally, social media use is dependent on a "critical mass" of one's friends and acquaintances also using the technology (Gibson et al. 2010; Hargittai

2008); if one's social network is not reflected in the users of a particular social media platform, nonuse will likely result.

How Is Older Adults' Social Media Use Different from Younger Users?

Several studies have detailed the marked differences in Internet and social media use between youth and young adult and older adult users in the United States and Europe (e.g., Arjan, Pfeil, and Zaphiris 2008; Duggan and Brenner 2013; European Commission 2012; Ofcom 2013), yet few scholarly attempts have sought to place these differences in the context of life experiences. Older adults spend less time on social media than younger persons and have fewer connections on these platforms; yet while using these platforms, they spend more time interacting with other individuals and looking at family photos (McAndrew and Jeong 2012). Younger adults find entertainment value in all types of social media platforms including social networking sites, blogs, and Internet forums, while older adults find Internet forums to be most entertaining (Leung 2013).

Generational differences in Internet and social media use are often attributed to access and literacy issues, with older adults lacking both access to broadband and the necessary literacy skills to navigate the emerging environment (Bloch and Bruce 2011; Cresci, Yarandi, and Morrell 2010; van Deursen and van Dijk 2009). Older adults are less likely than the general population to have access to broadband Internet connections (Smith 2010), often a critical component for optimized social media use; those with broadband connections however, use the Internet in their daily lives at rates that approach those of younger users and are slightly more likely to use social media than those Internet users without a high speed connection (Madden 2010). Distinctions are made between "young-older adults" (under sixty-five years) and "old-older adults" (over sixty-five years) regarding social media use, with those in young-older groups reporting higher use levels (Bell et al. 2013; Madden 2010; Sundar et al. 2011). These reports are consistent with findings of reduced Internet use at old-older ages generally (Charness and Boot 2009; European Commission 2012; Ofcom 2013). More frequent Internet users report higher levels of social media use at older ages (Braun 2013), as do those with higher confidence in using technology (Bell et al. 2013). Older adults are less likely to share and consume created content, such as photos, videos, and status updates, often due to lower levels of technology proficiency and concerns about privacy (Brandtzæg, Lüders, and Skjetne 2010; Karahasanović et al. 2009).

Research on social media use has indicated that characteristics of social networks represented through social media differ between younger and older adult users too. Older adults have fewer connections with others on these platforms and the age dispersion among those connections is wider (Arjan, Pfeil, and Zaphiris 2008); that is, youth have more connections with other users of a similar age than do older adult users. This difference perhaps may be attributable to the lower levels of social media adoption among the older adult population: with fewer social media users at older ages, the available number of similarly aged social media connections is less. Simply put, if an individual's social network is not represented in a social media platform, he or she cannot connect with them.

Motivations for using social network sites differ between older and younger users, with older adults indicating they use these platforms to stay in touch with family while younger users look to stay in touch with friends (Bell et al. 2013; Zickuhr and Madden 2012). Unlike youth and younger adults however, older adults use social media to maintain connection with extended family and friends who are not in everyday circles, that is, their weaker connections (Brandtzæg, Lüders, and Skjetne 2010). An emerging use of social media at older ages is reconnection with friends and colleagues from one's past (Madden 2010; Quinn 2013; Shklovski 2010), a practice that may be more limited with younger social media users due to less life experience and an introduction to these connection-preserving technologies at younger ages.

How Does Social Media Use Relate to Sociality and Social Well-Being?

Somewhat surprisingly, while research on social relationships and social well-being strongly indicates that individuals with larger and stronger networks are healthier, and experience greater social support, and reduced levels of cognitive decline (Cherry et al. 2013; Smith and Christakis 2008; Wilhelmson et al. 2005), research on the role of mediated communication in enhancing life quality has provided mixed results. Early studies on younger adult use of social media suggested that it is positively related to social capital creation and maintenance (Ellison, Steinfield, and Lampe 2007; Steinfield, Ellison, and Lampe 2008; Valenzuela, Park, and Kee 2009); these effects have been demonstrated to generalize to older adult populations as well (Burke, Marlow, and Lento 2010). Other studies have found that Internet and social network site use is not related to quality of life at older ages, perhaps due to relatively fewer available connections and more limited forms of engagement (Lee et al. 2010; Leung 2010; Slegers, van Boxtel, and Jolles 2008; Sundar et al. 2011). A critical factor in these conflicting results may lay in the studied samples; many social media studies to date have focused on novice participants (Leist 2013) or have limited sample frames due to low adoption rates of the Internet and social media at older ages. As greater numbers of older adults engage in these platforms, there will be increased opportunities to provide clarity.

Social media use has been connected with reduced feelings of loneliness for both younger and older adults (Ballantyne et al. 2010; Burke, Marlow, and Lento 2010; Sheldon 2012) and, in particular, those with greater numbers of connections report lower levels of loneliness (Burke, Marlow, and Lento 2010). Communication through social media platforms enhances feelings of social connectedness (Ballantyne et al. 2010; Bell et al. 2013), a finding related to research that suggests Internet-using older adults incur higher contact frequency with friends and family than non-Internet users and that Internet use strengthens one's social network (Hogeboom et al. 2010). Social media use by older adults also encourages self-disclosure, which in turn may lead to higher levels of social support (Lee, Noh, and Koo 2013); this is consistent with studies on young adults that have demonstrated a positive relationship between levels of self-disclosure, social support, and subjective well-being (Lee, Lee, and Kwon 2011). These findings on social connectedness have positive implications for aging social media users. Maintaining social connections often becomes more difficult at older ages due to factors such as retirement, bereavement, mobility limitations, and chronic disease; social disconnectedness and loneliness are, in turn, associated with poorer mental and physical health outcomes (Cornwell and Waite 2009; Lee, Noh, and Koo 2013). These recent findings suggest that additional research on the relationship between social media use and adaptive mechanisms to sustain social connection may be an important future direction of study.

CRITICAL JUNCTURES:
THE PAST AND FUTURE OF RESEARCH

Two dominant disciplinary thrusts are evident in the research surrounding social media and older adults, and these differ by an overarching emphasis on either the practical use of a medium or the consequences of its use. Surprisingly few studies on social media and older adults have utilized theories related to aging and the life course, with the exception of studies related to the physical and cognitive aspects of aging and their implications for technology use.

Studies that center on the use of social media platforms are often functional in nature; these studies explore the practical stumbling blocks that impede social media use at older ages and the types of learning environments older adults require. Emanating from disciplines such as computer science and information systems, the conceptual thrust is one of technology adoption and resistance; hence attitudes and perceptions are an important component. The Technology Acceptance Model (TAM; Davis 1989) is one theoretical framework that relates attitudes toward social media and its use. Studies under this paradigm converge on the perceived utility of social media forms and removal of the physical and psychological barriers to use.

The TAM is based on the theory of reasoned action (Ajzen and Fishbein 1980), and attempts to identify a causal relationship between a technology user's perceptions and actual use, specifically the perceptions of the benefit of using such technology and its ease of use (Davis, Bagozzi, and Warshaw 1992). Though developed to understand technology adoption in the work-place, TAM has been demonstrated to predict use of a wide variety of tech-nologies with populations of varying ages, including applications such as email, voice mail, personal computers, user-generated video sharing sites, and telemedicine technology (Braun 2013; Yousafzai, Foxall, and Pallister 2007).

"Perceptions of benefit" have been identified as important to technology adoption by older adults (Czaja et al. 2006; Melenhorst, Rogers, and Bohuis 2006) and have consistently surfaced as relevant in social media usage stud-ies as well (Braun 2013; Lampe, Vitak, and Ellison 2013; Sundar et al. 2011). These benefits to older adults include "keeping up" with the everyday lives of younger family members, sharing photos and videos with individuals seen less frequently, and being able to contact multiple people simultaneous-ly (Gibson et al. 2010). "Ease of use" appears to be less closely tied to voluntary social media adoption for older adults than perceived utility (Braun 2013); however, factors associated with aging such as declines in vision, cognitive processing speed, and psychomotor function make use of certain technologies more difficult for older adults (Charness and Holley 2004). Computer anxiety, a determinant factor of ease of use (Venkatesh 2000), has been found to be significantly reduced through experience and group training activities (Braun 2013; Gibson et al. 2010; Xie et al. 2012).

A second conceptual approach concerns the benefits of using social me-dia. Springing from sociology and social psychology, the focus of these studies is the advantages that are engendered through social media use. So-cial capital theory (Lin 1999) argues that informational and social resources are embedded in one's relationships with others, and that these resources may be converted into life enhancements or other quality-of-life reserves. Studies under this approach often hold an underlying premise that social media platforms provide critical support to realizing these resources by pro-viding access to information and enhanced social connection.

Social scientists have argued that because social media provides low-cost support to weaker relationships (Donath 2007; Donath and boyd 2004), these technologies should be beneficial as users age to fulfill increasing needs for support. Social capital theory (Lin 1999) connects social media use to the health and psychological benefits derived from sociability and underscores much of the research that involves motivation for social media use. Under this theory, investment in one's network of relationships provides a mechanism through which advantage may be gained and resources developed (Lin 2008): by engaging in relationship building, individuals gain access to resources, in the form of more varied and greater information sources, social credentialing, and social and emotional support (Lin 1999). Through the use of social media, two forms of social capital are typically facilitated: bonding social capital, which is typically found in strong relationships and provides access to social and emotional support; and bridging social capital, which is typically found in more diverse and weaker relationships and provides access to broader worldviews or more varied information resources (Putnam 2000). Social media use is seen as integral to forming and maintaining both types of social capital, but use especially supports bridging social capital for adults of all ages (Burke, Marlow, and Lento 2010).

These dominant conceptual approaches to the study of social media and older adults have provided a foundation to understand the functional and operative considerations surrounding older adults' social media engagement, but are limited in helping us to understand the place of technology in the everyday life of older adults. Use of a broader range of theoretical frameworks would provide richer perspective on how social media use compliments, supplements, and in some cases, complicates social behaviors throughout one's life course and direct attention to the complexities of how life experience shapes and is shaped by these media forms.

Aging theories present a promising avenue of study that would expand our understanding of the complexity of social media use in ways that cannot be adequately explored with an exclusive focus on younger users. For example, use of the life course paradigm (Elder 1998) would enable examination of the temporal dimensions of media use, perhaps in a study of past identity as expressed in user profiles. Future research might explore how age is represented differently in social media than other more traditional platforms such as film and television, and how user agency in such representations alters conceptions of aging. Alternatively, the impact of social media on relationships might be examined over time, and include how these media contribute to or diminish relational elasticity over lifelong relational processes. The relationship of life experience and social media use, the temporal trajectory of media motivations and fulfillment, and media support of relationships at all ages are all potential agendas for future study under a paradigm of aging.

Social media platforms are growing increasingly more mobile and visual as recent entrants such as Instagram and Pinterest have joined with longer-standing platforms such as YouTube and Flickr in the arena of social media options. Yet, the visual aspects of social media engagement have been underexplored, despite their significance to maintaining connection with distant friends and family over time. As these more visual platforms gain prominence, it will become important to understand the attributes that appeal to older users, qualities that extend beyond conventional notions of sharing and entertainment. For older adults, understanding how these visual media contribute to the acquisition of information, enhance social connectedness, and permit the ability of friends and family to maintain and sustain connection, will further our understanding of how these media can be used to provide support and augment life quality.

Finally, the opportunity divides that result from a lack of engagement in social media and the literacies required for its productive use are poorly understood, particularly at older ages. Recent research has demonstrated that those with lower digital skill levels report fewer privacy-enhancing behaviors while using social media sites (boyd and Hargittai 2010) and, when added to the privacy concerns related to social media use (Brandtzæg, Lüders, and Skjetne 2010; Braun 2013; Gibson et al. 2010), highlight the complexities of more widespread engagement in social media for older users. The path toward digital inclusion must encompass an understanding of the perceptions and attitudes of older adults in addition to building literacy skills, a path that may be less accessible and more challenging than previously understood.

CONCLUSION

In conclusion, as social media continue to gain in relevance and importance to everyday living, research involving older adults faces substantial future opportunities for evolution and progression. We have yet to ascertain how life experience intersects with the use of these media platforms or how they can more successfully enhance and sustain connection at older ages. Yet, the potential to impact life quality is significant. To date, research has been concentrated in three areas of older adult social media practice: nonuse of social media by older adults, generational differences between social media users, and the beneficial aspects of social media use. Future research programs should key on the intersection of aging theories and social media use, the implications of increasingly visual social media platforms, and the complexities of achieving digital inclusion.

Chapter Fifteen

Polite Pigs and Emotional Elves

Age in Digital Worlds

Rosa Mikeal Martey

When I was playing the massively multiplayer game *World of Warcraft* (WoW), one of the leaders of my guild (a formally grouped set of players) was a fantastic leader and organizer. He demonstrated an amazing level of patience, care, and sensitivity when leading groups of ten or twenty-five players in the complex dance of swords, arrows, and spells that are required for difficult WoW battles. He had a deft hand at gently shutting down insulting tirades or overlong complaints from guild members; he was incredibly generous with new folks (like me at the time); he was well organized and very reliable. When I discovered that this guild leader was only twenty-three years old, I was shocked.

I had assumed that my guild leader was closer to my own fortyish years than twenty-three in part because of the way he led. Even more influential on my perceptions was the fact that he was always careful with spelling and grammar (even correcting other guild members), had a broad vocabulary, and almost never used chat slang such as "ppl" (people) or "ur" (your). The cues I assumed were telling me he was close to my own age were not telling me that at all.

I was basing my impressions and assumptions on cultural expectations about age in relation to my own and others' age identity. Age identity, explain McCann et al., "acts as a 'pre-interactional' tendency whereby a strong sense of identification with a particular group (e.g., young adults) influences communication with out-group members (e.g., older people)" (2004, 89).

Age is part of our cultural expectations, shaped by beliefs, customs, and traditions. In fact, some scholars have pointed out that numerical age is not as meaningful as life stage, such as adolescence, young adulthood, middle age, et cetera. The number of birthdays a person has had is a relatively recent way to classify people that arose from the need to create legal and bureaucratic boundaries for certain groups like voters, drivers, and workers (Morgan and Kunkel 2007). Our own age identity, of course, changes across our lifetimes, although there is nothing that requires our "felt" age to be the same as our numerical age. Indeed, plenty of research shows that many older people feel younger than their chronological age (Westerhoff and Barrett 2005), and many young people believe others see them as older than they are (Montepare 1991). People have age-related crises and often resist the implications of "acting their age" (Westerhoff and Barrett 2005). There are also profound differences in age-based roles in different cultures, such as high status for elders in some cultures, which is often contrasted with the US "ageism" that leads to tucking its elderly away (Sokolovsky 2009). Age roles in societies change over time, as well (Hareven 1994). Overall, our age identity reflects how we see ourselves in social contexts and in relation to those we encounter (Logan, Ward, and Spitz 1992).

We develop a sense of others' age from cues—largely physical cues—that we observe when we interact with them. In physical spaces, someone's age appearance drives our sense of their age identity (McCann et al. 2004; Ryan et al. 1986). In online spaces such as WoW, where physical cues from the body, including apparent age and facial expressions aren't generally seen, age cues necessarily shift to language- and behavior-based ones.

Considerable research shows that people find a range of ways to communicate information in online spaces, including information about themselves (Joinson 2001; Walther 1992). Joseph Walther points out that not only language use, including spelling, punctuation, emoticons and the like, but also the structure of communication—longer, more frequent—serve as cues that facilitate meaning making among people in those spaces. Social information processing theory (SIPT; Walther 1992) explains how offline nonverbal cues are translated into language in text-only online spaces in order to form relationships. In text-only chat spaces, Walther argues, people adapt their use of such cues to exchange important personal information and build relationships with great success (Tidwell and Walther 2002).

In digital worlds where people use avatars to move around richly detailed visual environments, this translation can be extended an additional step: offline nonverbal cues can also be replaced with online nonverbal cues. The ways we learn about people we meet in an online game, then, are also based on a range of visual cues, which in an online world can include the style of your avatar's hair, an animation, where you stand, and how you name yourself.

A big benefit of finding ways to build meaningful relationships through online communication, Walther argues, is that online interaction can facilitate the growth of relationships that might not have developed because of intergroup differences, geographic distance, or the like. I assumed my guild leader was my own age, which had an effect on my interactions with him. Perhaps I was more comfortable, more open, and more willing to listen to his advice than I might have been otherwise. I was probably overestimating how much we had in common, which, as Postmes, Spears, and Lea (1998) point out, happens frequently in online interaction and leads us to create an idealized image of others. Their social identity of deindividuation effects model (SIDE) suggests that when group identity is strong, people tend to feel an exaggerated sense of similarity and connection, especially absent information that would contradict that sense. Focusing on, for example, participation and fitting into the guild group can increase the sense that fellow guild members share ideas, values, perspectives—and perhaps age identity.

Communicating who we are contributes to social identity more generally, as suggested by Tajfel and Turner (1986). Social identity influences group interaction because people associate specific behaviors with particular identities, from how they speak (LeBoeuf, Shadfir, and Bayuk 2010) to the clothes they wear and accessories they use (Shavitt and Nelson 2000). These associations are especially relevant to what people see as appropriate and inappropriate behaviors in specific settings (Turner and Oakes 1986), which in turn affect which identities are activated and performed. Social identity, then, is part of how we position ourselves in relation to other people and objects, how we see our role in those spaces. As a part of social identity, our own age identity as well as our perceptions of others' ages can affect how we behave.

Overall, then when we interact in an online world without the physical age markers we are otherwise accustomed to, we can turn to other cues to detect and express age, from language style to avatar appearance. To be sure, people who interact in WoW and other online worlds often have clear ideas about how you can know how old someone is. When someone misbehaves, an oft-heard response is, "Ah, that person is probably a fourteen-year-old." Sometimes people actively communicate their age with cues such as mentioning music or movies that were popular when they were a teenager, or aligning or distancing themselves from an age group (*Kids today, I tell ya!*) (Harwood, Giles, and Ryan 1995).

How much of age identity comes through in digital spaces? Can players accurately identify others' age, and do they communicate their own? Are there patterns in language, movement, and appearance that correspond consistently with the age of the person behind the avatar? We sought to answer these questions in a two-year study of player behavior in the online worlds *World of Warcraft* and *Second Life* (SL) through analyses of surveys, click logs, and interviews. We interviewed participants and asked them if and how they knew the age of others in these spaces and examined patterns in actual behavior to test those theories. We found that although explicit age identity cues were rare, there were some age-related patterns in how people look, chat, and move that people use with varying degrees of success to figure out the age of their online companions.

Theoretical models of communication and aging suggest that physical cues are key markers of age identity that trigger social stereotypes in encounters between generations (Hummert 1994; McCann et al. 2004; Ryan et al. 1986). Correspondingly, visual cues about age identity may have a strong influence on how we see each other online. In highly customizable digital worlds such as SL, players customize their appearance to fit in with specific cultures or portray a specific persona (Merola and Peña 2010). Messinger and colleagues (2008) found that although most people create avatars based on their offline appearance, many make themselves more attractive, including appearing younger. Reed and Fitzpatrick (2008) asked twenty-two older people without experience in SL to design an avatar and found that the majority felt their avatar looked younger than them, in spite of the fact that they felt the avatar also looked extremely similar to them. Sometimes avatar design is carefully crafted around a person's goals, such as creating a more attractive avatar for dating (Vasalou and Joinson 2009) or a more frightening avatar to play "the bad guy" (Salazar 2009). Other times, avatar designs are selected on a whim, or to enjoy the aesthetic of the digital object itself, rather than as a representation of the self (Banks 2013; Boler 2007; Yee 2008). Not only the avatar's design but also its movements serve as cues about who we are in digital worlds. Nonverbal expressions including avatar movement and proxemics, gestures, and facial expressions can communicate emotions, identities, and attitudes (Antonijevic 2008; Koda et al. 2006; Yee and Bailenson 2007; Yee et al. 2007). It is not clear if use of these nonverbal expressions differ by age, however.

Language is one of the key ways used to signal membership in specific age categories. We express and interpret ideas, emotions, and identities online using text-based cues such as writing style, emoticons, vocabulary, and even timing (Walther 1992). Often, language play such as slang or "like" is considered a marker of youth culture (Moore 2004), and along with profanity, has been found to be more common among younger users in online communication (Barbieri 2008; Jones and Schieffelin 2009). Schler and colleagues (2006) found that older bloggers tended to use more prepositions and articles and fewer pronouns and assent/negation words in online blogs. Automatic text categorization techniques have successfully predicted participant age groups by counting punctuation, capital letters, sentence length, and word types (Tam and Martell 2009). Several other studies have argued that youth are more fluent in the use of online-specific language, including emoticons (Derks, Bos, and von Grumbkow 2007; Huffaker and Calvert 2005; Lin 2007).

The literature suggests that identifying who is older and younger, even in this space of limited identity cues, is quite straightforward. And there are some differences in how people design their avatars, speak in text chat, and use their avatar, which was the focus of our research. But we also found that age is not always easy to determine.

METHODS

Between 2010 and 2012, we studied the chat, appearance, and movement of nearly six hundred participants in a study of social interaction in the digital worlds SL and *World of Warcraft*. The study was reviewed and approved according to federal human subjects guidelines through university institutional review boards (IRBs). For the study, we designed and programmed a three- to five-person multiplayer game in each world and asked groups to play through a series of quest tasks while we recorded their chat, clicks, avatar movement, and avatar appearance. Surveys before and after the session assessed demographics, experience in online worlds, and other characteristics. We conducted fifty SL sessions with 220 people and 110 WoW sessions with 370 people. A week or two after their session, a total of eighty participants were interviewed one-on-one for about twenty minutes each, selected to balance age, gender, and experience with games.

SL is a visual, digital world where users or "residents" can design and create avatars, environments, and objects. We used the SL programming language to build and program buildings and objects that populated a point-and-click mystery game on a private island. In the game, *The Madness Machine: Case of the Missing Moonstone*, players were positioned as detectives in training who were assigned to track down the thief of the valuable "Moonstone diamond." Players ranged in age from eighteen (our minimum for the study) to sixty-four, averaging about thirty-seven years old. They were about half women, half men, 69 percent had at least some college education, and most played SL at least once a day.

SL is an unusual game in how much control it gives participants over their avatar's appearance, and in the fact that it has no built-in goals. We conducted a second study with parallel design in the more traditional multiplayer online game WoW to find out if what we observed in SL would hold true in a world oriented around quests to kill monsters and gain character power. In WoW, players perform quests and do battle with various creatures to improve their character's strength. Players can select a race, such as a troll, elf, or human, and they have some control over their age appearance in selecting one of a dozen or so face designs specific to each race.

In WoW, we programed an add-on, which is a piece of software that alters players' screens but not the game world itself, to record player behavior and display text, sound, images, and buttons in the form of a ring and notebook to click for activating quest events. The WoW game was also a mystery players had to solve by clicking objects and working together to collect information and solve puzzles. Players created a new level one character and joined a session group to explore the shops and streets of Dalaran and track down the details of the Marauders' evil plot, confront their leader, and defeat him in a final battle. Participants ranged in age from eighteen to fifty-nine, with an average age of twenty-nine. About 44 percent were women, 56 percent men, 85 percent had at least some college education, and 85 percent played WoW at least three to five days per week.

To analyze the data from both studies, we used a combination of content analysis and automatic calculations to create a series of chat, movement, and appearance variables. Human coded categories include conventional phrases, which are greetings and closings such as "hello" and "good-bye," as well as those that fulfill conventional social functions including thanks and apology. Hedges are linguistic softeners such as "sort of" or "maybe" that reduced the power of a statement. Action directives are commands such as "go over there." Attention-getting phrases include "hey" or "you guys." Emotional phrases are a word or phrase that conveys emotional state, such as "ewww" or "cool!" Computer coded variables included punctuation, word length, and objects clicked. Lexicons were created to automatically count emoticons, shouts, profanity, praise, and laughter (see Martey et al. [2013] for a detailed description). All chat measures were calculated per utterance to take chat volume into account. Movement variables were calculated from player location coordinates, identified every two seconds.

We also content analyzed avatar attractiveness in SL and in WoW. For the SL sessions, we identified whether or not participants used a gender-idealized avatar, which was defined as an idealized humanoid body, but not clothing (see Martey and Consalvo [2011] for detailed description). In WoW, appearance coding was somewhat different, because players do not have as many customization options there. We coded avatar attractiveness based on selection of face appearance and whether or not the avatar was of a normatively attractive race (night elves, blood elves, humans, gnomes, and draenei). We developed a coding scheme for traditional age appearance such as use of avatars with gray hair and wrinkles, and found that all but one avatar across the two studies appeared as youthful adults. For all human coding, researchers coded approximately 10 percent of the full dataset to establish intercoder reliability using a threshold of Krippendorff's alpha of 0.8.

KEY MARKERS OF AGE IN DIGITAL WORLDS

In the post-session interviews we asked participants how they know how old someone is and received a range of answers. Although few felt they could say for sure, most had theories of what older and younger people do in SL and WoW. Most common was the idea that older people talk less, and type well, with fewer errors and more clarity. Many interviewees told us that they assumed the more polite players were older, and that those who were more comfortable with leadership, more easygoing, and had more knowledge about the world were older. They also assumed that those who had a harder time understanding directions and got confused with the more technical aspects of the experience were probably older. Participants said that younger players exhibited needs for attention and approval, seemed more insecure, used profanity, were more likely to wander or rush around on their own, and were generally more independent. Some of our interviewees also said they thought younger players used more terse chat-speak such as abbreviated words and emoticons.

In our SL sessions, not a single participant, even those well over fifty years of age, used an avatar that appeared older than early to mid-adulthood. In fact, we found that the older a participant was, the more likely he or she would use a traditionally attractive avatar. Appearance was the strongest differentiator between those over and under thirty years old, but not through the use of traditional age cues: younger participants were more likely to have avatars with a playful or nontraditional appearance, such as using animal avatars, distorted faces, or less modelesque bodies.

Our SL research did find some support for our players' theories about age. Older players were indeed more polite, addressing other players by name more often, and using more "hellos" and "goodbyes," as well as more "thank yous" and "you're welcomes." They were less likely to use emoticons such as a smiley face, and used fewer emotional phrases in their chat. Older players also clicked the quest and puzzle objects less than younger ones, although those differences were rather small. What we didn't see were differences in how much punctuation players used, how much they talked, how large their vocabulary was, or how much they wandered around the game world. Table 15.1 shows the list of the behaviors that differed significantly by age in SL, and the Pearson correlation with age for each.

In some ways, what we found in WoW was similar to what we found in SL. First, just as in SL, players over thirty were more likely to use an attractive avatar than younger players (46 percent of younger and 59 percent of older players used more attractive avatars). Interestingly, younger players were also more likely to use an avatar opposite their reported gender than older players: 18 percent of younger and only 5 percent of older players did so. Older participants were similarly more polite, using more conventional,

Chat Measures (per 100 Utterances)	Correlation with Age	Movement, Click, and Appearance Measures	Correlation with Age
Conventional phrases (hello, bye, thanks etc.)	0.285**	Avatar form furry	−0.377**
Appreciation	0.278**	Idealized gender appearance	0.300**
Use of player names	0.245**	Rabbit clicks	−0.246**
Emoticons	−0.193**	Vault button clicks	−0.194**
Emotional phrases	−0.171*	Object clicks	−0.140*

*$p < 0.05$. **$p < 0.01$. Two-tailed.

Table 15.1 Correlation Coefficients for Coded Variables and Age in *Second Life*.

appreciative, and apology phrases. Younger players talked more, and were more emotionally expressive, using more emotional phrases, shouts, attention-getting statements, and avatar gestures. Emoticon use did not differ by age in WoW, however. Younger players in WoW were also a lot bouncier than older players: Players under thirty jumped an average of 130 times an hour, and those over thirty only fifty-four times, and younger players moved around the game space a bit more during the session. In WoW, punctuation and vocabulary did differ by age, but not always in the way our interviewees assumed. Younger WoW participants used more profanity, but also more punctuation and had larger vocabularies with longer words than older players. Older players clicked the ring and notebook game objects less than younger players, at forty and fifty clicks, respectively. Table 15.2 shows the correlations between age and in game behaviors for key variables. Many of the variables in the WoW study were modestly correlated with age, but we focused on those that corresponded with the literature, player theories about age differences, or what was found in SL for this analysis.

AGE, SOCIAL ROLES, AND ACCOMMODATION

Overall, there were clear patterns in differences by age in how polite, attractive, expressive, and, in WoW, jumpy, players were (as we could not measure jumps in SL, we could not compare this behavior across the two worlds). Although both SL and WoW players believed younger players used less punctuation and had smaller vocabularies than older ones, this was not the case: only in WoW did we see differences in these variables, and younger players were *more* likely to use punctuation and a wider variety of words. In both worlds older players were more polite, with more conventional phrases such as "thank you," "hello," and "good-bye," and more appreciation phrases such as "nice job!"; in WoW, older players were also more likely to apologize than younger players, and less likely to use profanity, as players theorized. Player theories about younger players talking more and moving around

Chat Measures (per 100 Utterances)	Correlation with Age	Movement, Click and Appearance Measures	Correlation with Age
Conventional phrases (hello, bye, thanks etc.)	0.277**	Jumps	−0.308**
Hedges	−0.185**	Notebook clicks	−0.254**
Chat lines	−0.180**	Distance moving backwards	−0.204**
Emotional phrases	−0.172**	Distance traveled	−0.154**
Average word length	−0.169**	Ring clicks	−0.150**
Vocabulary size	−0.169**	Gender switch	0.141**
Punctuation (commas, periods, question marks)	−0.155**	Attractive avatar	0.139**
Capital Letters	−0.147**	Staying close to the group	0.109*
Shouts	−0.145*	Combat with bunnies, squirrels	0.102*
Appreciation phrases	0.141***		
Action directives	−0.128*		
Attention Getting phrases	−0.124*		
Apologies	0.108*		
Profanity	−0.105*		

*$p < 0.05$. **$p < 0.01$. Two-tailed.

Table 15.2. Correlation Coefficients for Coded Variables and Age in *World of Warcraft*.

more held true for our WoW participants, although not in SL. In both games, younger players were more likely to click the objects associated with the game such as clues in SL and the ring and notebook in WoW. The most powerful differences in SL were in avatar appearance: older players were more likely to use an attractive avatar. In WoW, this held true, but clicks and movement were stronger age indicators than attractiveness, as might be expected where avatars are less customizable.

Statistically, we can model these differences and do a pretty good job of predicting whether someone is over or under thirty years old (see Martey et al. 2013). Players, however, were not particularly good at guessing each other's age. In the eighty post-session interviews we conducted, about 75 percent of participants said they generally can't tell how old other people are in these digital worlds. In some interviews, participants made guesses about group members' age. When group members were significantly older or younger than our participants, those guesses were usually off by about a decade. In general, those we interviewed who were in their twenties and thirties assumed that the other people in their group were close to their own age. Those who were in their late forties and fifties assumed most people were in their late twenties or early to mid-thirties.

People may not be quite as good at guessing others' age in SL and WoW because the differences in these behaviors are relatively small and difficult to observe. For example, older people use about two fewer emotional phrases (six versus eight), and thirty-four versus forty-seven punctuation marks in one hundred lines of chat. Systematic analyses show these as significant differences, but people would be hard-pressed to notice them while they play. The only easily seen way we found to identify who was younger was jumps in WoW; in SL, the differences were all small enough that they were difficult to track during play.

It may be that age is generally difficult to identify through speech or behavior because people adapt their language to the norms of the online space they are in, which may well include perceptions of which age group is most likely to be playing. Communication accommodation theory (Giles, Coupland, and Coupland 1991) says that we adjust our speech style depending on who we're talking to and our perceptions of the prevailing norms of the space. In SL, people of all ages might be more mature and polite to fit perceived norms of that space (Martey et al. 2013), and in WoW they might use more functional chat and slang because they feel task achievements are more important than socializing (Yee 2007). It is possible, then, that age identity cues, including the more subtle differences in language and behavior we examined in this study, are reduced as people seek to fit into the group and follow group norms rather than assert individual age identities, as SIDE would suggest.

This adjustment could be a two-way street, as well. A model of communication and age, the communication predicament model (CPA; Ryan et al. 1986), says that people observe age cues, usually physical ones, and then modify their speech behavior by, for example, speaking more slowly and loudly to elders and in a higher voice to little children. This shift in language might include adjusting topics, vocabulary, and style of speech, and serves to reinforce stereotypes about the other person. Others then respond to those adjustments in various ways, from emphasizing their age to feeling self-conscious about it (Ryan et al. 1986). This way, age becomes more salient in the interaction, and cultural and social barriers are reinforced. Online, absent those physical cues of age, that process of adjustment might be interrupted, and age becomes less salient than, say, how well you healed the main warrior tank when he was fighting the ogre. In other words, if we never treat others as older or younger than we are, we avoid triggering some of the social and cultural roles that age position entails.

Those social roles related to age matter. Age is thought to differentiate our relationships, knowledge, our responsibilities, our capabilities, and our credibility (Morgan and Kunkel 2007). Age is a primary way family roles are determined (Burton 1995), and is a fundamental component of the social structures of education, work, and law (Neugarten and Moore 1968). Age intersects with gender, class, and race to influence the norms of behavior for different groups, and specific age groups have even been defined as "special" groups within society with their own perspectives, needs, and subcultures (Neugarten and Moore 1968). Plenty of research tells us that youth, or seniors, or middle-aged people have different attitudes, behaviors, and habits than others (Westerhoff and Barrett 2005). In short, age tells us whom someone is supposed to love, what someone should wear, how someone should speak, how trustworthy someone is supposed to be, and what someone is supposed to believe.

But what happens when we experience people's love, appearance, language, activities, and beliefs without that "preinteractional" age information? Do we smooth out some of those differences in deference to the different norms of the group or according to what we believe others are expecting? In WoW, many of our participants said they assumed most people were relatively young. Do older players call up their younger selves when they run through that dungeon? Do younger players attending an elegant tea party in SL strive for a more mature exchange of pleasantries? It is possible that the consistent but small differences we found in our research were not more substantial because of a kind of flattening of age identity. Perhaps the absence of those physical age cues lets everyone inhabit more fully that old maxim, "you're only as old as you feel."

In our research, most participants said they had some ideas about others' age, but didn't really think about it much. My play experience made me realize I was prone to assuming people who acted similar to me were also of a similar age. Maybe the reason I was so wrong about my guild leader's age was because, more than anywhere else in my life, I regularly interact with people far younger and far older than I as peers. Fundamentally, my experiences in digital worlds and my research on age cues make me question how useful this age business really is in the first place. Do I want an eighteen-year-old "kid" in charge of the complex, challenging, and high-pressure activities that are such a fun and important part of my life? Put it that way, and I'll probably say no. But give me a "kid" with the experience, knowledge, and leadership skills to run a successful twenty-five person raid and kill the big boss, and I'll sign right up.

NOTE

This study was funded by the Air Force Research Labs and was conducted with Jennifer Stromer-Galley, Mia Consalvo, Kelly Reene, Tomek Strzalkowski, and Michelle Weihmann-Purcell. Valuable insight and discussion throughout the project were also contributed by Jingsi Wu and Jaime Banks. Special thanks also to R.B. for his insight, leadership, and inspiration.

Chapter Sixteen

Afterword

A View from Media Studies

Cornel Sandvoss

The starting point for this book could not be more apparent and pressing at the same time. Among the many changes to modern life in the latest phase of modernity and consumer capitalism, two transformations have changed everyday life practices and identity more than any other: First, life expectancy has dramatically increased and, second, everyday life is increasingly structured around the use of communication media.

Put simply, we get older and use more media while we do so. Yet, this is not a coincidental correlation, but one in which both processes profoundly shape each other. The wealth of data and concepts introduced across the chapters of this book highlight the many complexities, variations, and nuances of the interplay between media and the life course. As elsewhere in the study of modern media and communication systems, there are no simple, dichotomous moral judgments that can be drawn. Media are neither the saviour nor the curse of later life. However, simply acknowledging complexity is no sufficient *raison d'etre* for media and cultural studies, albeit something that the field for its theoretical and methodological foundations has occasionally been prone to. Instead, we need to explore complexity and identify patterns, themes, and clusters. And while we are still on thin empirical ice, this volume alongside the growing number of studies concerned with the interplay of aging, media, and popular culture, allows for a number of observations which indicate emerging patterns and point toward the key themes at the heart of the field's future research agenda.

At first sight, this volume alongside the growing number of studies concerned with the interplay of aging confirm a fault line between two different groups of media and communication practices that will be familiar to scholars of media and cultural studies: the distinction between "old" and "new" media, mass communication, and convergence culture. Mass media appear as a strong contributor to a cultural frame in which aging is portrayed and experienced as *decline* and as *a state of lack*—a lack of youth, which in turn serves as a yardstick for the construction of beauty and desirability (see Bauman and de Laat; Barrett et al.; Balasz, all this volume). In a visually dominated cultural landscape (television, film, magazines, advertising) the image is central, and the fundamental category through which the image is evaluated is youthfulness. Both the emphasis of youth and image are in turn firmly rooted in the wider hedonist frame of consumer culture alongside freedom, pleasure, luxury, and mobility (Featherstone 1991). The paradox, while obvious, is nevertheless worth noting: as societies grow older, their *leitmotif* is youthful mass mediated imagery. And as this volume (Bardo; Marshall; Marshall and Swinnen) illustrates, it is in this idealization of the *image of youth*, rather, *pace* Debord (1995), youth itself, that patriarchal inequality and discrimination still reign strongest. These studies of the nexus of mass media, aging, and gender thus illustrate how in some respects we have moved on remarkably little since the important analyses of power in visual culture nearly half a century ago by Berger (1972) and Mulvey (1975).

Digital media on the other hand, as Scodari, Quinn, and Harrington and Bielby indicate—alongside, as Katz reminds us, traditional face-to-face forms of interpersonal communication (all this volume)—have created communicative spaces which rather than problematizing aging as a state of lack can offer alternative discourses and allow for the articulation of personal experiences and narratives of aging as well as help media users address particular challenges of later life such as maintaining social capital and interaction. Moreover, online communication in particular in its virtual, disembodied form offers participants the chance to escape the shell of the aging body that Featherstone and Hepworth (1991) fittingly labeled the "mask of aging," if not, as Martey (this volume) suggests, all of the social, cultural, and behavioral context that shapes us in different life phases.

Yet, on closer inspection, much as in media studies at large, mass media and convergence culture are less easily separable than such a binary classification suggests. Firstly, social media such as Twitter, Facebook, YouTube, Tumblr, fan fora, and others do allow users to share and repost content. Yet, much of this content is either created by professional media organizations and for traditional mass media such as television, radio, or print media, or commentary on such industry produced content. In the inherently intertexual field of convergence culture, there is, therefore, no clear ideological dividing line between social media and mass media content. This is not to claim that user generated content does not facilitate challenges to dominant mass media representations of aging—it very much can and does so. But the capacity to frame discourses about the life course and later life phases remains firmly with mass media and advertising as central pillars of consumer culture; the latter of which of course also has a significant presence within online spaces.

Secondly, in the age of convergence culture, mass media are undergoing profound transformations themselves. While mass media have largely remained channels of one-way communication, digitization, alongside neoliberal regulatory changes, has driven the fragmentation, specialization, and personalization of the delivery of media content. Broadcasting has turned into narrowcasting with steadily declining audiences for major networks and the emergence of niche channels, many of which either in their explicit mode of address and branding or through their genre orientation attract audiences that cluster in particular age groups; from the BBC's CBeebies via the adolescents-centered MTV and the distinctly middle-aged "Dave" TV to UKTV's "Gold." Streaming services such as Netflix exponentially advance the capacities of customization through tens of thousands of subgenres (Madrigal 2014). Digitization has also strengthened access to markets (if not necessarily larger audiences) of independent media producers and public service coproductions that offer more nuanced representations of aging, gender and sexuality (Marshall and Swinnen, this volume), while other niche media targeted at older audiences, such as *Zoomer* magazine in Marshall's study, fail to break free from a wider cultural frame of aging as lack that is best negotiated through the prolongation of youth. As mass media thus become increasingly specialized and divisions between professional and user generated content are eroded (with the latter itself now frequently the subject of mass media discourses), distinctions between mass media and social media content are increasingly futile.

Thirdly, media are more than the sum of mediated content. They are technologies and social practices, manifested in habits, rituals, and performances, embedded not only in the fabric of modern everyday life (e.g., Moores 2000; Scannel 1996; Silverstone 1994) but also in the life course. The example of media use in advanced old age highlights their importance lucidly. To many in the final stages of their life television takes on the role of a last companion, radio the voice that keeps one company, long after children have left and life partners have passed away or are too ill to offer sustained interpersonal communication. Even if vision and hearing limit comprehension and no longer allow watching television or listening to the radio in the way that is presupposed in textual analysis of these media, television, and radio remain sources of entertainment, happiness, and indeed security and shelter. These particular emotive qualities of television and hence its importance in the life course and particularly so in late life solitude, are still best captured in Roger Silverstone's analysis (1994) of the medium as a transitional object. And like the original transitional object of early childhood in Winnicott's work, television serves as a means of negotiating transitions of life phases through maintaining (proxy) attachments that allow for the maintenance of a sense of ontological security. It provides a sense of home and belonging throughout the life course, a quality that becomes of greatest importance when other bonds disappear and other past practices and hobbies become unsustainable. In turn, as both Silverstone's (1999) and Hartley's (1999) analyses of the historic context of early television remind us, television is of course part of the precise sociocultural forces of suburbanization, consumerism, the formation of the nuclear family, and of technologies of "mobile privatisation" (Williams 1974), that have fuelled the rapid growth of single person households in late age. In studying the interplay between media and the life course, we hence need to broaden the research agenda beyond the study of media representations of aging and the life course and engage in the wider sociological study of the relevance of media—as texts *and* technologies—in different life phases.

This leads me to my fourth and final point: not only does the need for the analysis of interplay between media and aging extend beyond the study of representations of aging, but media are intrinsically embedded in the contemporary life course and the process of aging through two fundamental dimensions in the constitution of the modern self: memory and identity. Media and cultural studies have long paid particular attention to early life phases. The fact that childhood and youth have been a particular focus of the field is to be explained through social and policy concerns over the vulnerability of children and adolescents as much as the particular historical context in which the discipline formed: the 1960s, 1970s, and 1980s, were indeed the age of new, and highly visible youth cultures driving profound social and cultural change. Today, as baby boomers are the first generation which has grown up fully immersed in (mediated) popular culture and consumerism, to approach retirement and late life, subcultures, fan cultures, and affective and intensive media engagements are no longer the prerogative of the young. Discourses about celebrity as a means of participation in wider public debate, for instance, are now utilized in later life phases, too (Claessens; van den Bulck, this volume). Similarly, Scodari (this volume) maps out some of the conflicts arising from fan communities in middle or later age claiming affiliation to aspects of popular culture aimed at adolescents. In the cases of many music subcultures such as punks (Bennett 2006) or goths (Hodkinson 2011; see also Hodkinson and Bennett 2012) the power to set the symbolic canon within interpretative communities and thus to shape the norms and practices of fans and subcultures appears to rest yet more firmly with the generation who were engaged in the formation of these cultures and now have progressed deep into adulthood. Sports fandom (e.g., Sandvoss 2003; 2012) has long been a means to narrate one's life course, as is illustrated by the not uncommon practice in Britain and North America of having a deceased fan's ashes scattered in their favorite team's stadium or ballpark.

What follows is that media use is now a viable identity position in all life phases across different genres and cultural forms, as Harrington and Bielby (this volume) insightfully document. Affective engagements with media and popular culture thus offer a structure to both inward and outward-looking dimensions of identity: inward-looking as media and popular culture offer chronological markers of life phases and historical eras (such as the attendance at memorable music festivals, an important sports event, film release, or the songs associated with falling in or out of love, etc.) and thus offer a syntax to the ordering of our memory that also functions as an indexical trigger through which memories can be accessed and nostalgia is lived (listening to that special song, the ritual viewing of annually occurring sports or media events, and so on); outward-looking as our media use, fandom and fan practices are shared with, and visible to, those around us. From everyday life talk about our favorite television show or celebrity, sharing content from blogs to remixes online, via the events we attend, hobbies we have (see Katz, this volume), and the way we dress, to holidays and fan pilgrimages (see Adams, this volume), we communicate aspects of our identity and self-image. Let me illustrate this with a final example: few places are more firmly associated with seemingly hedonistic youth culture than the Balearic party island of Ibiza which over the past three decades has become the global center of electronic dance and house music. Yet rather than serving as an ephemeral space for the neotribal gathering of adolescents as Bennett (2004) suggested, I found that house music fandom and accompanying pilgrimages to the island served as a central identity resource through which transitions of the life course were formulated and negotiated by participants in my recent study of regular visitors to the island (Sandvoss 2013). Their photographs from previous travels, the careful cataloging of past songs, and online discussions about past and present in Ibicencan travel all served to form a frame in which memories were ordered into a coherent self-narrative. Through their past visits to the island, important life phases—graduating from school and moving to university, meeting a life partner or breaking up with someone, or making new friends—were marked and positioned within an overall life trajectory. In turn such inward-looking memories formed the basis of outward-looking practices: visiting clubs, attending parties, discovering new music, sharing memories through social media, even holding significant life events such as weddings on the island. The fact that house music and travelling to Ibiza played a sustained central role in the everyday life and identity of these participants, some of whom were now in their forties and fifties (and who reported meeting regular visitors to the island in their sixties and older) reflected the wider social and cultural change, which Jonathan Gray, Lee Harrington, and myself (2007) pointed to, in assessing the causes for the now near ubiquity of contemporary fandom: in a world in which traditional markers of identity such as employment, kinship, and nationality are declining in stability and/or relevance, the voluntary communities (e.g., Sandvoss 2003; 2005a) and identity positions derived from media use and engagements with popular culture are of growing centrality. Rather than being a contributing factor, such media use and consumption are thus a consequence of and reaction to the increasing liquidity of our life worlds as Bauman (2005) observes. This, in conclusion, underlines Harrington and Bielby's call for a greater synthesis between studies of the life course and media studies, in which each field has much to gain from the other. Almost univocally, for example, participants in my study praised what they had experienced as the "ageless" spirit of clubbing and partying in Ibiza in which all generations mixed freely and all forms of expressions and preferences—from sartorial to sexual— appeared permissible to any age group. It is in light of Featherstone and Hepworth's (1991) above-mentioned notion of the "mask of aging" that we can fully appreciate the importance that these experiences hold to participants in later life phases as they enable one to break restrictive social and cultural norms and practices which, alongside physical limitations, form part of the restrictive shell of later life. If aging creates a mask that is felt to conceal the "true self"—and thus ruptures the link between inward and outward-looking identity and self-narratives—then affective media consumption and cultural engagements serve as a mirror of consumption (Sandvoss 2005a) in which the inner self can recognize itself as much as project this inner self outwards.

As societies grow older and media permeate most aspects of everyday life, this is one of many conceptual syntheses that will be needed to further our understating of transformations to the self and its life world in the twenty-first century. It is time for the study of the interplay of aging, media, and culture to come of age.

Chapter Seventeen

Afterword

A View from Gerontology

Merril Silverstein

Almost forty years ago, Robert Butler (1975) established the modern era of gerontology in his Pulitzer Prize-winning book *Why Survive? Being Old in America*. Dr. Butler, who coined the term "ageism," wrote about the old as a marginalized population subject to the "painful, humiliating, debilitating, and isolating" insensitivities of the wider world (Butler 1975, 2). Since that time much has changed for the old and the societies within which they reside. Just the existence of a scholarly volume dedicated to aging, media, and culture attests to this change. It is nearly impossible to imagine that in 1975 older adults would be treated in cultural terms, let alone analyzed with respect to their media representation.

Aging is now big business and mature adults are its consumers. We are told in countless ads in electronic and print media that aging can be stalled or even reversed, and that youth culture is alive and well and residing in the hearts, minds, and bodies of aging baby boomers. And yet as the chapters in this volume show, ageism still resonates in media images of the old, both propagating and reflecting ageist attitudes in the general public. Perhaps these contradictory trends should not be surprising as aging is replete with paradoxes and ironies. For instance, why do our minds and bodies fail just at the time that we approach our fullest understanding of life?

In this afterword, I draw out several gerontological themes and orientations, each with similar dynamic tensions echoed in the preceding chapters. These are: (1) diversity in aging; (2) success and failure paradigms of aging; and (3) the life course perspective of aging.

DIVERSITY IN AGING

The growth of the older population since the beginning of the twentieth century is unprecedented in human history. The sheer increase in the relative size of the older population has been driven in part by reductions in fertility, reductions in infant and childhood mortality, and increases in adult life expectancy (in that order), producing a robust consumer market to which marketers can cater. As we have seen cited in several chapters, the use of aspirational images predominates as a marketing tool, creating attractive models of old age but also producing unrealistic, and for some, unattainable ideals of aging well. On the other hand, negative media images of older adults as sick, frail, confused, and demented are also documented. Yet both types of depictions are particularly poor representations of the old. Much research has demonstrated that across many dimensions of the human condition, diversity increases with age (Nelson and Dannefer 1992). Physical health, mental health, and cognitive ability all show more variation as age increases.

The theory of cumulative advantage and disadvantage posits a widening of inequality gaps with aging, as the rich get richer and preserve their health longer and the poor get poorer and experience more rapid health deterioration (Ferraro and Shippee 2009). This produces something of a conundrum in that it is more wrongheaded to treat older people as if they were alike than to treat younger people as a homogeneous mass. Late life diversity makes stereotypical portrayals of the old particularly egregious. In the language of advertisers, there are more market segments among the old than among the young.

However, the media do not represent demographic truths, the most dramatic example cited in several chapters being the continued underrepresentation of older women in television programming and movie production. Yet, older widowed women are among the poorest population segments of society (Cellini, McKernan, and Ratcliffe 2008), which limits their purchasing power and makes them a less attractive market to cater to. This is not to say that the double jeopardy of sexism and ageism is absent as a reason for the underrepresentation of older women in mass media; nevertheless it behooves cultural critics to separate out rational market decisions from discriminatory cultural ones, though the two likely interact and reinforce each other.

SUCCESS AND FAILURE PARADIGMS OF AGING

The paradigm of *successful aging* is arguably the single model of aging that has most crossed over into the public discourse. Formalized by Rowe and Kahn (1997), the successful aging paradigm is widely accepted as the central framework for how to age well. Set up as a prescriptive plan for success for growing old, this paradigm focuses on behaviors that help avoid disease and disability, maintain high cognitive and physical functioning, and promote engagement in social and productive activities. The explicit message is that aging is under volitional control and that adhering to these dictates will extend middle age as long as possible and forestall entry into disability and dependence. The implicit message, and one that guides a quintessentially American take on aging, is a culling of winners from losers in the game of life, where the winners are hale and hearty and the losers are sick and frail. Regardless of whether its cause is genetic, environmental, or due to random determinants, senescence is considered a defeat that could have been avoided by following "the rules."

From a more macro perspective, the meme of winners and losers is found in the pessimistic scenario offered by Fries (1983) who characterized the aging revolution of the twentieth century as "the failure of success." He noted quite accurately that many older adults will be living out their longer lifetimes with cognitive and physical impairments. Although Fries meant his statements to mobilize medicine and public health to pay attention to chronic and degenerative diseases, we again see how ingrained the discourse of success and failure is built into the schemas of professional gerontologists struggling to make sense of the conundrum of human aging. As noted in this volume's chapters, media messages play on the yearning for success and the fear of failure by presenting aspirational images of an active, wrinkle-free, and body-toned old age, as if death were not the great equalizer. The so-called failures in the aging game are portrayed as frail, confused, and sometimes farcical figures. Aspiration and anxiety are two sides of the same coin, reflecting ambivalences arising from a socially constructed cultural position of the old that is reified by the internalization of damaging societal images and a false consciousness of everlasting youth (Hazan 1994).

Much scholarly attention has been devoted to the compression of morbidity or a reduction in the amount of extended life that will be spent in poor health. The assumption built into the desire to compress morbidity is that extending life without commensurately maintaining quality of life is not a desirable outcome; however, this begs the question as to what exactly is meant by *quality*? Often missing in the debate on successful aging are the intangible positive qualities often associated with old age such as gaining wisdom, perspective, satisfaction, and a sense of meaningfulness in life. Understanding that each progressive life stage involves a reappraisal of personal expectations is key to explaining why late life frailty—that may seem abhorrent to the young—may indeed be a richly rewarding time of life. That satisfaction with life increases with age is known as "the paradox of aging" (Charles and Carstensen 2010); but even the word *paradox* tells us much about our assumptions about the capacity of older adults to be happy, as if we should be surprised that the old are happy! To be sure, some cultural constructions of old age go beyond the simple dichotomy of success and failure to a more nuanced view of aging. For instance, one can imagine that Far East societies that profess filial piety as a cultural goal are less apt to view aging as negatively as it is in the West and perhaps portray less negative images of the old in their media as well.

With regard to the future, there is some debate as to whether or not healthy life expectancy will continue to increase in the United States (Zeng, Crimmins, and Robine 2006), but at best it is a mixed picture: for many, living longer will increase the time spent with a disabling condition. It is unarguable that the sheer size of the aging population insures that there will be more adults aging with a disability and in need of long-term and expensive end-of-life care. This growth in the frail older population may reintroduce a culture of "generational warfare" and return "greedy geezer" as a media trope if older adults come to be viewed as responsible for the economic distress of youth—a form of public discourse that seems to emerge during times of economic austerity.

THE LIFE COURSE PERSPECTIVE ON AGING

The life course perspective is creatively employed in several chapters of this volume, particularly in analyzing how the adoption of a cultural identity stands at the intersection of personal biography and history. The life course perspective is a comprehensive, almost hegemonic framework that has served as an analytical lens for much social gerontological research over the past several decades. In part it focuses on how attitudes, beliefs, values, and social action are shaped by exposure to historical events at an impressionable age. Cultural imprinting is hypothesized to take place at the critical period of early adulthood and is then thought to endure over the adult life span. The *impressionable youth phenomenon* specifies a similar dynamic as applied to the socialization of youth to core values. Research has demonstrated that political and social values are established early and once established are not susceptible to great change (Alwin and Krosnick 1991). However, altruistic values—defined as egalitarianism and universalism—have been found to strengthen with aging even as the broader social environment becomes *less* altruistic over historical time (Roberts and Bengtson 1999). That several dynamic tempos related to biographical and historical time are simultaneously at work is a theoretical and empirical insight that has relevance for cultural studies of aging.

The life course perspective for all its emphasis on the dynamic properties of biography and history, is however, rather static when it comes to cultural considerations. The idea of impressionable youth rarely accounts for drift or transformation in how cultural constructs are differently embodied and enacted with the passage into new life stages. Consumer culture may rid cultural objects of their original galvanizing charge. A recent personal example is revealing on this count: Watching Super Bowl XLVIII, I took note of a commercial with a seventy-two-year-old Bob Dylan hawking cars for Chrysler. As an aging baby boomer myself, I was forced to confront the contradiction between Dylan, a cultural icon of the 1960s protest generation, and this corporatized version of Dylan selling luxury cars with the jingoistic message to buy American. Perhaps my mental representation of Dylan was revealed to be a chimera built on the façade of what after all is an adopted poetic name (he was born Robert Zimmerman). Or with his own aging, Dylan's professed values diverged from those of his origins and his most loyal fans. In either case, the culture of our youth may take on new meanings as it is reinterpreted in light of new historical-cultural contexts.

Karl Mannheim (1952/1998) carved out the intellectual space for understanding how social change is driven by a self-conscious cohort, galvanized by a common cause, and radicalized by a fresh interpretation of the world. Mannheim's notion of an *actualized* generation is embodied by baby boomers who in their earlier years exerted social, sexual, and political opposition to the status quo. Famously, the generation gap between the baby boom generation and their parents is often described in terms of a wedge that drove apart younger and older generations. Yet, research documents that the social and religious values of baby boomers, even in their youth, were substantially influenced by their parents (Min, Silverstein, and Lendon 2012). Cohort differences and parent-child similarities are not incompatible truths as the former applies to unrelated individuals in each generation and the latter to linked generations within common lineages. In this sense, what we glean from our family members about aging may offer resistance to dominant cultural messages from the media about growing old.

Mass entertainment, including rock concerts and football games, are sources of cross-generational integration in a sphere outside the family. For instance, the Rolling Stones (with Mick Jagger clearly aging successfully) have become a multigenerational draw, with older, middle-aged, young adults, and adolescents in attendance at their concerts. Fandoms of this type—with their own rituals, logos, electronic networks, and websites—may well continue to function as microforums of age integration. Such age mixing is rare in a society where age segmentation is common and is viewed as an underlying source of ageism (Hagestad and Uhlenberg 2005).

Finally, the role of human agency, another life course precept, is not to be underestimated. Older individuals, as do all individuals, make choices in their adaptation to the challenges and changing conditions of life. We know that the aging process is not a steady march downhill but one characterized by adaptations to the physical and mental vicissitudes of growing old. One vivid example of this plasticity in aging is Vladimir Horowitz, the celebrated classical pianist who continued to perform on the world's stages well into his

80s. Horowitz attributed his seemingly miraculous continuity on the stage to three adaptive strategies: increasing his practice time, concentrating on pieces he knew best, and "fooling" the audience by playing slower segments of the music extra slowly so that the rapid tempos sounded faster by contrast (Baltes and Staudinger 1993). Perhaps had Jerry Garcia survived into old age, he too would have used such a set of strategies to match his older fans who themselves adapted their concert behavior to better suit their aging bodies.

CONCLUSION

In bringing together several scholarly communities that rarely interact, this volume has created an intellectual agenda that is at once refreshing and challenging. Ageism is the last "ism" not to be politically incorrect; free market mechanisms that guide the entertainment and advertising industries have not lost revenue offending older adults. Media depictions of old age represent a great feedback mechanism both magnifying and distorting public conceptualizations of aging. Yet, as we have seen described in the preceding chapters, the older population is diverse and likely to become more diverse, making cultural considerations of aging increasingly difficult to summarize. This volume has produced much to consider about how the old are depicted in media and represented in the cultural Zeitgeist. That the constitution of the older population is not synchronized with media representations of it should be cause for concern, but this is also not inconsistent with the paradoxes and contradictions of what is a dynamic population that is redefined with every cohort that replenishes it.

References

Adams, Rebecca G. 1991. "Experiential Consumption: The Meaning of Expenditures in a Music Subculture." Presentation at the Annual Meeting of the American Sociological Association, Cincinnati, OH.

———. 1992. "The Persistence of Deadhead Subculture." Presentation at the Annual Meetings of the American Sociological Association, Pittsburgh, PA.

———. 1998. "Inciting Sociological Thought by Studying the Deadhead Community: Engaging Publics in Dialogue." *Social Forces* 77 (1): 1–25.

———. 1999. "A Portable Community: Facilitating Repeated Interactions at Grateful Dead Shows." Presentation at the Annual Meetings of the American Sociological Association, Chicago, IL.

———. 2003. "Stigma and the Inappropriately Stereotyped: The Deadhead Professional." *Sociation Today* 1 (1).

———. 2012. "Terrapin Station Demographics and 'Deadication': The Furthur Festival '98 Data." *Dead Letters* IV (2010): 51–62. Reprinted in *Reading the Grateful Dead: A Critical Survey*, edited by Nicholas Meriwether, 193–205. Lanham, MD: Scarecrow Press.

Adams, Rebecca G., Amy M. Ernstes, and Kelly M. Lucey. 2014. "After Jerry's Death: Achieving Continuity in Deadhead Identity and Community." In *Popular Music Fandom: Identities, Roles and Practices*, edited by Mark Duffett, 186–206. London: Routledge.

Adams, Rebecca G., and Jane Rosen-Grandon. 2002. "Mixed Marriage: Music Community Membership as a Source of Marital Strain." In *Inappropriate Relationships*, edited by Robin Goodwin and Duncan Cramer, 79–100. Mahwah: Lawrence Erlbaum.

Adams, Rebecca G., and Emily M. Taylor. Forthcoming. "Aging and Happiness in the Third Age." In Melikşah Demir, *Friendship and Happiness: Across the Life-Span and in Different Cultures*. New York: Springer.

Addison, Heather. 2010. "'That Younger, Fresher Woman': *Old Wives for New* (1918) and Hollywood's Cult of Youth." In *Staging Age: The Performance of Age in Theatre, Dance, and Film*, edited by Valerie B. Lipscomb and Leni Marshall, 11–26. New York: Palgrave Macmillan.

Agogo, David, George R. Milne, and Charles D. Schewe. 2013. "Who Wants to Age? Maybe You Will!" Presentation at the Association for Marketing and Health Care Research Conference, Big Sky, MT.

Ajzen Icek, and Martin Fishbein. 1980. *Understanding Attitudes and Predicting Social Behavior.* Englewood Cliffs: Prentice-Hall.

Allen, Robert C. 1985. *Speaking of Soap Operas.* Chapel Hill: University of North Carolina Press.

———. 2004. "Conversations with Scholars of American Popular Culture." *Americana: The Journal of American Popular Culture (1900–Present)* 3 (1). www.americanpopularculture. com/journal/articles/spring_2004/allen.htm.

Allergan Annual Report. 2012. "Innovation for the Future." 6.

Almerico, Gina M., and H. Thompson Fillmer. 1989. "The Portrayal of the Elderly in the U.S. Print Media." *Reading* 23 (2): 98–104.

Alwin, Duane F., and Jon A. Krosnick. 1991. "Aging, Cohorts, and the Stability of Sociopolitical Orientations Over the Life Span." *American Journal of Sociology* 97 (1): 169–95.

American Free Press. "US actress vows appeal over film database age ruling." *Hindustan Times*, April 13, 2013. www.hindustantimes.com/Entertainment/Tabloid/US-actress-vowsappeal-over-film-database-age-ruling/Article1-1043720.aspx.

American Society for Aesthetic Plastic Surgery. "The skinny on why women use Botox." October 15, 2012. www.surgery.org/consumers/plastic-surgery-newsbriefs/skinnywomen-botox-1038510.

Angel, Katherine. 2012. "Contested Psychiatric Ontology and Feminist Critique: 'Female Sexual Dysfunction' and the *Diagnostic and Statistical Manual*." *History of the Human Sciences* 25 (4): 3–24.

Anisiobi, J. J. "Simon Cowell embraces his grey hair . . . as he reveals he's back in touch with Cheryl Cole." *Mail Online*, January 25, 2012. www.dailymail.co.uk/tvshowbiz/article-2091397/Cheryl-Cole-misses-saysSimon-Cowell-reveals-theyre-touch.html#ixzz2aXK JKYqh.

Ansello, Edward. 1977. "Age and Ageism in Children's First Literature." *Educational Gerontology* 2: 255–74.

Antonijevic, Smiljana. 2008. "From Text to Gesture Online: A Microethnographic Analysis of Nonverbal Communication in the Second Life Virtual Environment." *Information, Communication and Society* 11 (2): 221–38.

Arjan, Rajiv, Ulrike Pfeil, and Panayiotis Zaphiris. 2008. "Age Differences in Online Social Networking." In *Proceedings of the Twenty-Sixth Annual CHI Conference on Human Factors in Computing Systems*, 2739–44. New York: ACM Press. doi: 10.1145/13586 28.1358754.

Atchley, Robert. 1989. "A Continuity Theory of Normal Aging." *The Gerontologist* 29 (2): 183–90.

———. 2009. *Spirituality and Aging.* Baltimore: Johns Hopkins Press.

Ayalon, Liat, Israel Doron, Ehud Bodner, and Noit Inbar. 2013. "Macro- and Micro-Level Predictors of Age Categorization: Results from the European Social Survey." *European Journal of Ageing*. Advance online publication. doi: 10.1007/s10433-013-0282-8.

Bailey, Steve. 2005. *Media Audiences and Identity: Self-Construction in the Fan Experience.* New York: Palgrave Macmillan.

Balasubramani, Venkat. "Actress suing IMDb takes the witness stand." *The Hollywood Reporter*, April 9, 2013. www.hollywoodreporter.com/thr-esq/actress-suing-imdbtakes-witness-435230.

Balazs, Anne L. 1995. "The Use and Image of Mature Adults in Health Care Advertising (1954–1989)." *Health Marketing Quarterly* 12 (3): 13–26.

Ballantyne, Alison, Luke Trenwith, Samara Zubrinich, and Megan Corlis. 2010. "'I Feel Less Lonely': What Older People Say about Participating in a Social Networking Website." *Quality in Ageing and Older Adults* 11 (3): 25–35. doi: 10.5042/qiaoa.2010.0526.

Baltes, Margaret, and Frieder Lang. 1997. "Everyday Functioning and Successful Aging: The Impact of Resources." *Psychology and Aging* 12: 433–43.

Baltes, Paul B. 1997. "On the Incomplete Architecture of Human Ontogeny: Selection, Optimization, and Compensation as Foundation of Developmental Theory." *American Psychologist* 52: 366–80.

Baltes, Paul B., Ulman Lindenberger, and Ursula M. Staudinger. 2006. "Life-Span Theory in Developmental Psychology." In *Handbook of Child Psychology: Vol. 1. Theoretical Models of Development*, edited by William Damon and Richard M. Lerner, 569–664. Hoboken: Wiley.

Baltes, Paul B., and Ursula M. Staudinger. 1993. "The Search for a Psychology of Wisdom." *Current Directions in Psychological Science* 2 (3): 75–80.

Bandura, Albert, and Richard H. Walters. 1963. *Social Learning and Personality Development.* New York: Holt, Rinehart and Winston.

Banks, Jaime. 2013. "Close Intimate Playthings? Understanding Player-Avatar Relationships as a Function of Attachment, Agency, and Intimacy." Presentation at the Association of Internet Researchers Conference. Denver, CO.

Banner, Lois. 1993. *In Full Flower: Aging Women, Power, and Sexuality.* New York: Vintage.

Barak, Benny. 2009. "Age Identity: A Cross-Cultural Global Approach." *International Journal of Behavioral Development* 33 (1): 2–11.

Barak, Benny, and Leon Schiffman. 1981. "Cognitive Age: A Nonchronological Age Variable." In *NA-Advances in Consumer Research*, Volume 8, edited by Kent B. Monroe, 602–6. Ann Arbor, MI: Association for Consumer Research.

Barba, Beth, and Anita Tesh. 2011. "Making Community Events Accessible to Older Adults." In *Aging Well: Gerontological Education for Nurses and Other Health Professionals*, edited by May Wykle and Sarah Gueldner, 191–98. Burlington, MA: Jones and Bartlett Learning.

Barbieri, Federica. 2008. "Patterns of Age-Based Linguistic Variation in American English." *Journal of Sociolinguistics* 12 (1): 58–88.

Bargh, John A., Mark Chen, and Lara Burrows. 1996. "Automaticity of Social Behavior: Direct Effects of Trait Construct and Stereotype Activation on Action." *Journal of Personality and Social Psychology* 71: 230–44.

Barlow, John Perry. 1987. "Throwing Stones." In *Songs for the Dead.* Wyoming: Self-Published.

Barnes, Barry. 2011. *Everything I Know about Business I Learned from the Grateful Dead.* New York: Business Plus.

Barrett, Anne E. 2003. "Socioeconomic Status and Age Identity: The Role of Dimensions of Health in the Subjective Construction of Age." *Journals of Gerontology: Psychological Sciences and Social Sciences* 58: 101–9.

———. 2005. "Gendered Experiences in Midlife: Implications for Age Identity." *Journal of Aging Studies* 19: 163–83.

Barrett, Anne E., and Cheryl Robbins. 2008. "The Multiple Sources of Women's Aging Anxiety and their Relationship with Psychological Distress." *Journal of Aging and Health* 20: 32–65.

Barrett, Anne E., and Carmen von Rohr. 2008. "Gendered Perceptions of Aging: An Examination of College Students." *International Journal of Aging and Human Development* 67: 359–86.

Barrett, Julia, and Stuart Kirk. 2000. "Running Focus Groups with Elderly and Disabled Elderly Participants." *Applied Ergonomics* 31: 621–29.

Bartsch, Anne. 2012. "As Time Goes By: What Changes and What Remains the Same in Entertainment Experience Over the Life Span?" *Journal of Communication* 62: 588–608.

Bauman, Zygmunt. 2005. *Liquid Life.* Cambridge: Polity Press.

Baumann, Shyon, and Kim de Laat. 2012. "Socially Defunct: A Comparative Analysis of the Underrepresentation of Older Women in Advertising." *Poetics* 40: 514–41. doi: 10.1016/j.poetic.2012.08.002.

Baym, Nancy. 2000. *Tune In, Log On: Soaps, Fandom, and Online Community.* Thousand Oaks: Sage.

Bazzini, Doris G., William D. McIntosh, Stephen M. Smith, Sabrina Cook, and Caleigh Harris. 1997. "The Aging Woman in Popular Film: Underrepresented, Unattractive, Unfriendly, and Unintelligent." *Sex Roles* 36 (7–8): 531–43. doi: 10.1007/BF02766689.

BBC News. "Acting unions criticise IMDb in age row." *BBC News*, October 28, 2011. www.bbc.co.uk/news/entertainment-arts-15492579.

Behm-Morawitz, Elizabeth, Melissa A. Click, and Jennifer S. Aubrey. 2010. "Relating to *Twilight*: Fans' Responses to Love and Romance in the Vampire Franchise." In *Bitten by Twilight: Youth Culture, Media, and the Vampire Franchise*, edited by Melissa A. Click, Jennifer S. Aubrey, and Elizabeth Behm-Morawitz, 137–54. New York: Peter Lang.

Bell, Caroline, Cara Fausset, Sarah Farmer, Julie Nguyen, Linda Harley, and W. Bradley Fain. 2013. "Examining Social Media Use Among Older Adults." In *Proceedings of the 24th ACM Conference on Hypertext and Social Media,* 158–63. New York: ACM Press. doi: 10.1145/2481492.2481509.

Bender, Mike, Paulette Bauckham, and Andrew Norris. 1999. *The Therapeutic Purposes of Reminiscence.* London: Sage.

Bennett, Andy. 2004. "Chilled Ibiza?: Dance Tourism and the Neo-Tribal Island Community?" In *Island Musics,* edited by Kevin Dawe, 123–36. Oxford: Berg.

———. 2006. "Punk's Not Dead: The Continuing Significance of Punk Rock for an Older Generation of Fans." *Sociology* 40 (2): 219–35.

———. 2013. *Music, Style, and Aging: Growing Old Disgracefully?* Philadelphia, PA: Temple University Press.

Benning, Ashley. 2011. "'How Old Are You?' Representations of Aging in the Saga." In *Theorizing* Twilight: *Critical Essays on What's At Stake in a Post-Vampire World,* edited by Maggie Parke and Natalie Wilson, 87–101. Jefferson, NC: McFarland. Kindle edition.

Benyon, Caryl. 2009. "Drug Use and Ageing: Older People Do Take Drugs!" *Age and Ageing* 38: 8–10.

Berger, John. 1972. *Ways of Seeing.* London: Penguin.

Berlatsky, Noah. "'Twilight' vs. 'Hunger Games': Why do so many grown-ups hate Bella." *The Atlantic,* November 15, 2011. www.theatlantic.com/entertainment/archive/2011/11/twilight-vs-hunger-games-why-do-so-many-grown-ups-hate-bella/248439/.

Beugnet, Martine. 2006. "Screening the Old: Femininity as Old Age in Contemporary French Cinema." *Studies in the Literary Imagination* 39 (2): 1–20.

Bielby, Denise D. 2009. "Gender Inequality in Culture Industries: Women and Men Writers in Film and Television." *Sociologie du Travail* 51: 237–52.

Bielby, Denise D., and William T. Bielby. 1996. "Women and Men in Film: Gender Inequality Among Writers in a Culture Industry." *Gender and Society* 10: 248–70.

———. 2001. "Audience Segmentation and Age Stratification Among Television Writers." *Journal of Broadcasting and Electronic Media* 45 (3): 391–412. doi: 10.1207/s15506878jobem4503_2.

———. 2002. "Hollywood Dreams, Harsh Realities: Writing for Film and Television." *Contexts* 1 (4): 21–27.

———. 2004. "Audience Aesthetics and Popular Culture." In *Matters of Culture: Cultural Practices in Sociology,* edited by Roger Friedland and John Mohr, 295–317. Cambridge: Cambridge University Press.

Bielby, William T., and Denise D. Bielby. 1999. "Organizational Mediation of Project-Based Labor Markets: Talent Agencies and the Careers of Screenwriters." *American Sociological Review* 64 (1): 64–84.

Biggs, Simon, Chris Phillipson, Rebecca Leach, and Anne-Marie Money. 2007. "The Mature Imagination and Consumption Strategies: Age and Generation in the Development of a United Kingdom Baby Boomer Identity." *International Journal of Ageing and Later Life* 2 (2): 31–60.

Bildgårdt, Torbjörn. 2000. "The Sexuality of Elderly People on Film—Visual Limitations." *Journal of Aging and Identity* 5 (3): 169–83. doi: 10.1023/A:1009565321357.

Blaikie, Andrew. 1999. *Ageing and Popular Culture.* Cambridge: Cambridge University Press.

Blau, Zena S. 1956. "Changes in Status and Age Identification." *American Sociological Review* 20: 198–202.

Bloch, Naomi, and Bertram C Bruce. 2011. "Older Adults and the New Public Sphere." In *Proceedings of the 2011 iConference—iConference,* 1–7. New York: ACM Press. doi: 10.1145/1940761.1940762.

Blum, Virginia L. 2003. *Flesh Wounds: The Culture of Cosmetic Surgery.* Berkeley: University of California Press.

Boler, Megan. 2007. "Hypes, Hopes and Actualities: New Digital Cartesianism and Bodies in Cyberspace." *New Media and Society* 9 (1): 139–68.

Bonner, Frances, and Susan McKay. 2000. "Challenges, Determination and Triumphs: Inspirational Discourse in Women's Magazine Health Stories." *Continuum: Journal of Media and Cultural Studies* 14 (2): 133–44.

Booth, Paul. 2008. "Rereading Fandom: MySpace Character Personas and Narrative Identification." *Critical Studies in Media Communication* 25 (5): 514–36.

boyd, danah, and Eszter Hargittai. 2010. "Facebook Privacy Settings: Who Cares?" *First Monday* 15 (8): 1–17. firstmonday.org/htbin/cgiwrap/bin/ojs/index.php/fm/article/view/3086.

Bradley, Peter. 2007. "Performance and Property: Archive.org, Authorship, and Authenticity." In *Grateful Dead and Philosophy*, edited by Steven Gimbel, 37–48. Peru: Open Court Publishing.

Bramlett-Solomon, Sharon, and Vanessa Wilson. 1989. "Images of the Elderly in *Life* and *Ebony*, 1978–1987." *Journalism Quarterly*, Spring: 185–88.

Branchik, Blaine J. 2010. "Silver Dollars: The Development of the US Elderly Market Segment." *Journal of Historical Research in Marketing* 2 (2): 174–97.

Brandtzæg, Petter Bae, Marika Lüders, and Jan Håvard Skjetne. 2010. "Too Many Facebook 'Friends'? Content Sharing and Sociability Versus the Need for Privacy in Social Network Sites." *International Journal of Human-Computer Interaction* 26 (11–12): 1006–30. doi: 10.1080/10447318.2010.516719.

Braun, Michael T. 2013. "Obstacles to Social Networking Website Use Among Older Adults." *Computers in Human Behavior* 29 (3): 673–80. doi: 10.1016/j.chb.2012.12.004.

Brooker, Will. 2002. *Using the Force: Creativity, Community and* Star Wars *Fans*. New York and London: Continuum.

Brookes, Fiona, and Peter Kelly. 2009. "Dolly Girls: Tweenies as Artefacts of Consumption." *Journal of Youth Studies* 12 (6): 599–613. doi: 10.1080/13676260902960745.

Bruford, Bill. 2009. *Bill Bruford: The Autobiography*. London: Jawbone Press.

Bruggeman, Daniëlle, and Anneke Smelik. 2010. "De Esthetiek en Erotiek van Ouderdom in de Beeldcultuur Ontrafeld." In *Seksualiteit van Ouderen: Een Multidisciplinaire Benadering*, edited by Aagje Swinnen, 267–90. Amsterdam: Amsterdam University Press.

Bull, Sarah. "'My bikini shot will haunt me for the rest of my life': Helen Mirren admits she will never live up to THAT photograph." *Mail Online*, February 22, 2011. www.dailymail.co.uk/tvshowbiz/article-2040108/Helen-MirrenBikini-photo-haunt-rest-life.html.

Burke, Moira, Cameron Marlow, and Thomas Lento. 2010. "Social Network Activity and Social Well-Being." In *Proceedings of the 28th International Conference on Human Factors in Computing Systems*, 1909–12. New York: ACM Press. doi: 10.1145/1753326.1753613.

Burton, Linda M. 1995. "Age Norms, the Timing of Family Role Transitions, and Intergenerational Caregiving Among Aging African American Women." *The Gerontologist* 36 (2): 199–208.

Butler, Robert N. 1975. *Why Survive? Being Old in America*. New York: Harper and Row.

Butt, Alex. "Jane Fonda: 73 and a half, and almost certainly hotter than you." *Grazia*, August 5, 2011. www.graziadaily.co.uk/fashion/archive/2011/08/05/janefonda-73-and-a-half-and-almost-certainly-hotter-than-you.html.

Cacchioni, Thea. 2007. "Heterosexuality and 'The Labour of Love': A Contribution to Recent Debates on Female Sexual Dysfunction." *Sexualities* 10 (3): 299–320.

Calasanti, Toni. 2007. "Bodacious Berry, Potency Wood and the Aging Monster: Gender and Age Relations in Anti-Aging Ads." *Social Forces* 86: 335–55.

———. 2009. "Theorizing Feminist Gerontology, Sexuality and Beyond: An Intersectional Approach." In *Handbook of Theories of Aging*. 2nd ed., edited by Vern L. Bengtson, Daphna Gans, Norella M. Putney, and Merril Silverstein, 471–85. New York: Springer.

Calasanti, Toni, and Neal King. 2005. "Firming the Floppy Penis: Age, Class, and Gender Relations in the Lives of Old Men." *Men and Masculinities* 8 (1): 3–23. doi: 10.1177/1097184X04268799.

Calcutt, Andrew. 1998. *Arrested Development: Pop Culture and the Erosion of Adulthood*. Washington, DC: Cassell.

Callens, Marc, and Koenraad Pauwels. 2006. "LOVO-2: De Steekproeven [the samples]." In *Het Leefsituatieonderzoek Vlaamse Ouderen (Lovo): LOVO-2 Rusthuis-en RVT-bewoners*

[The Life Situation Research of Flemish Older Adults: LOVO-2 Nursing Home Residents], edited by Lut Vanden Boer, Koenraad Pauwels, Marc Callens, and Valérie Carrette, 15–34. Brussel: CBGS.

Carmichael, Carl W. 1976. "Communication and Gerontology: Interfacing Disciplines." *Western Speech Communication* 40 (2): 121–29.

Carr, David. "New rules for the way we watch." *New York Times*, December 24, 2011. www.nytimes.com/2011/12/26/business/media/rules-for-the-new-ways-of-watching-david-carr.html?pagewanted=all&_r=0.

Carr, Dawn C., and Kathrin Komp, eds. 2011. *Gerontology in the Era of the Third Age*. New York: Springer.

Carr, Revell. 1999. "Deadhead Tales of the Supernatural: A Folklorist Analysis." In *Perspectives on the Grateful Dead: Critical Writings*, edited by Robert Weiner, 203–13. Westport: Greenwood.

Carrigan, Marylyn, and Isabelle Szmigin. 1998. "The Usage and Portrayal of Older Models in Contemporary Consumer Advertising." *Journal of Marketing Practice: Applied Marketing Science* 4 (8): 231–48. doi: 10.1108/EUM0000000004544.

———. 1999. "In Pursuit of Youth: What's Wrong with the Older Market?" *Marketing Intelligence and Planning* 17 (5): 222–30.

Carstensen, Laura L., Helene H. Fung, and Susan T. Charles. 2003. "Socioemotional Selectivity Theory and the Regulation of Emotion in the Second Half of Life." *Motivation and Emotion* 27 (2): 103–23.

Carstensen, Laura L., Derek M. Issacowitz, and Susan T. Charles. 1999. "Taking Time Seriously: A Theory of Socioemotional Selectivity." *American Psychologist* 54: 165–81.

Cashmore, Ellis. 2006. *Celebrity Culture*. New York: Routledge.

Caspi, Avshalom. 2000. "The Child Is the Father of the Man: Personality Continuities from Childhood to Adulthood." *Journal of Personality and Social Psychology* 78 (1): 158–72.

Cassata, Mary, Patricia A. Anderson, and Thomas Skill. 1983. "Images of Old Age on Daytime." In *Life on Daytime Television: Tuning in American Serial Drama*, edited by Mary Cassata and Thomas Skill, 37–44. Norwood: Ablex Publishing Corp.

Cavicchi, Daniel. 1998. *Tramps Like Us: Music and Meaning Among Springsteen Fans*. New York and Oxford: Oxford University Press.

Celebrity Beauty Buzz. "Celebrity youth secrets revealed." *Celebrity Beauty Buzz*, 2012. www.celebritybeautybuzz.com/2012/01/celebrity-youth-secrets-revealed/.

Cellini, Stephanie Riegg, Signe-Mary McKernan, and Caroline Ratcliffe. 2008. "The Dynamics of Poverty in the United States: A Review of Data, Methods, and Findings." *Journal of Policy Analysis and Management* 27: 577–605.

Centers for Disease Control. 2013. Healthy Places Terminology. www.cdc.gov/healthyplaces/terminology.htm.

Chambers, Deborah. 2012. "Sexist Ageing Consumerism and Emergent Modes of Resistance." In *Aging, Performance, and Stardom: Doing Age on the Stage of Consumerist Culture*, edited by Aagje Swinnen and John A. Stotesbury, 161–76. Vienna: LIT Verlag.

Chapman, Jane. 2005. *Comparative Media History: An Introduction*. Cambridge: Polity Press.

Charles, Susan T., and Laura L. Carstensen. 2010. "Social and Emotional Aging." *Annual Review of Psychology* 61: 383–409.

Charness, Neil, and Walter R. Boot. 2009. "Aging and Information Technology Use: Potential and Barriers." *Current Directions in Psychological Science* 18 (5): 253–58. doi: 10.1111/j.1467–8721.2009.01647.x.

Charness, Neil, and Patricia Holley. 2004. "The New Media and Older Adults: Usable and Useful?" *American Behavioral Scientist* 48 (4): 416–33. doi: 10.1177/0002764204270279.

Chayko, Mary. 1993. "How You 'Act Your Age' When You Watch TV." *Sociological Forum* 28 (4): 573–93.

Cherry, Katie E., Erin Jackson Walker, Jennifer Silva Brown, Julia Volaufova, Lynn R. Lamotte, David A. Welsh, L. Joseph Su, S. Michal Jazwinski, Rebecca Ellis, Robert H. Wood, and Madlyn I. Frisard. 2013. "Social Engagement and Health in Younger, Older, and Oldest-Old Adults in the Louisiana Healthy Aging Study (LHAS)." *Journal of Applied Gerontology* 32 (1): 51–75. doi: 10.1177/0733464811409034.

Chivers, Sally. 2011. *The Silvering Screen: Old Age and Disability in Cinema.* Toronto: University of Toronto Press.

Cieply, Michael. "Actress's privacy lawsuit challenges a web site." *New York Times*, March 4, 2012. www.nytimes.com/2012/03/05/business/media/junie-hoangs-imdblawsuit-and-internet-privacy.html?_r=2&.

Claessens, Nathalie. 2013a. *Celebrity, Media, and Audiences: Social and Cultural Meaning in Contemporary Western Societies.* Antwerp: Universitas.

———. 2013b. "Nursing Home Residents' Media Use from a Life Course Perspective." *Northern Lights: Film and Media Studies Yearbook* 11 (1): 35–50.

Clarke, Laura Hurd. 2010. *Facing Age: Women Growing Older in Anti-Aging Culture.* Lanham, MD: Rowman and Littlefield Publishers.

Coffman, Don. 2002. "Music and Quality of Life in Older Adults." *Psychomusicology* 18: 76–88.

Cohen, Patricia. 2012. *In Our Prime: The Invention of Middle Age.* New York: Scribner.

Cohen-Shalev, Amir. 2012. *Visions of Aging: Images of the Elderly in Film.* 2nd ed. Brighton: Sussex Academic Press.

Cohler, Bertram J., and Andrew Hostetler. 2003. "Linking Life Course and Life Story: Social Change and the Narrative Study of Lives Over Time." In *Handbook of the Life Course*, edited by Jeylan T. Mortimer and Michael J. Shanahan, 555–76. New York: Kluwer Academic/Plenum Publishers.

Collins, Suzanne. 2008. *Hunger Games.* New York: Scholastic Press.

Connidis, Ingrid Arnet. 1989. "The Subjective Experience of Aging: Correlates of Divergent Views." *Canadian Journal on Aging* 8: 7–18.

———. 2006. "Intimate Relationships: Learning from Later Life." In *Age Matters: Realigning Feminist Thinking*, edited by Toni M. Calasanti and Kathleen F. Slevin, 123–54. New York: Routledge.

Cooke, Marie, Wendy Moyle, David Shum, Scott Harrison, and Jenny Murfield. 2010 "A Randomized Controlled Trial Exploring the Effect of Music on Quality of Life and Depression in Older People with Dementia." *Journal of Health Psychology* 15 (5): 765–76.

Cornell, Dracula. 2009. *Clint Eastwood and Issues of American Masculinity.* New York: Fordham University Press.

Cornet, Roth. 2011. "Interview: 'Twilight' Scribe Melissa Rosenberg on 'Breaking Dawn' and Feminism." Screen Rant October 19, 2011. screenrant.com/twilight-breaking-dawn-interview-melissa-rosenberg-rothc-140261/.

Cornwell, Erin York, and Linda J. Waite. 2009. "Social Disconnectedness, Perceived Isolation, and Health Among Older Adults." *Journal of Health and Social Behavior* 50 (1): 31–48. doi: 10.1177/002214650905000103.

Costa, Paul T., and Robert R. McCrae. 1980. "Influence of Extraversion and Neuroticism on Subjective Well-Being: Happy and Unhappy People." *Journal of Personality and Social Psychology* 38 (4): 668–78.

Cox, David. "Twilight: The franchise that ate feminism." *The Guardian*, July 12, 2010. www.guardian.co.uk/film/filmblog/2010/jul/12/twilight-eclipse-feminism.

Cravit, David. 2008. *The New Old: How the Boomers Are Changing Everything . . . Again.* Toronto: ECW Press.

Creech, Andrea, Susan Hallam, Hilary McQueen, and Maria Varvarigou. 2013. "The Power of Music in the Lives of Older Adults." *Research Studies in Music Education* 35 (1): 87–102.

Crenshaw, Kimberlé Williams. 1993. "Beyond Racism and Misogyny: Black Feminism and 2 Live Live Crew." In *Words That Wound: Critical Race Theory, Assaultive Speech, and the First Amendment*, edited by Mari J. Matsuda, Charles R. Lawrence III, Richard Delgado, and Kimberlé Williams Crenshaw, 111–32. Boulder: Westview.

Cresci, M. Kay, Hossein N. Yarandi, and Roger W. Morrell. 2010. "The Digital Divide and Urban Older Adults." *Computers, Informatics, Nursing* 28 (2): 88–94. doi: 10.1097/NCN.0b013e3181cd8184.

Cuddy, Amy J. C., Michael I. Norton, and Susan T. Fiske. 2005. "This Old Stereotype: The Pervasiveness and Persistence of the Elderly Stereotype." *Journal of Social Issues* 61: 267–85.

Cumming, Elaine, and William Henry. 1961. *Growing Old: The Process of Disengagement.* New York: Basic Books.

Czaja, Sara J. 2005. "The Impact of Aging on Access to Technology." *Accessibility and Computing* 83: 7–11. doi: 10.1145/1102187.1102189.

Czaja, Sara J., Neil Charness, Arthur D. Fisk, Christopher Hertzog, Sankaran N. Nair, Wendy A. Rogers, and Joseph Sharit. 2006. "Factors Predicting the Use of Technology: Findings from the Center for Research and Education on Aging and Technology Enhancement (CREATE)." *Psychology and Aging* 21 (2): 333–52. doi: 10.1037/0882-7974.21.2.333.

Czaja, Sara J., and Chin Chin Lee. 2006. "The Impact of Aging on Access to Technology." *Universal Access in the Information Society* 5 (4): 341–49. doi: 10.1007/s10209-006-0060-x.

Dannefer, Dale, and Casey Miklowski. 2006. "Developments in the Life Course." In *The Futures of Old Age*, edited by J. A. Vincent, C. Phillipson, and M. Down, 30–39. London: Sage Publications.

Danowski, Jessica, and Tom Robinson. 2012. "The Portrayal of Older Characters in Popular Children's Picture Books in the US." *Journal of Children and Media* 6: 333–50.

Darnell, Emily A., Susan E. Mason, and Krisioloa Prifti. 2010. "Stereotypes and Representations of Aging in the Media." *Journal of Instructional Psychology* 37 (2): 189–90.

Davis, Fred D. 1989. "Perceived Usefulness, Perceived Ease of Use, and User Acceptance of Information Technology." *MIS Quarterly* 13 (3): 319–40.

Davis, Fred D., Richard P. Bagozzi, and Paul R. Warshaw. 1992. "Extrinsic and Intrinsic Motivation to Use Computers in the Workplace." *Journal of Applied Social Psychology* 22 (14): 1111–32. doi: 10.1111/j.1559-1816.1992.tb00945.x.

Davis, Kathy. 1995. *Reshaping the Female Body: The Dilemma of Cosmetic Surgery*. London: Routledge.

Davison, W. Phillips. 1983. "The Third Person Effect in Communication." *Public Opinion Quarterly* 47: 1–15.

De Backer, Charlotte J. S., Marc Nelissen, Patrick Vyncke, Johan Braeckman, and Francis T. McAndrew. 2007. "Celebrities: From Teachers to Friends." *Human Nature* 18 (4): 334–54.

de Medeiros, Kate. 2007. "Beyond the Memoir: Telling Life Stories Using Multiple Literary Forms." *Journal of Aging, Humanities and the Arts* 1, 159–67.

De Nora, Tia. 2000. *Music in Everyday Life.* Cambridge: Cambridge University Press.

Deaux, Kay. 1991. "Social Identities: Thoughts on Structure and Change." In *The Relational Self: Theoretical Convergences in Psychoanalysis and Social Psychology,* edited by Rebecca Curtis, 77–93. New York: Guildford Press.

Debord, Guy. 1995. *The Society of Spectacle.* New York: Zone Books.

Demakakos, Panayotes, Edlira Gjonca, and James Nazroo. 2007. "Age Identity, Age Perceptions, and Health: Evidence from the English Longitudinal Study of Ageing." *Annals of the New York Academy of Sciences* 1114: 279–87.

Derks, Daantje, Arjan E. R. Bos, and Jasper von Grumbkow. 2007. "Emoticons and Social Interaction on the Internet: The Importance of Social Context." *Computers in Human Behavior* 23 (1): 842–49.

Dietz, Tammy. 2011. "Wake Up, Bella! A Personal Essay on *Twilight*, Mormonism, Feminism, and Happiness." In *Bringing Light to* Twilight: *Perspectives on the Pop Culture Phenomenon*, edited by Giselle Liza Anatol, 99–112. New York: Palgrave Macmillan. Kindle edition.

DiMaggio, Paul. 1997. "Culture and Cognition." *Annual Review of Sociology* 23: 263–87. doi: 10.1146/annurev.soc.23.1.263.

Dimery, Martin. 2002. *Being John Lennon.* London: SAF Publishing.

Dolan, Josephine. 2011. "Firm and Hard: Old Age, the 'Youthful' Body and Essentialist Discourses." In *Pasado, Presente y Future de la Cultura Popular: Espacios y Contextos: Actas del IV Congreso de la SELICUP*, p. 1. Universitat de les Illes Balears.

Dolan, Josie. 2012. "The Queen, Aging Femininity and the Recuperation of the Monarchy." In *Aging, Performance, and Stardom: Doing Age on the Stage of Consumerist Culture*, edited by Aagje Swinnen and John A. Stotesbury, 39–52. Vienna: LIT Verlag.

———. Forthcoming. "(Re)visioning the Gaze: The Feminist Aesthetics of *The Best Exotic Marigold Hotel* and *The Whales of August.*" *Age, Culture, Humanities: An Interdisciplinary Journal.*

Dolan, Josie, and Estella Tincknell. 2012. *Aging Femininities: Troubling Representations.* Cambridge: Cambridge Scholars Press.

Domínguez-Rué, Emma. 2012. "Mothers, Daughters and Midlife (Self)-discoveries: Gender and Aging in the Amanda Cross' Kate Fansler Series." *Journal of Aging Studies* 26: 428–37.

Donath, Judith S. 2007. "Signals in Social Supernets." *Journal of Computer-Mediated Communication* 13 (1): 231–51. doi: 10.1111/j.1083-6101.2007.00394.x.

Donath, Judith S., and danah boyd. 2004. "Public Displays of Connection." *BT Technology Journal* 22 (4): 71–82. doi: 10.1023/B:BTTJ.0000047585.06264.cc.

Donlon, Margie M., Ori Ashman, and Becca R. Levy. 2005. "Re-Vision of Older Television Characters: A Stereotype-Awareness Intervention." *Journal of Social Issues* 61: 307–19.

Donnelly, Ashley. 2011. "Denial and Salvation: The *Twilight* Series and Heteronormative Patriarchy." In *Theorizing* Twilight: *Critical Essays on What's at Stake in a Post-Vampire World,* edited by Maggie Parke and Natalie Wilson, 178–93. Jefferson: McFarland. Kindle edition.

Drageset, Jorunn. 2004. "The Importance of Activities of Daily Living and Social Contact for Loneliness: A Survey Among Residents in Nursing Homes." *Scandinavian Journal of Caring Sciences* 18: 65–71.

Drake, Philip, and Andy Miah. 2010. "The Cultural Politics of Celebrity." *Cultural Politics* 6 (1): 49–64.

Dufault, Monica. 2011. "Nasty Old Things: The True Monsters of the *Twilight* Saga." *Inter-disciplinary.net.* www.inter-disciplinary.net/wpcontent/uploads/2011/08/dufaltmpaper.pdf.

Duggan, Maeve, and Joanna Brenner. 2013. "The Demographics of Social Media Users—2012." *Pew Internet and American Life Project.* Washington, DC: Pew Research Center. pewinternet.org/~/media/Files/Reports/2013/PIP_SocialMediaUsers.pdf.

Dyer, Richard. 1987. *Heavenly Bodies: Film Stars and Society.* London: Macmillan.

———. 1998. *Stars.* London: British Film Institute.

Ehrenreich, Barbara, Elizabeth Hess, and Gloria Jacobs. 1992. "Beatlemania: Girls Just Want to Have Fun." In *The Adoring Audience: Fan Culture and Popular Media,* edited by Lisa A. Lewis, 84–106. New York: Routledge.

Eibach, Richard P., Steven E. Mock, and Elizabeth A. Courtney. 2010. "Having a 'Senior Moment': Induced Aging Phenomenology, Subjective Age, and Susceptibility to Ageist Stereotypes." *Journal of Experimental Social Psychology* 46: 643–49.

Elder, Glen H. 1994. "Time, Human Agency, and Social Change: Perspectives on the Life Course." *Social Psychology Quarterly* 57 (1): 4–15.

———. 1998. "The Life Course as Developmental Theory." *Child Development* 69 (1): 1–12.

Elder, Glen H., Monica Kirkpatrick Johnson, and Robert Crosnoe. 2003. "The Emergence and Development of Life Course Theory." In *Handbook of the Life Course,* edited by Jeylan T. Mortimer and Michael J. Shanahan, 3–19. New York: Springer.

Ellison, Nicole B., and danah boyd. 2013. "Sociality through Social Network Sites." In *The Oxford Handbook of Internet Studies,* edited by William H. Dutton, 151–72. Oxford, UK: Oxford University Press.

Ellison, Nicole B., Charles Steinfield, and Cliff Lampe. 2007. "The Benefits of Facebook 'Friends': Social Capital and College Students' Use of Online Social Network Sites." *Journal of Computer-Mediated Communication* 12 (4): 1143–68. doi: 10.1111/j.1083-6101.2007.00367.x.

Empire, Kitty. "David Bowie: The Next Day—Review." *The Observer,* March 10, 2013. www.guardian.co.uk/music/2013/mar/10/david-bowie-next-day-review.

Erikson, Erik H. 1959. *Identity and the Life Cycle: Selected Papers.* New York: International Universities Press.

European Commission. 2012. "Media Use in the European Union." *European Commission, Directorate—General Communication.* ec.europa.eu/public_opinion/archives/eb/eb78/eb78_media_en.pdf.

Evans, Adrienne, Sarah Riley, and Avi Shankar. 2010. "Technologies of Sexiness: Theorizing Women's Engagement in the Sexualization of Culture." *Feminism and Psychology* 20 (1): 114–31.

Evans, Jessica, and David Hesmondalgh. 2005. *Understanding Media: Inside Celebrity*. Maidenhead: Open University Press.

Fagerstrom, Lisbeth. 2010. "Positive Life Orientation—An inner Health Resource Among Older People." *Scandinavian Journal of Caring Sciences* 24: 349–56.

Fairclough, Kirsty. 2012. "Nothing Less Than Perfect: Female Celebrity, Ageing and the Hyper-Scrutiny in the Gossip Industry." *Celebrity Studies* 3 (1): 90–103.

Feasey, Rebecca. 2006. "Get a Famous Body: Star Styles and Celebrity Gossip in Heat Magazine." In *Framing Celebrity: New Directions in Celebrity Culture*, edited by Sue Holmes and Sean Redmond, 177–94. London: Routledge.

———. 2008. "Reading *Heat*: The Meanings and Pleasures of Star Fashions and Celebrity Gossip." *Continuum* 22 (5): 687–99.

———. 2012. "The Ageing Femme Fatale: Sex, Stardom, and Sharon Stone." In *Aging, Performance, and Stardom: Doing Age on the Stage of Consumerist Culture*, edited by Aagje Swinnen and John A. Stotesbury, 109–30. Vienna: LIT Verlag.

Featherstone, Michael. 1991. "The Body in Consumer Culture." In *The Body: Social Process and Cultural Theory*, edited by Michael Featherstone, Mike Hepworth, and Brian S. Turner, 170–96. London: Sage.

Featherstone, Mike, and Mike Hepworth. 1991. "The Mask of Aging and the Postmodern Life Course." In *The Body: Social Process and Cultural Theory*, edited by Mike Featherstone, Mike Hepworth, and Bryan Turner, 371–88. Thousand Oaks: Sage.

———. 1995. "Images of Positive Aging: A Case Study of Retirement Choice Magazine." In *Images of Ageing: Cultural Representations of Later Life*, edited by Mike Featherstone and Andrew Wernick, 29–47. London: Routledge.

———. 2009. "Images of Aging: Cultural Representations of Later Life." In *The Cultural Context of Aging*, 3rd ed., edited by Jay Sokolovsky, 134–44. Westport: Praeger.

Ferraro, Kenneth F., and Tettyana Pylypiv Shippee. 2009. "Aging and Cumulative Inequality: How Does Inequality Get Under the Skin?" *The Gerontologist* 49 (3): 333–43.

Finch, Janet. 1993. "It's Great to Have Someone to Talk to: Ethics and Politics of Interviewing Women." In *Social Research: Philosophy, Politics and Practice*, edited by Martyn Hammersley, 166–80. London: Sage.

Fischoff, Stuart, Alexandra Dimopoulos, Francois Nguyen, and Rachel Gordon. 2002. "Favorite Movie Monsters and Their Psychological Appeal." *Imagination, Cognition and Personality* 22 (4): 401–26.

Fiske, Susan T., Amy J. C. Cuddy, Peter Glick, and Jun Xu. 2002. "A Model of (Often Mixed) Stereotype Content: Competence and Warmth Respectively Follow from Perceived Status and Competition." *Journal of Personality and Social Psychology* 82: 878–902.

Fogel, Joshua, and Michelle C. Carlson. 2006. "Soap Operas and Talk Shows on Television are Associated with Poorer Cognition in Older Women." *Southern Medical Journal* 99 (3): 226–33.

Ford, Sam. 2008. "Soap Operas and the History of Fan Discussion." *Transformative Works and Cultures* 1 (1). journal.transformativeworks.org/index.php/twc/article/view/Article/42/50.

Freese, Jeremy, Salvador Rivas, and Eszter Hargittai. 2006. "Cognitive Ability and Internet Use Among Older Adults." *Poetics* 34 (4): 236–49.

Fricke, David. "John Fogerty: Wrote a song for everyone." *Rolling Stone Reviews*, May 23, 2013. www.rollingstone.com/music/albumreviews/wrote-a-song-for-everyone-20130523.

Fries, James F. 1983. "Compression of Morbidity." *Milbank Memorial Fund Quarterly: Health and Society* 61 (3): 397–419.

Frith, Simon. 1990. "Music and identity." In *Questions of Cultural Identity*, edited by Stuart Hall and Paul du Gay, 108–27. London: Sage.

———. 1998. *Performing Rites: On the Value of Popular Music*. Oxford: Oxford University Press.

———. 2007. *Taking Popular Music Seriously: Selected Essays*. Aldershot: Ashgate.

Fry, Christine L. 2003. "The Life Course as a Cultural Construct." In *Invitation to the Life Course: Toward New Understandings of Later Life*, edited by Richard A. Settersten, Jr., 269–94. Amityville: Baywood Publishing Co., Inc.

Fry, Richard, D'Vera Cohn, Gretchen Livingston, and Paul Taylor. 2011. "The Rising Age Gap in Economic Well-Being." *Pew Research: Social and Demographic Trends*. www.pewsocialtrends.org/2011/11/07/the-rising-age-gap-in-economic-well-being.

Fung, Helene H., Laura L. Carstensen, and Amy M. Lutz. 1999. "Influence of Time on Social Preferences: Implications for Life-Span Development." *Psychology and Aging* 14: 595–604.

Furnham, Adrian, and Twiggy Mak. 1999. "Sex-Role Stereotyping in Television Commercials: A Review and Comparison of Fourteen Studies Done on Five Continents Over 25 Years." *Sex Roles* 41: 413–37.

Gamson, Jusua. 1994. *Claims to Fame: Celebrity in Contemporary America*. Berkeley: University of California Press.

Ganahl, Dennis J., Thomas J. Prinsen, and Sara Baker Netzley. 2003. "A Content Analysis of Prime Time Commercials: A Contextual Framework of Gender Representation." *Sex Roles* 49: 545–51.

Gantz, Walter, Howard M. Gartenberg, and Cindy K. Rainbow. 1980. "Approaching Invisibility: The Portrayal of the Elderly in Magazine Advertisements." *Journal of Communication* 30: 56–60. doi: 10.1111/j.1460-2466.1980.tb01769.x.

Gantz, Walter, and Lawrence A. Wenner. 1991. "Men, Women, and Sports: Audience Experiences and Effects." *Journal of Broadcasting and Electronic Media* 35: 233–43.

Garde-Hansen, Joanne. 2012. "The 'Hip-op' Generation: Representing the Aging Female Body in *Saga* Magazine." In *Aging Femininities: Troubling Representations*, edited by Josephine Dolan and Estella Tincknell, 161–70. Newcastle upon Tyne: Cambridge Scholars Publishing.

Gardner, Eriq. "Actress suing IMDb for revealing her age gets trial date." *The Hollywood Reporter*, February 7, 2012a. www.hollywoodreporter.com/thr-esq/actress-suingimdb huang-hoang-age-trial-date-287603.

———. "Judge allows actress suing IMDb over age revelation to go forward on lawsuit." *The Hollywood Reporter*, March 30, 2012b. www.hollywoodreporter.com/thresq/judge-allows-actress-suing-imdb-306399.

———. "Actress details Amazon's alleged data-mining fraud in amended IMDb lawsuit."*The Hollywood Reporter*, April 27, 2012c. www.hollywoodreporter.com/thresq/amazon-fraud-lawsuit-huang-hoang-imdb-317492.

———. "IMDb ageism trial delayed by death of actress' lawyer." *The Hollywood Reporter*, August 21, 2012d. www.hollywoodreporter.com/thr-esq/imdb-ageismtrial-delayed-huong-hoang-364356.

———. "Actress demands probe of IMDb's 'misuse' of personal info." *The Hollywood Reporter*, October 4, 2012e. www.hollywoodreporter.com/thr-esq/huong-hoangdemands-probe-imdbs-376345.

———. "Big decision looms in actress' lawsuit against IMDb over age revelation." *The Hollywood Reporter*, December 12, 2012f. www.hollywoodreporter.com/thresq/big-decision-looms-actress-lawsuit-401259.

———. "IMDb wins lawsuit over actress age revelation." *The Hollywood Reporter*, April 11, 2013. www.hollywoodreporter.com/thr-esq/imdb-wins-lawsuit-actress-age437828.

Gardner, Eriq, and Venkat Balasubramani. "Trial alert! actress suing IMDb over age revelation gets day in court." *The Hollywood Reporter*, April 5, 2013. www.hollywoodreporter.com/thr-esq/imdb-lawsuit-actress-suing-age-433190.

Gatto, Susan L., and Sunghee H. Tak. 2008. "Computer, Internet, and E-mail Use Among Older Adults: Benefits and Barriers." *Educational Gerontology* 34 (9): 800–11. doi: 10.1080/03601270802243697.

Gauntlett, David, and Annette Hill. 1999. *TV Living: Television, Culture and Everyday Life*. London: Routledge.

George, Linda. 1998. "Self and Identity in Later Life: Protecting and Enhancing the Self." *Journal of Aging and Identity* 3 (3): 133–52.

————. 2003. "Life Course Research: Achievements and Potential." In *Handbook of the Life Course*, edited by Jeylan T. Mortimer and Michael J. Shanahan, 671–80. New York: Kluwer Academic/Plenum Publishers.

————. 2011. "The Third Age: Fact or Fiction—And Does It Matter." In *Gerontology in the Era of the Third Age*, edited by Dawn C. Carr and Kathrin Komp, 245–59. New York: Springer.

Gerbner, George. 1993. "Learning Productive Aging as a Social Role: The Lessons of Television." In *Achieving a Productive Aging Society*, edited by Scott A. Bass, Francis G. Caro, and Yung-Ping Chen, 207–19. Westport: Auburn House.

Gerbner, George, Larry Gross, Michael Morgan, Nancy Signorielli, and James Shanahan. 2002. "Growing Up with Television: Cultivation Processes." In *Media Effects: Advances in Theory and Research*, edited by Jennings Bryant and Dolf Zillman, 43–67. Mahwah: Lawrence Erlbaum Associates, Inc. Publishers.

Gerbner, George, Larry Gross, Nancy Signorielli, and Michael Morgan. 1980. "Aging with Television: Images on Television Drama and Conceptions of Social Reality." *Journal of Communication* 30 (1): 37–47.

Ghisletta, Paolo, Jean-Francois Bickel, and Martin Lovden. 2006. "Does Activity Engagement Protect Against Cognitive Decline in Old Age? Methodological and Analytical Considerations." *Journal of Gerontology: Psychological Sciences* 61B (5), 253–61.

Gibson, Lorna, Wendy Moncur, Paula Forbes, John Arnott, Christopher Martin, and Amritpal S. Bhachu. 2010. "Designing Social Networking Sites for Older Adults." In *Proceedings of the 24th BCS Interaction Specialist Group Conference*, 186–94. Swinton: British Computer Society.

Giddens, Anthony. 1991. *Modernity and Self Identity: Self and Society in the Late Modern Age*. Cambridge: Polity Press.

Gilberg, Michael, and Terence Hines. 2000. "Male Entertainment Award Winners Are Older than Female Winners." *Psychological Reports* 86: 175–78.

Giles, David. 2002. "Parasocial Interaction : A Review of the Literature and a Model for Future Research." *Media Psychology* 4: 279–305. doi: 10.1207/S1532 785 XMEP 0403_04.

————. 2003. *Media Psychology*. London: Routledge.

Giles, Howard, Justine Coupland, and Nikolas Coupland. 1991. "Accommodation Theory: Communication, Context, and Consequence." In *Contexts of Accommodation*, edited by Howard Giles, Justine Coupland, and Nikolas Coupland, 1–68. New York: Cambridge University Press.

Gill, Rosalind. 2007. "Postfeminist Media Culture: Elements of a Sensibility." *European Journal of Cultural Studies* 10 (2): 147–66.

Gilleard, Chris, and Paul Higgs. 2005. *Contexts of Ageing: Class, Cohort and Community*. Cambridge: Polity.

————. 2007. "The Third Age and the Baby Boomers: Two Approaches to the Social Structuring of Later Life." *International Journal of Ageing and Later Life* 2 (2): 13–30.

————. 2010. "Aging Without Agency: Theorizing the Fourth Age." *Ageing and Mental Health* 14 (2): 121–28.

————. 2011. "The Third Age as a Cultural Field." In *Gerontology in the Era of the Third Age*, edited by Dawn C. Carr and Kathrin Komp, 33–49. New York: Springer.

————. 2013. *Ageing, Corporeality and Embodiment*. London: Anthem.

Gilly, Mary, and Valarie Zeithaml. 1985. "The Elderly Consumer and Adoption of Technologies." *Journal of Consumer Research* 12: 353–57.

Goffman, Erving. 1963. *Stigma: Notes on the Management of Spoiled Identity*. Englewood Cliffs, NJ: Prentice Hall.

————. 1979. *Gender Advertisements*. Cambridge: Harvard University Press.

Goodenough, Mary. 1999. "Grateful Dead: Manifestations from the Collective Unconscious." In *Perspectives on the Grateful Dead: Critical Writings*, edited by Rob Weiner, 175–82. Westport, CT: Greenwood.

Goodwin, Paige E., Robert C. Intrieri, and Dennis R. Papin. 2005. "Older Adults' Affect While Watching Television." *Activities, Adaptation and Aging* 29 (2): 55–72.

Gorin, Valérie, and Annik Dubied. 2011. "Desirable People: Identifying Social Values through Celebrity News." *Media, Culture and Society* 33 (4): 599–618.

Gossip Cop. "Brad Pitt's wrinkles 'killing' his career?" *Gossip Cop*, January 5, 2013. www.gossipcop.com/brad-pitt-wrinkles-age-photoshop/.

Gott, M., and S. Hinchcliff. 2003. "How Important Is Sex in Later Life? The Views of Older People." *Social Science and Medicine* 56 (8): 1617–28.

Grajczyk, Andreas, and Oliver Zollner. 1998. "How Older People Watch Television: Telemetric Data on the TV Use in Germany in 1996." *Gerontology* 44: 176–81.

Gravagne, Pamela. 2013. *The Becoming of Age: Cinematic Visions of Mind, Body and Identity in Later Life*. Jefferson: McFarland.

Gray, Jonathan, Cornel Sandvoss, and C. Lee Harrington. 2007. "Introduction: Why Study Fans?" In *Fandom: Identities and Communities in a Mediated World*, edited by Jonathan Gray, Cornel Sandvoss, and C. Lee Harrington, 1–16. New York: New York University Press.

Greenberg, Bradley S., and Larry Collette. 1997. "The Changing Faces on TV: A Demographic Analysis of Network Television's New Seasons, 1966–1992." *Journal of Broadcasting and Electronic Media* 41: 1–13.

Greenfield, Robert. 1996. *Dark Star: An Oral Biography of Jerry Garcia*. New York: William Morrow and Company.

Grenier, Amanda G. 2007. "Crossing Age and Generational Boundaries: Exploring Intergenerational Research Encounters." *Journal of Social Issues* 63 (4): 713–27.

Grodin, Debra, and Thomas R. Lindlof, eds. 1996. *Constructing the Self in a Mediated World*. Thousand Oaks: Sage.

Groper, Jessica. 2011. "A Post-Feminist Romance: Love, Gender and Intertextuality in Stephenie Meyer's Saga." In *Theorizing* Twilight: *Critical Essays on What's At Stake in a Post-Vampire World*, edited by Maggie Parke and Natalie Wilson, 132–46. Jefferson: McFarland. Kindle edition.

Gubrium, Jaber F., and James A. Holstein. 2009. *Analyzing Narrative Reality*. Thousand Oaks: Sage Publications.

Guitar World. 2013. "Guitar World Presents Gone Too Soon: Remembering the Guitar Legends Who Died Before Their Time." New York: Time Home Entertainment.

Gullette, Margaret. 1988. *Safe at Last in the Middle Years: The Invention of the Midlife Progress Novel*. Berkeley: University of California Press.

———. 1998. "Midlife Discourses in the Twentieth Century United States: An Essay on the Sexuality, Ideology, and Politics of 'Middle-Ageism.'" In *Welcome to Middle Age! (And Other Cultural Fictions)*, edited by Richard Shweder, 3–44. Chicago: University of Chicago Press.

———. 2004. *Aged by Culture*. Chicago: Chicago University Press.

———. 2011. *Agewise: Fighting the New Ageism in America*. Chicago: University of Chicago Press.

Gupta, Kristina. 2011. "'Screw Health': Representations of Sex as a Health-Promoting Activity in Medical and Popular Literature." *Journal of Medical Humanities* 32 (2): 127–40.

Habermas, T., and S. Bluck. 2000. "Getting a Life: The Emergence of the Life Story in Adolescence." *Psychological Bulletin* 126: 248–69.

Haboush, Amanda, Cortney S. Warren, and Lorraine Benuto. 2012. "Beauty, Ethnicity, and Age: Does Internalization of Mainstream Media Ideals Influence Attitudes towards Older Adults?" *Sex Roles* 66: 668–76.

Haeusler, Debbie. "How IMDb cripples below-the-line talent too (opinion)." *The Hollywood Reporter*, January 12, 2012. www.hollywoodreporter.com/news/imdb-age-lawsuitactress-281329.

Hagestad, Gunhild O., and Peter Uhlenberg. 2005. "The Social Separation of Old and Young: A Root of Ageism." *Journal of Social Issues* 61 (2): 343–60.

Hajjar, Wendy J. 1998. *Television in the Nursing Home: A Case Study of the Media Consumption Routines and Strategies of Nursing Home Residents*. London: Routledge.

Hakkarainen, Päivi. 2012. "'No Good for Shovelling Snow and Carrying Firewood': Social Representations of Computers and the Internet by Elderly Finnish Non-Users." *New Media and Society* 14 (7): 1198–1215. doi: 10.1177/1461444812442663.

Halberstam, Judith. 2007. "Theorizing Gender, Culture, and Music: Keeping Time with Lesbians on Ecstasy." *Women and Music* 11: 51–58.

Hall, Stuart. 1980. "Encoding/Decoding." In *Culture, Media, Language: Working Papers in Cultural Studies*, edited by Stuart Hall, Dorothy Hobson, Andrew Lowe, and Paul Willis, 128–38. London: Hutchinson Publishing.

Hancock, Philip, Bill Hughes, and Elisabeth Jagger, E. 2000. *The Body, Culture and Society: An Introduction.* Buckingham: Open University Press.

Hant, Myrna. 2007. "Television's Mature Women: A Changing Media Archetype: From Bewitched to the Sopranos." Last modified January 1, 2007. escholarship.org/uc/item/3357r9nz.

Hareven, Tamara K. 1994. "Aging and Generational Relations: A Historical and Life Course Perspective." *Annual Review of Sociology* 20 (1): 437–61.

Hargittai, Eszter. 2008. "Whose Space? Differences Among Users and Non-Users of Social Network Sites." *Journal of Computer-Mediated Communication* 13 (1): 276–97. doi: 10.1111/j.1083-6101.2007.00396.x.

Harrington, C. Lee, and Denise D. Bielby. 1991. "The Mythology of Modern Love: Representations of Romance in the 1980s." *Journal of Popular Culture* 24 (4): 129–44.

———. 1995. *Soap Fans: Exploring Pleasure and Making Meaning in Everyday Life.* Philadelphia: Temple University Press.

———. 2005. "Flow, Home, and Media Pleasures." *Journal of Popular Culture* 38: 834–54.

———. 2010. "A Life Course Perspective on Fandom." *International Journal of Cultural Studies* 13 (5): 429–50.

Harrington, C. Lee, Denise D. Bielby, and Anthony R. Bardo. 2011. "Life Course Transitions and the Future of Fandom." *International Journal of Cultural Studies* 14 (6): 567–90.

Harrington, C. Lee, and Denise Brothers. 2010. "A Life Course Built For Two: Acting, Aging and Soap Operas." *Journal of Aging Studies* 24: 20–29.

———. 2011. "Constructing the Older Audience: Age and Aging on Soaps." In *The Survival of Soap Opera: Transformations for a New Media Era*, edited by Sam Ford, Abigail de Kosnik, and C. Lee Harrington, 300–314. Jackson: University Press of Mississippi.

Harrison, Jill, and John Ryan. 2010. "Musical Taste and Ageing." *Ageing and Society* 30 (4): 649–69.

Hartley, Jennifer. 2000. "We Were Given this Dance: Music and Meaning in the Early Unlimited Devotion Family." In *Deadhead Social Science: You Ain't Gonna Learn What You Don't Want to Know*, edited by Rebecca Adams and Robert Sardiello, 129–55. Lanham, MD: AltaMira.

Hartley, John. 1999. *The Uses of Television.* London: Routledge.

Harwood, Jake. 1997. "Viewing Age: Lifespan Identity and Television Viewing Choices." *Journal of Broadcasting and Electronic Media* 41: 203–13.

———. 2007. *Understanding Communication and Aging: Developing Knowledge and Awareness.* Thousand Oaks, CA: SAGE Publications Incorporated.

Harwood, Jake, and Karen Anderson. 2002. "The Presence of Portrayal of Social Groups on Prime Time Television." *Communication Reports* 15 (2): 81–97. doi: 10.1080/0893421 0209367756.

Harwood, Jake, and Howard Giles. 1992. "'Don't Make Me Laugh': Age Representations in a Humorous Context." *Discourse and Society* 3 (3): 403–36. doi: 10.1177/095792659 2003004001.

Harwood, Jake, Howard Giles, and Ellen B. Ryan. 1995. "Aging, Communication and Intergroup Theory: Social Identity and Intergenerational Communication." In *Handbook of Communication and Aging Research,* edited by Jon F. Nussbaum and Justine Coupland, 133–59. Hillsdale: Lawrence Earlbaum.

Harwood, Jake, and Abhik Roy. 1999. "The Portrayal of Older Adults in Indian and U.S. Magazine Advertisements." *Howard Journal of Communications* 10: 269–80. doi: 10.1080/106461799246753.

Havighurst, Robert. 1961. "Successful Aging." *The Gerontologist* 1: 8–13.

Havighurst, Robert, and Ruth Albrecht. 1953. *Older People.* New York: Longmans, Green.

Hawes, Janice. 2010. "Sleeping Beauty and the Idealized Undead: Avoiding Adolescence." In *The* Twilight *Mystique: Critical Essays on the Novels and Films,* edited by Amy M. Clarke and Marijane Osborne, 167–78. Jefferson: McFarland.

Haynes, Brad. "Innocence." *Orlando Weekly,* November 2, 2001.

Hazan, Haim. *Old Age: Constructions and Deconstructions.* Cambridge: Cambridge University Press.

Healey, T., and K. Ross. 2002. "Growing Old Invisibly: Older Viewers Talk Television." *Media Culture and Society* 24 (1): 105–20.

Heckhausen, Jutta, and Orville G. Brim. 1997. "Perceived Problems for Self and Other: Self-Protection by Social Downgrading throughout Adulthood." *Psychology and Aging* 12: 610–19.

Hellekson, K., and Busse, K. 2006. "Introduction." In K. Hellekson and K. Busse, *Fan Fiction and Fan Communities in the Age of the Internet,* 5–40. Jefferson: McFarland.

Hepworth, Mike, and Mike Featherstone. 1982. *Surviving Middle Age.* Oxford: Basil Blackwell.

Hermes, Joke. 1995. *Reading Women's Magazines: An Analysis of Everyday Media Use.* Cambridge: Polity.

Hermes, Will. "Black Sabbath: 13." *Rolling Stone Reviews,* June 3, 2013. www.rollingstone.com/music/albumreviews/13-20130603.

Hiemstra, Roger, Maureen Goodman, Mary Ann Middlemiss, Richard Vosco, and Nancy Ziegler. 1983. "How Older Persons Are Portrayed in Television Advertising: Implications for Educators." *Educational Gerontology* 9 (2–3): 111–22. doi: 10.1080/0380127830090202.

Higgs, Paul, and Ian Rees Jones. 2008. *Medical Sociology and Old Age: Towards a Sociology of Health in Later Life.* London: Routledge.

Hill Collins, Patricia. 2000. *Black Feminist Thought: Knowledge, Consciousness, and the Politics of Empowerment.* Reprint. New York: Routledge Classics, 2009.

Hills, Matt. 2002. *Fan Cultures.* London: Routledge.

———. 2005. "Patterns of Surprise: The 'Aleatory Object' in Psychoanalytic Ethnography and Cyclical Fandom." *American Behavior Scientist* 48 (7): 801–21.

———. 2007. "Essential Tensions: Winnicottian Object-Relations in the Media Sociology of Roger Silverstone." *International Journal of Communication* 1 (1): 37–48.

Hillsdon, Melvyn, Eric Brunner, Jack Guralnick, and Michael Marmot. 2005. "Prospective Study of Physical Activity and Physical Function in Early Old Age." *American Journal of Preventative Medicine* 28 (3): 245–50.

Hilt, Michael, and Jeremy Lipschultz. 2004. "Elderly Americans and the Internet: E-Mail, TV News, Information and Entertainment Websites." *Educational Gerontology* 30 (1): 57–72.

Hine, Rochelle. 2011. "In the Margins: The Impact of Sexualised Images on the Mental Heath of Ageing Women." *Sex Roles* 65: 632–46.

Hislop, Jenny, and Sara Arber. 2006. "Sleep, Gender, and Aging: Temporal Perspectives in the Mid-to-Later Life Transition." In *Age Matters: Realigning Feminist Thinking,* edited by Toni M. Calasanti and Kathleen F. Slevin, 225–46. New York: Routledge.

Hjarvard, Stig. 2009. "Soft Individualism: Media and the Changing Social Character." In *Mediatization: Concept, Change, Consequences,* edited by Knut Lundby, 159–77. New York: Peter Lang.

Hockey, Jenny, and Allison James. 2003. *Social Identities Across the Life Course.* Basingstoke: Palgrave Macmillan.

Hodgetts, Darrin, Kerry Chamberlain, and Graeme Bassett. 2003. "Between Television and the Audience: Negotiating Representations of Ageing." *Health* 7: 417–38.

Hodkinson, Paul. 2011. "Ageing in a Spectacular 'Youth Culture': Continuity, Change and Community Amongst Older Goths." *British Journal of Sociology* 62 (2): 262–82.

Hodkinson, Paul, and Andy Bennett. 2012. *Ageing and Youth Cultures: Music, Style and Identity.* London and New York: Berg.

Hoffman, Paul, and Cindy Cosgrove. 1990. *Outside the Show.* Berkeley, CA: Proper Publishing.

Hofstetter, C. Richard, William A. Schultze, Sean M. Mahoney, and Terry F. Buss. 1993. "The Elderly's Perception of TV Ageist Stereotyping: TV or Contextual Aging?" *Communication Reports* 6 (2): 92–100.

Hogeboom, David L., Robert J. McDermott, Karen M. Perrin, Hana Osman, and Bethany A. Bell-Ellison. 2010. "Internet Use and Social Networking Among Middle Aged and Older Adults." *Educational Gerontology* 36 (2): 93–111. doi: 10.1080/03601270903058507.

Holland, Janet, Caroline Ramazanoglu, and Sue Sharpe. 2004. *The Male in the Head: Young People, Heterosexuality and Power*, 2nd ed. London: Tufnell Press.

Holloway, Donell. 2007. "See Australia and Die: Shifting Discourses about Gray Nomads." *Consumerism, Culture and Communication* 7: 161–68.

Holmes, Su. 2005. "'Off-guard, Unkempt, Unready?': Deconstructing Contemporary Celebrity in Heat Magazine." *Journal of Media and Cultural Studies* 19 (1): 21–38.

Holmes, Su, and Sean Redmond. 2010. "A Journal in Celebrity Studies." *Celebrity Studies* 1 (1): 1–10.

Holmlund, Chris. 2002. *Impossible Bodies: Femininity and Masculinity at the Movies*. London: Routledge.

Holstein, Martha. 2011. "Cultural Ideal, Ethics and Agelessness: A Critical Perspective." In *Gerontology in the Era of the Third Age*, edited by Dawn C. Carr and Kathrin Komp, 225–43. New York: Springer.

Hoofnagle, Chris, Jennifer King, Su Li, and Joseph Turow. 2010. "How Different Are Young Adults from Older Adults When It Comes to Information Privacy Attitudes and Policies?" Working paper. papers.ssrn.com/sol3/papers.cfm?abstract_id=1589864.

Hopkins, Christopher D., Catherine A. Roster, and Charles M. Wood. 2006. "Making the Transition to Retirement: Appraisals, Post-Transition Lifestyle, and Changes in Consumption Patterns." *Journal of Consumer Marketing* 23 (2): 87–99.

Hornby, Nick. 1995. *High Fidelity*. New York: Riverhead Books.

Huffaker, David A., and Sandra L. Calvert. 2005. "Gender, Identity, and Language Use in Teenage Blogs." *Journal of Computer-Mediated Communication* 10 (2). jcmc.indiana.edu/vol10/issue2/huffaker.html.

Hummert, Mary Lee. 1990. "Multiple Stereotypes of Elderly and Young Adults: A Comparison of Structure and Evaluations." *Psychology and Aging* 5: 182–93.

———. 1993. "Age and Typicality Judgments of Stereotypes of the Elderly: Perceptions of Elderly vs. Young Adults." *International Journal of Aging and Human Development* 37 (3): 217–27.

———. 1994. "Stereotypes of the Elderly and Patronizing Speech." In *Interpersonal Communication in Older Adulthood: Interdisciplinary Research*, edited by Mary Lee Hummert, John M. Wiemann, and Jon F. Nussbaum, 162–84. Newbury Park: Sage

———. 2011. "Age Stereotyping and Aging." In *Handbook of the Psychology of Aging*, 7th ed., edited by K. W. Schaie and S. L. Willis, 249–62. San Diego: Academic Press.

Hummert, Mary Lee, Teri A. Gartska, Jaye Shaner, and Sharon Strahm. 1994. "Stereotypes of the Elderly Held by Young, Middle-Aged, and Elderly Adults." *Journals of Gerontology: Psychological Sciences* 49: 240–49.

Hunter, Robert. 1990. *A Box of Rain: Collected Lyrics of Robert Hunter*. New York: Penguin.

Ibarra, Sergio. "Nielsen: Older audiences getting bigger." *TVBizWire*, August 29, 2008. www.tvweek.com/blogs/tvbizwire/2008/08/nielsen_older_audiences_gettin.php.

Jackson, Stevi, and Sue Scott. 2004. "Sexual Antimonies in Late Modernity." *Sexualities* 7 (2): 233–48.

Jackson, Sue, Tiina Vares, and Rosalind Gill. 2013. "'The Whole Playboy Mansion Image': Girls' Fashioning and Fashioned Selves within a Postfeminist Culture." *Feminism and Psychology* 23 (2): 143–62. doi: 10.1177/0959353511433790.

James, E. L. 2011. *Fifty Shades of Grey*. New York: Random House.

Jameson, Frederic. 1991. *The Culture of Postmodernism: Or the Cultural Logic of Late Capitalism*. Durham: Duke University Press.

Jenkins, Henry. 1992. *Textual Poachers: Television Fans and Participatory Culture*. New York: Routledge.

Jennings, Ros, and Abigail Gardner, eds. 2012. *"Rock On": Women, Ageing, and Popular Music.* Farnham: Ashgate.

Jensen, Joli. 1992. "Fandom as Pathology: The Consequences of Characterization." In *The Adoring Audience: Fan Culture and Popular Media,* edited by Lisa A. Lewis, 9–29. London: Routledge.

Jermyn, Deborah. 2012a. "'Get a Life Ladies. Your Old One Is Not Coming Back': Ageing, Ageism and the Lifespan of Female Celebrity." *Celebrity Studies* 3 (1): 1–12.

———. 2012b. "'Glorious, Glamorous and That Old Standby, Amorous': The Late Blossoming of Diane Keaton's Romantic Comedy Career." *Celebrity Studies* 3 (1): 37–51.

John, Deborah Roedder, and Catherine Cole. 1986. "Age Differences in Information Processing: Understanding Deficits in Young and Elderly Consumers." *Journal of Consumer Research* 13: 297–315.

Johnson, Monica K., Justin Allen Berg, and Toni Sirotzki. 2007. "Differentiation in Self-Perceived Adulthood: Extending the Confluence Model of Subjective Age Identity." *Social Psychology Quarterly* 70: 243–61.

Joinson, Adam N. 2001. "Self-Disclosure in Computer-Mediated Communication: The Role of Self-Awareness and Visual Anonymity." *European Journal of Social Psychology* 31 (2): 177–92.

Jones, Graham M., and Bambi B. Schieffelin. 2009. "Enquoting Voices, Accomplishing Talk: Uses of Be + Like in Instant Messaging." *Language and Communication* 29 (1): 77–113.

Jones, Malcolm. "Harry Potter: The End Is Here: Darker, Deeper and Defying Expectation, 'The Deathly Hallows' Is Indeed Magic." *Newsweek,* July 30, 2007.

Jones, Stacy Holman. 1998. *Kaleidoscope Notes: Writing Women's Music and Organizational Culture.* Walnut Creek: AltaMira Press.

Kahana, Eva, Loren Lovegreen, Boaz Kahana, and Michael Kahana. 2003 "Person, Environment, and Person-Environment Fit as Influences on Residential Satisfaction of Elders." *Environment and Behavior* 35 (3): 434–53.

Kane, Kathryn. 2010. "A Very Queer Refusal: The Chilling Effect of the Cullens' Heternormative Embrace." In *Bitten by* Twilight: *Youth Culture, Media, and the Vampire Franchise,* edited by Melissa A. Click, Jennifer S. Aubrey, and Elizabeth Behm-Morawitz, 103–18. New York: Peter Lang.

Kaplan, E. Ann. 2010. "The Unconscious of Age: Performances in Psychoanalysis, Film and Popular Culture." In *Staging Age: The Performance of Age in Theatre, Dance, and Film,* edited by Valerie B. Lipscomb and Leni Marshall, 27–55, New York: Palgrave Macmillan.

Karahasanović, Amela, Petter Bae Brandtzæg, Jan Heim, Marika Lüders, Lotte Vermeir, Jo Pierson, Bram Lievens, Jeroen Vanattenhoven, and Greet Jans. 2009. "Co-creation and User-Generated Content–Elderly People's User Requirements." *Computers in Human Behavior* 25 (3): 655–78. doi: 10.1016/j.chb.2008.08.012.

Karp, David A. 1988. "A Decade of Reminders: Changing Age Consciousness Between Fifty and Sixty Years Old." *The Gerontologist* 28: 727–38.

Katz, Stephen. 2005. *Cultural Aging: Life Course, Lifestyle and Senior Worlds.* Peterborough: Broadview Press.

———. 2010. "Measuring Age Beyond Chronological Age: Functions, Boundaries, Reflexivity." Paper presented at the Gerontology Society of America 63rd Annual Scientific Meetings, New Orleans.

———. 2013. "Active and Successful Aging: Lifestyle as a Gerontological Idea." *Recherches Sociologiques et Anthropologiques* 44 (1): 33–49.

Katz, Stephen, and Barbara L. Marshall. 2003. "New Sex for Old: Lifestyle, Consumerism and the Ethics of Aging Well." *Journal of Aging Studies* 17 (1): 3–16.

Keegan, Rebecca, and Nicole Sperling. "'Fifty Shades of Grey' by E. L. James is selling books (and more)." *Los Angeles Times,* April 17, 2012. articles.latimes.com/2012/apr/17/entertainment/la-et-fifty-shades-of-grey-20120417.

Kellner, Douglas. 1995. *Media Culture: Cultural Studies, Identity and Politics Between the Modern and the Postmodern.* London: Routledge.

Kelly, John, Marjorie Steinkamp, and Janice Kelly. 1987. "Later-Life Satisfaction: Does Leisure Contribute?" *Leisure Sciences* 9: 189–200.

Kenneally, Tim. "Actress sues IMDb for $1M for revealing her age." *The Wrap*, October 18, 2011a. www.thewrap.com/movies/article/actress-wants-1m-because-imdb-revealedher-age-31951.

———. "IMDb Jane Doe case: Actress lied about her age, used fake passport, court papers claim." *The Wrap*, November 30, 2012. www.thewrap.com/tv/article/imdbjane-doe-case-actress-lied-about-her-age-used-fake-passport-court-papers-claim-67401.

———. "Judge: Actress must lose anonymity in IMDb age-reveal case." *The Wrap*, December 23, 2011b. www.thewrap.com/tv/article/judge-actress-must-loseanonymity-imdb-age-reveal-case-33915.

Kenneally, Tim, and Pamela Chelin. "IMDb Jane Doe plaintiff reveals her real name." *The Wrap*, January 6, 2012. www.thewrap.com/tv/article/imdb-jane-doe-defendant-revealsher-real-name-34152.

Kershaw, Sarah. "Notable deaths trouble self-reflective baby boomers." *New York Times*, September 17, 2009.

Kessler, Eva-Marie, Katrin Rakoczy, and Ursula Staudinger. 2004. "The Portrayal of Older People in Prime Time Television Series: The Match with Gerontological Evidence." *Ageing and Society* 24 (4): 531–52.

King, Neal. 2010. "Old Cops: Occupational Aging in a Film Genre." In *Staging Age: The Performance of Age in Theatre, Dance, and Film*, edited by Valerie B. Lipscomb and Leni Marshall, 57–81. New York: Palgrave Macmillan.

Kissling, Elizabeth A. 2006. "I Don't Have a Great Body but I Play One on TV." In *The Celebrity Culture Reader*, edited by P. David Marshall, 551–56. London: Routledge.

Kite, Mary E., Gary D. Stockdale, Bernard E. Whitley, and Blair T. Johnson. 2005. "Attitudes towards Younger and Older Adults: An Updated Meta-Analytic Review." *Journal of Social Issues* 61: 241–66.

Klara, Robert. "How Clairol hair color went from taboo to new you: Hair dyeing shifts from shameful secret to $1 billion bonanza." *Adweek*, February 28, 2013. www.adweek.com/news/advertising-branding/how-clairol-hair-color-went-taboo-new-you-147480.

Kleiber, Douglas, Francis McGuire, Begum Aybar-Damali, and William Norman. 2008. "Having More by Doing Less: The Paradox of Leisure Constraints in Later Life." *Journal of Leisure Research* 40 (3): 343–59.

Kleinplatz, P. J., A. D. Menard, N. Paradis, M. Campbell, T. Dalgleish, A. Segovia, and K. Davis. 2009. "From Closet to Reality: Optimal Sexuality Among the Elderly." *The Irish Psychiatrist* 10: 15–18.

Kleinspehn-Ammerlahn, Anna, Dana Kotter-Grühn, and Jacqui Smith. 2008. "Self-Perceptions of Aging: Do Subjective Age and Satisfaction with Aging Change During Old Age?" *Journals of Gerontology: Psychological Sciences and Social Sciences* 63: P377–85.

Koda, Tomoko, Toru Ishida, Matthias Rehm, and Elisabeth Andre. 2006. "Avatar Culture: Cross-Cultural Evaluations of Avatar Facial Expressions." *AI and Society* 24 (3): 237–50.

Kohlbacher, Florian, Michael Prieler, and Shigeru Hagiwara. 2011. "The Use of Older Models in Japanese TV Advertising: Practitioner Perspective vs. Consumer Opinions." *Keio Communication Review* 33: 25–42.

Korzenny, Felipe, and Kimberly Neuendorf. 1980. "Television Viewing and Self-Concept of the Elderly." *Journal of Communication* 30: 71–80.

Kotarba, Joseph A. 2013. *Baby Boomer Rock 'N' Roll Fans*. Lanham: Scarecrow Press.

Kotarba, Joseph A., and Phillip Vannini. 2009. *Understanding Society Through Popular Music*. New York and London: Routledge.

Kotter-Grühn, Dana, Anna Kleinspehn-Ammerlahn, Denis Gerstorf, and Jacqui Smith. 2009. "Self-Perceptions of Aging Predict Mortality and Change with Approaching Death: 16-year Longitudinal Results from the Berlin Aging Study." *Psychology and Aging* 24: 654–67.

Krainitzki, Eva L. 2011. "Exploring the Hypervisibility Paradox: Older Lesbians in Contemporary Mainstream Cinema." PhD dissertation, University of Gloucestershire.

Kuhn, Annette. 2002. *An Everyday Magic: Cinema and Cultural Memory*. London: I. B. Tauris.

Kurutz, Stephen. 2008. *Like a Rolling Stone: The Strange Life of a Tribute Band*. New York: Broadway Books.

La Ferle, Carrie, and Steven M. Edwards. 2013. "Women's (40+) Perceptions of Digitally Retouched Models in Product Relevant vs. Product Irrelevant Advertisements." Working paper.

Ladd, Paddy. "When There Were No Ears to Hear." *Spiral Light* 20 (June 1990): 18.

———. "Seeking All That's Still Unsung." *Spiral Light* 35 (May 1996): 60–65, 78.

Lamb, Erin. 2014. "'Polyester Pants and Orthopedic Shoes': Introducing Age Studies to Traditional Undergraduates." *Age, Culture, Humanities* 1 (1): In press.

Lampe, Cliff, Jessica Vitak, and Nicole Ellison. 2013. "Users and Nonusers: Interactions Between Levels of Facebook Adoption and Social Capital." In *Proceedings of the 2013 Conference on Computer Supported Cooperative Work*: 809–19. New York: ACM Press. doi: 10.1145/2441776.2441867.

Lang, Frieder, Nina Rieckmann, and Margaret Baltes. 2002. "Adapting to Aging Losses: Do Resources Facilitate Strategies of Selection, Compensation, and Optimization in Everyday Functioning." *Journal of Gerontology: Psychological Sciences* 57B: 501–9.

Langer, Ellen. 2009. *Counterclockwise: Mindful Health and the Power of Possibility*. New York: Ballantine Books.

Langmeyer, Lynn. 1983. "Age Role Portrayals in Magazine Advertisements: A Content Analysis." In *Marketing: Theories and Concepts for an Era of Change*, edited by John H. Summey, 286–89. Carbondale: Southern Marketing Association.

———. 1993. "Advertising Images of Mature Adults: An Update." *Journal of Current Issues and Research in Advertising* 15 (2): 81–91. doi: 10.1080/10641734.1993.10505005.

Lash, Scott. 1999. *Another Modernity: A Different Rationality*. Oxford: Blackwell.

Laslett, Peter. 1987. "The Emergence of the Third Age." *Ageing and Society* 7: 133–60.

Lauzen, Martha M., and David M. Dozier. 2002. "Equal Time in Prime Time? Scheduling Favoritism and Gender on the Broadcast Networks." *Journal of Broadcasting and Electronic Media* 46 (1): 137–53.

———. 2005a. "Recognition and Respect Revisited: Portrayals of Age and Gender in Prime-Time Television." *Mass Communication and Society* 8: 241–57.

———. 2005b. "Maintaining the Double Standard: Portrayals of Age and Gender in Popular Films." *Sex Roles* 52: 437–46.

Lauzen, Martha M., David M. Dozier, and Nora Horan. 2008. "Constructing Gender Stereotypes\ Through Social Roles in Prime-Time Television." *Journal of Broadcasting and ElectronicMedia* 52 (2): 200–14.

Lauzen, Martha M., David M. Dozier, and Barbara Reyes. 2007. "From Adultescents to Zoomers: An Examination of Age and Gender in Prime-Time Television." *Communication Quarterly* 55 (3): 343–57.

Leahy, Sarah. 2006. "Simone Signoret: Aging and Agency." *Studies in the Literary Imagination* 39 (2): 21–42.

LeBoeuf, Robyn A., Eldar Shafir, and Julia B. Bayuk. 2010. "The Conflicting Choices of Alternating Selves." *Organizational Behavior and Human Decision Processes* 111 (1): 48–61.

Lee, Gyudong, Jaeeun Lee, and Soonjae Kwon. 2011. "Use of Social-Networking Sites and Subjective Well-Being: A Study in South Korea." *Cyberpsychology, Behavior and Social Networking* 14 (3): 151–55. doi: 10.1089/cyber.2009.0382.

Lee, Kyung-Tag, Mi-Jin Noh, and Dong-Mo Koo. 2013. "Lonely People Are No Longer Lonely on Social Networking Sites: The Mediating Role of Self-Disclosure and Social Support." *Cyberpsychology, Behavior and Social Networking* 16 (6): 413–18. doi: 10.1089/cyber.2012.0553.

Lee, Monica M., Brian Carpenter, and Lawrence S. Meyers. 2007. "Representations of Older Adults in Television Advertisements." *Journal of Aging Studies* 21: 23–30. doi: 10.1016/j.jaging.2006.04.001.

Lee, Paul S. N., Louis Leung, Venhwei Lo, Chengyu Xiong, and Tingjun Wu. 2010. "Internet Communication versus Face-to-Face Interaction in Quality of Life." *Social Indicators Research* 100 (3): 375–89. doi: 10.1007/s11205-010-9618-3.

Lehtinen, Vilma, Jaana Näsänen, and Risto Sarvas. 2009. "'A Little Silly and Empty-Headed'—Older Adults' Understandings of Social Networking Sites." In *Proceedings of the*

23rd British HCI Group Annual Conference on People and Computers, 45–54. Swinton: British Computer Society.

Leist, Anja K. 2013. "Social Media Use of Older Adults: A Mini-Review." *Gerontology* 59 (4): 378–84. doi: 10.1159/000346818.

Leogrande, Cathy. 2010. "My Mother, Myself: Mother-Daughter Bonding via the *Twilight* Saga." In *Bitten by* Twilight: *Youth Culture, Media, and the Vampire Franchise*, edited by Melissa A. Click, Jennifer S. Aubrey, and Elizabeth Behm-Morawitz, 155–72. New York: Peter Lang.

Lena, Jennifer C. 2012. *Band Together: How Communities Create Genres in Popular Music.* Princeton: Princeton University Press.

Lesh, Phil. 2006. *Searching for the Sound: My Life with the Grateful Dead.* New York: Back Bay Books.

Leung, Louis. 2010. "Effects of Internet Connectedness and Information Literacy on Quality of Life." *Social Indicators Research* 98 (2): 273–90. doi: 10.1007/s11205-009-9539-1.

———. 2013. "Generational Differences in Content Generation in Social Media: The Roles of the Gratifications Sought and of Narcissism." *Computers in Human Behavior* 29 (3): 997–1006. doi: 10.1016/j.chb.2012.12.028.

Levin, Jack. 2013. *Blurring the Boundaries: The Declining Significance of Age.* New York: Routledge.

Levy, Becca R. 2003. "Mind Matters: Cognitive and Physical Effects of Aging Self-Stereotypes." *Journals of Gerontology: Psychological Sciences and Social Sciences* 58: 203–11.

———. 2009. "Stereotype Embodiment: A Psychological Approach to Aging." *Current Directions in Psychological Science* 18 (5): 332–36.

Levy, Becca R., Martin D. Slade, and Stanislav V. Kasl. 2002. "Longitudinal Benefit of Positive Self-Perceptions of Aging on Functional Health." *Journals of Gerontology: Psychological Sciences and Social Sciences* 57: 409–17.

Levy, Becca R., Martin D. Slade, Suzanne R. Kunkel, and Stanislav V. Kasl. 2002. "Longevity Increased by Positive Self-Perceptions of Aging." *Journal of Personality and Social Psychology* 83: 261–70.

Lewis, John. "Todd Rundgren: State." *Uncut*, May 2013, 76.

Lin, Jane. 2007. "Automatic Author Profiling of Online Chat Logs." Unpublished master's thesis, Naval Postgraduate School, Monterey, California.

Lin, Nan. 1999. "Building a Network Theory of Social Capital." *Connections* 22 (1): 28–51.

———. 2008. "A Network Theory of Social Capital." In *The Handbook of Social Capital*, edited by Dario Castiglione, Jan W. van Deth, and Guglielmo Wolleb, 50–69. Oxford: Oxford University Press.

Lincoln, Anne E., and Michael Patrick Allen. 2004. "Double Jeopardy in Hollywood: Age and Gender in the Careers of Film Actors, 1926–1999." *Sociological Forum* 19 (4): 611–31.

Lindstrom, Heather A., Thomas Fritsch, Grace Petot, Kathleen A. Syth, Chien H. Chen, Sara M. Debanne, Alan J. Lerner, and Robert P. Friedland. 2005. "The Relations Between Television Viewing in Midlife and the Development of Alzheimer's Disease in a Case Control Study." *Brain and Cognition* 58: 157–65.

Linton, Ralph. 1942. "Age and Sex Categories." *American Sociological Review* 7 (5): 589–603.

Livingstone, Sonia. 2009. "On the Mediation of Everything: ICA Presidential Address 2008." *Journal of Communication* 59: 1–18.

Lloyd, Vicki, Amanda Gatherer, and Sunny Kalsy. 2006. "Conducting Qualitative Interview Research with People with Expressive Language Difficulties." *Qualitative Health Research* 16 (10): 1386–1404.

Logan, John R., Russell Ward, and Glenna Spitze. 1992. "As Old as You Feel: Age Identity in Middle and Later Life." *Social Forces* 71 (2): 451–67.

Lowe, Melanie. 2004. "'Tween' Scene: Resistance within the Mainstream." In *Music Scenes: Local, Translocal, and Virtual*, edited by Andy Bennett and Richard A. Peterson, 80–95. Nashville: Vanderbilt University Press.

Lumme-Sandt, Kirsi. 2011. "Images of Aging in a 50+ Magazine." *Journal of Aging Studies* 25 (1): 45–51.

Lynch, Scott M. 2000. "Measurement and Prediction of Aging Anxiety." *Research on Aging* 22: 533–58.

Macrae, C. Neil, and Galen V. Bodenhausen. 2000. "Social Cognition: Thinking Categorically about Others." *Annual Review of Psychology* 51: 93–120. doi: 10.1146/annurev .psych.51.1.93.

Madden, Mary. "Older Adults and Social Media." *Pew Internet and American Life Project* August 27, 2010. pewinternet.org/~/media//Files/Reports/2010/Pew%20Internet%20-%20 Older%20Adults%20and%20Social%20Media.pdf.

———. "Privacy Management on Social Media Sites." *Pew Internet and American Life Project*, February 24, 2012. www.pewinternet.org/Reports/2012/Privacy-management-on-so cial-media.aspx.

Madrigal, Alexis C. "How Netflix reverse engineered Hollywood." *The Atlantic*, January 2, 2014. www.theatlantic.com/technology/archive/2014/01/how-netflix-reverse-engineered-hollywood/282679/.

Mannheim, Karl. 1952/1998. "The Sociological Problem of Generations." In *Essays on the Sociology of Knowledge*, edited by Paul Kecskemeti, 163–95. London: Taylor and Francis (Routledge).

Mares, Marie-Louise, and Joanne Cantor. 1992. "Elderly Viewers' Responses to Televised Portrayals of Old Age: Empathy and Mood Management versus Social Comparison." *Communication Research* 19: 459–78.

Mares, Marie-Louise, and Ye Sun. 2010. "The Multiple Meanings of Age for Television Content Preferences." *Human Communication Research* 36: 372–96.

Mares, Marie-Louise, and Emory H. Woodard IV. 2006. "In Search of the Older Audience: Adult Age Differences in Television Viewing." *Journal of Broadcasting and Electronic Media* 50 (4): 595–614.

Markson, Elizabeth W., and Carol A. Taylor. 1993. "Real versus Reel World." *Women and Therapy* 14 (1–2): 157–72.

Marshall, Barbara L. 2010. "Science, Medicine and Virility Surveillance: 'Sexy Seniors' in the Pharmaceutical Imagination." *Sociology of Health and Illness* 32 (2): 211–24.

———. 2011. "The Graying of 'Sexual Health': A Critical Research Agenda." *Canadian Review of Sociology* 48 (4): 390–413.

———. 2012. "Medicalization and the Refashioning of Age-Related Limits on Sexuality." *Journal of Sex Research* 49 (4): 337–43.

Marshall, Barbara L., and Stephen Katz. 2005. "Forever Functional: Sexual Fitness and the Aging Male Body." In *Cultural Aging: Life Course, Lifestyle, and Senior Worlds*, edited by Stephen Katz, 161–87. Peterborough: Broadview Press.

———. 2012. "The Embodied Life Course: Post-Ageism or the Renaturalization of Gender?" *Societies* 2: 222–34. www.mdpi.com/2075–4698/2/4/222/pdf.

Marshall, P. David.1997. *Celebrity and Power*. Minneapolis: Univeristy of Minnesota Press.

———. 2006a. *The Celebrity Culture Reader*. London: Routledge.

———. 2006b. "Intimately Intertwined in the Most Public Way: Celebrity and Journalism." In *The Celebrity Culture Reader*, edited by P. David Marshall, 315–23. London: Routledge.

Martey, Rosa M., and Mia Consalvo. 2011. "Performing the Looking-Glass Self: Avatar Appearance and Group Identity in Second Life." *Popular Communication* 9 (3): 165–80.

Martey, Rosa M., Jennifer Stromer-Galley, Kelly Reene, Mia Consalvo, Tomek Strzalkowski, Jingsi Wu, Jaime Banks, and Michelle Weihmann-Purcell. 2013. "Communicating Age in Second Life: The Contributions of Textual and Visual Factors." *New Media and Society*. doi: 10.1177/1461444813504270.

Martin, Douglas. "Richie Havens, folk singer who riveted Woodstock, dies at 72." *New York Times*, April 22, 2013. www.nytimes.com/2013/04/23/arts/music/richie-havensguitarist -and-singer-dies-at-72.html?_r=0.

Mather, Mara, and Laura L. Carstensen. 2005. "Aging and Motivated Cognition: The Positivity Effect in Attention and Memory." *Trends in Cognitive Science* 9: 496–502.

McAdams, Dan P. 2006. "The Role of Narrative in Personality and Psychology Today." *Narrative Inquiry* 16 (1): 11–8.

McAdams, Dan P., Jack J. Bauer, April R. Sakaeda, Nana Akua Anyidoho, Mary Anne Macha-do, Katie Magrino-Failla, Katie W. White, and Jennifer L. Pals. 2006. "Continuity and Change in the Life Story: A Longitudinal Study of Autobiographical Memories in Emerging Adulthood." *Journal of Personality* 74 (5): 1371–1400.

McAndrew, Francis T., and Hye Sun Jeong. 2012. "Who Does What on Facebook? Age, Sex, and Relationship Status as Predictors of Facebook Use." *Computers in Human Behavior* 28 (6): 2359–65. doi: 10.1016/j.chb.2012.07.007.

McCann, Robert M., Kathy Kellermann, Howard Giles, Cynthia Gallois, and M. Angels Vila-dot. 2004. "Cultural and Gender Influences on Age Identification." *Communication Studies* 55 (1): 88–105.

McKim, A. Elizabeth, and William J. Randall. 2007. "From Psychology to Poetics: Aging as a Literary Process." *Journal of Aging, Humanities, and the Arts* 1: 147–58.

McNally, Dennis. 2003. *A Long Strange Trip: The Inside History of the Grateful Dead.* New York: Three Rivers Press.

Meiners, Norbert H., and Bernd Seeberger. 2010. "Marketing to Senior Citizens: Challenges and Opportunities." *Journal of Social, Political and Economic Studies* 35 (3): 293–328.

Meisner, Brad A. 2012. "A Meta-Analysis of Positive and Negative Age Stereotype Priming Effects on Behavior Among Older Adults." *Journals of Gerontology: Psychological Sciences and Social Sciences* 67: 13–17.

Melenhorst, Anne-Sophie, Wendy A. Rogers, and Don G. Bouwhuis. 2006. "Older Adults' Motivated Choice for Technological Innovation: Evidence for Benefit-driven Selectivity." *Psychology and Aging* 21 (1): 190–95. doi: 10.1037/0882-7974.21.1.190.

Melina, Lois Ruskai. 2008. "Backstage with the Hot Flashes: Performing Gender, Performing Age, Performing Rock 'N' Roll." *Qualitative Inquiry* 14 (1): 90–110.

Mellor, David, Lucy Firth, and Kathleen Moore. 2008. "Can the Internet Improve the Well Being of Elderly?" *Ageing International* 32 (1): 25–42.

Mendoza, Nadia. "Nicole's face looks like a bat." *The Sun*, March 14, 2008. www.thesun.co. uk/sol/homepage/showbiz/bizarre/918232/BOTOX-expert-reckons-Nicole-Kidman-looks-like-a-bat.html.

Merkin, Daphne. "Can anyone make a movie for women?" *New York Times Magazine*, December 15, 2009.

Merola, Nicholas, and Jorge Peña. 2010. "The Effects of Avatar Appearance in Virtual Worlds." *Journal of Virtual Worlds* 2 (5). journals.tdl.org/jvwr/index.php/jvwr/article/view/779/717.

Merom, Dafna, Robert Cumming, Erin Mathieu, Kaarin Anstey, Chris Rissel, Judy Simpson, Rachel Morton, Ester Cerin, Catherine Sherrington, and Stephen Lord. 2013. "Can Social Dancing Prevent Falls in Older Adults? A Protocol of the Dance, Aging, Cognition, Economics (DAnCE) Fall Prevention Randomised Controlled Trial." *BMC Public Health* 13: 1–9.

Messinger, Paul R., Xin Ge, Eleni Stroulia, Kelly Lyons, Kristen Smirnov, and Michael Bone. 2008. "On the Relationship Between My Avatar and Myself." *Journal of Virtual Worlds Research* 1 (2). journals.tdl.org/jvwr/article/view/352.

Meyer, Stephenie. 2005. *Twilight.* New York: Little, Brown.

———. 2006. *New Moon.* New York: Little, Brown.

———. 2007. *Eclipse.* New York: Little, Brown.

———. 2008a. *Breaking Dawn.* New York: Little, Brown.

———. "Frequently asked questions: *Breaking Dawn.*" *The Official Website of Stephenie Meyer*, 2008b. www.stepheniemeyer.com/bd_faq.html.

Migliaccio, John. 2004–2005. "Media Connections, Marketing, and Managing Obstacles in Reaching the Older Consumer." *Generations* 28 (4): 20–25.

Milkie, Melissa. 1999. "Social Comparisons, Reflected Appraisals, and Mass Media: The Impact of Pervasive Beauty Images on Black and White Girls' Self-Concepts." *Social Psychology Quarterly* 62: 190–210.

Miller, Darryl W., Teresita S. Leyell, and Juliann Mazachek. 2004. "Stereotypes of the Elderly in U.S. Television Commercials from the 1950s to the 1990s." *International Journal of Aging and Human Development* 58 (4): 315–40.

Miller, Melissa. 2011. "Maybe Edward Is the Most Dangerous Thing Out There: The Role of Patriarchy." In *Theorizing* Twilight: *Critical Essays on What's at Stake in a Post-Vampire World,* edited by Maggie Parke and Natalie Wilson, 165–77. Jefferson: McFarland. Kindle edition.

Miller, Nancy K. 1980. *The Heroine's Text: Readings in the French and English Novel 1722–1782.* New York: Columbia University Press.

Mills, C. Wright. 1959/2001. "The Promise of Sociology." In *Sociological Odyssey: Contemporary Readings in Sociology,* edited by Patricia A. Adler and Peter Adler, 10–15. Belmont: Wadsworth/Thompson Learning.

Min, Joohong, Merril Silverstein, and Jessica P. Lendon. 2012. "Intergenerational Transmission of Values Over the Family Life Course." *Advances in Life Course Research* 17: 112–20.

Moen, Phyllis. 2001. "Constructing a Life Course." *Marriage and Family Review* 30 (4): 97–109.

Molloy, Tim. "IMDb: Actress suing over age reveal is 'selfish,' trying to commit fraud." *The Wrap,* November 14, 2011. www.thewrap.com/tv/article/imdb-actress-suing-overage-reveal-selfish-trying-commit-fraud-32764.

Montepare, Joann M. 1991. "Characteristics and Psychological Correlates of Young Adult Men's and Women's Subjective Age." *Sex Roles* 24 (5/6): 323–33.

———. 1996. "Variations in Adults' Subjective Ages in Relation to Birthday Nearness, Age Awareness, and Attitudes toward Aging." *Journal of Adult Development* 3: 193–203.

———. 2009. "Subjective Age: Toward a Guiding Lifespan Framework." *International Journal of Behavioral Development* 33 (1): 42–46.

Moore, Robert L. 2004. "We're Cool, Mom and Dad Are Swell: Basic Slang and Generational Shifts in Values." *American Speech* 79 (1): 59–86.

Moores, Shaun. 2000. *Media and Everyday Life in Modern Society.* Edinburgh: Edinburgh University Press.

Morgan, David L. 1997. *Focus Groups as Qualitative Research,* 2nd ed. London: Sage.

Morgan, Leslie A., and Susanne R. Kunkel. 2007. *Aging, Society, and the Life Course.* New York: Springer Publishing.

Morgan, Michael, and James Shanahan. 2010. "The State of Cultivation." *Journal of Broadcasting and Electronic Media* 54 (2): 337–55.

Mulvey. Laura. 1975. "Visual Pleasures and Narrative Cinema." *Screen* 16 (3): 6–19.

———. 1992. "Visual Pleasure and Narrative Cinema." In *The Sexual Subject: A Screen Reader in Sexuality,* edited by Mandy Merck (Screen), 22–34. London: Routledge.

Myers, Hayley, and Margaret Lumbers. 2007. "Silver Consumers Find Leisure and Socialization in Shopping: Insights from a U.K. Survey." *Research Review* 14 (3): 25–27.

Negra, Diane, and Susan Holmes. 2008. "Going Cheap? Female Celebrity in the Reality, Tabloid and Scandal Genres." *Genders* 48. www.genders.org/g48/g48_negraholmes.html.

Nelson, E. Anne, and Dale Dannefer. 1992. "Aged Heterogeneity: Fact or Fiction? The Fate of Diversity in Gerontological Research." *The Gerontologist* 32 (1): 17–23.

Nelson, Todd D. 2004. *Ageism: Stereotyping and Prejudice Against Older Persons.* Cambridge: MIT Press.

Neugarten, Bernice L. 1974. "Age Groups in American Society and the Rise of the Young-Old." *Annals of the American Academy of Political and Social Science* 415 (1): 187–98.

———. 1982. *Age or Need?: Public Policies for Older People.* Beverly Hills: Sage.

Neugarten, Bernice L., and Joan W. Moore. 1968. "The Changing Age-Status System." In *Middle Age and Aging: A Reader in Social Psychology,* edited by Bernice L. Neugarten, 5–20. Chicago: University of Chicago Press.

New York Post. "50 fat celebrities." *New York Post,* 1999. www.nypost.com/p/pagesix/celebrity_photos/item_v61Jthev4lGuTQOmdOgoL?.

Newitz, Annalee. "In *Twilight: Breaking Dawn,* Bella becomes a supernatural version of Octomom." *io9,* November 11, 2011. io9.com/5860947/in-twilight-breaking-dawn-bella-be comes-a-supernatural-version-of-octomom.

NewsCore. "Jane Doe actress suing IMDb for revealing age identifies herself." *The Telegraph,* January 8, 2012. www.dailytelegraph.com.au/news/jane-doe-actress-suing-imdbfor-reveal

ing-age-identifies-herself/story-e6freuy9-1226238925358.

Nicol, Rhonda. 2011. "'When You Kiss Me I Want to Die': Arrested Feminism in *Buffy the Vampire Slayer* and the *Twilight* Series." In *Bringing Light to* Twilight: *Perspectives on the Pop Culture Phenomenon*, edited by Giselle Liza Anatol, 113–24. New York: Palgrave Macmillan. Kindle edition.

Nimrod, Galit, and Douglas Kleiber. 2007. "Reconsidering Change and Continuity in Later Life: Toward an Innovation Theory of Successful Aging." *International Journal of Aging and Human Development* 65 (1): 1–22.

North, Michael, and Susan Fiske. 2013. "Act Your (Old) Age: Prescriptive Ageist Biases Over Succession, Consumption, and Identity." *Personality and Social Psychology Bulletin* 39 (6): 720–34.

NY Daily News. 2013a. "Bo Derek appears ageless at 56: Stars who stay forever young." www.nydailynews.com/life-style/ageless-celebs-secret-staying-young-gallery-1.31328.

———. 2013b. "Fit and fabulous over 40." www.nydailynews.com/lifestyle/health/celebrities-40-fit-fabulous-gallery-1.1080906.

O'Brien-Suric, Nora. 2013. "A Cross-National Comparison of Perceptions of Aging and Older Adults. Discussion of Comparative Analysis and Findings of the Five Countries: Part 2." *Care Management Journals* 14: 89–107.

O'Connor, Clare. "Undercover billionaire: Sara Blakeley joins the rich list thanks to Spanx." *Forbes*, March 7, 2012. www.forbes.com/sites/clareoconnor/2012/03/07/undercover-billionaire-sarablakely-joins-the-rich-list-thanks-to-spanx/.

Ofcom. "Adults' Media Use and Attitudes Report." *Ofcom*, April 2013. stakeholders.ofcomorg.uk/binaries/research/media-literacy/adult-media-lit-13/2013_Adult_ML_Tracker.pdf.

Ong, Fon Sim, and H. K. Chang. 2009. "Older People as Models in Advertisements: A Cross-Cultural Content Analysis of Two Asian Countries." *Journal of Business and Policy Research* 4 (2): 1–15.

Orimo, Hajime, Hideki Ito, Takao Suzuki, Atsushi Araki, Takayuki Hosoi, and Motoji Sawabe. 2006. "Reviewing the Definition of 'Elderly.'" *Geriatrics and Gerontology International* 6: 149–58.

Osbourne, Sharon. 2006. *Extreme: My Autobiography*. New York: Springboard Press.

O'Shea, Helen. 2012. "'Get Back to Where You Once Belonged!' The Positive Creative Impact of a Refresher Course for 'Baby-Boomer' Rock Musicians." *Popular Music* 31 (2): 199–215.

Panis, Koen, and Hilde Van den Bulck. 2012 "Celebrities' Quest for a Better World: Understanding Flemish Public Perceptions of Celebrities' Societal Engagement." *Javnost* 19 (3): 75–92.

Pardoe, Iain, and Dean K. Simonton. 2008. "Applying Discrete Choice Models to Predict Academy Award Winners." *Journal of the Royal Statistical Society: Series A (Statistics in Society)* 171 (2): 375–94.

Paterline, Brent. 2000. "Community Reaction to Deadhead Subculture." In *Deadhead Social Science: You Ain't Gonna Learn What You Don't Want to Know*, edited by Rebecca Adams and Robert Sardiello, 183–201. Lanham: AltaMira.

Pearson, Allison. 2011. *I Think I Love You*. London: Vintage Books.

Perdue, Charles W., and Michael B. Gurtman. 1990. "Evidence for the Automaticity of Ageism." *Journal of Experimental Social Psychology* 26 (3): 199–216. doi: 10.1016/0022-1031(90)90035-K.

Perkins, Rosie, and Aaron Williamson. 2013. "Learning to Make Music in Older Adulthood: A Mixed-Methods Exploration of Impacts on Wellbeing." *Psychology of Music*. doi: 10.1177/0305735613483668.

Perry, Vanessa G. and Joyce M. Wolburg. 2011. "Aging Gracefully: Emerging Issues for Public Policy and Consumer Welfare." *Journal of Consumer Affairs* 45 (3): 365–71.

Peterson, Robin T. 1992. "The Depiction of Senior Citizens in Magazine Advertisements: A Content Analysis." *Journal of Business Ethics* 11: 701–6.

Peterson, Richard, and N. Anand. 2004. "The Production of Culture Perspective." *Annual Review of Sociology* 30: 311–34. Palo Alto: Annual Reviews, Inc.

Pettijohn, Terry F. 2003. "Relationships Between U.S. Social and Economic Hard Times and Popular Motion Picture Actor Gender, Actor Age, and Movie Genre Preferences." *North American Journal of Psychology* 5 (1): 61–66.

Platt, Carrie Anne. 2010. "Cullen Family Values: Gender and Sexual Politics in the Twilight Series." In *Bitten by* Twilight: *Youth Culture, Media, and the Vampire Franchise,* edited by Melissa A. Click, Jennifer S. Aubrey, and Elizabeth Behm-Morawitz, 71–96. New York: Peter Lang.

Postmes, Tom, Russell Spears, and Martin Lea. 1998. "Breaching or Building Social Boundaries? SIDE-Effects of Computer-Mediated Communication." *Communication Research* 25 (6): 689–715.

Preiler, Michael, Florian Kohlbacher, Shigeru Hagiwara, and Akie Arima. 2011. "Gender Representation of Older People in Japanese Television Advertisements." *Sex Roles* 64: 405–15. doi: 10.1007/s11199-010-9923-y.

Putnam, Robert D. 2000. *Bowling Alone: The Collapse and Revival of American Community.* New York: Simon and Schuster.

Quinn, Kelly. 2013. "We Haven't Talked in 30 Years! Relationship Reconnection and Internet Use at Midlife." *Information, Communication and Society* 16 (3): 397–420. doi: 10.1080/1369118X.2012.756047.

Randall, William L., and A. Elizabeth McKim. 2004. "Toward a Poetics of Aging: The Links Between Literature and Life." *Narrative Inquiry* 14 (2): 235–60.

Reed, Darren J., and Geraldine Fitzpatrick. 2008. "Acting Your Age in Second Life." In *Fun and Games 2008*, edited by Panos Markopoulos, 158–69. Berlin: Springer-Verlag.

Rheingold, Howard. 1991. *Virtual Reality.* New York: Summit Books.

Rice, Anne. 1976. *Interview with the Vampire.* New York: Alfred A. Knopf.

Richards, N., L. Warren, and M. Gott. 2012. "The Challenge of Creating 'Alternative' Images of Ageing: Lessons from a Project with Older Women." *Journal of Aging Studies* 26 (1): 65–78.

Richins, Marsha L. 1991. "Social Comparison and the Idealized Images of Advertising." *Journal of Consumer Research* 18: 71–83. doi: 10.2307/2489486.

Ridgeway, Cecelia, and Shelley Correll. 2004a. "Motherhood as a Status Characteristic." *Journal of Social Issues* 60 (4): 683–700. doi: 10.1111/j.0022-4537.2004.00380.x.

———. 2004b. "Unpacking the Gender System: A Theoretical Perspective on Gender Beliefs and Social Relations." *Gender and Society* 18: 510–31. doi: 10.1177/0891243204265269.

Riggs, Karen E. 1998. *Mature Audiences: Television in the Life of Elders.* New Brunswick: Rutgers University Press.

Roalf, David, Suzanne Mitchell, William Harbaugh, and Jeri Janowsky. 2012. "Risk, Reward, and Economic Decision Making in Aging." *Psychological Sciences and Social Sciences* 67 (3): 289–98.

Roberts, Robert E. L., and Vern L. Bengtson. 1999. "The Social Psychology of Values: Effects of Individual Development, Social Change, and Family Transmission Over the Life Span." In *The Self and Social Processes in Aging*, edited by Carol D. Ryff and Victor W. Marshall 453–82. New York: Springer.

Roberts, Scott D., and Nan Zhou. 1997. "The 50 and Older Characters in the Advertisements of *Modern Maturity*: Growing Older, Getting Better?" *Journal of Applied Gerontology* 16 (2): 208–20. doi: 10.1177/073346489701600205.

Robinson, Thomas E. 1998. *Portraying Older People in Advertising: Magazine, Television, and Newspaper.* New York: Garland.

Robinson, Tom, and Caitlin Anderson. 2006. "Older Characters in Children's Animated Television Programs: A Content Analysis of Their Portrayal." *Journal of Broadcasting and Electronic Media* 50 (2): 287–304.

Robinson, Tom, Mark Callister, Dawn Magoffin, and Jennifer Moore. 2007. "The Portrayal of Older Characters in Disney Animated Films." *Journal of Aging Studies* 21: 203–13.

Robinson, James D., and Thomas Skill. 1995a. "Media Usage Patterns and Portrayals of the Elderly." In *Handbook of Communication and Aging Research*, edited by Jon F. Nussbaum and Justine Coupland, 359–91. Mahwah: Erlbaum.

————. 1995b. "The Invisible Generation: Portrayals of the Elderly on Prime-Time Television." *Communication Reports* 8 (2): 111–19. doi: 10.1080/08934219509367617.

Rock Med. n.d. "Rockmed." Accessed on December 19. www.rockmed.org.

Rogers, Wendy A., Arthur D. Fisk, Anne Collins McLaughlin, and Richard Pak. 2005. "Touch a Screen or Turn a Knob: Choosing the Best Device for the Job." *Human Factors* 47 (2): 271–88. doi: 10.1518/0018720054679452.

Rojek, Chris. 2001. *Celebrity*. London: Reaktion Books.

————. 2007. *Cultural Studies*. Cambridge: Polity Press.

Rooke, Constance. 1988. "Hagar's Old Age: The Stone Angel as *Vollendungsroman*." In *Crossing the River: Essays in Honour of Margaret Laurence*, edited by Kristjana Gunnars, 25–42. Winnipeg: Turnstone.

Rosenberg, Alyssa. "Katniss Everdeen v. Bella Swan, or, there's not one perfect way to be feminine." *Think Progress*, November 17, 2011. thinkprogress.org/alyssa/2011/11/17/369148/katniss-everdeen-v-bella-swan-or-theres-not-one-perfect-way-to-be-feminine/.

Rotfeld, Herbert J., Leonard N. Reid, and Gary B. Wilcox. 1982. "Effect of Age of Models in Print Ads on Evaluation of Product and Sponsor." *Journalism Quarterly* 59 (Autumn): 374–81.

Rowe, John, and Robert Kahn. 1987. "Human Aging: Usual and Successful." *Science* 237 (4811): 143–49.

————. 1997. "Successful Aging." *The Gerontologist* 37 (4): 433–40.

Roy, Abhik, and Jake Harwood. 1997. "Underrepresented, Positively Portrayed: Older Adults in Television Commercials." *Journal of Applied Communication Research* 25: 35–56. doi: 10.1080/00909889709365464---.

Rubin, David C., and Dorthe Berntsen. 2006. "People over Forty Feel 20% Younger than Their Age: Subjective Age across the Life Span." *Psychonomic Bulletin and Review* 13: 776–80.

Rubin, Gary S., Sheila K. West, Beatriz Muñoz, Karen Bandeen-Roche, Scott Zeger, Oliver Schein, and Linda P. Fried. 1997. "A Comprehensive Assessment of Visual Impairment in a Population of Older Americans: The SEE Study." *Investigative Ophthalmology and Visual Science* 38 (3): 557–68.

Ryan, Ellen B., Howard Giles, Giampiero Bartolucci, and Karen Henwood. 1986. "Psycholinguistic and Social Psychological Components of Communication By and With the Elderly." *Language and Communication* 6 (1–2): 1–24.

SAG–AFTRA. "Screen actors guild and AFTRA deplore age discrimination facilitated by IMDb.com and similar online databases." *Hot News* (Los Angeles), October 27, 2011. www.sagaftra.org/screen-actors-guild-and-aftra-deplore-agediscrimination-facilitated-imdbcom-and-similar-online-data.

Salazar, Javier A. 2009. "Analyzing Social Identity (Re)production: Identity Liminal Events in MMORPGs." *Journal of Virtual Worlds Research* 1 (3). journals.tdl.org/jvwr/article/viewArticle/353.

Salzberg, A. 2012. "'The Spirit Never Really Ages': Materiality and Transcendence in Three Rita Hayworth Films." In *Aging, Performance, and Stardom: Doing Age on the Stage of Consumerist Culture*, edited by Aagje Swinnen and John A. Stotesbury, 77–92. Vienna: LIT Verlag.

Sandberg, Linn. 2011. *Getting Intimate: A Feminist Analysis of Old Age, Masculinity and Sexuality, Lingkoping Studies in Arts and Science*. Linkoping, Sweden: Linkoping University.

Sandvoss, Cornel. 2003. *A Game of Two Halves: Football, Television, and Globalisation*. London and New York: Routledge.

————. 2005a. *Fans: The Mirror of Consumption*. Cambridge: Polity Press.

————. 2005b. "One Dimensional Fan: Toward an Aesthetic of Fan Texts." *American Behavioral Scientist* 49 (3), 822–39.

————. 2008. "On the Couch with Europe: The Eurovision Song Contest, the European Broadcast Union, and Belonging on the Old Continent." *Popular Communication* 6 (3): 190–207.

————. 2012. "Liquid stars, Liquid Identities: Political Discourse in Transnational Media Sport." In *Bodies of Discourse: Sports Stars, Media and the Global Public*, edited by Cornel Sandvoss, Alina Bernstein, and Michael Real, 171–92. New York: Peter Lang.

————. 2013. "'I ♥ Ibiza": Music, Place and Belonging." In *Popular Music Fandom: Identities, Roles and Practices*, edited by Mark Duffett, 115–45. New York: Routledge.

Scannell. Paddy. 1996. *Radio, Television and Modern Life: A Phenomenological Approach.* Oxford: Blackwell.

Scardaville, Melissa. 2005. "Accidental Activists: Fan Activism in the Soap Opera Community." *American Behavioral Scientist* 48 (7): 881–991.

Schafer, Markus H., and Tetyana P. Shippee. 2009. "Age Identity, Gender, and Perceptions of Decline: Does Feeling Older Lead to Pessimistic Dispositions about Cognitive Aging?" *Journal of Gerontology: Social Sciences* 65B (1): 91–96.

————. 2010. "Age Identity in Context: Stress and the Subjective Side of Aging." *Social Psychology Quarterly* 73: 245–64.

Schäfer, Thomas, Mario Smukalla, and Sarah-Ann Oelker. 2013. "How Music Changes Our Lives: A Qualitative Study of the Long-Term Effects of Intense Musical Experiences." *Psychology of Music*. doi: 10.1177/0305735613482024.

Schwartzman, Sarah. 2010. "Is Twilight Mormon?" In *The* Twilight *Mystique: Critical Essays on the Novels and Films*, edited by Amy M. Clarke and Marijane Osborne, 121–36. Jefferson: McFarland.

Schewe, Charles D., and Anne L. Balazs. 1992. "Role Transitions in Older Adults: A Marketing Opportunity." *Psychology and Marketing* 9 (2): 85–99.

Schimmel, Kimberly S., C. Lee Harrington, and Denise D. Bielby. 2007. "Keep Your Fans to Yourself: The Disjuncture Between Sport Studies and Pop Culture Studies' Perspectives on Fandom." *Sport in Society* 10 (4): 580–600.

Schler, Jonathan, Moshe Koppel, Shlomo Argamon, and James Pennebaker. 2006. "Effects of Age and Gender on Blogging." *Proceedings of AAAI Spring Symposium on Computational Approaches for Analyzing Weblogs*. Menlo Park.

Schudson, Michael. 1984. *Advertising: The Uneasy Persuasion*. New York: Basic.

Scodari, Christine. 1998. "'No Politics Here': Age and Gender in Soap Opera 'Cyberfandom.'" *Women's Studies in Communication* 21 (September), online version.

————. 2003. "Resistance Re-Examined: Gender, Fan Practices, and Science Fiction Television." *Popular Communication* 1: 111–30.

————. 2004. *Serial Monogamy: Soap Opera, Lifespan, and the Gendered Politics of Fantasy.* Cresskill: Hampton Press.

————. 2007. "Yoko in Cyberspace with Beatles Fans: Gender and the Re-Creation of Popular Mythology." In *Fandom: Identities and Communities in a Mediated World*, edited by Jonathan Gray, Cornell Sandvoss, and C. Lee Harrington, 48–59. New York: New York University Press.

————. 2008. "Frozen in Time: Gender, Fan Culture, and a Young Widow's Icy Terrain." *Communication, Culture, and Critique* 1: 143–162.

————. 2012. "'Nyota Uhura Is Not a White Girl': Gender, Intersectionality, and *Star Trek* 2009's Alternate Romantic Universes." *Feminist Media Studies* 12: 352–70.

Scodari, Christine, and Jenna Felder. 2000. "Creating a Pocket Universe: 'Shippers,' Fan Fiction, and *The X-Files* Online." *Communication Studies* 51: 238–57.

Scodari, Christine, and Becky Mulvaney. 2005. "Nothing's Gonna Give: Age, Gender, and Cultures of the Screen." *Reconstruction* 2 (5). reconstruction.eserver.org/052/scodari.shtml.

Scott, John W., Mike Dolgushkin, and Stu Nixon. 1997. *Deadbase X: The Complete Guide to Grateful Dead Song Lists*. Cornish: Deadbase.

Sedgley, Diane, Nigel Morgan, and Annette Pritchard. 2007. "Insights into Older Women's Leisure: Voices from Urban South Wales." *World Leisure Journal* 49 (3): 129–41.

Segal, Judy. 2011. "The Sexualization of the Medical." *Journal of Sex Research* 49 (4): 369–78.

Settersten, Richard A. 2007. "The New Landscape of Adult Life: Road Maps, Signposts, and Speed Lines." *Research in Human Development* 4 (3–4): 239–52.

————. 2008. "Navigating the New Adulthood." *The Futurist*, March/April: 21– 28.

Settersten, Richard A., and Barbara Ray. 2010. "What's Going on with Young People Today? The Long and Twisting Path to Adulthood." *The Future of Children* 20 (1): 19–41.

Settersten, Richard A., Jr., and Molly E. Trauten. 2009. "The New Terrain of Aging: Hallmarks, Freedoms and Risks." In *Handbook of Theories of Ageing*, 2nd ed., edited by Vern L. Bengsten, Daphna Gans, Norella M. Putney, and Merril Silverstein, 455–69. New York: Springer.

Sewell, William H. 1992. "A Theory of Structure: Duality, Agency, and Transformation." *American Journal of Sociology* 98 (1): 1–29. doi: 10.2307/2781191.

Sharit, Joseph, Mario A. Hernández, Sara J. Czaja, and Peter Pirolli. 2008. "Investigating the Roles of Knowledge and Cognitive Abilities in Older Adult Information Seeking on the Web." *ACM Transactions on Computer-Human Interaction* 15 (1). doi: 10.1145/135 2782.1352785.

Shavitt, Sharon, and Michelle R. Nelson. 2000. "The Social-Identity Function in Person Perception: Communicated Meanings of Product Preferences." In *Why We Evaluate: Functions of Attitudes*, edited by Greg Maio and James M. Olson, 37–57. Mahwah: Lawrence Erlbaum Associates, Inc.

Sheldon, Pavica. 2012. "Profiling the Non-Users: Examination of Life-Position Indicators, Sensation Seeking, Shyness, and Loneliness Among Users and Non-Users of Social Network Sites." *Computers in Human Behavior* 28 (5): 1960–65. doi: 10.1016/ j.chb.2012.05.016.

Shenk, David, and Steve Silberman. 1994. *Skeleton Key: A Dictionary for Deadheads*. New York: Doubleday.

Sheptoski, Matthew. 2000. "Vending at Dead Shows: The Bizarre Bazaar." In *Deadhead Social Science: You Ain't Gonna Learn What You Don't Want to Know*, edited by Rebecca Adams and Robert Sardiello, 157–81. Lanham: AltaMira.

Shklovski, Irina. 2010. "Social Ties for the Soul: How Russians Reconnect with the Past Through Social Network Sites." Presented at the Annual Meeting of the International Communication Association, Suntec City, Singapore.

Signorielli, Nancy. 2004. "Aging on Television: Messages Relating to Gender, Race, and Occupation in Prime Time." *Journal of Broadcasting and Electronic Media* 48 (2): 279–301.

Silcoff, Mireille. "Against Zoomerism." *The National Post*, 2010. www.nationalpost.com/life/story.html?id=2944021.

Silverstein, Rebecca. "Foxy over 50." *Wonder Wall*, 2011. wonderwall.msn.com/Movies/foxy-50-over-50_13505.gallery#!wallState=0_%2Fmovies%Ffoxy-50-over-50-13505. gallery%3Fphotold%3D57263.

Silverstone, Roger. 1994. *Television and Everyday Life*. London: Routledge.

Simcock, Peter, and Lynn Sudbury. 2006. "The Invisible Majority? Older Models in UK Television Advertising." *International Journal of Advertising* 25 (1): 87–106.

Simon, Scott. "Actress sues IMDb, but it's internet privacy on trial." *National Public Radio March*, 10, 2012. www.npr.org/2012/03/10/148354091/internet-privacy-whats-vitalinfor mation.

Sisario, Ben. "Ex-bassist for Grateful Dead strikes a deal." *New York Times*, November 4, 2013.

Slegers, Karin, Martin P. J. van Boxtel, and Jelle Jolles. 2008. "Effects of Computer Training and Internet Usage on the Well-Being and Quality of Life of Older Adults: A Randomized, Controlled Study." *Journals of Gerontology Series B, Psychological Sciences and Social Sciences* 63 (3): P176–84.

———. 2009. "The Efficiency of Using Everyday Technological Devices by Older Adults: The Role of Cognitive Functions." *Ageing and Society* 29: 309–25.

Slevec, Julie, and Marika Tiggeman. 2010. "Attitudes Toward Cosmetic Surgery in Middle-Aged Women: Body Image, Aging Anxiety, and the Media." *Psychology of Women Quarterly* 34: 65–74.

Sloane, Stephanie. 2007. "Mama Kass." *Soap Opera Digest* 33 (20): 39–41.

Smith, Aaron. "Home Broadband 2010." *Pew Internet and American Life Project*, August 11, 2010. pewinternet.org/Reports/2010/Home-Broadband-2010.aspx.

Smith, Kirsten P., and Nicholas A. Christakis. 2008. "Social Networks and Health." *Annual Review of Sociology* 34 (1): 405–29. doi: 10.1146/annurev.soc.34.040507.134601.

Smith, Marc, and Peter Kollock (editors). 1999. *Communities in Cyberspace.* London: Routledge.

Smith, Susan. 2012. "'Getting Off Your Arses for These Old Broads!': Elizabeth Taylor,
Ageing and the Television Comeback Movie." *Celebrity Studies* 3 (1): 25–36.

Sokolovsky, Jay. 2009. *The Cultural Context of Aging: Worldwide Perspectives.* Westport:
Greenwood Publishing Group.

Sontag, Susan. 1972. "The Double Standard of Aging." *Saturday Review*, September 23,
29–38.

———. 1979. "The Double Standard of Aging." In *Psychology of Women: Selected Readings*,
edited by Juanita H. Williams, 462–78. New York: Academic Press.

Steinfield, Charles, Nicole B. Ellison, and Cliff Lampe. 2008. "Social Capital, Self-Esteem,
and Use of Online Social Network Sites: A Longitudinal Analysis." *Journal of Applied
Developmental Psychology* 29 (6): 434–45. doi: 10.1016/j.appdev.2008.07.002.

Stephan, Yannick, Aïna Chalabaev, Dana Kotter-Grühn, and Alban Jaconelli. 2013. "Feeling
Younger, Being Stronger: An Experimental Study of Subjective Age and Physical Function-
ing Among Older Adults." *Journals of Gerontology: Psychological Sciences and Social
Sciences* 68: 1–7.

Stephens, Nancy. 1991. "Cognitive Age: A Useful Concept for Advertising?" *Journal of Advertising* 20 (4): 37–48.

Stevenson, Nick. 2009. "Talking to Bowie Fans: Masculinity, Ambivalence and Cultural Citi-
zenship." *European Journal of Cultural Studies* 12 (1): 79–98.

Strahan, Erin J., Anne E. Wilson, Kate E. Cressman, and Vanessa M. Buote. 2006. "Comparing
to Perfection: How Cultural Norms for Appearance Affect Social Comparisons and Self-
Image." *Body Image* 3: 211–27.

Sundar, S. Shyam, Anne Oeldorf-Hirsch, Jon Nussbaum, and Richard Behr. 2011. "Retirees on
Facebook: Can Online Social Networking Enhance Their Health and Wellness?" In *Pro-
ceedings of the 2011 Annual Conference on Human Factors in Computing:* 2287–92. New
York: ACM Press. doi: 10.1145/1979742.1979931.

Sutton, Shan. 2000. "The Deadhead Community: Popular Religion in Contemporary American
Culture." In *Deadhead Social Science: You Ain't Gonna Learn What You Don't Want to
Know*, edited by Rebecca Adams and Robert Sardiello, 109–27. Lanham: AltaMira.

Swayne, Linda E., and Alan J. Greco. 1986. "The Portrayal of Older Americans in Television
Commercials." *Journal of Advertising* 16 (1): 47–54.

Swinnen, Aagje. 2010. *Seksualiteit van Ouderen: Een Multidisciplinaire Benadering.* Amsterdam: Amsterdam University Press.

———. 2012. "Benidorm Bastards, Or the Do's and Dont's of Aging." In *Aging, Performance
and Stardom*, edited by Aagje Swinnen and John A. Stotesbury, 7–14. Zurich: LIT Verlag.

Swinnen, Aagje, and John A. Stotesbury, eds. 2012. *Aging, Performance and Stardom: Doing
Age on the Stage of Consumerist Culture.* Berlin: LIT Verlag.

Szmigin, Isabelle, and Marylyn Carrigan. 2000. "Does Advertising in the UK Need Older
Models?" *Journal of Product and Brand Management* 9 (2): 128–43.

Tajfel, Henri, and John C. Turner. 1986. "The Social Identity Theory of Intergroup Behavior."
In *Psychology of Intergroup Relations*, edited by Stephen Worchel and William G. Austin,
7–24. Chicago: Nelson-Hall.

Tally, Margaret. 2006. "'She Doesn't Let Age Define Her': Sexuality and Motherhood in
Recent 'Middle-Aged Chick Flicks.'" *Sexuality and Culture* 2: 33–55.

Tam, Jenny, and Craig H. Martell. 2009. "Age Detection in Chat." In *Semantic Computing,
2009. ICSC '09. IEEE International Conference on Semantic Computing.* Berkeley.

ter Bogt, Tom F. M., Loes Keijsers, and Wim H. J. Meeus. 2013. "Early Adolescent Music
Preferences and Minor Delinquency." *Pediatrics.* doi: 10.10542/peds.-2012-0708.

The Capitol Theatre. n.d. "The Capitol Theatre." Accessed on December 19. www.the
capitoltheatre.com.

Thorsheim, Howard, and Bruce Roberts. 1995. "Finding Common Ground and Mutual Social
Support Through Reminiscing and Telling One's Story." In *The Art and Science of Remi-
niscing: Theory, Research, Methods, and Applications*, edited by Barbara K. Haight and
Jeffrey D. Webster, 193–200. New York: Taylor and Francis.

Tian, Qing, and Cynthia A. Hoffner. 2010. "Parasocial Interaction with Liked, Neutral, and Disliked Characters on a Popular TV Series." *Mass Communication and Society* 13 (3): 250–69. doi: 10.1080/15205430903296051.

Tidwell, Lisa C., and Joseph B. Walther. (2002) "Computer -Mediated Communication Effects on Disclosure, Impressions, and Interpersonal Evaluations : Getting to Know One Another a Bit at a Time." *Human Communication Research* 28 (3): 317–48.

Tiggeman, Marika, and Belinda McGill. 2004. "The Role of Social Comparison in the Effect of Magazine Advertisements on Women's Mood and Body Dissatisfaction." *Journal of Social and Clinical Psychology* 23: 23–44.

Tincknell, Estella. 2011. "Scourging the Abject Body: Ten Years Younger and Fragmented Femininity Under Neoliberalism." In *New Femininities: Postfeminism, Neoliberalism and Subjectivity*, edited by Rosalind Gill and Christina Scharff, 83–98. New York: Palgrave Mcmillan.

———. 2012. "Goldie Hawn: An Ageless Blonde for the Baby Boomer Generation." In *Aging, Performance, and Stardom: Doing Age on the Stage of Consumerist Culture*, edited by Aagje Swinnen and John A. Stotesbury, 93–108. Berlin: Lit Verlag.

Tolson, Andrew. 2001. "'Being Yourself': The Pursuit of Authentic Celebrity." *Discourse Studies* 3 (4): 443–57.

Tornstam, Lars. 2005. *Gerotranscendance: A Developmental Theory of Positive Aging.* New York: Springer.

Toscano, Margaret M. 2010. "Mormon Morality and Immortality in Stephenie Meyers' *Twilight* Series." In *Bitten by* Twilight: *Youth Culture, Media, and the Vampire Franchise*, edited by Melissa A. Click, Jennifer S. Aubrey, and Elizabeth Behm-Morawitz, 21–36. New York: Peter Lang.

Treme, Julianne, and Lee A. Craig. 2013. "Celebrity Star Power: Do Age and Gender Effects Influence Box Office Performance?" *Applied Economics Letters* 20 (5): 440–45.

Trevorrow, Jennifer. "Madonna jealous of daughter Lourdes' youth and beauty?" *Entertainmentwise*, February 6, 2009. www.entertainmentwise.com/news/47016/Madonna-Jealous-Of-DaughterLourdes-Youth-And-Beauty.

Troy, Sandy. 1991. *One More Saturday Night: Reflections with the Grateful Dead, Dead Family, and Dead Heads.* New York: St. Martin's Press.

Tulloch, John. 1989. "Approaching the Audience: The Elderly." In *Remote Control: Television, Audiences and Cultural Power*, edited by Ellen Seiter, Hans Borchers, Gabriele Kreutzner, and Eva-Maria Warth, 180–202. London and New York: Routledge.

Turner, Graeme. 2004. *Understanding Celebrity.* London: Sage.

———. 2010. "Approaching Celebrity Studies." *Celebrity Studies* 1 (1): 11–20.

Turner, Graeme, Frances Bonner, and P. David Marshall. 2000. *Fame Games: The Production of Celebrity in Australia.* Cambridge: Cambridge University Press.

Turner, John C., and Penelope J. Oakes. 1986. "The Significance of the Social Identity Concept for Social Psychology with Reference to Individualism, Interactionism, and Social Influence." *British Journal of Social Psychology* 25 (3): 237–52.

United Press International. "SAG asks IMDb to stop posting ages." *United Press International*, October 28, 2011. www.upi.com/Entertainment_News/TV/2011/10/28/SAG-asks-IMDb-to-stopposting-ages/UPI-40951319839488/.

Unruh, David. 1983. *Invisible Lives: Social Worlds of the Aged.* Beverly Hills: Sage Publications.

Ursic, Anthony C., Michael L. Ursic, and Virginia L. Ursic. 1986. "A Longitudinal Study of the Use of the Elderly in Magazine Advertising." *Journal of Consumer Research* 13 (1): 131–33.

US Bureau of Labor Statistics. 2006. Consumer Expenditure Survey. www.bls.gov/cex/.

US Census Bureau. 2011. Current Population Survey, Annual Social and Economic Supplement, 2011. Internet release date: November 2012.

———. 2011. *The Older Population: 2010.* Washington, DC: US Department of Commerce.

Vaisey, Stephen. 2008. "Socrates, Skinner, and Aristotle: Three Ways of Thinking about Culture in Action." *Sociological Forum* 23 (3): 603–13. doi: 10.1111/j.1573-7861.2008.00079.x.

————. 2009. "Motivation and Justification: A Dual-Process Model of Culture in Action." *American Journal of Sociology* 114: 1675–1715. doi: 10.2307/20616040.

Valenzuela, Sebastián, Namsu Park, and Kerk F. Kee. 2009. "Is There Social Capital in a Social Network Site?: Facebook Use and College Students' Life Satisfaction, Trust, and Participation." *Journal of Computer-Mediated Communication* 14 (4): 875–901. doi: 10.1111/j.1083-6101.2009.01474.x.

Van den Bulck, Hilde, and Nathalie Claessens. 2013. "Celebrity Suicide and the Search for the Moral High Ground: Comparing Frames in Media and Audience Discussions of the Death of a Flemish Celebrity." *Critical Studies in Media Communication* 30 (1): 69–84.

Van den Bulck, Hilde, and Sil Tambuyzer. 2008. *The Celebrity Supermarket*. Berchem: EPO.

Van den Bulck, Hilde, and Jasmijn Van Gorp. 2011. "Eternal Fandom: Elderly Fans, the Media, and the Staged Divorce of a Schlager Singer." *Popular Communication* 9 (3): 212–26.

Van der Goot, Margot J. 2009. *Television Viewing in the Lives of Older Adults*. Nijmegen: Radboud University.

Van der Goot, Margot J., Johannes W. J. Beentjes, and Martine van Selm. 2012. "Meanings of Television in Older Adults' Lives: An Analysis of Change and Continuity in Television Viewing." *Ageing and Society* 32: 147–68.

Van Deursen, Alexander, and Jan van Dijk. 2009. "Improving Digital Skills for the Use of Online Public Information and Services." *Government Information Quarterly* 26 (2): 333–40. doi: 10.1016/j.giq.2008.11.002.

Van Deursen, Alexander, Jan van Dijk, and Oscar Peters. 2011. "Rethinking Internet Skills: The Contribution of Gender, Age, Education, Internet Experience, and Hours Online to Medium- and Content-Related Internet Skills." *Poetics* 39 (2): 125–44.

Vandebosch, Heidi, and Steven Eggermont. 2002. "Elderly People's Media Use: At the Crossroads of Personal and Societal Developments." *Communications: The European Journal of Communication Research* 27: 437–55.

Vasalou, Asimina, and Adam Joinson. 2009. "Me, Myself and I: The Role of Interactional Context on Self-Presentation through Avatars." *Computers in Human Behavior* 25 (2): 510–20.

Vasil, Latika, and Hannelore Wass. 1993. "Portrayal of the Elderly in the Media: A Literature Review and Implications for Educational Gerontologists." *Educational Gerontology* 19: 71–85. doi: 10.1080/0360127930190107.

Venkatesh, Viswanath. 2000. "Determinants of Perceived Ease of Use: Integrating Control, Intrinsic Motivation, and Emotion into the Technology Acceptance Model." *Information Systems Research* 11 (4): 342–65.

Venn, Susan, Robert Meadows, and Sara Arber. 2013. "Gender Differences in Approaches to Self-Management of Poor Sleep in Later Life." *Social Science and Medicine* 79: 117–123.

Vernon, JoEtta A., J. Allen Williams, Jr., Terri Phillips, and Janet Wilson. 1990. "Media Stereotyping: A Comparison of the Way Elderly Women and Men Are Portrayed on Prime-Time Television." *Journal of Women and Aging* 2 (4): 55–68.

Vroomen, Laura. 2004. "Kate Bush: Teen Pop and Older Female Fans." In *Music Scenes: Local, Translocal, and Virtual*, edited by Andy Bennett and Richard A. Peterson, 238–53. Nashville: Vanderbilt University Press.

Wahl, Hans-Werner, Agneta Fänge, Frank Oswald, Laura Gitlin, and Susanne Iwarsson. 2009. "The Home Environment and Disability-Related Outcomes in Aging Individuals: What Is the Empirical Evidence?" *The Gerontologist* 49 (3): 355–67.

Walling, Anne, and Gretchen Dickson. 2012. "Hearing Loss in Older Adults." *American Family Physician* 85 (12): 1150–156.

Walther, Joseph B. (1992). "Interpersonal Effects in Computer-Mediated Interaction: A Relational Perspective." *Communication Research* 19 (1): 52–90.

Walz, Thomas. 2002. "Crones, Dirty Old Men, Sexy Seniors: Representations of the Sexuality of Older Persons." *Journal of Aging and Identity* 7 (2): 99–112.

Waters, Mary, Patrick J. Carr, Maria J. Kefalas, and Jennifer Holdaway. 2011. *Coming of Age in America: The Transition to Adulthood in the Twenty-First Century*. Berkeley: University of California Press.

Waxman, Barbara Frey. 1990. *From the Hearth to the Open Road: A Feminist Study of Aging in Contemporary Literature*. London: Greenwood Press.

Wearing, Sadie. 2007. "Subjects of Rejuvenation: Aging in Postfeminist Culture." In *Interrogating Postfeminism: Gender and the Politics of Popular Culture*, edited by Yvonne Tasker, 277–310. Durham: Duke University Press.

———. 2012. "Exemplary or Exceptional Embodiment? Discourses of Aging in the Case of Helen Mirren and *Calendar Girls*." In *Aging Femininities: Troubling Representations*, edited by Josie Dolan and Estella Tincknell, 145–57. Cambridge: Cambridge Scholars Press.

Weber, Brenda R. 2012. "Reality (Celebrity) Check: Fat, Death and the Ageing Female Body." *Celebrity Studies* 3 (1): 64–77.

Westerhof, Gerben J. 2010. "'During my life so much has changed that it looks like a new world to me': A Narrative Perspective on Migrating in Time." *Journal of Aging Studies* 24: 12–19.

Westerhoff, Gerben, and Anne E. Barrett. 2005. "Age Identity and Subjective Well-Being: A Comparison of the United States and Germany." *Journals of Gerontology Series B: Psychological Sciences and Social Sciences* 60 (3): S129–36.

Westerhof, Gerben J., Anne E. Barrett, and Nardi Steverink. 2003. "Forever Young: A Comparison of Age Identities in the United States and Germany." *Research on Aging* 25: 366–83.

Westerhof, Gerben J., Karolien Harink, Martine Van Selm, Madelijn Strick, and Rick Van Baaren. 2010. "Filling a Missing Link: The Influence of Portrayals of Older Characters in Television Commercials on the Memory Performance of Older Adults." *Ageing and Society* 30: 897–912.

Westerhof, Gerben J., Susan Krauss Whitbourne, and Gillian P. Freeman. 2012. "The Aging Self in a Cultural Context: The Relation of Conceptions of Aging to Identity Processes and Self-Esteem in the United States and the Netherlands." *Journals of Gerontology, Series B: Psychological Sciences and Social Sciences* 67 (1): 52–60.

Wetherington, E., H. Cooper, and C. S. Holmes. 1997. "Turning Points in Midlife." In *Stress and Adversity Over the Life Course: Trajectories and Turning Points*, edited by I. H. Gotlib and B. Wheaton, 215–31. New York: Cambridge University Press.

Wiersema, Robert J. 2011. *Walk Like a Man: Coming of Age with the Music of Bruce Springsteen*. Vancouver: Greystone Books.

Wilhelmson, Katarina, Christina Andersson, Margda Waern, and Peter Allebeck. 2005. "Elderly People's Perspectives on Quality of Life." *Ageing and Society* 25 (4): 585–600. doi: 10.1017/S0144686X05003454.

Williams, Angie, Paul M. Wadeigh, and Virpi Ylänne. 2010. "Images of Older People in UK Magazine Advertising: Toward a Typology." *International Journal of Aging and Human Development* 71: 83–114.

Williams, Carol Traynor. 1980. *The Dream Beside Me: The Movies and the Children of the Forties*. Rutherford, NJ: Fairleigh Dickinson University Press.

Williams, Linda. 2008. *Screening Sex*. Durham: Duke University Press.

Williams, Raymond. 1974. *Television: Technology and Cultural Form*. London: Fontana.

Wilson, Sherryl. 2003. *Oprah, Celebrity and Formations of Self*. Hampshire: Palgrave Macmillan.

Wohlmann, Anita. 2014. *Aged Young Adults: Age Readings of Contemporary American Novels and Films*. New York: Columbia University Press.

Woodward, Kathleen. 1999. *Figuring Age: Women, Bodies, Generations*. Bloomington: Indiana University Press.

———. 2006. "Performing Age, Performing Gender." *NWSA Journal* 18 (1): 162–89.

Wurm, Susanne, Clemens Tesch-Romer, and Martin J. Tomasik. 2007. "Longitudinal Findings on Aging-Related Cognitions, Control Beliefs, and Health in Later Life." *Journals of Gerontology: Psychological Sciences and Social Sciences* 62: 156–64.

Xie, Bo, Ivan Watkins, Jennifer Golbeck, and Man Huang. 2012. "Understanding and Changing Older Adults' Perceptions and Learning of Social Media." *Educational Gerontology* 38 (4): 282–96. doi: 10.1080/03601277.2010.544580.

Yarnal, Careen. 2006. "The Red Hat Society: Exploring the Role of Play, Liminality and Communitas in Older Women's Lives." *Journal of Women and Aging* 18 (3): 51–73.

Yee, Nick. 2007. "Motivations of Play in Online Games." *Journal of CyberPsychology and Behavior* 9 (6): 772–75.

———. 2008. "Maps of Digital Desires: Exploring the Topography of Gender and Play in Online Games." In *Beyond Barbie and Mortal Kombat: New Perspectives on Gender and Gaming*, edited by Yasmin Kafai, Carrie Heeter, Jill Denner, and Jennifer Y. Sun, 83–96. Cambridge: MIT Press.

Yee, Nick, and Jeremy N. Bailenson. 2007. "The Proteus Effect: The Effect of Transformed Self-Representation on Behavior." *Human Communication Research* 33 (3): 271–90.

Yee, Nick, Jeremy N. Bailenson, Mark Urbanek, Francis Chang, and Dan Merget. 2007. "The Unbearable Likeness of Being Digital: The Persistence of Nonverbal Social Norms in On-line Virtual Environments." *CyberPsychology and Behavior* 10 (1): 115–21.

Ylanne, Virpi. 2012. "Introduction." In *Representing Ageing: Images and Identities*, edited by Virpi Ylanne, 1–16. New York: Palgrave Macmillan.

Young, Steven Dine. 2000. "Movies as Equipment for Living: A Developmental Analysis of the Importance of Film in Everyday Life." *Critical Studies in Media Communication* 17 (4): 447–68.

Yousafzai, Shumaila Y., Gordon R. Foxall, and John G. Pallister. 2007. "Technology Acceptance: A Meta-Analysis of the TAM: Part 1." *Journal of Modelling in Management* 2 (3): 251–80. doi: 10.1108/17465660710834453.

Zender, Carrie. "Catherine Deneuve looking good with plastic surgery." *Make Me Heal*, September 21, 2010. news.makemeheal.com/celebrity-plastic-surgery/catherine-deneuve-looking-good-with-plastic-surgery/1293.

Zeng, Yi, Eileen M. Crimmins, and Jean-Marie Robine. 2006. *Longer Life and Healthy Aging*. Dordrecht: Springer.

Zhang, Yan Bing, Jake Harwood, Angie Williams, Virpi Ylanne-McEwen, Paul Mark Wadleigh, and Caja Thimm. 2006. "The Portrayal of Older Adults in Advertising: A Cross-National Review." *Journal of Language and Social Psychology* 25: 264–82.

Zickuhr, Kathryn. "Generations 2010." *Pew Internet and American Life Project*, December 16, 2010. pewinternet.org/~/media//Files/Reports/2010/PIP_Generations_and_Tech10.pdf.

Zickuhr, Kathryn, and Mary Madden. 2012. *Older Adults and Internet Use*. Washington, DC: Pew Research Center.

FILMOGRAPHY

The Best Exotic Marigold Hotel. Directed by John Madden. 2012. UK: Participant Media, 2012. DVD.

The First Wives Club. Directed by Hugh Wilson. 1996. USA: Paramount Pictures.

High Fidelity. Directed by Stephen Fears. 2000. USA: Touchstone Pictures, Working Title Films, Dogstar Films, New Crime Productions.

The Hunger Games. Directed by Gary Ross. 2012. USA: Lionsgate, 2012. DVD.

Innocence. Directed by Paul Cox. 2000. Australia: Strand/New Oz Productions, 2002. DVD.

Metal Evolution. Directed by Sam Dunn and Scot McFadyen. 2011. Canada: Banger Films.

The Mother. Directed by Roger Michell. 2003. UK: BBC Films, 2004. DVD.

Something's Gotta Give. Directed by Nancy Meyers. 2003. USA: Columbia Pictures, 2004. DVD.

Sunset Boulevard. Directed by Billy Wilder. 1950. USA: Paramount Pictures.

Twilight (1). Directed by Catherine Hardwicke. 2008. USA: Summit Entertainment, 2008. DVD.

The Twilight Saga: Breaking Dawn—Part 1. Directed by Bill Condon. 2011. USA: Summit Entertainment, 2011. DVD.

The Twilight Saga: Breaking Dawn—Part 2. Directed by Bill Condon. 2012. USA: Summit Entertainment, 2012. DVD.

La Veuve Couderc [*The Widow Couderc*]. Directed by Pierre Granier-Deferre. 1971. France: Lira Films, 2005. DVD.

Wild Strawberries. Directed by Ingmar Bergman. 1957. Sweden: Svensk filmindustri, 2002. DVD.

Wolke 9 [*Cloud 9*]. Directed by Andreas Dresen. 2008, Germany: Peter Rommel Productions, 2009. DVD.

Index

AARP, 27, 40
activity theory, 107
age/aging: anxiety, 43, 45, 47, 213; appearance, 194, 197, 198; appropriateness, 31, 32, 66, 134; as comedic, 18, 19, 23, 24n1; as context for familial relationships, 21–22, 23; as context for occupational relationships, 21, 23; as incidental, 22, 23–24; as treatable condition, 20–21, 23; casting, 57, 61; chronological. *See* chronological age; discrimination, 54, 57, 58, 60; diversity in, 212; identity, 3–4, 23, 24, 32, 35, 43, 47, 51, 56, 60–61, 62, 152, 193, 194, 195, 195–196, 202, 203; markers, 26, 170, 195, 196, 209; norms, 128, 133, 134, 135, 136, 138, 140; representation of, 5, 6, 13–18, 14, 15–16, 18, 22, 27, 29, 30, 30–31, 31, 33–34, 34, 35, 40–41, 47, 57, 59, 67, 95, 124, 148, 159, 169, 171, 172, 176, 191, 206–208, 211, 212, 216; self-perceptions of, 42–44, 47–48; self-stereotypes of, 43; stereotypes, 13, 16, 19, 23, 31, 40, 41, 42, 46, 57, 59
age/gender nexus, 40, 49, 145, 148
ageism, 18, 23, 31, 51, 55, 157, 160, 194, 211, 212, 215, 216
age-related changes, 65, 112, 131
aging in place, 27, 117

age studies, 2, 9, 65, 93, 143, 145, 157, 166, 167, 169, 172, 179
aging spaces, 95
aide-memoire, 79, 80, 86, 88, 89
American Federation of Television and Radio Artists, 53
American Society for Aesthetic Plastic Surgery, 33
American Sociological Association, 1
Americans with Disabilities Act, 114
anti-aging culture, 174, 179
aspirational marketing, 13, 14, 15, 16, 212, 213
attitudes toward aging/older adults, 41–42; cross-national variations, 42, 43, 48; impact on older adults' health and well-being, 42, 44, 48; media effects on attitudes, 44–46, 47–48
avatars, 194, 195–196, 197, 198, 199, 201

baby boomers, 25, 25–26, 28, 33, 34, 35, 67, 94–104, 113, 125, 170–171, 171, 208, 211, 214–215
Bandura, Albert, 5
body as commodity, 71
Butler, Robert, 211

CBeebies, 207
celebritization, 66, 78
celebrity, 2, 9, 21, 33, 46, 65–76, 77–89; apparatus, 66, 67, 76, 78, 88; culture,

65–66, 66, 67–70, 70–71, 71, 73, 75, 76, 77, 83
celebrity as commodity thesis, 67
Chayko, Mary, 6, 7
Choice, 40
chronological age, 2, 4, 32, 51, 53, 55, 56, 61, 162, 194
chronological boundaries, 95, 180n2
cognitive age, 26, 32–34
cohort, 6, 25, 25–26, 33, 35, 95, 96, 99, 112, 113, 124, 166, 183, 215, 216
communication accommodation theory, 202
communication predicament model, 202
community participation, 107, 109
connectedness, 110, 184, 189, 191
consumer culture/consumption, 7, 13, 24, 25, 31, 172, 178, 205, 206, 214
content analysis, 5, 14, 15, 48
continuity, 96, 98, 107, 107–108, 111, 112, 115, 118, 138, 160, 215
convergence culture, 206, 207
cultivation theory, 5, 30, 31, 34, 44, 47
cultural schemas, 13, 14, 15, 17, 22–23, 23
cultural narratives, 94, 158, 168, 170
cultural objects/texts, 130, 131, 133, 136, 137, 139–140
cumulative advantage and disadvantage, 212

Dannefer, Dale, 1, 8
"Dave," 207
deadhead, 107, 108–119
digital worlds, 194, 196, 197, 201, 203
disengagement, 108
double standard of gender/aging, 40, 54, 57, 58, 60, 65, 68, 69–70, 76, 144, 152, 154, 160, 161, 212

elderly, definition of, 26–27, 27, 35
Erikson, Erik, 133, 141n8

fan, 7, 8, 52, 67, 78, 88, 94, 99, 102, 107, 108, 110, 111, 112, 115, 117, 123–140, 143–144, 145, 148–149, 150–151, 153, 154, 154n2, 208–209, 214, 215; community/culture, 2, 134, 140, 208; fan objects, 126, 128, 129, 132,

136–138, 138; long term fans, 130, 131, 136, 137, 138
fan-based identities, 109, 124, 125, 126, 127, 128, 129–130, 131, 132, 134, 135, 138, 140, 149
fan-consumers, 126, 139–140
fandom, 2, 9, 86, 88, 106n7, 123–140, 144, 145, 153, 208–209, 215; mainstreaming of, 126, 132, 135, 139; physical expression of, 129
The First Wives Club, 59
fountain of youth, 29

generation, 6, 21, 25, 32–33, 47, 83, 87, 93–104, 106n8, 124, 127, 129, 130, 133, 145, 171, 173, 185, 196, 208–209, 214–215; affiliation, 126; divides, 100, 124; identity, 94, 96; fantasy, 101, 102
Generation X, 35
Generation Y, 35
Gerbner, George, 5, 8, 30, 44
Goffman, Erving, 18
"Gold," 207
The Golden Girls, 20, 57
goodness of fit, 108, 118
Goodwin, Paige E., 7
The Graduate, 57
Gray Panthers, 27
"graying" of America, 27

Hall, Stuart, 7
Harwood, Jake, 16, 19–20
healthy aging, 28
hippies, 99, 109, 113, 115, 117–118
human agency, 215
human development, 133, 140n1

ideal age, 4, 61
identity maintenance, 107
IMDb, 51, 52, 53–56, 56, 61, 62n1
impressionable youth phenomenon, 214
inclusiveness, 114
in-group symbols, 111
Innocence, 158, 159, 161, 165
intergenerational, 80, 93, 95, 96, 100, 100–101, 119
intergenerational transfers, 115
internet use, 6, 117, 184, 185, 186, 187, 188–189

invisible lives, 108, 117

life: milestone, 128, 131, 138; narratives, 93, 96, 99, 131, 137, 138, 166; phases, 59, 124, 132–133, 134, 206, 207–209; transitions, 3, 32, 34, 47, 60, 95, 124, 127, 129, 131, 138–139, 140, 170, 207, 209

life course, 1, 1–3, 3–4, 8, 47, 51, 60–61, 93, 95, 105n1, 123–124, 125–126, 127–128, 130–134, 134, 136, 137–140, 140n1, 170, 172, 179, 180n2, 189, 191, 205, 206, 207–209, 211, 214, 215; development, 125; identities, 95; trajectories, 95, 96, 124, 129, 131, 137, 139, 209

life-span approach, 3–4, 47, 125, 140n1, 145, 168n2

linked lives, 1, 124

Livingstone, Sonia, 2, 8

loser/lunatic stereotype, 132

mainstream, 5, 46, 66, 105n6, 106n9, 109, 111, 113, 157, 162, 163, 168n9

Mannheim, Karl, 215

marketing segmentation, 25–26, 27, 32

mask of aging, 206, 210

mature market, 4, 26, 27, 29, 32, 33, 171, 177

media/cultural studies, 1–2, 44, 123, 130, 140n3, 157, 166, 167, 169, 172, 179, 188, 206, 209

mediation/mediatized, 1, 2, 4, 8, 9n1, 68, 172, 205

midlife industrial complex, 172

Miklowski, Casey, 1, 8

The Mother, 158, 159, 161, 165

National Academies of Sciences, 7

National Institute of Aging, 7

new-old, 27

nostalgia industries, 98, 153, 209

old-old, 27, 41, 78, 105n2, 187

online communication, 195, 196, 206

online games, 194, 197

ordinary-extraordinary celebrity paradox, 85, 88

parasocial relationships/parasociality, 77, 79, 82, 83, 84, 85, 86, 88, 133

period, 58, 95

person-environment fit, 116–117

Peterson, Richard, 8

popular media, 41, 61, 124, 145, 146, 172, 175

population pyramid, 28

positive life orientation, 32

postageist ageism, 169, 178, 179

posttraditional aging culture, 99

reminiscence, 79, 82, 86–87, 89, 144, 151, 153, 154, 173

retirement, 3, 20, 21–22, 26, 27, 34, 40, 47, 61, 70, 94–96, 112, 113, 115, 116–117, 131, 163, 170, 171, 176, 189, 208

Screen Actors Guild (SAG), 53, 54, 56

Second Life (SL), 195, 196, 197, 198, 199–203, 200

self-stereotyping theory, 46

senior market. *See* mature market

sexual activity, 59–60, 129, 143, 157, 158, 158–160, 160–161, 162–163, 164–165, 166–167, 167, 170–171, 173, 174, 175, 177, 179

sexual bodies, 19, 158, 160–161, 179

sexual engagement, 158, 167

sexualization of culture, 178, 179

sexualization of the third age, 169

Silverstone, Roger, 207–208

social capital, 40, 184, 188, 190, 206

social comparison theory, 45

social media networks, 183, 188

social media ubiquity, 183, 185

social media use, 48, 187

socioemotional selectivity theory, 48

sociological imagination, 93, 104

stereotype content model, 41

subjective age, 4, 61

successful aging, 67, 68, 71, 76, 107, 108, 118, 167, 168n3, 169, 170, 172, 173, 178, 179, 211, 212–213, 215

technology and aging, 6, 28, 32, 206, 207

third age, 94, 96, 99, 105n2, 113, 169, 170–171, 172–173, 178, 179

transitional object, 207

tribal stigma, 113
Twilight Moms, 143, 148

van der Goot, Margot, 7

Walters, Richard, 5
Westerhof, Gerben J., 4, 60
Wolke 9, 158
World of Warcraft (WoW), 193, 194, 195, 197, 197–203, 201

Writers Guild of America, 53

youthful aging, 65, 67, 68, 71, 73, 74, 75, 76

zoomer philosophy, 173, 173–174, 174, 175, 176
Zoomer magazine, 169, 171–172, 172, 173, 175–176, 178–179, 180n1, 207
zoomers, 95, 169, 171–177, 180n3

About the Contributors

Rebecca G. Adams is professor and director of gerontology at the University of North Carolina at Greensboro. Her research interests include older adult friendship and music fan communities. She is co-author or co-editor of the following publications: *Deadhead Social Science* (2000), *Placing Friendship in Context* (1998), *Adult Friendship* (1992), and *Older Adult Friendship: Structure and Process* (1989).

Anne L. Balazs is head of the Department of Marketing at Eastern Michigan University in Ypsilanti, MI, and vice president of EMU's women in philanthropy group. She served as an ACE fellow during 2013–2014 at Bowling Green State University and the University of Toledo. Her research interests include elderly consumer behavior, health care marketing, and sales management.

Anthony R. Bardo is a doctoral candidate in social gerontology at Miami University. He is interested in fostering multi- and interdisciplinary approaches to advance the study of aging as a lifelong process. His work focuses on cultural studies, global aging, social policy, health, and the intersections of subjective well-being.

Anne Barrett, professor of sociology at Florida State University, studies subjective experiences of aging, particularly their social structural antecedents and their health and behavioral consequences. Her current projects include an examination of women's aging anxieties and a content analysis of aging images reflected in *Modern Maturity/AARP Magazine* from the 1960s to present.

Shyon Baumann is associate professor of sociology at the University of Toronto. He works in the area of arts, media, culture, and consumption, and addresses questions of cultural evaluation and classification with the goal of increasing our understanding of social and cultural hierarchies and inequalities. To this end, he has done work on Hollywood cinema, gourmet food culture, and television advertising. His most recent book, co-authored with Josée Johnston, is *Foodies: Democracy and Distinction in the Gourmet Foodscape* (Routledge, 2010). He is associate editor of *Poetics: Journal of Empirical Research on Culture, the Media, and the Arts* from 2013–2015.

Denise D. Bielby is professor of sociology at the University of California, Santa Barbara, and Affiliated Faculty in the Department of Film and Media Studies. With C. Lee Harrington she is the co-author of *Soap Fans* (1995) *and Global TV* (2008) and the co-editor of *Popular Culture: Production and Consumption* (2001). She is the author is numerous scholarly articles on the culture industries of television and film, audiences and popular criticism, and aging and the life course.

Nathalie Claessens is a senior year research assistant at the research group media, policy, and culture of the University of Antwerp. She has recently completed a PhD on the mediated relationships between audiences and celebrities, part of which focuses on the meaning of celebrities in the everyday lives of nursing home residents.

Justine Gunderson is a graduate student in sociology at Florida State University. Her research interests center on family ideologies, particularly those surrounding women's roles. Her master's thesis was a quantitative assessment of the relationship between intensive mothering practices and women's emotional well-being.

Justin Harmon is a doctoral student at Texas A&M University in the Recreation, Park, and Tourism Sciences Department. His current lines of research include understanding the role of music in enhancing quality of life, which includes music as a conduit for secular spirituality, and identity maintenance through the continued practice of leisure activities for people with terminal diseases.

C. Lee Harrington is professor of sociology and affiliate of the Women's, Gender, and Sexuality Studies Program at Miami University. With Denise Bielby she is co-author *of Soap Fans* (1995) and *Global TV* (2008) and co-editor of *Popular Culture* (2001); she is also co-editor of *Fandom* (2007) and *The Survival of Soap Opera* (2011). Her sole-authored work has appeared in journals such as *Media, Culture and Society*, *Feminist Media Studies*, *Jour-*

nal of Broadcasting and Electronic Media, and *International Journal of Cultural Studies*.

Stephen Katz is professor of sociology at Trent University, Peterborough, Canada. He is author of *Disciplining Old Age, Cultural Aging: Life Course, Lifestyle and Senior Worlds*, and numerous book chapters and articles in *Generations, Journal of Aging Studies, Body and Society, History of the Human Sciences, Dementia*, and *Journal of Women and Aging*. His current research is on cultural aspects of aging, memory, and cognitive impairment. In 2009 he received the prestigious Trent University Distinguished Research Award for his work in critical aging studies.

Kim de Laat is a sociology doctoral candidate at the University of Toronto. Her research, supported through the Social Sciences and Humanities Research Council and an Ontario Graduate Scholarship, lies at the intersection of cultural sociology, organization theory, communication, gender, and economic sociology. Using the music industry as a case study, she is examining processes of organizational change to discern how the devaluation of creative labor is experienced by songwriters, as well as how record label executives adjust shared beliefs about the boundaries in which they work and compete. In her work with Shyon Baumann, she studies representations of gender, age, and motherhood in television advertising. The first article from this project, "Socially defunct: A comparative analysis of the underrepresentation of older women in advertising" was published in *Poetics: Journal of Empirical Research on Culture, the Media, and the Arts*.

Barbara L. Marshall is professor of sociology at Trent University in Peterborough, Canada. Co-editor of the recently published *Ageing Men, Masculinities and Modern Medicine* (2013, with A. Kampf and A. Peterson), she has also authored numerous publications on feminist theory, sexuality, and the body. With her colleague Stephen Katz, she has co-authored a series of articles exploring aging, embodiment, and sexuality. In 2006 she was honored with Trent's Distinguished Research Award.

Leni Marshall, is professor of English at the University of Wisconsin-Stout. Her research focuses on age studies in North American minority and majority literatures and cultures. She is advisory editor for *Age, Culture, Humanities,* and has served at the leadership level for AGHE, ENAS, GSA, NANAS, NWSA, and MLA. She edited *Staging Age: The Performance of Age in Theatre, Dance, and Film* with Valerie Lipscomb. Her next book, *Age: Of Bodies, Gender, and Construction,* is forthcoming.

Rosa Mikael Martey's research focuses on social interaction in online contexts, from virtual worlds and games, to Facebook and online information. Recent work examines communication and behavior in custom-built games in Second Life and in World of Warcraft using a variety of methodologies including participant-observation, online surveys, and game-play logs. Current projects include project designing, developing, and experimentally examining features of an educational game that trains people to minimize reliance on cognitive biases when dealing with incomplete information.

Kelly Quinn is a visiting assistant professor in communication at the University of Illinois at Chicago. She has an interdisciplinary research focus on new media and how it intersects with such diverse areas as the life course, social capital, friendship, and privacy. Quinn's recent work has centered on midlife and older adults and their use of internet communication technologies in their relationships. Her publications have been included in *Information, Communication and Society*, the *International Journal of Emerging Technologies and Society* and in edited volumes.

Alexandra Raphael is a graduate student in sociology at Florida State University. Her research interests focus on gender, aging, and retirement. Her master's thesis used a sample of middle-aged married adults to examine the relationship between division of household labor and sexual relationship quality. She is currently working on projects about debt and relationship satisfaction, self-perceptions of aging and retirement savings, and the division of household labor and leisure time in retirement.

Cornel Sandvoss is senior lecturer in sociology at the University of Surrey. He has published widely on fans and fan cultures (*Fans: The Mirror of Consumption* [2005] and *Fandom: Identities and Communities in a Mediated World* [2007, with Lee Harrington and Jonathan Gray]) and the interplay between media, sport, and identity, including *Bodies of Discourse: Sport Stars, Media and the Global Public* (2012, with Michal Real and Alina Bernstein) and *A Game of Two Halves: Football, Television and Globalization* (2003). He is a former Chair of the Popular Communication Division of ICA and is currently working on an AHRC funded project on the aesthetics of participatory culture.

Christine Scodari is an associate of the Center for Women, Gender, and Sexuality Studies and professor in the School of Communication and Multimedia Studies at Florida Atlantic University. Her work on gender and/or age in media fandom includes *Serial Monogamy: Soap Opera, Lifespan, and the Gendered Politics of Fantasy* (Hampton, 2004) and essays on film, television, sports media, and popular books in such journals as *Communication, Culture, and Critique*, *Feminist Media Studies*, and *Reconstruction*.

Merril Silverstein is the Marjorie Cantor Professor of Aging Studies in the Department of Sociology and School of Social Work at Syracuse University. Prior to this appointment he was professor of gerontology and sociology at the University of Southern California. He received his doctorate in sociology from Columbia University. His research focuses on aging within the context of family life, including intergenerational relationships over the life course, and international perspectives on aging families.

Aagje Swinnen is an assistant professor at Maastricht University (Netherlands). She has published on the representation of age and gender in literature, film, and photography (in *The Gerontologist*, *Journal of Aging Studies*, and the volume *Aging, Performance and Stardom*, with J. A. Stotesbury). Swinnen has acquired numerous competitive research grants, is current chair of the European Network in Aging Studies (ENAS) and is co-editor of the new journal *Age, Culture, Humanities*.

Hilde Van den Bulck is professor of communication studies, head of the research group media, policy, and culture, and dean of the Faculty of Social Sciences at the University of Antwerp. She combines complementary expertise in media policy and structures with expertise in media culture and identity. In the latter field she has specialized in recent years in the role of mediated celebrity culture in people's (collective) identity work, including that based on age.

CPSIA information can be obtained at www.ICGtesting.com
Printed in the USA
BVOW01*0905100614

355926BV00003B/3/P

9 780739 183632